John C. Brown of Tennessee

John C. Brown
of Tennessee

Rebel, Redeemer, and Railroader

Sam Davis Elliott

Knoxville • The University of Tennessee Press

Frontispiece: John C. Brown's official portrait as governor (Credit: Tennessee State Library and Archives/Courtesy of Tennessee Historical Society).

Library of Congress Cataloging-in-Publication Data

Names: Elliott, Sam Davis, 1956– author.

Title: John C. Brown of Tennessee : rebel, redeemer, and railroader / Sam Davis Elliott.

Description: First edition. | Knoxville: The University of Tennessee Press, 2017. | Includes bibliographical references and index.

Identifiers: LCCN 2017009051| ISBN 9781621902874 (hardcover : alk. paper) | ISBN 9781621902898 (ebook/kindle)

Subjects: LCSH: Brown, John C. (John Calvin), 1827–1889. |

Generals—Confederate States of America—Biography. | United States—History—Civil War, 1861–1865—Campaigns. | Confederate States of America. Army of Tennessee—Biography. | Governors—Tennessee—Biography. | Texas & Pacific Railway—Biography.

Classification: LCC E467.1.B769 E45 2017 | DDC 973.7/468092 [B]—dc23

LC record available at https://lccn.loc.gov/2017009051

Contents

Illustrations

Figures

Maps

Preface

John Calvin Brown is little known to today's Americans. Those who are most likely to recognize him are students of the Civil War, whose usual frame of reference is that Brown was one of the Rebel generals who fell wounded at the Battle of Franklin. Tennessee lawyers who take the trouble to look at the signatories of the state constitution may note that Brown was the president of the constitutional convention of 1870. Visitors to the state capitol in Nashville can see his portrait as governor hanging in the hallway near the entrance to the present governor's office. Historians studying the financial and railroad interests of the 1870s and 1880s might take note of his role in the effort to fund and develop a transcontinental railroad through Texas to the Pacific Ocean.

His contemporaries knew him as John C. Brown, likely to differentiate him from a plethora of other men named John Brown. And his was a name well recognized by his contemporaries, including millions in the state of Tennessee, and millions more in Texas. While he maintained a home and frequently returned to his native Giles County, he trod the halls of power in Washington, presided over the Volunteer State from the stately capitol in Nashville, interacted with rich financiers in Philadelphia, New York, and St. Louis, argued cases before the United States Supreme Court, and was for a number of years the face of the Texas and Pacific Railway. During the Civil War, he rode, in the words of his successor as governor, "up and down the line like Henry of Navarre," and fought on every major battlefield of the Western Theater except where imprisonment or wounds intervened.

From the standpoint of contemporary historiography, however, John C. Brown is in a virtual void. As a Confederate officer, it was his fate to fight with the Army of Tennessee. Historians Thomas Lawrence Connelly and Richard McMurry have outlined the significant disadvantages suffered by the Army of Tennessee, both as to its performance during the Civil

War, and in the history books thereafter. In their view, the lack of good and, moreover, concentrated source material, attractive personalities, and overall success have in the past made the officers of the Army of Tennessee unappealing subjects for historians. Connelly first published this thesis in 1967, and McMurry elaborated on it in 1989. Fortunately, since then a number of the previously neglected corps and division commanders of the Army of Tennessee have biographies. Recently, the University of Tennessee's *Confederate Generals in the Western Theater* series has brought to light significant aspects of more prominent officers, and provided the more obscure biographical treatment where there was none. But John C. Brown, one of only eight Confederate Tennesseans at the rank of major general or above, has been ignored. In a sense, this is understandable, as he left no cache of papers, diaries, or memoirs, and died relatively young, leaving his voice silent while historical debate raged over events in which he was a significant, if not a major player.[1]

Brown also played a substantial role in the ex-rebel resistance to Governor William G. Brownlow's postwar Radical government. The lack of historical record here, however, was likely intentional. If not an actual night-rider himself, the weight of the evidence supports the conclusion that Brown was a leader of the Ku Klux Klan. The Klan had the political goal of removing Brownlow's Radical regime. But the Klan employed means other than politics to undermine Brownlow's rule and to restore the prewar social order, including violence and intimidation against the Radicals and their new allies, the freed blacks of Tennessee. From the perspective of Brown's times, notoriety as a leader of the Klan would not only make Brown a Radical target, it also might raise his profile should the Federal government take control of Tennessee, as it did other former Rebel states. It is therefore not a surprise that the historical record of that phase of Brown's life is at best incomplete.

Brown was one of many men of ability to lead the anti-Radical party, which later became the Conservative Party and, eventually, the Democratic Party. It was a phenomenon of the times that Brown was uniquely situated to assume leadership of the Conservative or "Redeemer" coalition that regained control in 1869–1870. While he served honorably as a Confederate general, he was not counted among the discredited secessionists. He was not disqualified by Article III of the Fourteenth Amendment, which at the time prevented the majority of former Confederate leaders from holding office. These factors put him in position to be selected president of the constitutional convention in 1870 and then be elected governor in the election held later that year. His role in the convention is perhaps dimmed by the fact that he was but one of several luminaries among the delegates. Although president of the convention, Brown was obscured by men who were much more experienced politicians, including his brother, former governor Neill S. Brown. And because the sitting governor, De Witt C. Senter, was left to serve the entirety of his term under the new convention, Brown spent over a year as governor-elect, and first took office for a shortened term. While the state was in dire straits at that time, it was not under the threat of invasion or insurrection faced by Brown's recent predecessors. Instead, it was faced with an enormous and crushing debt. Only two scholarly works published in the mid-1970s addressed the years of Brown's governorship, and they largely focus only on specific issues, such as the efforts to confront the debt, and do not provide an overall evaluation of Brown's governorship.[2]

Brown appears in the history books only rarely after his term as governor ended in 1875. In *Reunion and Reaction: The Compromise of 1877 and the End of Reconstruction* (1951), historian C. Vann Woodward identifies Brown as one of the politicians from the old Confederacy seeking to obtain Federal funding for a southern transcontinental railroad in connection with the last of the great political compromises between the sections in the 1800s.[3] He had a role in the struggle between rival financiers for control of the southern route to the Pacific, and was in the front lines of management on behalf of the Texas and Pacific Railway during the Great Southwest Railroad Strike of 1886. Brown's lengthy absences from Tennessee on these railroad endeavors, as well as the 1882 eclipse of the faction of the Tennessee Democrats who were former Whigs by Bourbon Democrats led by Isham G. Harris diminished, but did not eradicate, his influence in the Volunteer State. Indeed, he returned to Tennessee in the spring of 1889 as president of the Tennessee Coal, Iron, and Railroad Company, at that time the largest corporation in the South. Brown's early death at age sixty-two, however, cut short any plans he may have had to reestablish himself in his home state.

Brown's only prior biographical treatment, aside from a few encyclopedia entries, was a master's thesis submitted by Margaret Butler, "The Life of John C. Brown" (1936). Butler lived in Pulaski, and likely knew persons who had known Brown in life. Light on Brown's role in the Civil War and in connection with the Texas and Pacific, the thesis is commendably extensive on Brown's role as governor. Butler's account relies in large amount on publicly available sources, but contains information which, while uncited, appears to come from local sources. With all due respect, while valuable for this work, Butler's text is insufficient and dated for today's reader. Perhaps one reason that Brown has not had a modern examination is that there are virtually no personal papers. There is an unsubstantiated story that his wife burned them after his death, which, at least at it relates to his wartime activities, appears to be untrue—they were actually lost in a house fire in 1871. Accordingly, his life can only be reconstructed from newspaper accounts, his governor's papers, his reports as a soldier, and what glimpses can be afforded of the man in the writings of others.[4]

Rebel general, Redeemer politician, railroad executive, and lawyer. All identified Brown at various times of his life, and all indicate a man who had reached a high level of distinction. At the time of Brown's death, an admiring Texas newspaperman wrote: "Governor Brown was a great man, and had achieved a more varied success and distinction than the majority of great men . . . ."[5] A man of consequence in his time, John C. Brown deserves to be remembered in ours.

This project started in 2011 after I completed a tour of duty as president of the Tennessee Bar Association. It was a welcome relief to retreat back into nineteenth-century Tennessee after being mired in the ethical and political issues faced by lawyers in our state during the eight years I served on the TBA board. Fortunately, neither my devoted wife, Karen, nor my loving daughters, Mary Claire and Sarah Anne, disowned me for my rapid immersion in John C. Brown's life and times. As always, I am grateful for their love and support.

Another crucial group that understood my need to refocus was my law partners, Wayne Peters, Wade Cannon, Bob Lockaby, Lee Ann Adams, Beverly Edge, David McDowell, Gary Henry, and Ellie LaPorte. I am grateful to them and our associate attorneys and staff for the collegial atmosphere in our workplace. Of the latter group, I greatly appreciate three who have been around for many years of my practice, Kim Keylon, Vicki Jackson, and Melanie Young. Our IT person, Patti Russell, helped with the computer-related issues raised in connection with a twenty-first century writing project. And my paralegal and assistant, Jill Townsend, cheerfully assisted with various tasks of great utility to me.

Living near Chattanooga, Tennessee, as I do, I am a member of overlapping history communities. The Chickamauga and Chattanooga National Military Park is a center of gravity for historians with an interest in the Civil War. Park historian Jim Ogden is an inexhaustible resource for the Western Theater and is selfless in his efforts to be of assistance. Ranger Lee White is only slightly less so. Dave Powell of Chicago is down here so much that he is an honorary citizen of the Chattanooga area. And Keith Bohannon of West Georgia University also counts as such, and only needs to know what one is working on to bring from him a welcome flood of wonderful materials from his years of meticulous research on the Army of Tennessee. I am indebted to each of these men as sources and sounding boards.

Within the greater confines of the state of Tennessee, my prolific friend Tim Smith of the University of Tennessee at Martin is full of insights on the Civil War in the West, and in the course of research for his new book on the Fort Henry and Fort Donelson campaign, was kind enough to lend some insight as to Brown's role at Fort Donelson. Other members of our state's history community are equally quick to encourage and assist with inquiries. My thanks go to Chuck Sherill of the Tennessee State Library and Archives and his wonderful staff for maintaining and making accessible the rich sources of Tennessee history stored there. Megan Spainhour and Karina McDaniel of Chuck's staff were particularly helpful. My friends Ann Toplovich of the Tennessee Historical Society and Dan Pomeroy of the Tennessee State Museum greatly aided me in making available some of the illustrations in this volume. I enjoyed meeting Paul Bergeron, professor emeritus of history at the University of Tennessee, Knoxville, in 2010 at the initial Tennessee Sesquicentennial event, and he was kind enough, almost five years later, to read two chapters of the book and provide many helpful insights.

Larry Daniel, whose real job, at least until his recent retirement as a United Methodist minister, was outside the history profession, provided references to useful materials. I have worked for over ten years with the too numerous to mention members and staff of the Tennessee Historical Commission. Their dedication to the interpretation and preservation of our state's history has always been a great inspiration to me. Finally, it has been my privilege to serve on the boards of the Friends of the Chickamauga and Chattanooga National Military Park and the Tennessee Civil War Preservation Association. The individual past and present members of these boards are also too numerous to mention, but I am grateful to them just the same.

Outside of Tennessee, my friend Mike Peters of Columbus, Ohio, provided access to an obscure article from his vast holdings of Civil War literature. David Holmgren of Des Moines, Iowa, very efficiently researched the Grenville Dodge Papers at the State Historical Society of Iowa. Maury Klein, professor emeritus at the University of Rhode Island, kindly responded to inquiries relating to Jay Gould. Mastin Combs of Haiku, Hawaii, and Zack Watters of Rome, Georgia, both William B. Bate men, provided assistance as to source materials of great usefulness. Sara Keckeisen and Lisa Keys of the Kansas Historical Society very patiently handled a research request that suddenly appeared from Tennessee, and John Coski, historian at the American Civil War Museum (formerly the Museum of the Confederacy), kindly answered questions relative to research I did there over fifteen years ago. Fellow Western Theater historian Alex Mendoza is also a talented military cartographer, and very patiently translated my rude scratches into the maps that appear herein—although I alone am responsible for the content. And I would be remiss if I did not collectively mention the members of the Forlorn Hope discussion group, who have been friends in the Civil War realm for many years now.

Institutionally, Mary Helms and the staff of the Local History Department of the Chattanooga Public Library provided their usual cheerful assistance, as did the staff at the Lawson-McGhee Library, Knoxville, and the Giles County Public Library in Pulaski, Tennessee. The libraries of the University of Tennessee at Chattanooga, Middle Tennessee State University, and my two alma maters, the University of the South (Sewanee) and the University of Tennessee, Knoxville, provided valuable access to various research materials. I am also grateful to the other institutions listed in the bibliography who made their materials available to me.

It eventually came to my attention that I actually was acquainted with a direct descendant of John C. Brown, Norman Blake, who was more or less a contemporary of mine at Sewanee. Norman was kind enough to discuss his great-grandparents with me, and to refer me to his cousin, Rt. Rev. Henry Parsley, with whom, unfortunately, I was never able to fully connect.

For some years, I have had a relationship with the University of Tennessee Press, either as a manuscript reader, or as a contributor to the *Confederate Generals in the Western Theater* series. I am very pleased to add a new layer to that relationship with this book, and I appreciate the cheerful patience demonstrated by Scot Danforth and his staff. I also appreciate the useful suggestions made by the Press's outside readers concerning the book, which have added to both the content and the clarity of what was presented.

I have already mentioned the three persons who mean the most to me in this world, my wife and daughters, but other members of my family have provided their encouragement during this project, including, most significantly, my father, Gene Elliott. Thanks are also due to my brother, Jeff Elliott, who has finally quit making fun of my inordinate interest in history. I have long appreciated the great relationship I have had with my father-in-law, Arvid Honkanen, and my recently departed and very much missed mother-in-law, Claire Honkanen.

Finally, the several years I spent working on this book marked the loss of several friends and mentors who have had an important role in my life. In 2012 we lost Nathaniel Cheairs Hughes Jr., an eminent historian of the Civil War and fellow resident of Chattanooga, who took a phone call out of the blue from a stranger in 1996 and guided and encouraged me in my first writing projects. The year 2013 was particularly hard. In May, Tennessee lost its longtime state historian, Walter Durham, who was always willing to share his wide-ranging knowledge of the history of the Volunteer State. In June, my law partner and longtime mentor in the legal profession, Charles J. Gearhiser, passed. Charlie's renowned sense of humor doubtlessly gave him the patience he needed to foster my growth as a lawyer, for which I will always be indebted to him. November of that year saw the passing of Joseph D. Cushman, a professor at the University of the South who gave considerable focus to my interest in the Civil War. While I enjoyed his classes, I particularly appreciated the time I was able to spend with him in later years discussing southern history and our beloved alma mater. Finally, and most profoundly, in December 2014, I lost my dear mother, Ruth Davis Elliott. Her influence, encouragement, teaching, and incomparable love were of incalculable benefit to me. I scarcely can go a day without thanks to God for her indelible imprint on my life.

It is with great appreciation and sense of loss that I dedicate this book to these lost mentors and friends.

1

Desires the Perpetuity and Integrity of Our Union

1827–1861

Slowly the fallen leaders of the 3rd Tennessee Regiment were brought home from the old battlefields of Georgia. Almost two years after his death at Resaca, Major Flavel Barber, who kept a diary that told so much about his regiment's history during the war, was reburied in Pulaski. A formerly "wicked" and "profane" man who found religion during the great revival of the Army of Tennessee in the winter of 1864, Col. Calvin H. Walker was killed a few weeks after Barber at Kolb's Farm, and was reburied in Tennessee in January 1867. Now, finally, Lt. Col. Calvin Clack was at last brought home to Pulaski from the grave where he was laid after his death at Jonesboro. In 1860, Clack was a lawyer living in a boarding house in Pulaski with twenty other men, including fellow attorney John Calvin Brown. On November 10, 1883, Clack's former comrades gathered to honor him. Brown, the 3rd Tennessee's first commander, spoke of the choice that his friend Clack, Brown himself, and the men of Giles County faced in the frantic days of April and May 1861.[1]

Brown related that Clack "believed secession was not a remedy for any of the real or fancied wrongs of his section," and continued to hope, as the crisis deepened, for peace within the Union. Only when President Abraham Lincoln called for troops to "coerce" the departed southern states did Clack, Brown, and the assembled veterans of the regiment go to war on the side of the South. That day, over eighteen years after the defeat of their cause, Brown conceded "[w]hether we acted wisely will be fairly and truthfully answered only after we have joined our comrade. That we were inspired by an honest sense of duty, and yielded to the appeals of our manhood, none but the fanatic will deny."

As the assembled throng remembered their fallen friend, Brown recalled the mass meeting occasioned by the "great emergency" of 1861. He observed that it was a "people's meeting," and the people included "our fathers, our brothers, our kindred, our friends," the "sons and grandsons of the men of the Revolution." These veterans and pioneers claimed no ancestral nobility. "Theirs was an ancestry of honor, truth, courage, and tireless energy. They scaled the mountains, felled the forests, crossed the rivers, subdued the savage and the wild beasts, and in the dark savannahs of southern wilds made castles of their own humble cabins, and in the awe inspiring stillness of nature's solitude consecrated their sons to God and their country."[2]

On January 6, 1827, John Calvin Brown was born of the very pioneer stock to which he would refer in 1883. He was the tenth and last child of his parents, Duncan and Margaret Smith Brown. Duncan and Margaret, who were both of Scotch descent, moved to Tennessee from Robeson County, North Carolina, in 1808, settling briefly in Sumner County before moving south to the "howling wilderness" of Giles County in the fall of 1809, along with Margaret's sister and her husband, Daniel McCallum, and other family members. Born in 1780, Duncan was the son of Angus Brown, who was likely a North Carolina veteran of the Revolution, while Margaret, born in 1782, was the granddaughter of Colonel Archibald Lyttle, who commanded North Carolina Continentals during the Revolution.[3]

While explorers traversed the area in prior years, white settlers first came into what would be established a few years later as Giles County in 1805 or 1806. The country "was a dense cane-break, inhabited only by wild beasts of the forest, with the Indians living in near proximity, and occasionally passing through it on their hunting or marauding excursions." A settler arriving in the area would find cane growth in the rich bottoms from twelve to twenty feet high, and on the thinner soil on the hills and ridges from four to seven feet high. Stopping on December 11, 1809, in the southern part of the county, near where Richland Creek flows into the Elk River, Duncan and Margaret would have likely cleared a space in the cane next to a spring or other water source sufficient to erect a temporary shelter prior to building a log cabin. Margaret at that time

Desires the Perpetuity and Integrity of Our Union

was pregnant with her third child, Neill Smith Brown, who was born on April 18, 1810. Eventually the Browns moved about two miles southeast to another farm, where their son John was born and raised.[4]

The rich land claimed from the cane brakes brought abundant crops of corn. With a large family, Duncan became a farmer of moderate circumstances. Both Duncan and Margaret were credited by Neill as "strict disciplinarians, instilling correct morals." Much later, the elder brother attributed his own considerable success to "native ambition," that "[a] pains-taking father and mother inculcated moral and religious principles, without which no success is worth anything," and desire imposed by his relative poverty. Doubtless similar motivations existed for the younger brother. John was first educated in the "old field schools" near his home, named for the practice of erecting a log cabin in a fallow field for the purposes of very elementary education. He also labored on his parents' farm while young. As indicated by the 1840 census, Duncan worked his farm with Margaret and four slaves. By that time, young John was living with his sister Mary Ann, his elder by fifteen years, and her husband, Edward McMillan, who was a minister at a Presbyterian church in the northern part of Giles County. The McMillans attended to John's education from that point.[5]

While Duncan and Margaret farmed, their oldest surviving son, Neill, managed to complete his education and become a member of the bar. After a brief relocation to Texas in 1835, where unsettled conditions were not to his liking, Neill returned to Pulaski and then volunteered for the Seminole War, where he earned a promotion to sergeant-major of the First Tennessee Regiment. He entered politics in 1836 as an elector on the ticket of Andrew Jackson's Tennessee antagonist, Hugh Lawson White, and in 1837 was elected to the Tennessee legislature. In 1843, Neill ran for Congress against another Pulaski lawyer, Aaron V. Brown, and lost, but was an elector for Henry Clay in 1844.[6]

While at the time of John's birth Democrat Andrew Jackson was the political colossus of Tennessee, when Neill ran for Congress, he ran as a Whig, a national label that Tennessee's anti-Jacksonian faction was late to adopt. The Whigs coalesced around their opposition to various policies pursued by Jackson, such as his destruction of the Bank of the United States and his disfavor of internal improvements, which was cemented by their dislike of Old Hickory, who they deemed to be arbitrary, especially in his choice of his presidential successor, Martin Van Buren. During the 1840s, as John grew to manhood, the Whigs and the Democrats contended for control of the state, with Democrat James K. Polk first being elected governor in 1839, and then losing his bid for reelection in 1841. His successor, Whig James C. "Lean Jimmy" Jones, was in turn defeated in 1845 by Neill's former congressional opponent, Democrat Aaron V. Brown.[7]

Likely in 1842, John entered Jackson College in Columbia, Tennessee. The institution was founded in 1809 as the Manual Labor Academy, and later became the Jackson Seminary before it became Jackson College in 1830. The college educated both university and preparatory students. Brown and his fellow students studied classical authors, mathematics, and science, and practical subjects including surveying and topography. The college also required courses in politics, laws of nations, and the US Constitution. Tuition was $20 a session.[8]

During John's senior year, Lawrence O'Bryan, a member of the junior class, wrote a friend about college life in Columbia in the fall of 1845. O'Bryan noted that there were at that time only eighteen or twenty young men at the college, although they expected more soon. "Of these, there are only four or five professors of Religion. There are two debating Societies held here every Friday night. There is also a Prayer Meeting held here on Saturday nights by the students." O'Bryan found "Columbia to be a very pleasant and handsome place" that was a grander place for girls than Franklin. O'Bryan also related to his friend that "[w]e have a brother of Neil S. Brown of Giles County, but he has not yet given any indication of an intellect equal to his distinguished brother."[9]

Upon graduation, John returned to Pulaski, and was one of two men placed in charge of the local school. The institution was chartered by the legislature in 1809 as Pulaski Academy, but the name changed to Wurtemburg Academy in 1812.

John was reported to have "exhibited remarkable talent as an instructor" and "evinced thorough knowledge of books." Although he only remained in charge of the school for one or two sessions, for several years afterward he maintained a relationship with the school, serving as a member of the committee that examined the students on a semi-annual basis.[10]

Desires the Perpetuity and Integrity of Our Union

Neill S. Brown (Credit: Tennessee
State Library and Archives)

At some point, John decided to follow Neill into the practice of law, and read law under his brother's tutelage. Neill, however, was approaching the apogee of his political career, and spent much of the period between mid-April and early August 1847 campaigning for governor against Aaron V. Brown. On October 16, 1847, having been elected by the narrowest of margins, the "tall, spare and thoughtful" Neill took office as governor. It is uncertain how John finished his apprenticeship. One local account indicates that he completed the process with an "uncle," Hugh Brown of Spring Hill, Tennessee. Hugh Brown was not actually an uncle, but was a more distant family connection from Robeson County, North Carolina. Further, in 1847 Hugh Brown was eighty-five years old. In any event, John completed his studies, and was licensed to practice law in either September or October of 1848. One of his first tasks was to act as administrator of his father's estate, as Duncan Brown died in March of that year. Duncan's will, written the year before, left John a horse. Other items were left to his sister Eliza and their mother, with the property to be sold and the proceeds equally divided among the children at Margaret's death.[11]

Evidently, much of John's early work as a lawyer was helping Neill keep his law practice going in Pulaski while Neill attended to his business as governor in Nashville. In January 1849, John exchanged a series of letters with Neill reporting on his legal work, the first letter detailing efforts to collect a note due Neill and describing a suit on which a client employed the brothers to collect a debt secured by a slave. John's second letter described an effort to use court process to levy on a judgment, and expressing the frustration of a young lawyer, he confessed: "It was my first effort to force matters & if it is uniformly as difficult to make levies I do not care to make any more, soon." John's final letter was in response to a letter where his brother, the senior partner, admonished him on various matters, including the uncollected note, an unexplained bill for shoes, and a bill for some sort of purchase at the state penitentiary. As to the last, John explained his good faith efforts to pay the bill before he left Nashville, and then his receiving a promise from a friend that it would be paid from sums owed John. John promised to straighten matters out, complaining that the friend was "infernally mean" not to let him know the debt was unpaid. Exasperated, John closed his letter by observing: "It appears that when I would do right, some base dog invariably thwarts my purposes."[12]

Under the state constitution, Neill's term as governor was two years, during which the General Assembly met only once, from October 1847 to February 1848. As expressed in his initial legislative message, Neill's primary concerns were the status of the state's finances, internal improvements, and education, with lesser issues being the status and continuance of the Bank of Tennessee, the construction of the Capitol, the lunatic asylum, and the national issues raised by the Mexican War. Of immediate concern were obligations on the state to pay an installment on bonds used to purchase stock in the Union Bank (in order to help get it up and running) and a deficiency in the profits of the Bank of Tennessee, creating an anticipated loss of over $240,000 to be supplied by the treasury. While Neill thought that the shortage could be made up from existing resources, he was prepared to support an increase in taxes. Foreshadowing a future controversy, Neill stated: "I need not impress upon you the duty of promptly providing for all the public engagements, and of maintaining inviolate the public faith . . . The honor of the State has never made its silent but eloquent appeal in vain. . . ."[13]

In true Whig fashion, Neill also pressed for expenditures on internal improvements including railroads, removal of obstructions in the Tennessee River, and roads for West Tennessee. As for education, Neill made the groundbreaking proposal that a statewide tax be imposed for educational purposes. Neill deemed internal improvement and education the two pillars of the state's "local well-being and prosperity." Taxes "ought never to be resorted to, except to discharge existing obligations, and for objects which guarantee, at least, corresponding advantages." In the end, Neill got a yearly tax of one-tenth of a cent on each dollar in value of various forms of property, which brought in more revenue, but the state's expenditures for the two-year period of his administration exceeded the additional revenue. Neill's requests relative to education and river obstructions were not adopted, although eight laws were passed dealing with the incorporation, or the revisions thereof, of certain railroads. All was not fruitless, however, as real steps were taken toward the construction of a lunatic asylum, spurred, in large part, by a memorial to the General Assembly from philanthropist Dorothea Dix, who was a well-known advocate for the mentally ill.[14]

In April 1849, Neill was nominated by the Whigs for reelection. His Democratic opponent was General William Trousdale. The burning issue of the day, as it would be for the next decade and a half, was slavery, and as there was a wide range of views on the subject, Trousdale and Neill were careful in their comments on the campaign trail. The August 1849 election resulted in Trousdale defeating Neill by much the same narrow margin as Neill had defeated Aaron V. Brown. Freed from the need to skirt the issue by the result of the election, Neill's final message to the legislature maintained that Congress had no power to legislate upon slavery, as it was a matter left to the states. Slavery, whether right or wrong, should be left to run its course, as it had in the North. But Neill made it clear that he had "no sympathy with the threats of violence and disunion, that have been but too often been heralded forth, on both sides of the question, as the ultimate remedy . . . With the Union, we have everything to inspire the hopes and impel the energies of patriotism, amid the vast field of improvement that lies before us. Without it, we have nothing worth maintaining—worth living for—worth dying for!"[15]

Neill was a defeated politician at the age of thirty-nine, but the patronage of Tennessee's leading Whig, Senator John Bell, secured his appointment as United States minister to Russia in February 1850. Imperial Russia was confronting the after-effects of the European revolutions of 1848 and a concomitant new wave of liberalism, and it acted in a reactionary manner relative to such movements in Poland and Hungary. While many Americans condemned Russia's repressive actions, inherently conservative southern Whigs were not so quick to do so, making Neill an effective spokesman for his country in St. Petersburg. For over three years, Neill endured illness, the bitter cold, spying by the Tsar's agents, official censorship, and the State Department's failure to keep him fully informed of his country's policy. He concluded his mission in late June 1853, and returned to Tennessee, settling in Nashville rather than Pulaski.[16]

Long before that time, John made great strides in life. No doubt learning from his interaction with the "base dogs" of the world, John developed a "large and lucrative" law practice. By August 1850, he entered into a law partnership with John C. Walker, a lawyer of some substance who was about six years older than John. An admiring friend of later years explained that John was not a lawyer versed in various cases, but instead was "thoroughly versed" in the law's general principles. John was "a man of much force before a jury or an audience. His personal presence was majestic and commanding." Seeking to build his fortune, John argued cases, advertised land for sale, and later sold insurance on the side. He joined the Sons of Temperance, drafted resolutions for his fellow Whigs when President Zachary Taylor and, later, Henry Clay died, and participated in county meetings of the party. John was elected major of the "Pulaski Regiment," and joined in efforts to bring a railroad through Giles County.[17]

On November 5, 1850, John married nineteen-year-old Ann Eliza Pointer. Ann was the daughter of wealthy transplanted Virginians John H. and Martha A. Pointer. A great deal of the Pointers' property was in slaves. Their large holdings of bondsmen (fifty in 1840, ninety-nine in 1860) placed them in the top fifty or sixty slaveholders in the state. The Pointers' house in Pulaski was next door to the hotel where John lived, which doubtlessly provided him ample opportunity to court Ann. The couple eventually moved into a two-story frame house on East Madison Street near the Pointer residence. How his marriage into the upper crust of society was viewed by John's family probably depended on their situation. Neill, of course, from the viewpoint of his political and professional success, likely deemed it an advantageous match. Three of John's sisters, on the other hand, were married to clergymen, including his surrogate mother, Mary Ann McMillan, whose clergyman husband later viewed the slaveholding influence of the Pointers as pernicious. The next year, John further solidified his standing in the community by joining the local Masonic lodge, where he was eventually honored with several leadership positions.[18]

John followed Neill into the Whig Party. The 1850s started with a crisis over the issue of the admission of California as a free state. The crisis was defused by the Compromise of 1850, which was a series of congressional actions that divided irksome sectional issues into separate, more palatable measures. Tennessee Whigs praised the compromise as a "peaceful and honorable adjustment." Whig William B. Campbell ran for governor on the good faith acceptance of the compromise; Neill's successor, Governor Trousdale, took the position that it favored the North too much. Campbell won a narrow victory. The Whigs also took control of the legislature, and led by Representative Gustavus A. Henry, passed a legislative reapportionment (which was waggishly termed the "Henrymander") calculated to give the Whigs control of the General Assembly and the state's congressional delegation. As events would prove, this was the apogee of the influence of the Whigs in the state.[19]

With the Whig Party's decline, new parties arose to contest the Democrats. In areas of the North, the Republican Party formed, but was not attractive to southerners because of its anti-slavery principles. Elsewhere, the growing influx of foreign immigrants birthed the American Party, which had a nativist basis. While the anti-foreign and related anti-Catholic rhetoric of the party, also known as the "Know-Nothings" because of its initial secret meetings and rituals, likely appealed to some southerners, the ultimate true appeal of the party in Tennessee and other parts of the South was its provision of a political base for continued opposition to the Democrats. In 1855, Neill was a recognized leader of this new party in Tennessee, and published a letter in a Nashville newspaper exhorting readers to "make one unbroken effort to vindicate our rights against foreign aggression."[20]

Neill took to the stump in 1856 as the Elector for the State at Large for the American Party's presidential ticket of Millard Fillmore and Tennessean Andrew Jackson Donelson, the former president's nephew and private secretary. In accepting the post, Neill condemned those who agitated over the issue of slavery, asserting the "battle cry" of "the Union and the Constitution." But the party struggled, both because not all former Whigs supported the American Party and because some Democratic defectors who flirted with the Americans were returning to their former fold. Neill's statewide campaign was waged against Andrew Johnson's rival for leadership of the state's Democrats, Isham G. Harris. The argument was mostly over the protection of slavery, as Harris argued that James Buchanan and the national Democratic Party, north and south, were better situated to protect the institution. Neill maintained that northern Democrats had in fact voted against the South on slavery related issues in Congress, while Fillmore was perfectly sound on the issue. Buchanan eventually won, the first time a Democrat presidential candidate carried Tennessee in twenty-four years. Harris, whose political sphere had previously been largely limited to West Tennessee, raised his profile considerably, and would defeat an American Party candidate for governor the next year.[21]

Giles County's voting records indicate a consistent preference for the Democrats in the decade of the 1850s, generally in the 53 percent to 47 percent range, although in the 1856 presidential election and the 1857 gubernatorial election, the Democrats got a few more votes. The bitterness reflected in the rhetoric between the parties in other locations appears to have infected the county, as Democrats would "hurl all sorts of anathemas and vituperation at the Whigs," who in turn would "try to out-do" the Democrats. The rival adherents often physically fought in "fist and skull" encounters. A slave made the mistake of cheering for John C. Fremont, the 1856 candidate of the new Republican Party, and his owner whipped him until "blood ran down his heels." A Whig, replying to a claim that the local Democrats looked up to their leaders, remarked that the Democrats were "so low down that they could not look any other way."[22]

The extent of John's involvement in these rough and tumble politics is unknown. John had his young wife and professional obligations to take

Desires the Perpetuity and Integrity of Our Union

up his time. But John did not eschew politics completely; in 1856 or 1857, he served a term as mayor of Pulaski, being succeeded by his law partner, John Walker. And the family continued to have influence, as in 1855–57 Neill served a term in the state legislature and was elected Speaker of the House. In October 1857, Neill was a candidate for United States Senator, but was defeated for that office by Andrew Johnson. John likely would have supported Neill to the extent he could, which was limited by the fact that the senate seat was filled by a vote among the members of the Tennessee General Assembly.[23]

Ann died childless at age twenty-eight on June 29, 1858. A grieving John threw himself into his work, to the extent of impairing his health. Upon a physician's advice, he determined to travel abroad, so he sold his marital home and left Pulaski. Brown's passport file dated September 29, 1858, indicated he was age thirty-one, six and three quarters feet in height, with a full forehead, grey eyes, an aquiline nose, medium mouth, dark brown hair, "rather dark" complexion, and an oval face. A few days later, John boarded the steamship *Vanderbilt*, which sailed for Southampton, Havre, and Bremen. In the course of his travels, he visited Great Britain, the continent of Europe, the Holy Land, and Egypt. John kept a now-lost diary of his trip, reflecting a voyage up the Nile to the Second Cataract, and by means of a report in a Nashville newspaper, it can be deduced he was in Italy in March through May of 1859. He was back in Pulaski no later than December 1859.[24]

While John was gone, the remnants of the Whigs and Know-Nothings reorganized in Tennessee as simply the Opposition Party, and in 1859 unsuccessfully contested Isham Harris's hold on the governorship. Although the main state issue in the election related to the Democrats' insistence on hard money in the wake of the Panic of 1857, the looming sectional crisis continued to create the most interest, with the Democrats claiming the new party was allied with the abolitionists, while the Opposition advocated the maintenance of slavery under the federal constitution. Although the Opposition made some gains, Harris was re-elected, along with a Democratic majority in the legislature. The other great event of 1859 to put focus on the sectional crisis was John Brown's seizure of the Federal arsenal at Harper's Ferry, Virginia, in hopes of inciting a slave insurrection. While events proved that John Brown and his raiders were simply a small group of anti-slavery zealots, and Republicans convincingly showed they had no complicity in Brown's violent outburst, admiration of Brown's motives from many quarters convinced southerners that they were hated in the North, meaning another intangible tie of Union was lost. Politically, the raid meant that in Tennessee and other parts of the Upper South, any possibility that the Opposition might make common cause with the Republicans in the larger national struggle against the Democrats became impossible.[25]

Whether Ann's death removed an impediment or the crisis facing the country called for more political involvement, in 1860 John C. Brown (who will hereafter be referred to as "Brown") became much more active in politics. On January 14, he was elected to a one-year term as an alderman for Pulaski. Meanwhile, former senator John Bell, Tennessee's most recognizable anti-Jacksonian, perceiving that an alliance with northern Republicans was a non-starter, became a presidential contender. The state Opposition convention on February 22, to which Brown was a delegate from Giles County, resolved to support his candidacy, and that the injurious agitation over slavery should cease. Brown went to the Opposition convention in Baltimore in May, where the name Constitutional Union Party was adopted, with no platform but "The Constitution, the Union, and The Enforcement of its Laws." At the end, Neill, who was also present, "thanked God that he had at last found a Convention in which the 'nigger' was not the sole subject of consideration." Indeed, "[n]ot a word was said from the first to the last about the question of slavery in the Territories, or the execution of the Fugitive Slave law, and old John Brown was only referred to a couple of times."[26]

Conversely, the sectional crisis was at the forefront of the Democratic and Republican conventions, also held that spring. The Democratic convention met in April in unseasonably warm Charleston, South Carolina, hardly the place to expect sectional conciliation. The delegates wrangled over Illinois senator Stephen A. Douglas's concept of "popular sovereignty," whereby the choice of allowing slavery in a territory would be left up to its citizens. When the southern delegates could not get that concept removed from the party platform, they "retired" from the convention. The party reconvened in Baltimore, and again split. The northern faction nominated Douglas. The southern-dominated faction,

Desires the Perpetuity and Integrity of Our Union

including most of the Tennessee delegation, gathered in Richmond, Virginia, and adopted a platform requiring protection of slavery in the territories, and nominated Vice President John C. Breckinridge for president. The last national political party was fractured. As if to emphasize the southern extremists' view that they were a "sectional" party, the Republicans gathered in Chicago, adopted a platform that denied that slavery should be allowed in the territories, and nominated Abraham Lincoln of Illinois. Tennessee was unrepresented at the Republican convention, and no national committeeman was named for Tennessee. The election would go forward in Tennessee with Lincoln not even on the ballot.[27]

Brown returned from the National Union Convention at Baltimore and within the month was listed as a possible presidential elector for the 7th congressional district. On July 5, he was selected as a candidate for that position. Recovering at Bailey Springs, Alabama, from a bout of "ill-health," Brown wrote that he was "not only willing, but anxious to do battle in a cause that addresses itself to the heart of every man who loves his country, and desires the perpetuity and integrity of our Union, with all its constitutional rights." A month later, at Pulaski, Brown debated Breckinridge Democrat W. J. Sykes of Columbia for about five and a half hours. A correspondent of the Bell organ, the *Nashville Republican Banner*, observed that Sykes skillfully advanced a "specious and logical" argument that Breckinridge and his party were the only friends of the South. Brown was noted to have replied "with great ability," condemning Sykes's faction as promoting a "sectional candidate on a sectional platform." The writer observed that John's "urbane manner, cultivated intellect, and elevated patriotism all conspire to make him a 'tower' of strength in the present canvass." Brown also found time to represent, with his partner, Walker, a criminal defendant accused of raping a four year old girl. They lost, although they were able on appeal to the Tennessee Supreme Court to get a new trial on the basis of a statutory technicality.[28]

While the campaign started with Sykes, Brown's main opponent during the 1860 canvass was Nicholas Nichols Cox, a twenty-three year old lawyer serving as the Breckinridge elector for the district. Over the weeks between the end of August and the election on November 6, Cox and Brown traveled across the district speaking on behalf of their respective tickets. The states' rights Democratic organ, the *Nashville Union and American*, wrote that Cox destroyed Brown while debating Bell's positions for and against various issues in the long course of his public life, while papers friendly to the Constitutional Union Party extolled Brown's condemnation of Breckinridge's sectional platform. Acknowledging that Breckinridge was correct on his views of slavery, Brown lamented that he was unfortunately being used as a tool of the disunionists: "It is known that the leading Breckinridge democrats of the cotton states especially, have openly declared that the election of a black republican is just cause for disunion. Here, then, we have a party which has openly declared beforehand that it will subvert the ballot-box with the sword, and will declare an election void which is not in accordance with its wishes, and which at the same time is tending to produce that very event." Friendly correspondents condemned young Cox's passionate hatred of Bell, and contrasted that with Brown's sustaining his "high character for fairness, conservatism, patriotism and enlightened statesmanship." Another noted that Brown's "mild, gentlemanly appearance, his keen, fearless eye, clear and cogent reasoning, determined and dispassionate eloquence, command respect alike from friend and foe, and carries conviction home to the heart." Happily, a persistent bronchial condition that somewhat affected Brown early in the canvass resolved itself, and a correspondent observed that he looked better and appeared to be in better health "than he had been for years." Brown also was observed to have improved over the course of the debate in his public speaking powers. A good sign for future political prospects, an admirer wrote that "I have no doubt that John C. Brown is regarded as the ablest man of our party in this district. . . ."[29]

Although there was little movement in Bell's favor in Brown's district, Tennessee's favorite son won the state, with Breckinridge a fairly close second. Overall, Bell won the same proportion of the state vote that Fillmore got in 1856. The difference was that enough of the Democratic vote was siphoned from Breckinridge by Douglas to allow Bell to win the state. For the most part, Tennesseans deplored Abraham Lincoln's election, but did not see it as a reason to break the ties of Union. Unfortunately, the men who controlled South Carolina did not agree, and that state seceded on December 20, 1860. In the next six weeks, six other lower South states left the Union. Unionists and secessionists in Tennessee agreed that some sort of course should be charted, and there were widespread calls for Governor Harris to call the legislature into special session. In late November, Neill joined in a published appeal to the people of the state advocating such a call, which was accommodated by Harris in December, when he set a special session for January 7, 1861.[30]

In his message to the special session, Harris indicted the North for acts or omissions that hindered the enjoyment of "slave property" and tended to "exclude the slaveholder from the territory acquired by the common blood and treasure of all the States." Harris recommended a referendum which would determine whether a convention should be called "to take into consideration our federal relations, and determine what action shall be taken by the State of Tennessee for the security of the rights and the peace of her citizens." At the same time, delegates for the convention would be elected should it be approved. On January 19, an act was passed that called for the election Harris suggested, to be held February 9. But the Unionist element were able to insert a requirement that any action of the convention that changed the relationship between the state and the Union must be ratified by a vote, with a majority measured by the majority of all those voting in the gubernatorial election of 1859.[31]

Harris's speech reflected a substantial secessionist sentiment that was building in Tennessee, as well as other places in the Upper South. But antisecession forces were not yet defeated, although the depth of their commitment to the Union was of varying degrees. Basically, they were divided into unconditional Unionists, the most well-known of which in Tennessee was Senator Andrew Johnson, and conditional Unionists, who were inclined to stay with the Union so long as no effort was made to bring the seceded states back by force. All Unionists tended to reject the secessionist idea that the economic interests of the Upper South lay with the seceded states, believed that the fire-eating secessionists had conspired to frighten their fellow southerners, that secession was therefore a mass delusion, and that southern misunderstanding of northern intentions created a threat of war that only the Republicans could correct.[32]

The immediate issue for both sides was the February 9 election. The secessionist "Southern Rights Anti-Coercion" group were basically Democrats, and they urged the approval of the convention and the election of "men who will resist coercion to the death." The "Southern Rights

Unionists" split between those conservatives who thought a convention could be used to defuse the secessionists, and those who thought a convention was both unnecessary and might be seized by fire-eaters who would take Tennessee out of the Union. Just to be safe, the Unionist newspapers urged the election of a Unionist ticket regardless of whether the individual voter wanted a convention or not, but cautioned: "If you are opposed to a convention and vote against it, be sure to vote for the Union candidates. An omission to vote for these candidates is the same as a vote against them." Although the old party traditions were something of a basis for membership in either faction, the consensus in the state was that the old party distinctions were meaningless—one was either for or against the Union or secession. Neill was a Unionist candidate for the convention in Nashville, Brown for Giles County.[33]

The result was a resounding win for the Unionists. The convention lost by 11,589 votes, and a majority of Unionist delegates won. In Giles County, the voters were pro-convention by a margin of 1,531 to 550. But demonstrating that perhaps some of the pro-convention voters were Unionists who thought a convention would be of benefit, John was elected Giles County's delegate with 1,831 votes. On February 17, a joyous Neill wrote to his old political rival, Andrew Johnson: "The happiest day of my whole life was the 9th inst. when I witnessed the stern verdict of the people of my native state in behalf of the Union." But Isham Harris and the secessionists were confident that Tennessee would join the Confederacy. In a meeting with an envoy from Georgia, Harris "deeply deplored the result of the election" but "expressed the opinion that the withdrawal of Tennessee from the Government of the United States and its union with the Confederate States of America was only a question of time." Lincoln's inauguration on March 4 passed without any further significant developments in the state, although secessionists chose to interpret his inaugural speech as a threat of force. The Unionist party began to prepare for the gubernatorial and congressional elections scheduled for later in 1861. The Giles County Union party held a meeting on April 8, and determined to nominate Brown for Congress at the 7th District Union convention to be held May 11, passing a resolution asserting that "that secession is not a remedy either for existing evils or for anticipated dangers from the Administration of Mr. Lincoln, and in our opinion

Desires the Perpetuity and Integrity of Our Union

there is no adequate cause at present, for Tennessee to dissolve her connection with the Federal government." Ominously, the April 13 edition of the Nashville *Republican Banner* that reported on the Giles Union meeting also featured the headline: "Fort Sumter Attacked."[34]

Throughout the crisis, Neill, John Bell, and other prominent Whigs were the Unionist center of gravity. But the Confederate attack on Fort Sumter was met by President Lincoln's proclamation on April 15 requesting 75,000 troops to suppress the rebellion in the seceded states. Southern Unionists saw this naked threat of force as a betrayal. In his February letter to Johnson, Neill predicted that many Union men "would be carried off in a storm." For Neill, and many other Unionists, that prophecy came true. East Tennessee Unionist Oliver P. Temple deemed the Unionist leaders of Middle Tennessee "splendid leaders," but wrote of a private meeting with Neill and others in early May in which Temple judged his mid-state compatriots "paralyzed. They had not yet joined the enemy, and they declared they never would; yet they were evidently under the influence of the prevailing feeling in Middle Tennessee. They were timid, cautious, hesitating." Indeed, a few days earlier Neill wrote a letter advocating arming the state, because "the conviction is forced upon my mind that it is the settled policy of the Administration, and so far as I can see, of the whole North, to wage a war of extermination against the South." Yet, days later, with Temple present to stiffen his resolve, Neill "arose, and putting one hand behind him, and striding back and forth across the room, he poured forth an eloquent denunciation of secession, declaring in the most earnest terms his determination to stand by the Union." Temple concluded he "was wanting in the boldness necessary for a leader."[35]

Nine years later, Brown stridently stated that he "was *not* the advocate of secession, and *never was* in favor of secession." Brown advocated the Union almost to the bitter end, giving the very last Union speech in his congressional district. But in the end, whether in favor of secession or not, Brown joined the secessionist cause. The influence of friends and family likely came into play, as community political currents in that period had a role in changing Unionists into secessionists. Indeed, to that extent Brown may have been "forced" to join the rebels. Brown's surrogate father and brother-in-law, Edward McMillan, thought Ann's family influenced the decision. Neill's faltering support of the Union was likely of some influence as well. But to take Brown at his word some years later, for him and other Unionists in Giles County, Lincoln's proclamation calling for troops to invade the South indeed made the difference. "With one voice the multitude declared for resistance. In response to that universal sentiment . . . I . . . went to war." And thus it was that John C. Brown, who at the first of April 1861 was a Unionist candidate for Congress, was by the end of that month calling for the raising and equipping of a secessionist artillery company.[36]

Desires the Perpetuity and Integrity of Our Union

2

Fellow Victims
of the Fatal Blunder

Early Service and the Campaigns of 1862

On May 6, 1861, the Tennessee General Assembly passed a "declaration of independence" dissolving the state's relationship with the United States of America, which would be confirmed by a referendum held in June. That same day, the legislature authorized raising, arming, and equipping an army of 55,000 volunteers to defend the state. The next day, May 7, the state government moved to militarily ally itself with the Confederate States of America in its struggle with the United States. In short order, Tennessee joined its Confederate allies in a war with the Federal government.[1]

Anticipating the organization of a state army, on May 1, 1861, men from all over Giles County assembled in Pulaski and organized themselves into a company, which they styled the "Giles Boys." They elected John C. Brown as their captain, and his friend and fellow attorney Calvin J. Clack as first lieutenant. The men were presented with a "splendid gray jeans uniform" made up by the "noble and self-sacrificing ladies of the county." Prior to departing town, the company assembled at the Methodist Church in Pulaski, listened to a sermon, and "asked God to bless our efforts to defend our country and preserve our liberty." In the meantime, Brown received an appointment as an assistant adjutant general of the Provisional Army of Tennessee, which he quickly declined. On May 16, the Giles Boys assembled at Lynnville, and joined with four other companies from Giles County, three from Maury County, and one each from Lawrence and Lewis counties to organize as the 3rd Tennessee Regiment. Brown was unanimously elected the regiment's colonel, and Clack took over the captaincy of the company. The other officers of the regiment were Lt. Col. Thomas M. Gordon, a thirty-three-year-old Giles County farmer of some substance, and Major Nathaniel F. Cheairs, a forty-three-year-old Maury County farmer of wealth and social prominence who was a peacetime friend of Brown's.[2]

Seen off at the depot in Pulaski by a thousand well-wishers, the bulk of the regiment proceeded to Nashville, where they were sworn into the state service on May 19. They then immediately proceeded to the Capitol building and drew arms, which were described as "old United States muskets." The men were disappointed with the old smoothbores, although it was believed they would only have them for the purposes of drill. They then entrained for Camp Cheatham in Robertson County, near the Kentucky border. The camp was under the command of Brig. Gen. Robert C. Foster of the state army. There, the regiment pitched its tents, and "commenced the study and practice of Hardee's tactics." The men all voted in the June 8 election confirming the *fait accompli* of Tennessee's joining the Confederacy, and suffered from camp diseases, primarily measles. Brown undertook the "onerous and responsible duties of disciplining and instructing" his regiment, and read army regulations to the assembled men. The men graduated from squad drill to company drill, and finally to battalion drill after five weeks of hard work.[3]

On July 26, 1861, the 3rd moved from Camp Cheatham to Camp Trousdale, along the Louisville & Nashville Railroad in Sumner County, named after Neill's political rival in 1849. On August 7, the 3rd ceased its existence as a regiment of the Provisional Army of Tennessee and became a unit of the Confederate States Army. While at Trousdale, the health of the regiment began to improve, as the regiment camped on "high ground close to a spring of the purest water." In retrospect, a soldier of Company C deemed this period a "continuous holiday," although the men were too fresh from their civilian lives to comprehend that. Indeed, the 885 members of the regiment were served by almost 75 slaves, and were so situated along the railroad that visitors from Giles County were in camp almost every day, especially on the weekends, when they brought "luxuries in abundance." These amenities made their existence a "quasi-picnic." Their regimental surgeon, Samuel H. Stout, who later became the medical director of the Army of Tennessee, appreciated the "difficulty, delicacy and tediousness" of the work undertaken by Brown and his officers, as the men, or their parents, were mostly "well-to-do

Fellow Victims of the Fatal Blunder

Fragment of Flag of Third Tennessee Regiment captured at Fort Donelson
(Credit: Tennessee State Museum)

farmers" accustomed to "wholesome and nutritious food, and to the comforts of the best of moral homes." While his men had it relatively easy at Trousdale, Brown's duties increased substantially as he took command of all troops there as senior colonel.[4]

Governor Isham G. Harris's strategy for the defense of the state was to politically shield Tennessee's northern line from Federal invasion, hiding behind a "neutral" Kentucky in order to allow the Confederate government time to arm enough troops to defend the state, a policy with which Confederate president Jefferson Davis concurred. This strategy indeed bought the Confederacy time, at least until September 3, when Maj. Gen. Leonidas Polk occupied Columbus, Kentucky, with Confederate troops. With Kentucky neutrality thus dissolved, the new Confederate theater commander, Gen. Albert Sidney Johnston, determined to advance his line north into central Kentucky to Bowling Green, and secured the appointment of Brig. Gen. Simon Bolivar Buckner, a southern-sympathizing Kentuckian, as commander of the sector.[5]

On September 15, 1861, Buckner was ordered to assume command of the five thousand or so troops at Trousdale and another camp and occupy Bowling Green. At 8:00 a.m. on the morning of September 17, Brown gave orders to cook two days rations, and the men loaded their effects on to wagons for transportation to the depot. The move of the brigade-sized force took the rest of the day and into the next, Brown arriving in the Kentucky town on September 18. Brown's men found that the residents of Bowling Green were decidedly not secessionist, and only came around to tolerate and even compliment the men of the 3rd after they had an opportunity to appreciate their soldierly qualities and courtesy. Brown's men camped on the banks of the Barren River, and with a short exception, spent time drilling and building fortifications.[6]

Although it featured natural advantages that made it a strong defensive position in and of itself, Bowling Green was a difficult position for reasons relating to its suitability for overall defense and the road networks to both the north and south. Johnston was compelled to hold the place because of the need to support Polk's fortifications on the Mississippi River at Columbus. Johnston established his theater headquarters there, and there were discussions of possible offensive operations in the fall of 1861, which ceased as the Federal strength in north-central Kentucky grew. To what extent Brown would have been part of these discussions is not clear, and in any event he was away on unspecified detached service for a period in October. At the end of that month, though, Johnston had seen enough of Brown to recommend him for promotion to brigadier general, observing in a communication to Confederate adjutant general Samuel Cooper that Brown's "regiment is in excellent condition; its thorough instruction and discipline is a commendation indicating that he will make an efficient commander of a brigade."[7]

Unfortunately for Brown, there was no action on Johnston's request. Nonetheless, the commanding general thought enough of the Tennessean to have him accompany him on a reconnaissance early in November toward Glasgow, Kentucky. Johnston enjoyed being away from headquarters and while camped one night, the rebel force got word of Federal brigadier general Ulysses S. Grant's landing at Belmont, Missouri, across the Mississippi River from Polk's Columbus position. Anticipating the start of a larger Federal movement, Johnston ordered Brown to take a hundred horsemen, scout the various fords on the Big Barren River, and report to him at Bowling Green the next night. Brown expressed the thought that he could do the job quicker with only six men. Johnston replied "Well as my friend Captain Jack Hays used to say, on the plains of Texas when about leaving camp of a morning, looking at his revolvers—'Perhaps I will not need you to day but if I do I will need you damned badly'—so with you and the cavalry Colonel Brown; you may not need them at all; but if you do you will need them quick and very badly; so you had better take them along with you." Brown took the men and completed the mission.[8]

As reinforcements flowed into Bowling Green, a more formal organization of what became known as the Army Corps of Central Kentucky occurred, and Brown retained command of the Third Brigade of Buckner's Division, including his own 3rd Tennessee, as well as the 18th and 23rd Tennessee regiments. The 18th was under the command of Colonel Joseph B. Palmer, a thirty-six-year-old former Whig lawyer from Murfreesboro. The regiment was made up of companies from several Middle Tennessee communities, including Rutherford, Cannon, Davidson, Sumner, Cheatham, Bedford, and Wilson counties. The 23rd would eventually be replaced by the 32nd Tennessee, under the command of another former Whig, thirty-three-year-old Franklin lawyer Colonel Edmond C. Cook. The 32nd was also made up of men from Middle Tennessee, including Lincoln, Marshall, Lawrence, Williamson, and Franklin counties, as well as four companies from Giles County.[9]

While Brown and his men began the winter in their comfortable quarters in Bowling Green, theater commander Johnston's narrow focus on that position and Leonidas Polk's single-minded determination to base the defense of his West Tennessee district on his position on the Mississippi River at Columbus left the riverine invasion route between those two advanced positions in Kentucky with little attention. In May 1861, just a few days after Tennessee entered into its military alliance with the Confederacy, Governor Harris dispatched an engineer to "locate and construct defensive works on the Cumberland and Tennessee Rivers." Notwithstanding this quick start, for most of the rest of 1861, the Confederate effort to construct effective works to block the two rivers was hindered by lack of laborers, artillery, and troops, and by varying degrees of neglect, localism, and controversy from almost anyone with command authority over the two projects.[10]

Ultimately, Fort Henry was located on the east bank of the Tennessee River just a few miles south of the Kentucky line. Fort Donelson lay on the west bank of the Cumberland near the small town of Dover about twelve miles to the east of Fort Henry. By December 1861, the Federal leadership in the west was clearly beginning to focus on the two rivers as a means of penetrating the Confederate defense line. Troops under Brig. Gen. Ulysses S. Grant demonstrated toward Columbus on January 9, 1862, with no immediate result on the Union side except for muddying up roads and weather-related casualties. But on the Confederate side, Albert Sidney Johnston decided that the move might be a precursor to an advance around Polk's right flank toward Nashville, and on January 20 ordered a detachment of eight thousand men from Bowling Green southwest to Russellville, Kentucky, twenty-nine miles down the Memphis, Clarksville, and Louisville Railroad.[11]

Brown's three regiments were part of the force transferred to Russellville, arriving on January 22. While there, Brown and his men learned of a serious defeat of the Confederate forces guarding East Tennessee at Mill Springs, Kentucky, that occurred on January 19. Brown's fellow prewar Whig, Brig. Gen. Felix Zollicoffer, was killed, the rebel troops in that area scattered in retreat, and the eastern flank of Johnston's line of defense in southern Kentucky dissolved. Johnston realized that the result of the defeat was to either leave East Tennessee open to invasion, or to expose the right flank of his position shielding Nashville. And the department commander saw in Federal movements on his left threats to the positions at Fort Henry and Fort Donelson, which would indicate an advance on Nashville from that quarter. He called on the Richmond government for reinforcements, having just over a week before sent a member of his staff, Col. St. John Richardson Liddell to President Davis, who met a similar request with the exclamation, "Why did General Johnston send you to me for arms and reinforcements when he must know I have neither?"[12]

Johnston would have to make do with what he had, especially as the crisis he feared was at hand. On January 30, Grant received authorization to move against Fort Henry. Organizing his troops into two divisions,

Fellow Victims of the Fatal Blunder

Grant moved off up the Tennessee River from Paducah, Kentucky, on February 3. The Confederates at the fort, commanded by Brig. Gen. Lloyd Tighlman, had no warning of the invasion, and when the boats arrived and started debarking bluecoats, Tighlman was actually supervising work at Fort Donelson. As events transpired, the Federal infantry never got the chance to storm the fort, as the superior weight of the guns trained on the partially flooded works by the Union gunboats overwhelmed the defenders' cannon. Tighlman dispatched the bulk of Fort Henry's garrison east to join the troops at Fort Donelson, while he stayed with seventy-six officers and men to surrender Fort Henry to the Federal navy on February 6.[13]

Johnston knew that Fort Donelson was probably next, and was painfully aware of the consequence of the loss of that point. Indeed, Brown later related to Johnston's son and biographer that he was with Johnston the first few days of February, and the department commander anticipated even at that point the possible need to fall back far to the south, behind the Tennessee River, and concentrate at Corinth, Mississippi. Expecting the loss of the fort, he gave orders to begin the evacuation of Bowling Green. Disastrously, he abdicated responsibility for defense of Fort Donelson to Brig. Gen. John Buchanan Floyd and Brig. Gen. Gideon Johnson Pillow. Floyd was a veteran Virginia politician who just over a year before had been the United States secretary of war. Gideon Pillow was a friend and political ally of former president James K. Polk, and as a result of the same, achieved the rank of major general of volunteers in the Mexican War. On the strength of that, he was the senior officer of Isham Harris's Provisional Army of Tennessee, but only made the grade of Confederate brigadier general. As events would prove, neither was up to such an important command.[14]

Unfortunately for Simon Bolivar Buckner and the men under his command, even as he left the defense of the Cumberland sector to Floyd and Pillow, Johnston ordered Pillow to move to Donelson with the troops at Clarksville and Russellville and assume command. Brown's brigade accordingly traveled to Clarksville by rail and then up the river to the fort by steamer, the 3rd Tennessee taking passage on the *B. M. Runyan*. The bulk of the brigade appears to have reached the fort on February 8, in "cold and unpleasant" weather without food or tents. Giving three cheers

Simon B. Buckner (Credit:
Alabama Department of
Archives and History,
Montgomery, Alabama)

for their neighbors from Giles County, the men of the 53rd Tennessee shared food and tents with the men of the 3rd.[15]

The next day, a few of the men went out to inspect the defenses, and arrived in time to rapidly fall in on a false alarm. Pillow assigned Brown's brigade to the right, where it was posted on the crest of a hill. Woefully short of tools, the men began digging rifle pits and felling timber to build breastworks and form abatis, working night and day, "through rain and snow yet most of them bore it without a murmur." The timber in front of the line was cut about six hundred yards in front of the line to afford a clear field of fire. Buckner observed that as a whole, the army defended a space "quadrangular in shape," bounded on the north by the river, on the east and the west by streams "now converted into deep sloughs by . . . high water," and on the south by the line then being constructed. The whole purpose of the fort was to interdict the Cumberland with artillery. The line being built by Brown's brigade and the rest of Buckner's command shielded the land approach to the water batteries.[16]

Fellow Victims of the Fatal Blunder

Buckner arrived at the fort on February 11, the same day as Brown, possibly because Buckner kept the colonel with his staff. The Kentuckian had Floyd's blessing to remove his division from the potential trap at Fort Donelson. Pillow refused to allow Bucker's men to leave, however, directing him to stay at the fort until he had a chance to discuss the matter with Floyd. Floyd and Buckner thought a concentration downriver at Cumberland City would allow for a more flexible defense of the area, and planned to leave only enough men at Donelson to defend the water batteries. Appealing to Johnston, Pillow insisted that he could hold the fort with Buckner's men, but not otherwise. But as the Confederate high command debated, Grant and the Federals acted. On the morning of February 12, Lt. Col. Nathan Bedford Forrest, commanding the cavalry screen to the west of the fort, reported the bluecoats were advancing in force toward the rebel defenses. Johnston therefore decided to make the fight for the Cumberland at Fort Donelson, and directed Floyd to go to the fort.[17]

The arrival of the Federals made the work to complete Brown's line of defense difficult during daylight hours, so the next three nights many men worked in the intense cold to improve the works. Although incomplete, the fortifications proved to be a sufficient impediment to the first Federal advance, which occurred at two points on the Confederate line the morning of February 13. Brown's force was strengthened that morning by the temporary attachment of two additional regiments, the 14th Mississippi and the 41st Tennessee. Grant made two advances that day, one on the Confederate center held by Col. Augustus Heiman's brigade, and the other on the extreme right, held by Col. Roger Hanson's 2nd Kentucky. Brown directed Capt. Rice E. Graves and his Kentucky light artillery to provide fire support for Heiman's line, which helped break up the Federal attack, while Hanson was effectively supported by fire from Captain Thomas K. Porter's Tennessee light artillery. Besides the two batteries, the only part of Brown's brigade that was engaged on February 13 were two companies of Palmer's 18th Tennessee, which, along with fire from Porter's cannon, helped Hanson repulse the attack on his line. When the woods over which the Federals made this second advance caught fire, Captain Flavel C. Barber of the 3rd's Company K "agoniz[ed]" over "the groans and the screams of the poor helpless men suffering this double torture." On the river, a federal gunboat directed long range fire into the water batteries, which resulted in a few casualties on each side. The day ended with Grant realizing that Fort Donelson would be a tougher nut to crack than Fort Henry.[18]

That night, it snowed, and the temperature, already cold, dropped to around twelve degrees Fahrenheit. The work continued on the fortifications, although the men suffered terribly. Dawn of February 14 came with icy grounds and cold winds, and the only action on the land side of the fort was occasional sharpshooting on both sides. Floyd and Pillow summoned Buckner to a council of war, and it was determined to attack on the Confederate left to open a line of communication to Charlotte, toward Nashville. But after preparations got under way, the attack was called off, as Pillow thought it too late in the day. In any event, all attention soon became focused on the river, as the Federal gunboat flotilla steamed down to engage the water batteries. While the Federal shells were directed at the water battery, overshots resulted in explosions away from the battery, causing Brown's slave Ned to jump in a hole where one of the black cooks was hiding. The cook complained that Ned was "mashin the life outen me," causing the frightened Ned to offer to switch places with the cook. An afternoon's fighting resulted in the almost total defeat of the naval attack, as three of the four ironclads in the six gunboat attack were disabled.[19]

Notwithstanding the victory over the feared gunboats, however, the Confederate council of war reconvened that night. Convinced that Grant had been significantly reinforced, the senior commanders settled on a plan that was essentially Pillow's, calling for an attack by most of both divisions on the left early the next morning. The brigade commanders were summoned and given instructions, but there was no clear direction relative to what would happen if the way to Nashville was opened. Buckner's front was to be almost completely evacuated but for a single regiment, and he seems to have believed that certain units would have to be sacrificed to save the whole of the army. For his part, Brown thought the purpose of the attack "to turn the enemy's right wing and march out on the Wynn's Ferry road to fall back upon Nashville." Apparently not expecting to spend another night in Fort Donelson, Brown had his men cook three days rations and bring their knapsacks.[20]

Fellow Victims of the Fatal Blunder

The movement on February 15 started with an almost unendurable delay. Brown's orders were to move his command to the left as soon as the 30th Tennessee, from the garrison proper of the fort, occupied his lines. Exasperated by the 30th's tardiness, Brown finally put his column into motion, leaving the men then in the rifle pits to hold the line until the 30th arrived. Brown admitted that his men moved out "in some disorder," likely caused by slippery conditions and the disruption of leaving a portion of the command in the entrenchments. At Buckner's direction, Brown deployed the 3rd in the rifle pits of Pillow's men, who were then concentrated on the left, and kept the rest of the brigade in reserve, waiting for "the proper moment of coordination." In the meantime, Buckner directed the placement of Graves's battery and ordered it to fire on two Federal artillery positions visible from his position.[21]

Pillow's attack on the left started around daylight, striking Brig. Gen. John A. McClernand's reinforced Federal division. While the rough terrain, pockets of Federal resistance, and the inexperience of the rebel officers and men hindered the Confederate advance, the superior numbers of butternut soldiers bent McClernand's line at a right angle. Buckner was somewhat intimidated by the Federal batteries in his front, so no advance came from his lines against the imperiled Union front until Pillow asked for help. Indeed, in the case of the 32nd Tennessee, Pillow bypassed Buckner and directly ordered Col. Cook to attack one of the Federal batteries in his front. Buckner and Brown arrived and confirmed the order, having, it seems, already ordered the 14th Mississippi to advance and the 3rd and then the 18th Tennessee to support it.[22]

The men surged forward, met, as Brown observed, by a "murderous fire." Louis Adams of the 3rd Tennessee wrote that "[t]here was a million of balls fired at us." The rebels "returned a steady fire," and a slugfest went on, in the view of Col. Palmer of the 18th, "for a considerable time." Eventually, the Federal battery and its supporting line retreated, threatened by other Confederates on their right, and by the exhaustion of ammunition. One of Buckner's staff, Maj. Alexander Casseday, ordered the 14th Mississippi back into the entrenchments, in Buckner's words "under a misapprehension of instructions," requiring their Tennessean compatriots to follow. Brown deemed "further pursuit . . . impracticable in that direction," especially as "the companies [became] separated and somewhat intermixed" in the advance. One of the soldiers in the 3rd put it more bluntly: the Confederates were "scattered badly."[23]

As the Federal flank was pushed more to the Confederate right, Buckner determined to launch another attack to affect the Union line of retreat along the Wynn's Ferry Road. Buckner organized artillery support, and then ordered Brown and his brigade forward. At least part of the 3rd was under "furious" shelling, keeping the men pinned down in their rifle pits. Brown jumped from his horse, waved his sword over his head, and cried: "Men of the 3rd Tenn., come out of the pits." The 3rd formed a line in back of their fortifications, and Brown left the conduct of the regiment to Lt. Col. Gordon. Crossing the trenches, and forming into double column, the brigade advanced toward the supposed position of a Federal battery. The 3rd was deployed on the left, the 18th in the center, and the 32nd on the right. The advance went across an open field and then up a hill, where it overran a section of Federal artillery and drove the Federal line up a densely thicketed hill. It appears that Brown and his men encountered very little resistance at this phase of the battle, as their opponents from Col. W. H. L. Wallace's brigade were at that time in retreat. At this point, as the Federals in their front were falling back, it became difficult to determine the new Federal position or the numbers Brown and his men faced. Brown moved his men forward on the best information that he had, after Palmer and Cook had themselves personally scouted ahead to find the enemy. A Federal prisoner was captured and brought to Brown, who asked him a few questions and then sent him on to the rear.[24]

In the meantime, McClernand's hard-pressed troops were reinforced by nine regiments of Brig. Gen. Lew Wallace's division, which drew a new line perpendicular to the Wynn's Ferry Road. Under orders from Buckner, Brown ordered the advance resumed. The brigade soon came under fire within 100 to 150 yards of the enemy, and the men were ordered to lie down while the advance skirmishers tried to pick off the men serving their cannon. Brown then gave the command, "Forward! Storm the battery!" The bluecoats were on the higher ground, but most of their fire passed over Brown's line, although Lt. Col. Gordon of the 3rd and Lt. Col. W. P. Moore of the 32nd both fell wounded. The wounded Gordon ordered the 3rd to fall back under the cover of the hill, but Brown, after some difficulty, rallied his men with the help of Buckner and placed

Fellow Victims of the Fatal Blunder

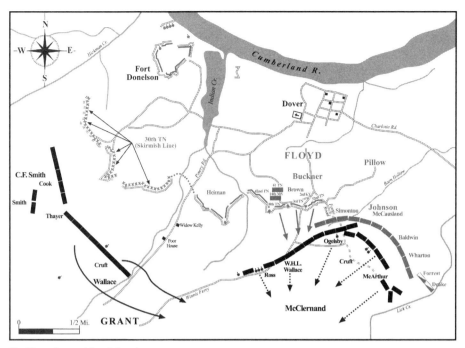

Ft. Donelson. Alex Mendoza.

them back in line of battle. With Gordon out, command of the 3rd fell to Maj. Cheairs. Col. Palmer had the impression that the rebel fire was more accurate than that of the Federals, an impression confirmed by at least one Federal witness. Cook reported that the 32nd was protected by the heavy timber and the hillside from the Federal fire. Both the 18th and the 32nd were mostly armed with ancient flint-lock muskets and their rate of fire was affected by their priming powder getting wet from the melting snow. The men of the 32nd fell back to clean their weapons, while the lack of ammunition and the disappearance of the Federals from their front essentially stopped the 18th. The Federals later claimed they had finally stopped the rebel attack, and Buckner and Brown reported the Wynn's Ferry Road was completely open. Both sides may have been partially right, as the final Federal position on the road was the place chosen to stop the rout of McClernand's men—not a position to prevent a rebel breakout. Critically, the way to Nashville was open.[25]

With escape made possible by the execution of Pillow's attack plan, the failure of the inexperienced Confederate commanders to completely define the particulars of the breakout and order of march from the lines around the fort now negated the morning's success. Without consulting Floyd or Buckner, Pillow began ordering the rebel troops back to their entrenchments, so that the second phase of the operation, gathering the whole Confederate force and their artillery and supplies for the march out of the perimeter, could begin. Buckner protested, but Pillow eventually convinced Floyd of the necessity to consolidate before the march began. Brown received orders to return to his jump-off point from both of those officers, which was effected while his troops tried to gather in their wounded comrades from the day's fighting and to collect the spoils of the battlefield.[26]

The Confederate attack caught Grant by surprise. The Federal commander was conferring with Flag Officer Andrew H. Foote on his flagship in the river. He did not make it back to the front lines until about 1:00 p.m., when Brown's final assault was under way. Correctly surmising that the Confederate right was stripped to make the assault, he ordered his left division, commanded by Brig. Gen. Charles F. Smith, to advance. The alarmed Confederate command reacted, and Pillow ordered Maj. Cheairs to double quick the 3rd Tennessee back to the rebel right. When Cheairs protested that he was there under Buckner's orders, Pillow insisted he was in command and directed Cheairs to obey his order. Cheairs agreed, with the qualification that his men could not double quick because they were "broke down & almost frozen & Starved to death." Smith pushed through the thinly held original line, and moved toward a ridge about five hundred yards to its rear. There they encountered the 2nd Kentucky, the lead element of Buckner's exhausted division, supported by the 3rd Tennessee, followed soon by Brown and the rest of the brigade. Captain Barber saw numerous examples of individual heroism from the outnumbered men of the 3rd. Supported by Porter's battery, the rebels succeeded in halting the Federal advance. The afternoon ended in darkness after a "long and desperate," but successful, struggle to restore the line.[27]

The men of Brown's brigade worked well into the night on the new line of breastworks confronting Smith's Federal division. With Cheairs exhausted in his tent, Brown exercised more direct supervision over the 3rd, leaving Barber in command of the five companies of the regiment on

Fellow Victims of the Fatal Blunder

"that cheerless hill" with orders to keep a "strict watch." Floyd gave orders that the army should prepare to break out of the perimeter, and it was 2:00 a.m. by the time Brown received that order. The orders were passed along to the regiments of the brigade, and in the early morning darkness the men moved back toward Dover. As Cheairs was conducting the 3rd Tennessee, he encountered one of Buckner's staff, who ordered him to halt his march and wait in place for orders. The officer then asked for the location of Brown's headquarters. Cheairs waited about an hour in the freezing cold, and then went to see Brown himself. Cheairs found the colonel "Mad as a hornet." Brown said: "We are going to Surrender, [and] I want you to take a flag of truce to Grant with some dispatches from Buckner." Cheairs could not believe his ears, but Buckner's staff officer confirmed the pending capitulation, and informed Cheairs that Floyd and the brigade of Virginians were leaving aboard a transport, that Pillow was also departing, and that Forrest, refusing to surrender, was escaping with his command.[28]

Earlier that night, there was a conference of the regimental, brigade, and division commanders, and orders were given to begin the breakout at 4:00 a.m. on February 16. At some point after these decisive orders, Floyd, Pillow, and Buckner began to waver, as reports relative to the presence of the Federals and the probable impassability of the roads around them began filtering in. These reports, as well as the clear fatigue of the men and the overestimated yet substantial Federal reinforcements, began preying on the minds of the Confederate leaders. Buckner, the only remotely competent general of the three, was most pessimistic, and contended that the army would be subject to a "massacre." Pillow, who entertained a mutual personal dislike of Buckner, disagreed. Finally, after a period of wrangling, Floyd agreed with Buckner, and Pillow gave in. But as Cheairs was told, Floyd and Pillow did not stay to surrender—they departed, leaving the already defeated Buckner to make the arrangements. Brown wrote his sister and brother-in-law a few days later to the effect that he was offered a chance to escape with the two generals, but that he "scorned to do so mean a thing."[29]

Cheairs agreed to take the flag of truce forward. Brown cut a strip off of his tent, fastened it to a hickory pole, and asked Lt. David Rhea to accompany the major as a bugler. None of the three knew what the surrender call was. As Cheairs recalled, the exasperated Brown "told the Bugler to blow everything he knew & if that did not do to blow his D.M. brains out." Reaching Federal lines about daylight, Cheairs encountered C. F. Smith and was sent on to Grant. Grant wrote out a response, and gave Cheairs an unreasonably short amount of time, given the rough country with patches of snow and sleet. Grant relented a bit, but said he would open his guns if Cheairs did not bring back a response within an hour and fifty minutes. Cheairs returned to Confederate lines, found Brown with his horse saddled, handed over the papers, and Brown took them on to Buckner. Buckner, though deeming Grant's terms of unconditional surrender harsh, surrendered. Eventually, Cheairs conducted Grant to confer with Buckner at his headquarters, and the surrender was formalized.[30]

The Confederate rank and file was "thunderstruck." Seeing "the white flag floating where the 'Bonnie Blue'" had waved," the "hearts sank" within the men of the 3rd. Louis Adams of the 3rd recorded in his diary that "I never saw men look as bad in my life." W. S. Jennings, 2nd Lieutenant of the regiment's Company C, the "Bigby Greys," wrote that "[s]hould the question of capitulation have been left to their decision, their reply would have been like that of the Old Guard of Napoleon—the Garrison can die but never surrender." Brown doubtlessly shared his troops' mortification, but also had the duty to honor the terms of the surrender. After Brown's death, a story appeared in the Memphis *Appeal* that was reprinted in the *National Tribune* that reflected this conflict between enmity and duty. In that account, Grant came through Brown's lines on the way to see Buckner. One of Grant's staff introduced them, and Brown gave a polite formal bow. Grant removed his hat, extended his hand, and complimented Brown on his "brave defense." Grant then rode on to his meeting. As Brown stood near his tent, he saw a young officer on a horse riding hard after the Federal general's party, with a drawn pistol. Brown grabbed the horse's bridle and asked the man where he was going. The man replied:

"To shoot that damned Yankee officer; now loose my
bridle or I'll shoot you."
"We have surrendered sir, and——

Fellow Victims of the Fatal Blunder

"Loose my bridle!

"I will not, sir; you shall not do——

"Col. Brown, for the third and last time, I tell you to loose my rein."

The man's horse made a sudden move, allowing Brown to draw his own pistol and order the man to dismount. If this story is true, Brown had likely saved the life of the general who proved to be his short-lived country's most effective enemy.[31]

Thus ended Brown's first campaign of the war. Buckner commended Brown and his other brigade commanders for "gallant and able conduct" during the battle. Cheairs later extolled: "no man or officer displayed more true courage, skill and gallantry" than Brown. Certainly, Brown was conspicuous in rallying his men under fire. The first attack the brigade launched on February 15 was a success; the second attack was hindered by the initial failure to locate the point of attack, and the absence of the enemy. The third was thrown into confusion by the wounded Lt. Col. Gordon's ill-considered order, but in any event was clearly halted by Federal reinforcements after helping achieve the rebel goal of opening an escape route. For a man who a year before was a lawyer rallying the Unionist cause, Brown's initial fight on behalf of the Confederacy showed capacity and room for growth.[32]

February 16 was spent with the Federals moving into possession of the rebel lines, taking possession of their camps, and in many cases plundering the personal possessions of the defeated. That night, the Confederate prisoners were loaded onto boats for control purposes, and the next day, were transferred to steamers for the ride north to prison camp. Brown accompanied the 3rd on the *Tecumseh*, which got under way early on the 18th. Barber recorded that the "boat was exceedingly crowded and filthy and many of the men were taken sick." Already there were plans to separate the officers from the men, with the Federal high command directing that the Confederate generals and field grade officers, as well as officers of the old army, be transported to Fort Warren at Boston, Massachusetts, doubtlessly hoping to deprive the men of leadership. The policy behind this move became apparent early in the trip up the rivers to the north. A Federal major was going about disarming the officers who had retained their sidearms. Brown made a comment which the officer did not appreciate, and when "hot words ensued," Brown "denounced" the major as "a cowardly meddlesome rascal." At one point, it appeared there would be violence, and Private Sam Mitchell recalled that if Brown had been harmed, the major "would have been torn to shreds in a moment."[33]

The *Tecumseh* sailed up the Cumberland to Smithland, Kentucky, and then down the Ohio past Paducah to Cairo, Illinois. Entering the Mississippi, the boat began encountering ice as it headed up river to St. Louis. It was at this point, on February 22, that the enlisted men were marched off the boat to be transported by rail to Chicago's Camp Douglas. As the men filed by, the officers of the 3rd lifted their hats in a silent tribute. The officers lingered at St. Louis, and moved from the *Tecumseh* to the *Nebraska*. As some residents of St. Louis were sympathetic to the southern cause, there were efforts to bring food and items of personal comfort to the officers, but the Federal authorities would not allow it. Some little boys were actually arrested for giving the officers apples.[34]

On February 27, the party left the boats and marched to the depot. Brown assembled his officers and "exhorted" them "to hold fast to [their] faith, never to disgrace [themselves or their] cause by accepting of release upon dishonorable conditions." The prisoners passed through Terre Haute and Indianapolis, arriving at Columbus, Ohio, on March 1. They were marched four miles to Camp Chase, where the Confederates were placed in "a pen or high enclosure containing some rough and filthy shantys where vermin and all manner of creeping things infested." After three days in the muddy, smelly enclosure, the field officers were put on the trains for the east, passing through Cleveland, Buffalo, Rochester, and Utica to Albany the afternoon of March 5. Leaving the train, the rebel prisoners crossed the Hudson River on the ice and went on to Springfield, Massachusetts, where they were given "the best supper . . . since leaving Ft. Donelson."[35]

Brown and his companions reached Boston early on the morning of March 6. They stayed on the cars for about six hours before they were conducted to a small steamer, the *Charles Fremont*, for the nine mile trip out to their new place of imprisonment, Fort Warren. Situated on Georges Island in Boston Harbor, the work was built of granite in the pentagon shape typical of nineteenth-century fortresses, and was completed about fifteen years prior to the arrival of the Fort Donelson prisoners. Lt. Col. Randal McGavock of the 10th Tennessee observed that the fort had a good view of the city, the Charlestown Naval Yard, and the Bunker Hill Monument. Major Cheairs wrote that the harbor traffic was also visible, "which helps a great deal to pass off the time." The fort was commanded by Colonel Justin E. Dimick, a Regular Army professional for whom the Confederate officers came to have a high regard. The rooms were relatively comfortable, and the prisoners divided into two messes of forty each, with two sets of four cooks each. While the government rations they got were good, the officers chipped in two dollars apiece a week to send over to Boston for alcohol, cigars, and other amenities. Access to even that meager sum was not available to all, and in early April, Brown along with forty-seven other officers petitioned President Davis to send some of their back pay to "add to their comfort." With the exception of Buckner and Tighlman, who were under a form of close arrest, the prisoners were allowed to walk "over and around the Fort from reveille in the morning untill [sic] retreat at 6 o'clock . . . which gives us very good exercise."[36]

In Brown's first days of imprisonment, efforts were made to secure his early release. As early as February 26, a request was made from an unknown quarter to release Brown, Palmer, and Hanson on parole, which the Federal department commander, Maj. Gen. Henry W. Halleck, declined, even though Halleck thought leniency toward the Kentucky and Tennessee officers might help Unionist sentiment there. Like Brown, Palmer was a prewar Unionist, which might explain the reason they were considered, and even Hanson, a member of the secessionist Kentucky State Guard, was originally an opponent of secession. A few weeks later, a much more serious effort was made, brought about by a letter from Brown to his sister, Mary Ann, and her husband Edward McMillan, who were then in Carlinville, Illinois. Written from Camp Chase, the letter led the McMillans to conclude that "repentance has already begun its salutary work" to bring Brown back to loyalty to the Union. On March 10, McMillan wrote his congressman, David A. Smith, asking that Brown be paroled into his custody. Smith, vouching for McMillan and Brown's prewar loyalty, wrote President Abraham Lincoln, whose secretary, John Hay, endorsed the letter to the secretary of war asking "the most favorable consideration" be given the request. While there is no further record after Hay's endorsement, it appears that the condition of release was taking an oath of allegiance, "and renouncing Jeff Davis and his crew." Brown was nowhere near that level of repentance.[37]

Late in March, Brown received a letter from his brother Neill providing a "gloomy account of things" in Nashville. Neill expressed the people's belief that Albert Sidney Johnston, then gathering forces at Corinth, Mississippi (as he had earlier predicted to Brown), would be whipped "and that the star of the Confederacy is set." Neill had also opposed secession, but when it occurred, he was named to Governor Harris's Military and Financial Board, which undertook to arm and equip the Provisional Army of Tennessee in 1861. Later, Neill was ironically, in light of his brother's predicament, involved in a project to build a gunboat for the Cumberland River. When Nashville fell to the Federals, however, Neill stayed in the city, and pursuant to a secret request from Harris, went to the capitol and destroyed papers that would have incriminated certain citizens with the Federal authorities. Eventually Neill, along with James Childress, the brother of President James K. Polk's widow, Sarah Childress Polk, was arrested for treason.[38]

Neill enjoyed the brief notoriety of a false report that he had, during his arraignment before Military Governor Andrew Johnson, drawn a pistol and shot Johnson dead, and that he was hung immediately afterward. The reality was much less heroic, at least from a Confederate standpoint. On June 2, 1862, at Columbia, Neill appeared on the rostrum with Johnson, lamenting that against his judgment, "[h]is only brother was a prisoner, and his two sons were in the Southern army." Neill pronounced it "his solemn duty to tell his old friends that the Confederate cause was ruined and hopelessly lost." The news reached Fort Warren the next day, but a "mortified" Brown did not believe it. A few days later, Brown received a letter from Neill claiming the papers misrepresented his speech. Neill apologized for the fact he made a speech at all, a fact that, in McGavock's estimation, damned him just the same.[39]

Brown was obviously still sensitive on the subject of Neill's rediscovered Unionism when John Hugh Smith, a former mayor of Nashville, recycled and placed in that job again by the Federals, visited the fort, after coming north to testify in an impeachment trial before the Senate

Fellow Victims of the Fatal Blunder

relating to the removal of United States District Judge West Humphries. Smith met with several old acquaintances among the prisoners, including McGavock, himself a former mayor of Nashville. Brown and Col. James E. Bailey of the 49th Tennessee refused to join the meeting because of Smith's Union loyalty. The next night, Brown and one of the men who met with Smith got into a discussion over the propriety of the meeting. McGavock remarked that his "record on the Southern Question was as good as anybody's." Just then, Cheairs entered the room, and asserted McGavock was a liar. McGavock bristled, called Cheairs a "G—d— liar and a scoundrel", and lunged at him. The other officers present intervened and conducted Cheairs from the room. In Brown and others, imprisonment seems to have increased Confederate loyalties.[40]

With the exception of these irritants, Brown's imprisonment at Fort Warren appears to have been quite tolerable. He received the good news that a horse and both slaves, Ned and Major, had gotten back to Pulaski from Fort Donelson. He remained generally in good spirits, and although he suffered occasional bouts of ill health throughout his life, all reports from the prison indicate he enjoyed good health while there. Brown bunked with Hanson, and McGavock recorded an evening in their room where the orators of Tennessee, Kentucky, and Mississippi were discussed in full. On another occasion, Brown shared a bottle of gin with McGavock, Col. Bailey, Col. John Gregg of the 7th Texas, and Col. Heiman, among others. Heiman reached the point where he made several attempts to sing "Old Tom Cat" before finally getting successfully all the way through the song.[41]

One of the pastimes of many of the Confederate officers at Fort Warren was to keep an autograph book, obtaining the signatures of their friends among the prisoners, who would also include a thought or two relating to their common circumstances and their hopes for the southern cause. Brown owned one, and collected several signatures, including the 26th Tennessee's John M. Lillard (who wished Brown a "speedy release . . . promotion in rank and a long and happy life"); Lt. Col. Robert G. McClure, an old friend from Marshall County; fellow Donelson brigade commander Col. William E. Baldwin of Mississippi; Palmer; Hanson; Cheairs (who wrote a useful and lengthy entry on their experiences to that point in the war); Col. Alfred H. Abernathy of the 53rd Tennessee (even if not victorious, "we have not disgraced ourselves"); Buckner; Heiman; and McGavock. Palmer also kept a book, in which, on July 20, Brown wrote that he and Palmer were "fellow victims of the fatal blunder of that Ditch-digging Genrl, and are now inmates of the same prison. We never bargained for this!" Brown expressed his "warmest friendship and best wishes," and hoped "[m]ay we soon meet on victorious fields, in the sunny south, winning personal laurels, but more than all, aiding our bleeding and oppressed countrymen in their struggle for freedom!"[42]

On July 31, Brown and his fellow prisoners boarded the *Ocean Queen*, sailing away from Col. Dimick and his guards. On August 5, the party landed a few miles below Richmond, back in the Confederacy. The prisoners would all be officially exchanged as of August 27, 1862, in Brown's case, for three Federal lieutenants. Buckner met with President Davis and recommended Hanson, Brown, and another officer for promotion to brigadier general, inciting a jealous McGavock to observe that there were more generals than brigades and that Davis "might find better material than either of those gentlemen." Brown passed down through Knoxville, reaching Tunnel Hill, Georgia, on August 14 on his way to join his regiment at Vicksburg, Mississippi. The men of the 3rd Tennessee were at that time still in the process of being exchanged, 607 having survived their imprisonment.[43]

When the first elements of the 3rd Tennessee arrived at Vicksburg on September 16, they learned that they would need a new colonel. At some point in his journey to Mississippi, Brown received a telegram to join the rebel army then massing at Chattanooga. Notwithstanding McGavock's misgivings, Brown was promoted to brigadier general, to rank from August 30, 1862. Having just returned to Tennessee from the north, Brown was again marching in that direction with a new rank and assignment so that he might also return to Kentucky.[44]

In February 1862, when Brown stepped on the deck of the *Tecumseh* at Dover, the fortunes of the Confederacy were beginning a free fall that eventually included the loss of Nashville, Island No. 10, Memphis, Middle and West Tennessee, northern Virginia, and New Orleans, and Albert Sidney Johnston's death at Shiloh. As spring became summer, however, southern fortunes began to recover. In late June, General Robert E. Lee took command of the Confederate army defending Richmond and drove the advancing Federal Army of the Potomac away from the Confederate capital. In July, General Braxton Bragg boldly transferred the Confederate Army of the Mississippi from Tupelo, Mississippi, to Chattanooga, Tennessee. Bragg took a roundabout railroad route, but arrived before a Federal force under Maj. Gen. Don Carlos Buell.[45]

The Army of the Mississippi's move to Chattanooga not only relieved an immediate threat to Chattanooga, but opened up the possibility of offensive action, which suited the ambitions of Maj. Gen. Edmund Kirby Smith, the commander of the small Confederate force in East Tennessee. At some point between late June and mid-July, Kirby Smith developed the concept of a Confederate advance into Kentucky. Bragg expected that the goal of his cooperative effort with Kirby Smith was the recovery of Middle Tennessee. Since Bragg's army would not be ready to move for several days, Kirby Smith would in the meantime attack the Federal garrison at Cumberland Gap. But once unleashed, and reinforced by two of Bragg's brigades under the promising Brig. Gen. Patrick Cleburne, Kirby Smith deftly sidestepped Cumberland Gap and moved north into the Bluegrass, pursuing his own plan. Bragg soon warmed to the idea of the Kentucky scheme, and in any event did not intend to leave Kirby Smith without support. The Army of the Mississippi therefore left Chattanooga at the end of August, bound for the Bluegrass State.[46]

Bragg's Army of the Mississippi had its genesis in the troops called together from the far flung outposts of Albert Sidney Johnston's command in the aftermath of the disaster at Fort Donelson. With troops detached to support Kirby Smith and left to occupy East Tennessee, his mobile force consisted of four divisions, two of which were assigned to Maj. Gen. Leonidas Polk, who commanded the "right wing" of the army, while the remaining two were in the "left wing" under the command of Maj. Gen. William J. Hardee. In the space of a month, Hardee was assigned two new division commanders, Buckner and James Patton Anderson. Anderson was a native of Winchester, Tennessee. Trained as an attorney, Anderson's prewar experience included service in the Mississippi legislature, as United States marshal for the Washington Territory, and later as that territory's delegate to Congress. An ardent secessionist, he turned down an offer to become governor of the territory and in 1857 moved to Florida to manage the plantation of his wife's aunt. He served in Florida's secession convention and at the convention in Montgomery that formed the Confederate government, and then returned to be appointed colonel of the 1st Florida Infantry. He skirmished with the Federals at Pensacola in 1861, and commanded a brigade at Shiloh.[47]

Although exchanged, the regiments of Brown's original brigade were far to the south. He was therefore placed in command of a new formation of three regiments in Anderson's division. The 1st Florida was commanded by Col. William Miller, a native of New York and veteran of the Mexican War. A few companies of what became the 1st Florida Regiment fought at Shiloh and in the Federal approach to Corinth, Mississippi, in the weeks afterward. They were the brigade's only veterans of any fighting in the war so far. The 3rd Florida was mustered in August 1861, and reorganized for the war in 1862, leaving Florida to join the Army of the Mississippi at Chattanooga. As its colonel was under arrest, the regiment was commanded by Lt. Col. Lucius Church, a prewar planter. The last regiment was the 41st Mississippi, only in service since the spring of 1862. The 41st was commanded by Col. William F. Tucker, a lawyer who commanded a company in the Battle of Bull Run. Attached to the brigade was Battery A of the 14th Battalion of Georgia Light Artillery. Commanded by Capt. Joseph E. Palmer, the "Southern Rights Battery" was made up of men from the Southern Rights Guard, formerly Company C of the 1st Georgia Regiment, who reenlisted when their regiment disbanded that spring after its one year of service. The brigade appears to have numbered around one thousand officers and men.[48]

Brown's Brigade moved out of Chattanooga and crossed the Tennessee River on ferries. The march took them over Walden's Ridge into the Sequatchie Valley, and then onto the Cumberland Plateau. It was late summer, water was scarce, and the roads dusty. A veteran of the 3rd Florida recalled that he threw away part of his clothing, and that the road was strewn with old clothes, blankets, and "sick old men." The army reached Sparta, Tennessee, during the first week of September, where Bragg reevaluated his line of advance on account of reports that there was little means of feeding his men and animals along his intended route. The army was therefore diverted west, and its columns marched north to cross the Cumberland River. In the meantime, overly optimistic news came

Fellow Victims of the Fatal Blunder

that the Federals were evacuating Nashville, and from Kirby Smith of his victory at Richmond, Kentucky, at the end of August and his occupation of Lexington. On September 7, cavalryman Nathan Bedford Forrest reported that Buell was rapidly moving to Bowling Green. The Confederates had the opportunity to cut the Federals off from their main supply base at Louisville, and at the same time faced the risk of having Buell interpose himself between Bragg and Kirby Smith. Hard marching was called for, and on September 9 and 10, Brown's men marched from 3:00 a.m. to 10:00 a.m., rested, and then marched another five hours. The next day, they arose at 2:00 a.m. and marched until the next evening.[49]

Rewarding the men's exertions, on September 11, Bragg's advance troops made it to Glasgow, Kentucky, ahead of Buell and cut the railroad to Louisville. While he contemplated confronting Buell at that point, a false report that Maj. Gen. William S. Rosecrans's army from Mississippi had joined Buell, and the reality that supplies and forage in the Glasgow area were sparse, compelled Bragg to move east to effect a junction with Kirby Smith in the rich Bluegrass region of the state. Elements of the army diverted to gobble up a four-thousand-man garrison at Munfordville, Kentucky, on September 17. Some of Brown's Floridians marveled at the contrast between the well fed and dressed Federal prisoners and their "dirty, ragged, bare-footed and hungry" ranks. After a few days of vacillation, Bragg moved north to Bardstown, closer to both Louisville and Kirby Smith, his advance elements reaching that point on September 22, while Brown's men appeared on September 24. That day, there was a grand review of the army, and the men of the brigade marched through town with unfurled colors, fixed bayonets, and dressed files, while bands played "Dixie" and "The Bonnie Blue Flag." Notwithstanding this brave scene, for the first time Bragg was on the defensive, the advance on Louisville abandoned.[50]

Buell's tired men trudged into Louisville that same September 24, enthusiastically greeted by the citizens who to that point had relied on hastily assembled green troops for their defense. Buell took the next few days to allow his men to rest while he attempted to amalgamate the new levies with his veterans. Two issues of command arose during this interval. First, Union generals William "Bull" Nelson and Jefferson C. Davis had a heated confrontation prior to Buell's arrival in Louisville, which eventually resulted in Davis murdering Nelson. Second, the authorities in Washington, who thought the direction of the war in that quarter was not being energetically pursued, directed that Buell be relieved by his second in command, Maj. Gen. George Henry Thomas, unless Buell was already in the presence of the enemy. The message arrived the very day of Nelson's murder. Thomas protested that he was not sufficiently informed to take command, resulting in the "suspension" of the order. Buell therefore retained his command, and during the reorganization that followed named Thomas his second in command, which deprived Buell of a most effective battlefield commander.[51]

With his very status as a commander under threat, Buell marched out of Louisville on the morning of October 1 in four columns, one advancing against Kirby Smith, and three converging on Bragg at Bardstown. When word came that Buell was on the move, Bragg was away from the main body of his army, taking control of Kirby Smith's thitherto independent army at Lexington. By this time, the stark reality that his army would not gain huge numbers of recruits from its presence in the Commonwealth was apparent, causing Bragg to bitterly observe that Kentuckians "have too many fat cattle and are too well off to fight." Nonetheless, Bragg installed a Confederate governor at Frankfort, so that there would be a legal veneer to Confederate conscription in Kentucky. Soon thereafter, the Confederate dignitaries left town as one of Buell's columns neared. Bragg remained confused about the imminence of the threat, and gave Polk orders that the bishop disregarded because it was clear that Bragg did not know of the nearness of the Federals to the main body of the army. Polk withdrew to the southeast, even as Bragg, reversing a previous order, decided to move the Army of the Mississippi north to join Kirby Smith. On the morning of October 7, Bragg issued an order to that effect, even though his plans were already outdated. The night before, Hardee stopped at the small town of Perryville with three of Buckner's brigades, sketching out positions to meet the oncoming Federal pursuit.[52]

All through October 7, Hardee's cavalry brigade under Col. Joseph Wheeler fought a delaying action, enabling the wing commander to order Anderson's division forward. Retracing their steps from a day and a half before, Brown and his men arrived on the field the morning of

Fellow Victims of the Fatal Blunder

that day, taking position to the north of town. Even though Bragg still thought the main Federal effort was against Kirby Smith, the presence of the Federals near Perryville was sufficiently disturbing for Bragg to order Maj. Gen. Benjamin F. Cheatham's division back to that point. Bragg directed Polk to defeat the advancing blue column, and then move toward Versailles, to the west of Lexington. But at dawn on October 8, Polk and Hardee had information that heavy masses of Federal infantry were in their vicinity. The advanced position of Brig. Gen. St. John R. Liddell came under heavy attack. The two wing commanders conferred with the division commanders, and decided to go on the "defensive-offensive," and await developments. When an irritated Braxton Bragg arrived later that morning, he ordered an attack.[53]

Having learned that there was a large force of Confederates at Perryville, Buell ordered his three corps to concentrate at that point, anticipating that he would make a general attack the next day. Approaching the town on the Federal left was the corps of Maj. Gen. Alexander M. McCook, in the Federal center was a corps under Maj. Gen. Charles Gilbert, and approaching from the southwest was the corps of Maj. Gen. Thomas L. Crittenden. Bragg was blissfully unaware of Crittenden's approach, or of the fact that he faced the bulk of Buell's army. His plans, therefore, were formed by his alarm at Polk's disposition of his troops, lack of knowledge of Crittenden on his left flank, and the appearance of two Federal brigades of Brig. Gen. Lovell Rousseau's division on Buckner's right flank. Bragg therefore gave orders for Hardee to advance closer to the enemy, while Cheatham's Division marched around the rear of the army in order to attack the Federals on the rebel far-right flank.[54]

At about 11:00 a.m., Brown's Brigade advanced to a ridge west of the town and lay down on the east side awaiting orders, filling, along with the Mississippi brigade of Col. Thomas M. Jones, a gap between Buckner and Cheatham. The remaining two brigades of Anderson's Division were on Buckner's left. Elsewhere on the field, a fierce artillery battle took place, and Brown's regiments suffered some casualties from Federal overshots. During this interval, Cheatham's men filed into position on the Confederate right. The rebels expected that "Marse Frank" and his Tennesseans would fall on an unsuspecting Federal flank. But when Cheatham stepped off at about 2:00 p.m., he pitched head-on into

McCook's corps. When Cheatham attacked, Hardee directed Buckner to make his attack, and Jones moved forward with Buckner's assault force toward Col. Leonard A. Harris's brigade from Rousseau's division. Jones's men attempted to advance over a ridge line several times in an attempt to get at their adversaries, but in the end, they were repulsed with heavy casualties. Buckner's initial attack was made against Rousseau's flank, but was thrown into some confusion by strong Federal resistance and accidental shelling by friendly artillery.[55]

An hour into the struggle on Hardee's front, the time came for Brown to advance.[56] Admirably for previously unengaged troops, the men of the brigade stood up, and Brown placed them into line "as if on Drill." The brigade was in a single line, with the 41st Mississippi on the left and the two Florida regiments on the right. Drawing his sword, he gave the command "Forward, Guide right, March." The eager men, however, started from their orderly march, to a trot, and then, yelling, broke into a run, the raw 3rd Florida running into a patch of brambles. This put the line in "terrible bad order," and Brown stopped to reorder his line, cursing the Floridians for being too quick, warning them, "Dress up or you will be cut to pieces in such order." The brigade line descended into the dry bed of Doctor's Creek, and was faced with a bank on the other side about ten feet high. Palmer's battery accompanied the advance, but the creek bank kept it from moving forward as well. Brown, who Palmer deemed "a splendid officer," ordered Palmer to leave one section of the battery in the creek bed, and move the other to the right where the bluff was not as steep and engage the enemy. Palmer later wrote: *great God how the balls did whistle*!" It appears that the bluff in front of the Mississippians could be scaled, although Lt. Col. William C. Hearn found it necessary to dismount. The Floridians moved to the right along with Palmer's guns in order to ascend from the creek bed.[57]

Brown's men emerged onto a relatively flat area, and advanced up a slight ridge. There was a short flat interval between Brown and the Federals, then a steep ravine and a sinkhole, natural features which had helped the bluecoats defeat Jones's attack over the same ground. To compound the Federal advantage, the troops engaging Brown, two regiments of Harris's brigade, were behind a fence. Palmer's guns engaged the Federals, but soon a number of his men and horses were struck down by

Fellow Victims of the Fatal Blunder

Unionist fire. Out in the open, the rebels lay down and engaged the enemy, and were fortunate that Federal ammunition supplies were somewhat depleted from the earlier fighting. At some point during this interval, Brown, who remained mounted, was unhorsed by a shot that struck in the right thigh, just above the knee. The wound was severe enough for Brown to have "barely missed" death.[58]

With Brown out of action, command of the brigade fell on Col. Tucker of the 41st Mississippi, but soon Tucker, too, was wounded, and Col. Miller of the 1st Florida took command. Even though the Federals were getting low on ammunition, Lt. Col. Hearn deemed the Federal fire "most disastrous." On the Federal side, the flag of the 38th Indiana was riddled with bullets, and only one member of its nine member color guard came out unscathed. Both sides ran low on ammunition, Col. Miller blaming the lack of supply on the brigade ordnance officer, "a nephew of general Brown [who] was drunk." Eventually, however, Miller was able to resupply his men, and with the help of an attack by Brig. Gen. S. A. M. Wood's brigade (under the command of Col. Mark Lowery) and pressure from Cheatham's men, the brigade was able to push past the 10th Ohio of Col. William H. Lytle's brigade and pour fire on the men of Harris's Federal brigade.[59]

This fierce day of battle ended shortly after sundown, Brown's brigade having suffered a total of 239 casualties. That night, Bragg and his wing commanders learned that their battered three divisions faced most of Buell's army. Not only did he face a substantially superior force, but the army's line of retreat was in danger. Early the next morning, the rebels slowly pulled out of their lines, in the confusion forgetting to tell Col. Miller of the withdrawal. Only after the other troops around them had left the field did Brown's men pull back by the moonlight, unable to return to the previous night's camp to retrieve their personal belongings. As daylight broke, the first elements of the army began marching for Harrodsburg, unmolested by the Federals, leaving many of the spoils of war and, unfortunately, about nine hundred wounded comrades. There, on October 12, Bragg decided to abandon the Commonwealth and return to Tennessee.[60]

As a general officer, Brown was too important to leave behind. There is no account of his experience after his wound, but he probably was helped from the active line of battle by one of his staff. Because the nature of his wound is now uncertain, the type of treatment he would have received is also unknown, although even for the highest ranking officers treatment at a brigade- or division-level field hospital during battle was often a harrowing experience. When the army retreated, Brown would have been jostled in an ambulance, or if unlucky, a wagon, along the long, difficult road back to Tennessee. Indeed, the army's retreat from Kentucky was along the rough, mountainous roads of the eastern part of the state, down the old Wilderness Road to the Cumberland Gap. An early glut of food that existed when the army left Harrodsburg was quickly consumed, and the barren areas it passed yielded little sustenance for man or beast. Brown seems to have been fortunate to have traveled at the head of the column, even to the point of moving in an advance group, as he was reported in Knoxville on October 20, the same day Bragg's main body reached the Cumberland Gap.[61]

On November 9, Brown was granted thirty days leave. At some point after that, he went to the home of his sister, Anna Jane Bradshaw in Cleveland, Tennessee, where he was visited by local ladies on the cold, rainy morning of December 5. The general's recovery must have gone fairly well, as Bragg, who was short of competent officers, reported that Brown was expected within thirty days of November 22. Meanwhile, Bragg concentrated his army in and near Murfreesboro. Notwithstanding the lingering disappointment of the Kentucky campaign, the Confederacy had turned aside the early summer's imminent threat to Chattanooga and reoccupied a substantial portion of Middle Tennessee.[62]

While Brown convalesced, Bragg renamed and reorganized his army. On November 20, he issued a general order organizing his army into three corps, commanded by Polk, Hardee, and Kirby Smith, and renaming the whole the Army of Tennessee. By an order issued December 12, Patton Anderson's division was "broken up," and as part of its dissolution, the 41st Mississippi was transferred to Polk's Corps, the 1st and 3rd Florida to Hardee's. These units were to be assigned to their brigades and divisions by the corps commanders. The same order assigned Brown and other brigadier generals to the various corps, and Brown was to report to Hardee. On December 19, Hardee, in turn, announced the organization of the division of Maj. Gen. John C. Breckinridge, which included a new brigade to be commanded by Brown, consisting of the 18th, 26th, 28th, 32nd, and 45th Tennessee regiments, along with Captain S. A. Moses's Georgia battery. Thus, although the 3rd Tennessee remained in Mississippi, Brown was reunited with his former comrades in Col. Joseph B. Palmer's 18th Tennessee, and Col. Edmund C. Cook's 32nd Tennessee. New to Brown were Col. John M. Lillard's 26th Tennessee, who fought alongside Brown and the 18th and 32nd at Fort Donelson; Col. Preston D. Cunningham's 28th Tennessee, veterans of Mill Springs, Shiloh, and Breckinridge's campaign in Louisiana; and the 45th Tennessee, also veterans of Shiloh and Louisiana, commanded by Col. Anderson Searcy.[63]

At that point, Brown was still unable to assume command of his new brigade. Nonetheless, he was able to rejoin the army at some point before the end of the year, and Bragg assigned him to command the post at Murfreesboro. Whether he was able to join in the festivities surrounding a visit by President Jefferson Davis to the army, the wedding of a local belle to the cavalry's Brig. Gen. John H. Morgan, which was presided over by Polk in his bishop's role, and attended by much of the army's high command, or the other seasonal parties is unknown. Many of the men in his new brigade were able to visit with their families, as both the 18th and the 45th were composed of men from the Murfreesboro area. President Davis's visit was not all pomp and circumstance, however. He conferred with Bragg relative to the strategic situation in the Confederate West. Bypassing Gen. Joseph E. Johnston, his new Western Theater commander, the president directed that the largest division in Bragg's army, under Maj. Gen. Carter Stevenson, be sent to help counter a Federal threat against the key position of Vicksburg on the Mississippi River. As events would transpire, Bragg would need Stevenson and his men worse than the army at Vicksburg.[64]

On the Federal side, dissatisfaction with Buell led to his replacement at the end of October by Maj. Gen. William S. Rosecrans. On December 26, Rosecrans advanced out of Nashville, and the armies prepared for a general engagement. Bragg directed Hardee to attack the Federal right at daylight on December 31.[65]

As at Perryville, his attack struck the troops of the unlucky Alexander McCook, and after just under three hours of hard fighting, bent the Federal right back on its left in a manner similar to a jack-knife. The day ended after piecemeal attacks against the resulting concentration of blue troops. The attack cleaned out some pockets of Federals in the intervening area, but steered clear of a direct assault on the strong position in the Round Forest. The loss in Brown's Brigade was two killed, twenty wounded, and one missing.[66]

Although Rosecrans was not destroyed, he appeared sufficiently beaten for Bragg to send a telegram to Richmond: "God has granted us a happy New Year." Bragg fully expected Rosecrans to retreat back to Nashville, but Rosecrans and his commanders stubbornly remained the morning of January 1, 1863, consolidating their lines and crossing troops back over Stones River to occupy high ground that allowed them to control the river's east bank. Bragg determined to have Breckinridge attack and take it. Breckinridge protested to no avail, and to add insult to the coming injury to Palmer and many of his men, Palmer was supplanted in command of the brigade by Brig. Gen. Gideon Pillow, who many of the Fort Donelson veterans deemed responsible for their disgraceful surrender just over ten months before.[67]

The attack commenced at 4:00 p.m. on January 2. Brown's men, under Pillow, were the right brigade in the first line, next to the Kentucky Orphan Brigade of another Fort Donelson veteran, Brig. Gen. Roger W. Hanson. At the outset, Breckinridge was of the opinion that the usually brave Pillow showed some cowardice, and almost filed charges to that effect. In some disarray, the rebels crested a hill into the sights of a massed battery of Federal artillery, fifty-eight guns. The resulting storm of fire shattered Breckinridge's attack, and Brown's men, with much of the rest of Breckinridge's Division, were routed. It was a disastrous day for Brown's Tennesseans, who suffered 425 total casualties.[68]

On January 3, the cold, tired, and hungry Confederates faced what their commanders thought was already a vastly superior enemy, being reinforced from the Federal base at Nashville. While the reality was not as bad as the perception, that news, coupled with the fact that the battered Army of Tennessee could only put about twenty thousand men in line, was enough for Bragg to order a retreat to the southeast. He was at one point uncertain as to the extent of the retreat, but eventually settled on a line in the Duck River Valley, behind the Highland Rim. With there being little threat from Rosecrans's battle-depleted force, the next

Fellow Victims of the Fatal Blunder

weeks were spent in the throes of the first outburst of the ruinous infighting between Bragg and his detractors for which the high command of the Army of Tennessee became notorious. Although most of the struggle occurred within the higher command of the army, it is worthwhile to note that Brown returned from Kentucky as a supporter of the army commander. But others were not so inclined. The disappointments of the Kentucky campaign and the near-victory at Murfreesboro, coupled with Bragg's own personality defects resulted in President Davis directing theater commander Johnston to remove Bragg. Reluctant to do so, Johnston delayed the action until his own health suffered a relapse, thus sparing the divisive Bragg for the 1863 campaign.[69]

As was certainly true of thousands of other officers and men, the first year and a half of the war had put Brown through a wide range of experiences. Professionally, he was as an amateur a soldier as any lawyer who was called to the colors, yet before even 1861 was out, his leadership and efficiency resulted in brigade command and a recommendation for promotion to brigadier general, which eventually came after his exchange. He had seen near victory and crushing defeat at Fort Donelson, had nearly had lost his life while leading his men at Perryville, and was recognized as one of the army's competent brigadiers during its reorganization in November 1862. Ideologically, he started his service as a reluctant secessionist, yet by the time his imprisonment at Fort Warren ended, he was fully committed to the Confederate cause. Indeed, his experience in Boston Harbor hardened Brown's resolve for further service and allowed him to forge relationships that extended for decades after the war. Brown had been tested and had been found worthy to lead men in the coming struggle for Tennessee itself.

3

Boys, Them Damn Yanks Can't Whip You

The Campaigns of 1863

As the Army of Tennessee settled into its winter camps in January, Brown was finally able to assume command of his new brigade, while Gideon Pillow was detached for his only truly useful service to the Confederacy during the war, as head of the new Volunteer and Conscript Bureau of the Army of Tennessee. Bragg spent the remainder of the winter and most of the spring drilling his troops and erecting substantial fortifications. Yet, during this time period, the army commander struggled to keep his troops fed, as Confederate commissary agents stripped the area the Army of Tennessee was defending to send food to the Army of Northern Virginia. The Army of Tennessee's deployment was accordingly calculated not only to defend against a future move by Rosecrans, but also to most effectively gather food.[1]

Although he continued to struggle with his wound, Brown was fit enough to join Hardee on a visit with two young ladies in McMinnville in late January. Diarist and writer Lucy Virginia French recorded that it was said "that Gen. Brown was very much taken with Mary and was coming expressly etc. etc. etc!!! 'I tell you it tickled me.' Gen. Brown 'taken' with Mary Armstrong. He had seen her one day last week at Tullahoma. . . ." Romantic prospects aside, the first three months of 1863 were "cold, raw and disagreeable," and the army was generally confined, when not on duty, to their tents and cabins. The makeup of Brown's brigade changed in February as the 28th Tennessee was transferred out, and the 23rd Tennessee battalion transferred in. In camp that spring, the men listened to sermons that justified defending the Confederate cause, and the army was thrilled by news of Forrest's victory at Thompson's Station. Hardee's Corps, of which Brown's Brigade was a part, participated in a grand review at Tullahoma in March, an observer noting that "our troops are looking remarkably well." After an unseasonably heavy snow the night of March 30, the men spent the next day in a snowball fight "slightly wounding many (in fun)." The brigade stayed in the Tullahoma area until April, when Rosecrans made a demonstration on the Confederate right. Orders were dispatched moving Hardee's Corps forward to Wartrace, although Brown and another brigade of Breckinridge's Division marched through Manchester to Beech Grove, on the east side of the Highland Rim at Hoover's Gap. Eventually, Brown was placed at Fairfield, between Hoover's Gap and Wartrace, and moved yet again to Jacobs Store when the emergency subsided.[2]

The return of good weather presaged the resumption of the war in earnest. In Mississippi, Union major general Ulysses S. Grant embarked on a bold plan to take Vicksburg, which, by mid-May, resulted in the defeat of Lt. Gen. John C. Pemberton's efforts to stop the Federals short of the river fortress. On May 18, Pemberton retreated into Vicksburg and was invested by Grant's forces. On May 22, President Davis asked Bragg to "act on his judgment" and send whatever aid he could to Mississippi. Bragg accordingly ordered large elements of Breckinridge's and another division to Mississippi, including over 1,600 cavalry, weakening the Army of Tennessee by approximately 10,000 men. Retained with Bragg from the two infantry divisions were Breckinridge's Tennessee troops, Brown's Brigade, and much of Brig. Gen. William B. Bate's mostly Tennessean brigade. In the first week of June, Hardee assembled Brown's and three other brigades into a new division, commanded by the West Point–trained Tennessean Maj. Gen. Alexander Peter Stewart.[3]

An effort to continue Tennessee's Confederate state government resulted in a call for a convention to nominate suitable candidates for the elections, which should constitutionally be held in 1863. A piece appeared in the Memphis *Daily Appeal* (then published in Jackson, Mississippi) from a Richmond newspaper correspondent, who reported: "I have heard the mention of a dozen names. Gen. John C. Brown for one—a soldier, a gentleman, and a man of great business qualifications, he is commended to a select though strong body of admirers." A letter of endorsement appeared in the *Fayetteville Observer*, extolling Brown as a "brave soldier, sound lawyer and polished gentleman" who had "proved his patriotism and devotion to the South." The convention met at Winchester on June 17, with soldiers constituting many of its delegates, as a number of counties were behind enemy lines. Brown was a delegate from Giles County and was listed as a potential candidate for governor. Perhaps anticipating his future as a politician in Tennessee, Brown was among the delegates who addressed the convention. Eventually, the convention nominated candidates for the congressional seats, as well as a new governor, Robert L. Caruthers, who never was able to take office.[4]

No sooner had Brown finished with politics than his military duties intervened. In mid-June, a Federal cavalry force of 1,500 men rode across the Kentucky line onto the Cumberland Plateau in Tennessee. They captured isolated groups of Confederate soldiers and supplies, threatened sensitive areas such as the bridge over the Tennessee River at Loudon, and, on June 19 and 20, advanced on Knoxville. A hastily assembled force of infantry, convalescents, some artillery troops, and the home guard repelled the blue riders. The Federal force continued its raid for another few days, eventually being chased back into Kentucky by converging rebel forces. On June 20, Bragg dispatched reinforcements to Knoxville in the form of Brown and several of his regiments, with some of the men speculating they were off to Mississippi. The troops boarded the cars at Wartrace and traveled first to Chattanooga, then to Cleveland, where Brown was able to have a brief visit with his sister and nephew, before proceeding on to Knoxville. By that time, the Federal horsemen were riding away from Knoxville. Brown's men took advantage of being in town, "being flush with money and having good opportunities to purchase almost anything in town that our hearts could eat, drink or wear." The East Tennessee vacation, however, did not last long.[5]

Grant's Mississippi campaign also had an effect on the Federals facing the Army of Tennessee. President Lincoln urged Rosecrans to keep Bragg from sending reinforcements to help the rebels facing Grant. Rosecrans calculated he was doing so by doing nothing, and for various reasons his generals supported his inaction. Eventually, an ultimatum from Washington, coupled with Rosecrans's belief that Grant's capture of Vicksburg was only a matter of time, resulted in the execution of a bold plan to feint against the rebel left and attack the right, held by Stewart's Division. The attack occurred in the midst of a day of hard rain on June 24, 1863, with

Hoover's Gap captured in a quick stroke by mounted infantry armed with repeating rifles. An assault by two of Stewart's brigades failed to dislodge the Yankees, and Maj. Gen. George H. Thomas's corps poured through the gap. Accordingly, Brown and his men entrained once more, this time for Tullahoma, where, "greatly to our astonishment," they learned of the rapid Federal advance.[6]

By the time Brown returned, the army was concentrating, and Bragg had every intention of fighting at Tullahoma. But fearing that the army would be cut off from Chattanooga and forced into the relatively barren area of north Alabama, Polk, and to a lesser extent Hardee, counseled retreat. Bragg first considered withdrawing to a line along the Elk River, swollen by the torrential rains of the past week, but exhausted and suffering from a variety of infirmities, he ordered a retreat to Cowan, on the railroad at the foot of the Cumberland Plateau. There, on the evening of July 2, 1863, he ordered the army to retreat over the mountain to Chattanooga. At Cowan, Bragg confessed to Chaplain Dr. Charles Todd Quintard that he was "utterly broken down," and that the loss of Middle Tennessee was "a great disaster." The territory won by Bragg's bold move to Chattanooga the previous July was lost by a combination of poor planning and command instability at the highest level, and bold planning and execution on the Federal side.[7]

The new line of defense was the Tennessee River. With the bulk of the rest of Hardee's Corps, Brown's Brigade encamped near Tyner's Station, on the East Tennessee and Georgia Railroad outside of Chattanooga. No sooner had the corps settled into its camps than Hardee was transferred to Mississippi to help reorganize Confederate defenses there in the wake of the fall of Vicksburg on July 4. In Hardee's place, President Davis appointed Maj. Gen. Daniel Harvey Hill, a veteran of the Army of Northern Virginia, to the rank of lieutenant general (subject to confirmation by the Confederate Senate). Accompanied by Stewart, Brown, and two other of Stewart's brigade commanders, Hill rode through the camps of the various brigades of his corps on July 23, and "was enthusiastically received by both officers and men." Enthusiasm was an issue, as the army's succession of defeats inevitably had an effect on morale. There were desertions from the army that summer, although at least some of Brown's men remained defiant. R. D. Jamison of the 45th Tennessee wrote his

Boys, Them Damn Yanks Can't Whip You

wife that "every man who had any soul at all would rather die than be subject to the U. S. Government." G. W. Dillon of the 18th Tennessee expressed the sentiment that "all yet will be right to those that continue faithfully and cheerfully contending for our liberty glorious freedom and independence."[8]

Likely sensing the wavering morale of the army, Maj. Gen. Patrick Cleburne conceived of a fraternal order that aimed to foster "military brotherhood," "patriotic sentiment," and "strengthen the ties of army fellowship." The concept was taken to Bishop Polk, who was asked to attend a meeting on the subject at Tyner's Station. Polk sent Chaplain Quintard instead, who met with Cleburne, Brown, and several other officers. Cleburne, Brown, St. John R. Liddell, and Quintard were appointed to "draft a constitution and a plan of organization." They produced a document entitled "Constitution of the Comrades of the Southern Cross," dated August 28, 1863, but as Quintard later recalled, the advent of active operations kept the organization from taking root. Brown's participation in this effort, and his affixing his signature to a letter signed by Bragg, Polk, Hill, Stewart, Cleburne, and several other officers urging President Davis to tighten the exemptions granted from military service, was further indication that Brown, the former staunch Unionist, was totally dedicated to the Confederate cause.[9]

While Brown had proven his mettle for that cause in the cold at Fort Donelson, in imprisonment at Fort Warren, and in the heat of battle at Perryville, Neill still suffered from the "misrepresentations of his position toward his native South." Noting that Neill was in town in mid-July, the sympathetic editor of the *Chattanooga Daily Rebel* assured the paper's readers that Neill had "outlived all these misrepresentations, and his recent course by word and deed, not only puts them to silence forever, but proves how true he has ever been to that cause in which his distinguished brother has won such renown in the field, and in which his two gallant sons have been zealously engaged since the beginning of the war." With their sister in nearby Cleveland, and Neill's two sons in the army, it is possible that a significant portion of the Brown clan was able to enjoy some time together, although that time had to be limited by Brown's duties, especially in the first days of August, when he took command of Stewart's Division in "Old Straight's" temporary absence.[10]

Rosecrans's relatively bloodless conquest of Middle Tennessee earlier that summer only whetted Washington's appetite for the offensive. Rosecrans took his time getting his supplies up and his army in position, but by August 15, when one of his cavalry brigades attacked rebel cavalry at Sparta, on the western edge of the Cumberland Plateau about seventy miles north of Chattanooga, the Federal army was ready to advance. Having succeeded with a bold flanking movement in Middle Tennessee in June, Rosecrans intended to flank again, this time moving the bulk of his army southwest of Chattanooga in order to threaten Bragg's supply line to Atlanta. An elaborate demonstration by mounted forces, however, extended from the Chattanooga waterfront several miles north along the banks of the Tennessee, marked by a jarring bombardment of the little city on August 21.[11]

The Federal demonstrations on Bragg's front, as well as an advance into East Tennessee by Union forces under Maj. Gen. Ambrose Burnside led Bragg and Buckner, the latter of whom commanded in Knoxville, to believe that the Federals were making a concerted effort to isolate Buckner. Bragg ordered Buckner to the south, "so as to insure a junction at any time." This meant abandoning Knoxville to Burnside's advancing Federals, and severing Bragg's direct rail connection to Virginia. With reinforcements flowing in from Mississippi, Bragg assigned Stewart's Division to Buckner's command, creating a new corps. Stewart joined Buckner at his concentration point at Loudon, on the Tennessee River south of Knoxville, but only for a few days. Soon, Stewart, Brown, and the rest of Buckner's Corps were in motion for Charleston, on the Hiwassee River about thirty-five airline miles northeast of Chattanooga. In the meantime, Rosecrans began his major crossing of the Tennessee southwest of Chattanooga on August 29, but Bragg's first indication of the significance of the move did not come until early on the morning of September 1.[12]

Over the first few days of September, as part of Buckner's Corps, Brown and his men withdrew slowly out of Tennessee to the east of Chattanooga and into North Georgia. Although it was deemed necessary to (hopefully temporarily) abandon Chattanooga, Bragg, with the assurance of reinforcements, intended to turn and crush Rosecrans. The Federal commander's aggressive move across a wide front left large elements of

    Boys, Them Damn Yanks Can't Whip You

his army in danger of piecemeal destruction. After an initial bout of caution, Rosecrans, convinced that Bragg was in confused retreat, demanded a rapid pursuit, overruling the counsel of his senior corps commander, Maj. Gen. George H. Thomas. The Federals occupied Chattanooga, the ultimate prize of the campaign, on September 9.[13]

Even as Bragg suffered the blow of losing Chattanooga, a golden opportunity arose. As other elements of the Army of the Cumberland moved into the city, Maj. Gen. James S. Negley's division of Thomas's XIV Corps descended Lookout Mountain from Stevens Gap into McLemore's Cove, a small cul-de-sac valley formed between Lookout Mountain to the west and Pigeon Mountain to the east. Lafayette, Georgia, which would soon become Bragg's headquarters, was just to the east of Pigeon Mountain. And large elements of the Army of Tennessee were well within striking distance of Negley's isolated force. Bragg moved quickly, and on the evening of September 9 ordered an attack by Maj. Gen. Thomas C. Hindman's division from the north, and Maj. Gen. Patrick R. Cleburne's division from the east. Complications and misunderstandings arose during the night and early morning hours, and Bragg abandoned the thought of Cleburne being part of the attack, instead adding Buckner's entire corps to the operation. Hindman would remain in command as the senior major general.[14]

Hindman had a reputation as a bold and aggressive fighter, but failed to seize one of the Army of Tennessee's great opportunities of the war. On the evening of September 10, he called a council of war that included his three brigadiers, Patton Anderson, Zachariah C. Deas, and Arthur M. Manigault, and Buckner and his two division commanders, Stewart and William Preston. In the course of that council, it was determined to leave Negley unmolested and instead turn to face an imagined advance from the direction of Chattanooga. A message was sent to Bragg, who in the meantime had sorted out the confusion relating to Cleburne. Replying early the morning of September 11, Bragg forcefully confirmed his orders to attack, which were transmitted by a foreign staff officer who garbled them sufficiently to give Hindman pause. Later poorly drafted communications from headquarters increased Hindman's confusion. A timid forward movement, which involved Brown and the rest of Stewart's Division, was called to a halt, and an actual retreat was only averted by news that the Federals were retreating from the cove. In Patton Anderson's words, "[t]he bird had flown." September 11 closed with the great opportunity lost.[15]

Both sides recognized the significance of these events. Rosecrans finally realized that Bragg was not in headlong retreat, and began the concentration of his army that resulted in its reunification on the banks of South Chickamauga Creek at the end of the next week. On the Confederate side, there was cognizance, in the words of one of Buckner's staff, that "a great blunder had been made." Clearly, Hindman had been deficient in leadership, although the experienced generals in his council of war on September 10 failed to spur him to action. Bragg and his staff also bore some liability for the confusion created by their orders, but the conclusion reached by Hindman's council of war that Bragg's attack orders could be interpreted has been seen as continued evidence of the difficulties between Bragg and his higher officers.[16]

Over the next few days Rosecrans pulled his army together. His force swollen by reinforcements from Mississippi, and with the anticipation of further reinforcements from Robert E. Lee's Army of Northern Virginia, led by Lee's "War Horse," Lt. Gen. James Longstreet, Bragg abandoned the thought of defeating the Army of the Cumberland in detail in favor of interposing the Army of Tennessee between the Federals and Chattanooga. For that purpose, Bragg intended to send his troops across Chickamauga Creek at several points, placing the army in the area where the north/south Lafayette and Dry Valley roads ran closely together north of Lee and Gordon's Mill on the banks of the creek. The actual fighting for this territory started on September 18, when elements of the rebel army maneuvered to cross Chickamauga Creek at Reed's Bridge and Alexander's Bridge.[17]

With the rest of Stewart's Division, Brown's Brigade marched from Lafayette on September 17, and arrived near Thedford's Ford on the afternoon of September 18. Stewart deployed Bate's and Brig. Gen. Henry D. Clayton's brigades on the heights above the ford. As they moved into line, several cannon balls roared in from the direction of Alexander's Bridge and fell among the ranks. One came within five steps of striking Stewart and Brig. Gen. John Pegram of the cavalry, and then ricocheted and almost struck Capt. Hamp Cheney of Brown's staff. Eventually Clayton

         Boys, Them Damn Yanks Can't Whip You

was dispatched across the creek. Hungry soldiers of the 26th Tennessee went scavenging for food that night, and raided a local widow's potato patch. When an officer sought to interfere, the woman, recognizing her sons among the raiders, called him off with the admonition that they were her potatoes and her boys.[18]

Unfortunately for the Confederates, the Federals used the night of September 18/19 to move significant elements of Thomas's XIV Corps from Crawfish Springs north along the Lafayette Road to the Kelly Farm, over four miles closer to Chattanooga, in fact, further north than the mass of the Army of Tennessee. Bragg's plan of cutting Rosecrans off from Chattanooga was in great danger of frustration, although the Confederate commander was not cognizant of it as day dawned on September 19. With elements of three corps, and more to come, across the Chickamauga, he planned on launching a devastating attack against the Federal left where he perceived it to be—near Lee and Gordon's Mill. Fighting broke out that morning, however, far to the north, at Jay's Mill near Reed's Bridge. The struggle originally involved Confederate cavalry and Federal troops from Rossville, where the Lafayette Road crossed into Tennessee. As a result, the Federal command got the wrong impression that only a single rebel brigade was isolated across the creek. One of Thomas's divisions was accordingly dispatched to destroy the purportedly isolated brigade.[19]

The Federals found Nathan Bedford Forrest instead. A general engagement ensued, with both sides feeding brigades into the melee, the initial Confederate combatants being cavalry and the two small divisions of Maj. Gen. W. H. T. Walker's corps. While this struggle went on, Brown and Bate joined Clayton on the west side of Chickamauga Creek. Around noon, Stewart received orders from one of Bragg's staff officers to move to where the firing was, which seemed to Stewart to be "a considerable distance to the right and somewhat to the rear of us." Somewhat perplexed by these indefinite orders, Stewart conferred with Bragg personally, who informed him that "Walker was engaged on the right, was much cut up, and that the enemy threatening to turn his flank" and that the Tennessean "must be governed by circumstances." Stewart accordingly marched to the sound of the guns, his column passing "wounded men and mangled horses." Not being able to find Polk, Stewart found that the hottest fight was in the area of the Brock Field, where Cheatham's large division of mostly Tennessee troops was in a desperate fight with three Federal divisions. One of Brig. Gen. Marcus J. Wright's staff officers, Eugene Harris, the Tennessee governor's son, informed Stewart that Wright's brigade, which held Cheatham's left, "was much cut up by an enfilade fire; that Carnes' battery had been lost, and help was wanted." With the concurrence of one of Polk's aides, Stewart determined to support his fellow Tennesseans.[20]

The West Point–trained Stewart discerned that he had little room to deploy his three brigades in the space between Cheatham and Bushrod Johnson's provisional division further to the left. Stewart therefore directed Clayton to advance with his Alabamians, and sent one of his own staff officers to monitor this relatively inexperienced brigade. Following close behind, Stewart encountered General Wright, who confirmed young Harris's report. Clayton marched north through some woods, and was about to enter the Brock Field from the south, when John C. Carter, colonel of the 38th Tennessee of Wright's Brigade, informed Clayton that he was marching in a wrong direction, essentially going north when he should be going west. Clayton quickly obliqued his line, and almost as quickly became engaged with the Federals on his front. Clayton engaged first one, then two small Federal brigades, and an engagement estimated to last between a half-hour and an hour ensued, Clayton's men having the advantage of numbers but the enemy holding the high ground. In its firefight among the thick woods, Clayton's Brigade suffered four hundred casualties and exhausted its ammunition.[21]

With Clayton temporarily out of action, Stewart ordered Brown to advance. Brown's support of Clayton was so close that Brown's Brigade initially took some casualties without being able to return fire. Brown wrote that he and his men moved into "dense undergrowth which for more than 200 yards extended along my entire line." The battlefield was further obscured by the smoke of Clayton's contest with the Federals, and the burning of several small fires. Sergeant Major David S. Bodenhamer of the 32nd Tennessee deduced from the number of wounded being carried past them that "a frightful work of death" was going on. The brigade was deployed in a single long line with the 18th Tennessee on the right, with the 45th, the 32nd, the 23rd Battalion, and the 26th successively

Boys, Them Damn Yanks Can't Whip You

extending to the left. Brown's Tennesseans moved aggressively forward through Clayton's ranks, and steadily pushed the Federal skirmishers back on their main line. The Federals' "stubborn resistance" was "like a cyclone of fire," involving both small arms and the fire of three artillery batteries. Brown found that the dense undergrowth made it impossible to deploy his own battery, so his men forged on for four hundred yards, firing loads of "buck and ball" that was particularly effective in close quarters. Moving at the "double-quick" and raising the "rebel yell," they drove the Federals from the top of the low ridge they held. Two Federal brigades, those of Col. George Dick and Brig. Gen. Samuel Beatty, were pushed back to the Lafayette Road, and three cannon of the 26th Pennsylvania Independent Battery captured. Additionally, the Tennesseans rescued the four guns of Capt. W. W. Carnes's Tennessee battery, captured by the Federals during the collapse of Wright's line, and overran at least two other Federal pieces. Soon afterwards, the men of the 26th Tennessee were ordered to lay down to escape Federal fire. A soldier looked up, and saw Brown sitting on his horse, talking to his men and cursing the Yankees: "Boys, them damn Yanks cant whip you, G—damn them." When his men asked him to get down because they feared he would be killed, he made no reply.[22]

Although Brown's ability to command and control his brigade must have been severely tested by the length of his line, the undergrowth, the smoke, and the disruption of battle, he had utmost confidence in his veteran regimental commanders, particularly Col. Joseph B. Palmer of the 18th on the right, Col. Edmund C. Cook of the 32nd in the center, and Col. John M. Lillard of the 26th on the left. Unfortunately, Palmer, who had been wounded multiple times at Murfreesboro, was dangerously wounded in the shoulder early in the fight and only barely survived. On the left, just before the 26th reached the top of the low ridge, Lillard was mortally wounded by an exploding shell, and a destructive fire from a new line of Federals of Col. Edward A. King's brigade stopped the regiment's advance. Fearing that staying put would result in the loss of the regiment, its major ordered a retreat, which "was not executed in very good order."[23]

The situation rapidly changed on the right wing as well. The appearance of a fresh Federal regiment, the 75th Indiana, on the right and front of the 18th and 45th Tennessee threw the two regiments, likely very much disorganized by their losses and rapid advance, into confusion. The difficulties in the 18th were compounded not only by Palmer's wounding, but by the subsequent wounding of the unit's lieutenant colonel and major, requiring Brown to put one of his staff officers, Capt. Gid Lowe, in command. Indeed, it is likely Brown went to that side of his line to exercise closer supervision. The enfilade fire of these Federals, along with that of Battery H, 4th U. S. Artillery, forced the two regiments back a distance. In Brown's center, the 23rd Battalion's commander, Maj. Tazewell Newman, was also wounded, and his men were eventually withdrawn to procure more ammunition. Cook's 32nd Tennessee doggedly continued its advance and was preparing to engage yet another line of Federals supported by a battery when it was realized that it had no support on either the left or the right. An officer was dispatched to Brown for orders, and Cook was told to move to the rear and rejoin the rest of the brigade.[24]

General Stewart kept a watchful eye, however, and when he saw Brown's men beginning to falter, he ordered Bate's Brigade forward. Bate's men shored up Stewart's right, and then "Old Straight" ordered Clayton's resupplied Alabamians to advance in support of Bate on his left. While Bate's three right regiments attacked in a northwardly direction and eventually were stopped by a line of Yankee cannon, his remaining force, along with Clayton's men and elements of Col. James A. Sheffield's Alabama brigade who wandered into their midst, advanced across the Lafayette Road, piercing, for a short time, the Federal center. During this interval, Brown and his men replenished their ammunition and prepared to rejoin the fight in support of the other two brigades of the division, when a report came from one of Stewart's staff of a Federal advance in the interval on the left between Stewart's and Johnson's divisions. Brown therefore advanced to confront that threat, but found it was a false alarm. In the confusion and smoke, the 18th Tennessee mistakenly fired upon some of Sheffield's men, likely confused by their being out of place and wearing the new dark blue jackets and light blue pants that clothed the reinforcements from the Army of Northern Virginia. Brown reported to Stewart and was ordered to the front, basically along the ridge he had fought for earlier in the day. By that time, Clayton and Bate had withdrawn back across the Lafayette Road. Having placed his

Boys, Them Damn Yanks Can't Whip You

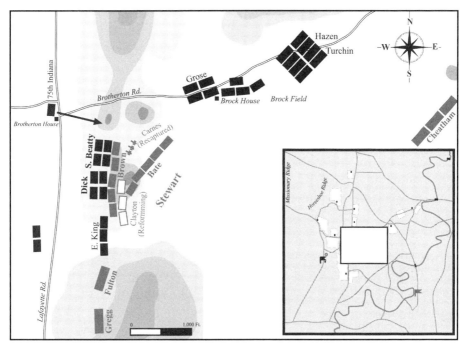

Chickamauga. Alex Mendoza.

artillery under Stewart's personal supervision, Brown held the left of the division's front line that night.[25]

Modern scholars have recognized the effectiveness of A. P. Stewart's tactical employment on September 19. And Stewart wrote that Brown and his two fellow brigadiers were due his "high appreciation." Indeed, Clayton's relatively inexperienced brigade fought well that bloody day and had supplied the bulk of the force Stewart used to penetrate the Union center. Bate's mixed brigade of Tennesseans and Georgians relieved the pressure on Brown and at least part of his men participated in Clayton's breakthrough, although Bate's unit fracturing into two attacks, one of which was bloodily repulsed by a line of Federal artillery, reduced the effectiveness of its contribution. Brown's veteran troops forced a federal retreat from the top of the low ridge they occupied, and not only captured Federal artillery, but also recovered Carnes's guns. The surprise attack of the 75th Indiana and the loss of three of his most experienced regimental commanders kept Brown and his Tennesseans from achieving more significant results.[26]

Darkness brought both respite and suffering. It had been a hard day for Brown's Brigade, as it suffered not only the loss of crucial officers, but almost 500 of the 1,210 men it took into battle that afternoon. R. D. Jamison of the 45th Tennessee recalled that "[i]t was a cold frosty night and we suffered extremely." As the night got colder, a few men of the 26th Tennessee "stirred some smoldering logs" and the ensuing flame brought fire from the Federals. Brown rushed to the scene and gave "a reprimand severe enough to settle the matter of having a fire the rest of the night." Major John P. McGuire of the 32nd Tennessee, who commanded Brown's line of skirmishers that night, recalled the "monotony [of the duty] was heavy, and stillness intense and painful." Wounded soldiers groaned, and unhurt horses were left in harness with dead and wounded animals and could not move. Sometimes the afflicted animals would join in "the most hideous and unearthly yells and groans imaginable."[27]

Even as Brown's Tennesseans endured that miserable night, William S. Rosecrans and Braxton Bragg planned for the next day. The fighting on September 19 extended generally from Jay's Mill southwest to the Viniard Farm, and included a rare night assault by Cleburne's Division. The Federal troops on the north end of the battlefield pulled back from their later afternoon positions to defensible high ground closer to the Lafayette Road, which in itself reflected the Federals' resolution to stay on the field and fight it out. For his part, Bragg had a significant number of troops that had not seen action on September 19 and expected yet another of Longstreet's brigades to arrive during the night, along with Longstreet himself. Bragg elected to stay on the offensive and decided to consolidate his command structure by dividing the Army of Tennessee into wings, with his two senior lieutenant generals, Longstreet and Polk, respectively commanding its left and right wings. Polk was to initiate the Confederate attack at "day dawn," approximately 5:30 a.m. on September 20, and the attacks would proceed down the line, forcing Rosecrans away from Chattanooga and, ideally, crushing the Army of the Cumberland against the mountains to the south.[28]

Stewart's Division was in Longstreet's left wing. Early that morning, riding alone and wearing an overcoat against the unseasonable chill, Longstreet met with Stewart, an old West Point classmate, and informed him of Bragg's plan for that day, and that he would be receiving orders directly from Longstreet himself. Stewart informed his friend that there were no Confederate troops to his immediate right and was directed to move his line a quarter-mile to the right, which moved the entire division north of the east-west Brotherton Road. Brown's Brigade moved along the crest of the same ridge it fought for the day before. During the move, Brown's skirmishers were driven in, with some casualties, by a force of Federals. Brown reinforced them, and they were pushed out about 150 yards, but no further, as Stewart did not want to bring on an engagement before his new line was established. While Brown's Tennesseans erected temporary breastworks of logs, rocks, and other "hastily collected material," Bate's men connected to their right, but his right angled off to the east, to protect against any Federal threat. In moving, Stewart had unknowingly masked part of Cleburne's line, however, and eventually Brig. Gen. S. A. M. Wood's brigade of Alabama and Mississippi men filed into place on Brown's right.[29]

Based upon a communication failure in the newly rearranged Confederate high command, the attack on the right did not begin at day-dawn. It began four hours later at 9:30 a.m., time which the Federals used to shore up their left flank. Breckinridge's and Cleburne's divisions advanced, and the day's fighting was on. As Bragg intended, Breckinridge turned the Federal left, but with insufficient force to drive Thomas's men out of their position. Cleburne's attacks were bloodily repulsed. Meanwhile, frustrated by the right wing's delay, Bragg instructed one of his staff officers to proceed down the line and order each division to attack. The officer found Stewart about 11:00 a.m. and told him to attack at once. Stewart related his orders from Longstreet, but to no avail. Securing the cooperation of S. A. M. Wood, Stewart ordered Brown to advance.[30]

Brown's men advanced off of their low ridge through the woods toward Brannan's Federal division, which was hunkered behind breastworks on the north and west edges of the small farm of Larkin Poe, consisting of a small log home on the west side of the Lafayette Road and cleared land on the east side. The brigade, aligned as it had been the previous day, advanced with the 18th, 45th, 32nd, 23rd Battalion, and the 26th in line from right to left. The Tennesseans' skirmishers drove in their Federal counterparts, and then merged into Brown's main line. The brigade advanced west at the double-quick, moving down off the ridge into a slight hollow through open woods before emerging at the Poe clearing. On its right, Wood's Brigade went forward, and soon encountered a particularly troublesome peculiarity in the Federal line. When viewed as a whole, the Army of the Cumberland's dispositions looked something like a large question mark, with three divisions located on high ground east of the Lafayette Road constituting the upper curved part of the question mark, and three more divisions in line extending southward from the Poe farm. S. A. M. Wood was not a particularly effective leader in battle, and his unfortunate men were situated to take fire from where the curved part of the line met the straight north-south part, and were therefore very effectively subject to fire from the front as well as their right flank. As his men advanced into the Poe Field, the crossfire was too much, and Wood's Brigade "broke in confusion."[31]

The right of Brown's Brigade was soon subject to this same convergence of fire. As Col. Searcy of the 45th later wrote in his report, "[t]he grape and canister coming from [the right and rear] was not at all agreeable." Still suffering from the loss of leadership the day before, and now without Wood's support on the right, the 18th was unable to take the punishment, and it, followed by the then-unsupported 45th, "broke and retired in disorder" to the temporary works erected that morning. The 45th's adjutant, future congressman James D. Richardson, impressed Bromfield Ridley with the almost casual remark, "This is hot, isn't it?" The next regiment in line, the 32nd Tennessee, or at least part of it, made it across the Lafayette Road, but in its turn was subject to fire from the right and rear. Sgt. Bodenhamer wrote that the most troublesome Federal battery was planted in the road itself, and "poured a heavy fire of grape and canister shots into our ranks and almost in our rear." At this point, Brown later wrote, "it became necessary to retire the remainder of the line, because to have advanced farther would have exposed it to the hazard of being cut off, while to have remainded [sic] stationary without shelter and under fire from a protected foe would have sacrificed the men without obtaining any compensating advantage."[32]

Stewart, in the meantime, ordered Bate and Clayton forward in support of Brown, but Brannan's line was too strong, and they, too, were forced to retire. While rallying and reorganizing his men, Brown was struck by a "spent grape" and disabled. Probably, Brown was knocked from his horse by the missile, with the resulting fall as likely as the projectile itself to have debilitated him. In any event, he was unable to command the brigade for the rest of the day, and with the senior colonel, Palmer, already wounded, Col. Cook of the 32nd assumed command. The brigade was not significantly engaged thereafter.[33]

With his division reformed, Stewart returned to the edge of the Poe Field, but facing more of the lower curve of the Federal question mark. His attack, in which Brown had played a prominent part, was not in and of itself successful, but it helped set the stage for the massive attack launched a short time later by Longstreet, which, catching the Federal troops in the line facing him in movement, was a spectacular success. A portion of the Army of the Cumberland was driven from the field, along with Rosecrans and two of his corps commanders, McCook and Crittenden. Only a brave stand by George H. Thomas and the men in blue under his command saved the Army of the Cumberland from complete destruction. Unfortunately for Bragg and the men who sacrificed so much for the Army of Tennessee's first major victory, the successful breakthrough was on the Federal right. The defeated bluecoats did not stream southward into the cul-de-sac of McLemore's Cove, as Bragg had planned. They instead retreated into Chattanooga, rendering the costly Confederate victory barren.[34]

The next day, it eventually became apparent the Federals had retreated back toward Chattanooga. Maj. Benjamin Franklin Carter, Brown's acting commissary, described in a letter to his wife the "awful spectacle the battle field presented on the retreat of the enemy . . . whole teams of artillery horses piled together, in one solid mass, the immense quantity of arms and accoutrements abandoned by the enemy in their wild retreat." While Bragg was criticized for his failure to follow up his hard-won victory, there was actually little Bragg could do. As in most Civil War battles, the winning side in a battle had suffered as much, or in the case of Chickamauga, a bit more than the losing side. Casualties were high among both officers and men, and the Army of Tennessee's chronic problems with wagon transportation were magnified by the addition of thousands of reinforcements to the army without their organic vehicles. The army was supplied by a single rail line to Atlanta, which itself was of dubious reliability. If these factors were not enough to limit Bragg's ability to maneuver across the Tennessee to the west of Chattanooga, at this point in time the army had no pontoon train. Bragg's best option was to invest the town and hope that the Federals, facing their own problems, would quit Chattanooga.[35]

Bragg's initial report of the battle on September 24 noted that Brown was "slightly wounded" during the battle, but at that point was back on duty. Stewart also reported that his casualty numbers did not include those slightly wounded who were not disabled, specifically mentioning Brown. Reports indicate Brown was on duty on September 27, and, as indicated below, he was back in Chattanooga either on October 4 or 5. Whether as a result of his wound or otherwise, apparently in this interval Brown went to Marietta, Georgia, "for a short rest." There, he met a young woman from Murfreesboro, Elizabeth Childress. Elizabeth, or "Bettie" as she was known, was the twenty-one-year-old daughter of John W. Childress and his wife, Sarah. Childress was the brother of Sarah Childress Polk, the widow of President James K. Polk. A gentleman farmer of substantial wealth, Childress was once a director of the Bank of Tennessee. His financial means and social standing provided Bettie with the advantages young women of her class had at that time. Bettie graduated with honors from Rev. C. D. Elliott's Nashville Female Academy, and was invited by President Davis to be present at his review of the troops when the executive visited the army in late 1862. Foreseeing that Murfreesboro would soon be a battleground, Childress removed his family to Georgia prior to the fighting.[36]

When Brown was introduced to Bettie, she was knitting a pair of socks with a pair of gold knitting needles given by her famous aunt. Purportedly, the socks were intended for Brown, and had a Confederate flag interwoven into its threads. Young, rich, and attractive, Bettie had many suitors among the officers who called on the Childress family. A story published fifty years afterward, but still during Bettie's lifetime, reported that it was a case of "love at first sight" and the couple was engaged within seven days of their first meeting. Their wedding would have to wait, however, as Brown was required to return to his duties at Chattanooga.[37]

Emboldened by his victory at Chickamauga, Bragg took the opportunity to remove those officers who he felt had kept it from being the complete victory he planned: Lt. Gen. Leonidas Polk and Maj. Gen. Thomas C. Hindman. Polk, who Bragg thought incompetent in any case, had been the center of anti-Bragg agitation for months. In the following days, a coterie of officers opposed to Bragg took the bold, and effectively mutinous, step of preparing a petition to ask President Davis to remove the general from command of the Army of Tennessee. The petition, a draft of which in Buckner's possession was dated October 4, was the culmination of months of ill feeling stretching back to the retreat from Kentucky, and involved not only officers who had served in the army from that time, but Longstreet and Hill as well. Although the instigators circulated the petition widely through the army's high command, only twelve officers signed the document: Longstreet, Hill, Buckner, Cleburne, William Preston, Archibald Gracie, James A. Smith, Marcellus Stovall, Lucius Polk, Bushrod Johnson, Randall Gibson, and John C. Brown. Brown's participation in this group is curious in one sense, in that the Tennessean was considered to have good relations with Bragg. Years later, Brown blandly explained: "The Army generally was dissatisfied with the operations directed by General Bragg after the victory [at Chickamauga] . . . Great demoralization prevailed, and the general desire was that General Bragg should be transferred to some other field of duty. . . ." The fact that Buckner was among the chief instigators of the petition must also be considered. Buckner was Brown's first commanding officer and had much to do with his promotion to brigadier general. He was also Brown's corps commander, and the two remained friends after the war. Bragg's chief of staff, Brig. Gen. William W. Mackall, marveled at Buckner's skill at political intrigue, writing to Joseph E. Johnston to that effect and observing to his wife that Bragg, who had "the misfortune of not knowing a friend from a foe," had to be talked out of promoting Buckner over one of the army's best officers just a few days before the petition.[38]

Bragg was not without those who wanted him sustained in command, chief among them being the man who counted most, President Jefferson Davis. On October 5, his aide, Col. James Chestnut, who was at Bragg's headquarters, thought Davis's presence was "urgently demanded." Davis therefore arrived on October 9, after conferring with Polk, Longstreet, and Breckinridge. After a meeting with Bragg to get his side of the story, Davis added the corps commanders, Longstreet, Cheatham (in Polk's place), Hill, and Buckner. None were favorable to Bragg. Davis later met with supporters of both sides, although there is no evidence he conferred with Brown. In the end, Bragg was sustained, and Davis left Bragg empowered to deal with the malcontents.[39]

While the Confederate president struggled with discontent in the army's high command, the men in the rebel ranks suffered nearly as much deprivation as their Federal counterparts in Chattanooga. Not only was the army tied to the single rickety railroad line to Atlanta, but its shortage of wagons and a period of heavy rains compounded the lack of food. The rains also made the lack of shelter and adequate clothing painfully apparent. One of Longstreet's division commanders, Maj. Gen. Lafayette McLaws, wrote in mid-October "the whole country is covered with water, the creeks are impassible . . . many of my command are without tents and hundreds are without blankets and shoes. Added to these wants, the ration is not sufficient, and hundreds are sick." In Brown's Brigade, G. W. Dillon of the 18th Tennessee recorded: "The rain was falling freely the weather cold and chilly and continued all day and night the water overflowing our various beds breaking our rest dampening our clothing and persons very much which rendered us quite uncomfortable for a time." A later period of rain was "awful beyond description."[40]

Rosecrans's absence from the field of Chickamauga during the crucial afternoon of September 20, his curious and less-than-reassuring dispatches since then, and reports from Assistant Secretary of War Charles A. Dana all led the administration in Washington to conclude that a reshuffling of the Federal command was required. A new Military Division of the Mississippi was created to coordinate the three major Western departments, and Maj. Gen. Ulysses S. Grant placed at its head. It was left to Grant to determine whether to keep Rosecrans or not, and as the two were old enemies, Rosecrans was promptly replaced with Thomas. Reinforcements were dispatched from the Army of the Potomac in Virginia, under its old commander, Maj. Gen. Joseph Hooker, and from the Army of the Tennessee in Mississippi and West Tennessee, under Maj. Gen. William T. Sherman. In late October, the Army of the Cumberland broke out to the west of Chattanooga into Lookout Valley, where it linked up with Hooker's men marching up from the railhead at

Boys, Them Damn Yanks Can't Whip You

Bridgeport, Alabama. A rebel counterattack failed to close this new line of communication. By the first of November, Grant was in Chattanooga and well on his way to rectifying the Federal situation.[41]

Notwithstanding his reverses in Lookout Valley, Bragg was not finished reckoning with his critics in the army, the most irritating of whom was Longstreet. In addition to Longstreet's aligning himself with Bragg's opposition and signing the petition, he had responsibility for the crucial sector in Lookout Valley. Bragg's solution, which had some practical basis in keeping the initiative and restoring direct communication with Virginia, involved sending Longstreet, his two divisions, and elements of the Army of Tennessee coincidentally commanded by certain of the petition signers, to retake Knoxville, given up in early September. Either oblivious of the danger of weakening the army in the face of the gathering Federal host, or calculating that Longstreet would be able to return in time for the ultimate struggle for Chattanooga, Bragg ultimately dispatched a force of 17,000 men with Lee's "War Horse." Sending Longstreet to Knoxville, Bragg confessed to Davis, "will be great relief to me." As for the disloyal officers who remained with the army, Bragg had "carte blanche" from Davis to do what he deemed necessary. On November 12, 1863, Bragg undertook a massive reorganization of the army, which broke up the blocs of Tennessee troops in Cheatham's and Stewart's divisions and placed his critics where his friends could watch them.[42]

Brown and his brigade were transferred to the division of Maj. Gen. Carter Littlepage Stevenson, recently returned from the area of East Tennessee around Sweetwater. The forty-five-year-old Stevenson was a West Point graduate who served with the Army of Tennessee in 1862. Stevenson's division was transferred to Mississippi before Murfreesboro, and was captured at Vicksburg earlier in the 1863 and then paroled. Declared exchanged by the Confederate government, the division was once more assigned to the Army of Tennessee. Subsequent to Bragg's reorganization, the division included Brown's Tennesseans, Brig. Gen. Alfred Cumming's Georgia brigade, and Brig. Gen. Edmund Pettus's Alabama brigade. The other two brigades were part of Stevenson's Vicksburg command, along with Brig. Gen. John C. Vaughn's brigade. Vaughn's men were nominally still part of the division, but were not fully reorganized and in any event remained in East Tennessee to assist Longstreet's campaign. By date of commission, Brown was the division's senior brigadier.[43]

Brown's disfavor with Bragg was not so comprehensive as to prevent a welcome addition to the brigade. When separated from Brown shortly after being exchanged in September 1862, the 3rd Tennessee was sent to Mississippi, where it was reorganized under Col. Calvin H. Walker and fought at Chickasaw Bayou, Port Hudson, Raymond, and Jackson. As part of Gregg's Brigade, the 3rd was transferred to north Georgia in time to fight at Chickamauga. Bragg's original order of reorganization of November 12 basically dissolved Gregg's Brigade and distributed its Tennessee regiments, including the 3rd, to Bate's command. But between November 12 and November 20, the much-diminished regiment, numbering less than two hundred men, was transferred to Brown's Brigade. Any increase in strength was of benefit to the brigade, but Brown was doubtlessly very pleased to be rejoined by his first command.[44]

Stevenson's Division was assigned to the top of Lookout Mountain. This eminence was part of a long ridge that stretched southwest over eighty miles from its dramatic point in Tennessee overlooking the Tennessee River at Chattanooga through the northwest corner of Georgia into Alabama. Linked to Chattanooga by a good road up the east side of the mountain, the mountaintop offered several reminders of peacetime, including the small village of Summertown, where a correspondent found a "most elegant summer resort, resembling in appearance a fashionable watering place, with beautiful and commodious hotel buildings, and all else to render the place attractive to seekers of pleasure." The reporter considered the views of the surrounding country spectacular, but was struck by the wartime view of forests and valleys filled by "ten thousand tents, and checkered with roads and entrenchments, and devastated by the scores of thousands of soldiers."[45]

Carter Stevenson (Credit: Alabama Department of Archives and History, Montgomery, Alabama)

Boys, Them Damn Yanks Can't Whip You

In September, Rosecrans's advance followed a road up Lookout Mountain from Johnson's Crook, a cove near Trenton, Georgia, to Stevens Gap, to descend on the east side the mountain into the near trap at McLemore's Cove. Having once had their position in Chattanooga made untenable by a Federal force taking that route, the Confederates were sensitive to Federal movements in that area, especially since Sherman's reinforcements from Mississippi would soon be marching through Lookout Valley from the railhead at Stevenson, Alabama. Accordingly, detachments of infantry and cavalry held the passes up the western face of the mountain from Johnson's Crook to the point overlooking Chattanooga, a distance estimated by Stevenson to be about eighteen miles. The length of the Confederate infantry line around Chattanooga and the logistical difficulty of maintaining a large cavalry force on the top of the mountain made Stevenson's dispositions quite thin.[46]

After making final arrangements relating to the transfer, Brown moved his men from Chattanooga Valley up onto the top of the mountain on November 15, his men chalking up to soldier's luck having to leave comfortable quarters upon which they had so recently labored. In accordance with Hardee's orders to Stevenson, Brown and most of his infantry stood watch on the mountain at Nickajack Pass, about ten miles from the point above Chattanooga. Brown was barely in place when, under orders from Bragg, Brig. Gen. St. John Richardson Liddell arrived on November 17 with a small force of cavalry with a plan to march north down the valley and burn a bridge on the line of Sherman's advance. Stevenson was ordered to provide two thousand men to support Liddell's expedition, and added Cumming's Brigade to Brown's for that purpose. Brown had not had time to visit the vital pass at Johnson's Crook himself, but the aggressive Liddell told Brown it could be held by "50 *resolute* men." In reporting the same to Stevenson, Brown confessed that "we are a little anxious on that subject."[47]

Liddell was frustrated by the "absurdity" of Bragg's orders. While Bragg had promised infantry support, positive orders had apparently not reached Liddell and Brown to allow them to move forward on the night of November 17. The frustrated Liddell went down into the valley to reconnoiter, even as Sherman's men started flooding into the valley from the west. Liddell determined that he could make an attempt on the bridge and return safely, but speed was essential. Finally, Bragg gave the necessary orders, and Liddell gave Brown and Cumming orders to post regiments at the foot of the mountain to support his return from the dash on the bridge. By this time, Federal strength had increased, and while Liddell thought he had an excellent chance for success with a surprise attack, Bragg ordered that the attack not be made, and ordered both Liddell and Brown to retire, which occurred about dusk on November 18. When later confronted by the disappointed Liddell, Bragg explained that he thought Liddell was going to attack a corps-sized force with only two brigades. When Liddell protested that the commanding general did not give him enough credit for common sense, Bragg asked him why he did not make the attack despite his orders. Liddell explained that Brown refused to disregard them, observing that he "did not stand too well to disobey an order."[48]

While Sherman had no intention of moving across Lookout Mountain at Johnson's Crook, he correctly perceived Bragg's sensitivity to that possibility, and ordered his brother-in-law, Brig. Gen. Hugh Ewing, to move his division south up the valley to Trenton to make the Confederates believe that "we were going to turn Bragg's left by pretty much the same road Rosecrans had followed." Accordingly, on November 19, Ewing sent troops to cover the trails descending from Lookout Mountain, and actually sent a small force up the trail at Johnson's Crook, driving a rebel cavalry force away. His purpose of "making a good demonstration" accomplished, Ewing called in his troops the next day and began marching down Lookout Valley toward the Federal lines nearer Chattanooga. Bragg was convinced that "a serious movement is being made on our left." On November 20, the same day Ewing started winding down his demonstration, another two rebel brigades were dispatched to the top of the mountain, and a brigade moved toward McLemore's Cove, should the Federals descend down Stevens Gap. Hardee and Stevenson were at Brown's position at Powell's Trail the morning of November 21. Ready for action, Brown's men spent the previous night camped in the rain in line of battle, but scouting parties through the 21st provided sufficient intelligence to conclude that the immediate threat was probably over. Brown reached that conclusion himself, but was not immediately informed of his superiors' plans, and therefore at 4:00 p.m. asked if he should coordinate an attack with the brigade coming up from McLemore's Cove or merely demonstrate.[49]

The next day, having deduced that the Federals had left the Trenton area, Brown gave orders to the cavalry pickets and ordered his brigade from its advanced position to its old camp on the mountain back toward Chattanooga. On November 23, as the immediate threat on his front was gone, Brown took the time to resolve personnel issues left over from the transfer from Stewart's Division. But elsewhere on the Chattanooga front, the Federals' sudden advance to capture an advanced outpost on Orchard Knob made Bragg realize that the true threat was on his right, and he began shifting troops in that direction. Hardee was sent to take command of the Confederate right wing, and troops preparing to board the train to reinforce Longstreet at Knoxville, primarily Cleburne's Division, were sent back into the line. Assigned the command of all troops west of Chattanooga Creek late in the afternoon, Stevenson accordingly directed Brown to assume command of his division the night of November 23.[50]

Ulysses S. Grant's plan for the final stage of the Battle of Chattanooga did not include an assault on Lookout Mountain. The troops under Hooker in Lookout Valley were intended to be passed across the Tennessee River and deployed against Missionary Ridge. Grant reasoned that a successful assault on Missionary Ridge would "unquestionably cause the evacuation by the enemy of his line across [Chattanooga] valley and on Lookout Mountain." Whatever the logic of that reasoning, a broken bridge left about ten thousand Federals in Lookout Valley, and Hooker was authorized to make a direct attack on Lookout Mountain with this force on the morning of November 24, supported by almost a quarter of the Federal artillery in the Chattanooga theater. Facing Hooker were Carter Stevenson's six brigades, manning positions from Nickajack Trail to the west side of Chattanooga Creek. On the top of the mountain, the day started with Brown in command of two brigades, his own and Pettus's, as well as Capt. Max Van Den Corput's battery of Napoleon cannon.[51]

About 8:30 a.m., in a heavy fog, Federal troops under Brig. Gen. John Geary began crossing Lookout Creek about two airline miles from the most recognizable point on the slope of Lookout Mountain, a house owned by local industrialist Robert Cravens. Geary's men formed a line that stretched up the side of the mountain to the steep wall of the cliffs extending below the top of the mountain, and reinforced by another Federal brigade, began an advance through the fog northward toward the Cravens house. Holding the northwest slope was Brig. Gen. Edward C. Walthall's Mississippi brigade, whose troops and works were oriented more to oppose an attack from the lower slope, not from the same elevation. Surging out of the fog, Geary's men overwhelmed Walthall's line, sending those Mississippians not killed or captured scurrying toward the Cravens house.[52]

In accordance with Stevenson's plan for the defense of the mountain, Walthall fell back on Brig. Gen. John C. Moore's brigade, concentrated near the Cravens house. Stevenson was on top of the mountain at this point, and ordered Brown to send the larger portion of Pettus's Brigade halfway down the mountain, leaving only two Alabama regiments who were tasked with defending the west face of the mountain nearer the point and with providing a reserve for the troops further south. The consolidated 18th and 26th Tennessee guarded the remote passes at Powell's and Nickajack trails, but the remainder of Brown's Brigade was "ordered under arms and marched from their encampments on Lookout Mountain to a point near Summertown at which the road reaches the summit of the mountain." Soon thereafter, Brown moved his largest regiment, the 32nd Tennessee, to the point of Lookout, where two of Corput's Napoleons were posted. While the majority of the 32nd formed a line of battle in support of the battery at the point, a company was deployed as skirmishers along the bluffs.[53]

Throughout the morning, Corput's battery looked for opportunities to engage the Federal advance. Occasionally a shell would do "good execution," but the extreme range, the thickness of the fog, and the inability to depress the guns kept the rebel guns from stemming the Federal advance. By 1:00 p.m., the Federals were in possession of the shelf of the mountain around the Cravens house. While the fog kept the bluecoats obscured from Brown's position on the point, Corput's Napoleons fired into the fog toward the Cravens house, assisted in fixing the direction by the signal corps. Brown also sent sharpshooters down the side of the mountain to fire on the Federal flank, and even ordered rocks rolled down the mountain. Both Brown and Corput believed that their efforts

Boys, Them Damn Yanks Can't Whip You

had some effect in slowing the Federal advance, although one Federal observer deemed the greater damage was done by shells hitting treetops that then fell upon the heads of Geary's men.[54]

As authorized by Bragg earlier that morning, Stevenson called on both the army commander and his corps commander, Maj. Gen. John C. Breckinridge, for reinforcements. With reinforcements, he planned to send a force down a trail on the west side of the mountain from a location near the point into the rear of the assaulting Federals. Bragg eventually informed him that no reinforcements were coming, and that Lookout Mountain was to be abandoned, a decision that Stevenson related to Brown late that afternoon. Around 7:00 p.m., Brown's regiments began descending the mountain by the main road from Summertown to Chattanooga, followed closely by the Alabama regiments Pettus left with the Tennessean. Because nearly all the brigade's wagons had been dispatched to the railhead at Chickamauga Station the night before for supplies, the sudden evacuation forced Brown to abandon his camp equipage and part of the baggage. Finally, word was dispatched to the 18th/26th, guarding the passes to the south, and those troops descended the mountain by another route, ending up just around daylight on November 25 at a point south of Rossville.[55]

While Brown and his men descended the mountain, Bragg, Hardee, and Breckinridge met to determine the Army of Tennessee's response to the loss of Lookout Mountain on its left and Sherman's massed troops on the right. While Hardee counseled retreat across rain-swollen South Chickamauga Creek, Bragg and Breckinridge were convinced that the strength of the rebel position on Missionary Ridge dictated that the army stay and fight the next day. Hardee successfully argued that he required heavy reinforcement to defeat the threat on the right, which resulted in Stevenson's and Cheatham's divisions being dispatched from the extreme left to the right. By the time these orders made their way down to John C. Brown, it was 4:00 a.m. on November 25, and he marched his Tennesseans from the east side of Chattanooga Creek to the position held by Maj. Gen. Patrick Cleburne's division on the northern end of Missionary Ridge, arriving there just after sunrise.[56]

On its northern end, Missionary Ridge ended in a jumble of hills just south of where South Chickamauga Creek flowed into the Tennessee

River. The highest elevation actually connected to Missionary Ridge was known as Tunnel Hill, although the railroad tunnel was about five hundred yards to the south of this high point, underneath a saddle in the ridge. A small valley separated Tunnel Hill from high ground seized by Sherman late the previous afternoon, now known as Billy Goat Hill. After a hard night of redeployment, Cleburne's men held the top of Tunnel Hill, another detached hill to the east close to Chickamauga Creek about a thousand yards from the high point of Tunnel Hill, and a position on the east side of Missionary Ridge facing north. Somewhat detached from the rest of Cleburne's position, a battery was positioned directly over the tunnel, facing west.[57]

Under Stevenson's direction, Brown formed his three regiments with the left resting over the tunnel, but Hardee soon changed the orientation of Brown's line so the Tennesseans would "be in position to support Cleburne's left or hold the railroad." As the railroad itself was at the bottom of Missionary Ridge, it appears at this point Brown's left was off the summit of the ridge somewhat, and his right not connected with Cleburne's left. A substantial force of skirmishers was advanced further downhill, covering the area from Cleburne's left out into the flat area around the Glass Farm. From the start, Brown's skirmishers engaged their counterparts in blue, but most of the Federal skirmishers probed Cleburne's position, which also received artillery fire from Billy Goat Hill. Likely anticipating the first major Federal attack of the day, an hour or two later Stevenson ordered Brown "to move up so at to occupy the interval between the left of Cleburne's line of defenses and the railroad, prolonging Cleburne's line to the railroad." Brown's right was in the wooded area on the hill next to Cleburne, and his left was "considerably advanced" down the hill, according to one observer off the hill and behind the railroad bank.[58]

Sherman's first assault was made by two brigades from Hugh Ewing's division, those of Brig. Gen. John M. Corse and Col. John M. Loomis. At about 10:30 a.m., Corse assaulted Tunnel Hill along a lower spur of Missionary Ridge that extended a few hundred yards to the north. In support, Loomis was to advance to strike at Tunnel Hill from the southwest, but had orders from Ewing "to push the enemy's skirmishers, but under no circumstances bring on a general engagement." Loomis's skir-

Boys, Them Damn Yanks Can't Whip You

mishers engaged their counterparts among Brown's Tennesseans, but when it became apparent that a heavier force was advancing, Brown reinforced his skirmishers until almost half the command was in advance of his main line. Loomis's men were subject to direct and cross fire of the massed rebel artillery, perhaps under the supervision of Hardee himself, as well as fire "from the infantry and sharpshooters of the enemy." One northern correspondent found Loomis's advance unimpressive, noting that it "resulted in a repulse of the brigade, after a short fight, so weakly made and as early dropped that I imagine it was intended to develop the enemy and his strength for the benefit of the [Federal] artillery."[59]

Brown proudly reported that his men "repulsed" the Federal attack, inflicting many casualties and capturing fifty prisoners. For his part, Loomis placed his brigade "under such cover as the low ground afforded." Loomis's predicament may have dictated a counterattack, but Brown felt his orders left him no discretion. While the conflict between Brown's and Loomis's skirmishers continued, from his vantage point on top of the ridge, Hardee ordered two regiments of Cumming's Brigade down to oppose an advance on the buildings of the Glass Farm by Loomis's support, Col. Adophus Buschbeck's brigade. From their position near the railroad, Brown's skirmish line doubtlessly participated in this contest, which temporarily left the Yankees in control of the buildings. Cumming later sent troops to burn the buildings.[60]

Sherman's second major attack of the day occurred in the early afternoon. Loomis was ordered to advance so his left was on the road that curled around the foot of Tunnel Hill and hold on. Not being satisfied with the security of his left, Loomis called on Buschbeck for support, and two Pennsylvania regiments were sent to that point. Meanwhile, the brigades of Brig. Gen. Charles L. Matthies and Col. Green B. Raum were also advanced to Loomis's support. Without any orders, the Pennsylvanians advanced far up the southwest face of Tunnel Hill, and first Matthies and then Raum moved to assist. With all of these troops coming to his aid, and his brigade already beaten up by the fighting to that point, Loomis hunkered down behind the railroad embankment where the track turned to go through the tunnel. This assault chased some of Brown's men up the face of the ridge, a shell beheading one brother in the 45th Tennessee and gruesomely wounding another. Cleburne

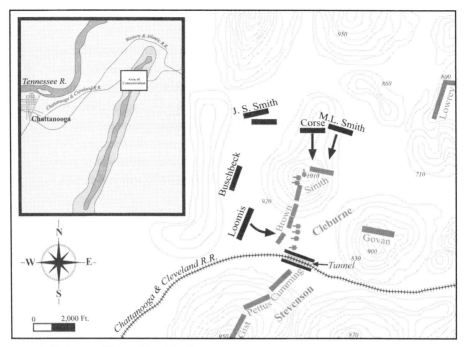

Missionary Ridge. Alex Mendoza.

approached Brown and suggested that the Tennessean's right flank could wheel out and attack the Federal assault column. Having been out on his skirmish line, Brown demurred, fearing that he would expose his men to a "terrible fire" from the flank, more than likely from Loomis's men. After considering Brown's objection, Cleburne directed the Tennessean to stay in position.[61]

Wisely, Hardee began sending Cleburne reinforcements. The Irishman determined a counterattack was in order. Elements of three rebel brigades charged down Tunnel Hill, engaging in savage and often hand-to-hand fighting, and enveloping the flanks of the Federal troops that had forged their way up the steep slopes of the hill. It was at this point that the detached 18th/26th Tennessee arrived on the scene, and shortly after its commander reported to Brown, Cleburne ordered it to a position on top of the hill supporting his attacking force. Although these late-arriving Tennesseans were not involved, Cleburne's attack was a great success, capturing "many prisoners and stand of colors." By 4:00 p.m., Sherman's attack, which Grant intended to be the main Federal effort against Missionary Ridge, was defeated.[62]

Boys, Them Damn Yanks Can't Whip You

The elation that the victorious troops on the Army of Tennessee's right felt at 4:00 p.m. changed to astonishment a few minutes later. At about the same time Cleburne's Confederates routed Sherman's men in a counterattack downhill, an attack uphill by the Army of the Cumberland against the Confederate center, aided to a lesser extent by an advance by Hooker's force from Lookout Mountain against the Confederate left, resulted in the collapse of Bragg's line on those portions of Missionary Ridge. Brown was ordered, probably by Hardee, to "move rapidly toward the center" and report to Cheatham. "Marse Frank" ordered Brown to form his brigade at right angles to what was left of Walthall's Brigade, facing southward against the Federals who had penetrated the main line along the crest of the ridge. In the gathering darkness, first an irregular line of rebel troops in Brown's front "retired in broken fragments" and then Walthall's men themselves "gave way in great disorder." While Brown's men, reinforced by Cumming's Brigade, were seeking to reform a new line, Cheatham ordered them to leave the ridge, abandoning it to the "shouting and victorious" Federals. The brigade, followed by the still separated 18th/26th, crossed the Chickamauga, some of the men by means of the railroad bridge, others being required to wade the stream, bivouacking for the night near the Shallow Ford Road. The next day, the brigade moved south to Ringgold, Georgia, and then further south to Dalton.[63]

Although the retreating Confederates were pursued by a Federal force under Hooker, the bluecoats suffered a sharp repulse at the hands of Cleburne's command at Ringgold Gap. The campaign for Chattanooga thereby came to an end, with the strategic little city a base for a future Federal advance into the heart of the Confederacy. Mortified by the collapse on Missionary Ridge, Bragg requested and was granted relief, and Hardee was placed in command of the army, but stipulated that it be only be temporary. After some period of deliberation in Richmond, President Davis appointed, with considerable reluctance, Gen. Joseph E. Johnston, with whom Davis shared a profound and mutual antipathy. As Confederate diarist Mary Chestnut famously observed, "The President detests Joe Johnston for all the trouble he has given him, and General Joe returns the compliment with compound interest." The Army of Tennessee, previously hobbled by the feuding between Bragg and many of his officers, now faced a new level of command discord.[64]

It was a dark December in Dalton. Major Barber of the 3rd Tennessee wrote that desertions were "frequent" and a "gloom rests upon the whole army." Major B. F. Carter, Brown's commissary officer, wrote his wife that the retreat from Chattanooga "depressed the feelings of our troops," but saw signs that Bragg's removal would restore confidence. Bad weather and news of ravages inflicted on the residents of Giles County by occupying Yankees also contributed to low morale. The brigade was assembled in a field near Dalton to witness the hanging of a deserter from Company D of the 18th Tennessee, who was executed wearing his Federal uniform. Not all was gloomy, however, as winter quarters were constructed and a ration of whiskey was issued to the men of the brigade on Christmas Eve.[65]

As his men adjusted to their new situation, Brown joined other officers in confronting the continuing manpower issues of the army. Before Johnston's arrival, Brown joined Hardee, Breckinridge, Stevenson, Cheatham, and three other brigadier generals in the army requesting that the Confederate Congress retain the troops then in service for the remainder of the war, expand the ages for conscription, limit exemptions, and "to place in service, as cooks, laborers, teamsters, and hospital attendants, with the army and elsewhere, able-bodied negroes and mulattos, bond and free." Twenty other officers stated various degree of qualification. Of these twenty, Patrick Cleburne had other, more revolutionary thoughts relating to manpower. Cleburne, believing that the independence of the Confederacy was at stake, favored arming slaves to fight for the South. It was a concept that the Irishman had been mulling for some time. At Wartrace earlier that year, Cleburne discussed the concept with Liddell. He began working on a memorandum to that effect in earnest in December, and secured the approval of a number, but not all, of his brigade and regimental commanders. Hardee requested that Johnston, who had assumed command on December 27, allow a meeting of the army's corps and division commanders on January 2, 1864, where Cleburne made his stunning proposal.[66]

All of the corps and division commanders were present except for Cheatham. After Cleburne read his paper, Hindman, for whom Cleburne had suffered a wound in a prewar Arkansas gunfight, spoke in support of the proposal, arguing at the very minimum the position taken by the

December 17 joint letter to the Confederate Congress. Indeed, Hindman had previously published an anonymous letter advocating arming black soldiers. Afterwards, Cleburne's chief of staff, Major Calhoun Benham, read a strong but respectful rebuttal. The response of his peers, however, was particularly disappointing to Cleburne. Southern rights fire-eaters W. H. T. Walker, James Patton Anderson, and William B. Bate spoke against the proposal. Walker in particular was exercised by the plan, and took it on himself to solicit a written response from each of the officers present. Stewart and Stevenson responded that they were also opposed, although Stevenson too was willing to consider something along the lines of the December 17 joint letter. Hardee and Cheatham did not respond to Walker's inquisition, and Hindman refused to recognize Walker's right to question him. Johnston ordered those present to keep quiet about the proposal, but Walker, perhaps secondarily motivated by the prospect of removing a rival for future promotion, insisted on informing President Davis. Davis soon thereafter ordered the proposal and the surrounding discussion hushed up.[67]

Although only corps and division commanders were at the meeting, news of the proposal must have leaked out. Whether Stevenson discussed it with his brigade and regimental commanders is unknown, and there is no contemporary record of Brown's views on the subject. But there is evidence Brown not only knew of the proposal, but approved of it as well. On July 24, 1891, nearly two years after Brown's death, Lucius E. Polk, one of Cleburne's brigadiers, wrote a letter to Campbell Brown with an account of the incident. Campbell Brown was unrelated to General Brown, and is best known as a staff officer for his stepfather, Lt. Gen. Richard S. Ewell, himself an early advocate for arming the slaves. He started the war, however, as a second lieutenant of Company F of the 3rd Tennessee. Polk's letter stated that Forrest, Cheatham, and Brown were in favor of the proposal, and at the end of the letter, Campbell Brown made the notation that Major Will Polk told him he applied to raise a negro regiment, and knew of others who did so. "He did it at the instance, or with the approval & suggestion of Gens. Cheatham and John C. Brown."[68]

There is reason to question Lucius Polk's recollection after twenty-eight years, not only on the basis of the passage of time, but also because of his inclusion of Forrest as a supporter, as the cavalryman was not with the army at that time. On the other hand, Lucius Polk's recollection was separately corroborated by his relative, Will Polk. And there are circumstantial factors to support the conclusion that Brown was in favor of Cleburne's proposal. Like Cleburne, Brown was not of the large slaveholding class, although he had married into it with Ann Pointer. As evidenced by his correspondence from Fort Warren, his feelings relating to southern independence were "doubly intensified" since the start of the war, and could only have increased with his service, his time in battle, and his wounds. Like Cleburne, Brown very well might have deemed southern independence more important than the racial issue involved, although Cleburne's concept was advanced with the theory that Confederate-emancipated slaves would be more easily controlled than those freed by the Federals. Finally, the proposal was supported by men who were known to be in the opposition to General Bragg—Hardee, Cheatham, and Hindman. The opponents were all Bragg friends. Brown's affixing his signature to the petition in October clearly staked out his position in that regard.[69]

On January 4, just two days after Cleburne aired his proposal, Maj. Barber of the 3rd Tennessee and Lt. Col. Charles G. Rogers, a cavalry-man who was formerly on Brown's staff, visited Brown in his headquarters. All were friends from Pulaski, and in the course of their "social chat" Brown and Rogers appeared to Barber to be "despondent, far too much so, I think, about our affairs." Certainly, if Brown and his friends expected an early return to Tennessee, there was reason for despondency. The Army of Tennessee was the shield for the vital communications center at Atlanta, and the munitions factories stretching from Augusta to Selma. Returning to Tennessee would require defeating the Federals in Georgia first.[70]

Boys, Them Damn Yanks Can't Whip You

4

A Military Convenience . . . in All the Hard Places

The Atlanta Campaign, 1864

Although the prospects of the Confederacy were uncertain in the winter of 1864, ambitious men continued to serve it. In the Army of Tennessee, the disruption in command wrought by Bragg's removal of D. H. Hill and reorganization of the army in late 1863 created opportunities for major generals to advance to corps command, and brigadier generals to become division commanders. Brown was a brigadier general who hoped for promotion, but he was not the only one. As in all human endeavors, while it was preferable to have merit, it was necessary to have political influence. And while Brown had powerful Tennesseans on his side, his public stance against Braxton Bragg and his heretical adherence to Cleburne's slave proposal cannot have been viewed favorably in Richmond.[1]

Maj. Gen. John C. Breckinridge commanded the corps consisting of Hindman's, Stewart's, and his own division in the fighting at Chattanooga, the first of which was led by Patton Anderson, and last of which fought under the command of its senior brigadier, William B. Bate. Bragg dropped charges against Hindman arising from the failure at McLemore's Cove, so he rejoined the army on December 15. Being senior to Breckinridge, the diminutive Arkansan assumed command of the corps. By the first of February, Breckinridge was gone from the army. Once it became apparent Breckinridge would be reassigned, his divisional command, and the promotion that came with it, was the subject of intense interest of two prominent Tennessee brigadiers. Bate was a few days junior to Brown as a brigadier, but had commanded the division for almost three months. He had the support of Tennessee's two Confederates senators and, without a doubt, Braxton Bragg. Brown got recommendations from Carter Stevenson (Brown was "energetic, faithful and indefatigable"), Hardee ("he will make an excellent division commander"), John Bell ("no officer . . . of greater promise"), and Governor Harris ("gallant, energetic and very efficient"), but to no avail. Patton Anderson was promoted to major general on February 9 for the purpose of commanding the former vice president's division, but due to Bragg's influence, and contrary to Joseph E. Johnston's preference, Anderson was almost immediately transferred to Florida, and Bate promoted to command the division. Brown had one last chance during this interval. When Lt. Gen. John B. Hood was assigned command of the corps in late February, Hindman tendered his resignation. A new round of letter writing on Brown's behalf came from several prominent Tennesseans, but Hindman's resignation was refused and he was returned to his division. Brown's ambitions for higher command would have to wait.[2]

Circumstances arose to satisfy another of Brown's ambitions, however. The previous fall, Federal Maj. Gen. William T. Sherman conceived of an idea of driving a force from Vicksburg eastward across Mississippi to Meridian, a small town where two railroads intersected and which therefore contained warehouses, depots, and other targets of military significance. Sherman gathered his forces, and started his advance on February 2, 1864. To keep Johnston from detaching troops from the Army of Tennessee to reinforce Leonidas Polk, who commanded in Mississippi, Federal commander Maj. Gen. Ulysses Grant planned two diversionary moves into North Georgia, one from the Chattanooga area toward Dalton, and another from Scottsboro, Alabama, toward Rome, Georgia. Rome was a significant part of the shrinking Confederate military industrial complex, and contained the South's second largest cannon foundry, the Noble Brothers Iron Works. The diversionary advance toward Rome commenced on January 25, which was of sufficient moment for Johnston to note it in a communication to Richmond on February 1. On February 4, he implored Polk, who had troubles of his own from Sherman, to send a division or at least a brigade to Rome. As the bishop was unable to comply, Johnston took other steps to protect the important West Georgia town.[3]

During this interval, morale continued to improve in the army, especially among the Tennessee troops, many of whom symbolically reenlisted for the war, as their original enlistments from 1861 had "expired." Legally, the distinction was meaningless, as under Confederate law, men who did not reenlist would be conscripted for the duration regardless. The units of Brown's Brigade all agreed to reenlist except for the 18th and the 45th, both still doubtlessly suffering from command losses at Chickamauga. On February 2, after the 3rd symbolically re-enlisted, most of the brigade went to Brown and called for a speech. Brown, Lt. Col. Calvin Clack of the 3rd, and Brig. Gen. Zachariah Deas of Alabama all spoke, and the men "dispersed in high good humor and with much enthusiasm." Major Barber wrote that " [t]he state of feeling among Tennessee troops is excellent now . . . [t]he old war spirit seems revived in full vigor." Three days later, Johnston reviewed the whole army in fine weather, and morale remained high.[4]

That night of February 5, the brigade was unexpectedly ordered to march to the depot and entrained for an all-night ride to Kingston, Georgia. After a layover through the morning, the men once again took to the cars, and arrived at Rome mid-afternoon on February 6. But the diversionary Federal advance on Rome that Brown was intended to counter soon dissipated. Away from the camps around Dalton, the men enjoyed a period of decent weather, and Major Barber noted that provisions in Rome were "cheaper and much more abundant." The 3rd Tennessee enjoyed quarters in buildings in town, while the other regiments camped in the outskirts. R. D. Jamison of the 45th Tennessee fondly recalled that Rome was a "nice town with intelligent inhabitants and they gave us a hearty welcome and treated us kindly." With things being quiet in Rome, Brown turned his attention to Bettie Childress. Plans were made to travel below Atlanta to Griffin, Georgia, where Bettie and her family and number of other expatriate Tennesseans resided. Frank Carter wrote his wife on February 21 that Brown was leaving for Griffin to marry Bettie on the 23rd, observing that she was "an excellent and accomplished lady, and his friends are all highly pleased with the match."[5]

The vicissitudes of war interfered with the couple's pleasant matrimonial plans. Sherman accomplished his goal of destroying the military usefulness of Meridian. It appeared to President Davis that the Federal commander would move on to Mobile, Alabama. He therefore ordered two divisions from the Army of Tennessee to join Polk in eastern Alabama. In the meantime, General Grant ordered George Thomas to move toward Dalton. After some delay, Thomas began his advance on February 22. The wedding was planned for the evening of February 23, but early that morning Johnston sent a telegram recalling Brown to Rome. Brown went to Bettie to explain the situation, and she acknowledged, "You will have to return to your command." Brown replied, "But not before you are my wife." Happily, she agreed, and Brown said, "God bless you, I knew that is what you would do." Chaplain Charles Todd Quintard, who was in town to perform the wedding but was then visiting one of the army hospitals, was summoned, and the wedding took place early in the afternoon, with a few friends in attendance. Brown and his staff then entrained for Rome.[6]

Four divisions of the Army of the Cumberland advanced toward Dalton. In skirmishing from February 24–26, the Federals accomplished little, although they gained valuable information as to the situation of the rebel defenses. But with two of his seven divisions gone, Johnston deemed it necessary to recall Brown's Tennesseans to the army. Brown was ordered to stop with most of his troops at Resaca, about eighteen railroad miles to the south of Dalton, and to watch for an advance from the direction of Villanow, Georgia, about fifteen road miles to the northwest through a pass that would later be famous, Snake Creek Gap. The crisis abated, and the brigade was moved back into its old camp. On March 4, the entire corps held a grand review for the benefit of its new commander, Lt. Gen. John Bell Hood.[7]

Soon thereafter, Brown was granted leave to enjoy a "wedding journey" with his new bride. The couple traveled to Charleston, South Carolina, and were rowed out to Fort Sumter under cover of night by oarsmen "who sang southern songs as they bent to their task." The fort was largely a ruin, having endured weeks of bombardment in the latter half of 1863. There, they were greeted by the fort's commander, Lt. Col. Stephen Elliott Jr. Elliott noted that Bettie was the first lady to visit the fort in several months, and there were a few anxious moments as a warning was received of a possible Federal naval attack. Just before dawn, the Browns were rowed back to the city, and attended a service at St. Michael's Church. As the Federals perceived that the Confederates were using the church's steeple as an observation post, it was a frequent target, and a shell indeed fell close by, "causing great excitement." The general and his bride then visited several other cities. They traveled through Montgomery, Alabama, where they were feted by Governor Thomas H. Watts. Upon their return to Dalton, they found Brown's headquarters decorated with Confederate flags and crossed sabers and guns. By March 22, Brown was back with his command.[8]

When Brown returned, the men were caught up in a great wave of revival that swept the camps. Although the army had experienced previous waves of religious fervor, the revival at Dalton that winter was the "greatest revival to touch the Army of Tennessee." Chaplain Thomas H. Deavenport of the 3rd Tennessee started the process in the brigade on February 28, writing on March 31 that "it has been a precious season." On March 19 Major Barber noted there was "more religious feeling in our army than there has been for a long time." The religious fervor lasted into April, when R. D. Jamison wrote his wife that it was "not mere excitement but it seems to be truly a revival by the spirit of God working in the heart." A number of men of the brigade assisted with the revival, including Major McGuire of the 32nd Tennessee. Chaplain Deavenport later wrote of the several men whose lives were changed by the revival before they met their Maker during the fighting to come. On March 22, the army was surprised by an early spring snowfall, and the troops, including the men of Brown's Brigade, frolicked with massive snowball fights. Brown's headquarters were about two miles outside of town in a large brick house, which must have accommodated Bettie quite well. She was noted to be present at a grand review of the army held in April, wearing a "brigidairs [sic] cap with a black vail [sic] which [was] very becoming, and is all the rage so to say. She was much praised."[9]

Soon after this review, however, the officers' wives and other female visitors were ordered away from the army. Johnston made other preparations for the coming battle, but planned on defending Dalton along a fortified line that started in Crow Valley, directly north of Dalton, extended west in a sort of fish hook to Rocky Face Ridge, then south along Rocky Face Ridge. The most logical point of passage, Mill Creek Gap, was both ingeniously and heavily fortified. Sherman had no intention of attacking at that point, which he termed a "terrible door of death." Instead, he adapted a proposal by George Thomas to flank Dalton by moving the Army of the Cumberland through Snake Creek Gap, which, as noted above, gave ready access to the railroad at Resaca, south of Dalton. But instead of the larger and presumably slower Army of the Cumberland, Sherman decided to use Maj. Gen. James B. McPherson's smaller and presumably nimbler Army of the Tennessee. While Johnston had his southwest flank in mind, his main focus was the bulk of the Federal force, which he anticipated would test his defenses in Crow Valley.[10]

The rebels confidently awaited the coming test. Captain George Wise, a staff officer of Stevenson's, recorded in his diary that the division moved into Crow Valley in preparation on April 26. He wrote that General Johnston was "wide awake," and "[t]he army is in splendid condition and ready for a trial of strength . . . We are ready to do or die." The last days of April and the first few days of May were spent in building fortifications and laying out a new camp. There were rumors and occasional gunshots, but the brigade did not go into action until the Federals effected a small lodgment on Rocky Face Ridge on May 8, taking advantage of a weak point in the line of Pettus's Brigade. After dark, Brown was ordered to ascend the ridge, reinforce Pettus, and assume command of that portion of the rebel line. The Federals could see into the rebel camps in Dalton, while that night, Brown and his men could see and smell the Federal campfires in the valley below. Desiring to know how many there were, Brown asked Sgt. Jamison if he would creep to the precipice to see, but the soldier demurred, as it was dangerous enough in the light. Brown did not order him to do so.[11]

The next few days, Brown and his men, with Pettus on their right and the Tennessee brigade of Brig. Gen. George Maney on their left, beat back Federal efforts to expand their foothold on Rocky Face Ridge. Federal activity eventually compelled the rebels to withdraw from this strong natural position, but it was McPherson's threat to Resaca from Snake Creek Gap and Sherman's march around Rocky Face Ridge to Resaca that required it, not direct attack. McPherson's relative weakness, timidity, and lack of cavalry scouts, as well as the providential arrival of Confederate reinforcements from Mississippi, kept the Army of Tennessee from potential destruction at the outset of the campaign. Brown and his men were largely ignorant of the situation, although they became aware of a failed attempt to cut the railroad at Resaca and of the rumored arrival of two divisions from Mississippi. They abandoned their line on

Rocky Face on the evening of May 12 and marched that night about nine miles to Tilton, Georgia, halfway to Resaca.[12]

The afternoon of May 13, the march to Resaca resumed, and Brown's Brigade was detached to provide infantry support to Confederate cavalry screening the rear of the army. At first, the retreating rebels were not pressed. Brown and his staff were sitting on their horses at the head of the brigade's column when a courier, likely from one of the cavalry commands, reported, "General, the Yankees have been marching parallel with you for two hours." Elements of the 18th Tennessee were sent out as skirmishers. Initially, they saw nothing, and then a volley rang out. Federal forces made a heavy attack on them as well as the cavalry they were supporting. It appeared that the Federals were making a move to cut off the Confederate rear guard. A newspaper reported that Brown was "ever cool and calm [and] equal to the emergency." The 32nd Tennessee was ordered forward, and the Federals repulsed. Brown's casualties were light, and the column made it safely to the main body of the army in the dark. A soldier remembered that the darkness confounded the Federals, as over a hundred of them fell in with the rebel column and became prisoners.[13]

At Resaca, Johnston faced Sherman's host with a significant enhancement to his forces. Large elements of Lt. Gen. Leonidas Polk's Army of Mississippi were present. When all his troops arrived, Polk's force amounted to an additional three division corps and another cavalry brigade. Somewhat emulating the inverted fishhook his troops occupied at Dalton, Johnston faced Sherman with the southern end of his line anchored on the Oostanaula River. The rebel line then extended northward, then hooked to the east, where Hood's line joined Hardee's. Hood's Corps faced the northwest as the right of the Confederate line. Hood was anchored on his right by a smaller stream, the Conasauga. The rebel right extended well past the Union left in Hood's sector, which created an opportunity for Johnston, even as the remainder of his army resisted strong attacks on Hardee's line near the point where it joined Hood's.[14]

Late in the afternoon of May 14, two of Hood's divisions, Stevenson's and Stewart's, formed for an attack on the Federal left. Johnston planned for them to move in a great left wheel with the intention of driving the Federals westward. On Stevenson's left, Cumming's Brigade held the pivot, while Brown, supported by Reynolds' Brigade, moved to attack the

Federal line. Brown's Tennesseans assaulted a ridge parallel to and east of the road leading from Resaca to Dalton, upon which were the troops of Brig. Gen. Charles Cruft's Federal brigade. Prior to moving against the hill, Brown briefly stopped in an open field to align his troops. N. J. Hampton of the 18th Tennessee recalled "We were dressed up in line, with our banners out six spaces in front of us. Gen. Brown rode down our line and said: 'Boys, when I give the command to move forward, I want every one of you to step as though your legs were hung on hinges.'" The Tennesseans' fierce attack forced Cruft back "in great disorder," exposing the flank of the next Federal brigade in line, that of Brig. Gen. Walter Whitaker. A correspondent wrote that "volley after volley was poured into [Brown's] advancing ranks," but the men "undauntedly moved forward." They drove the Federals "in utter confusion, muskets, canteens, knapsacks, blankets, etc., thrown off in their terror-stricken haste covered the ground while a number of prisoners added to the trophies." In Hampton's terms, "[w]e ran them as chaff before the wind."[15]

Stevenson's assault then chased the fleeing Yankees across the small valley through which the road ran, but a determined stand by the six-gun 5th Indiana Battery, timely reinforcements from the Federal 20th Corps, and ultimately darkness ended the Confederate attack. Stevenson recorded "[t]oo much praise cannot be awarded Brown's gallant brigade." The assault was costly, however, and resulted in the 3rd having three color bearers shot down and the mortal wounding of Brown's friend, Major Barber. Furthermore, it must have caused the men some frustration when they were ordered to withdraw from the hill they so gallantly assaulted late that evening. On orders from army headquarters, the brigade withdrew to their entrenchments, where they spent the night. Encouraged by the success of this attack, Johnston determined to make a more powerful assault on the Federal left the next day. Federal threats to cross the Oostanaula to the southwest made him rethink his plans, however, and to focus on countering that threat.[16]

The next morning, Hood directed Stevenson to reoccupy the hill taken and then abandoned the previous day. Happily, the Federals had not tried to reestablish their line there, and Brown's men erected "hasty breastworks of logs, planks and whatever came to hand." According to Stevenson, Hood ordered him to place a battery where it could engage

A Military Convenience . . . in All the Hard Places

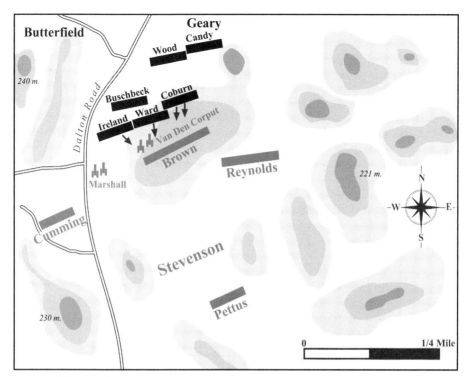

Resaca. Alex Mendoza.

the Federal artillery annoying Hindman's line, while Hood later recalled that the battery was placed to cover the reoccupation of the hill. The four pieces of Captain Max Van Den Corput's Cherokee Artillery were placed in advance of Brown's line, and began engaging the Federals. Skirmishers from the 32nd Tennessee were advanced, while others from the regiment helped scrape out a small lunette for the battery. The skirmishers found what proved to be two divisions of the Federal 20th Corps, those of Maj. Gen. Daniel A. Butterfield and Brig. Gen. John W. Geary, massing for an attack. Around noon, the heavy Federal column charged up the steep hill, and there was a brief hand-to-hand struggle, which some men of the 32nd fought with "picks, spades and rocks." The rebels were driven from their guns, but Brown's Tennesseans on the hill above the guns were able to keep the Federals from advancing further or removing their prizes.[17]

The contending parties spent the remainder of the afternoon of May 15 in a bitter struggle for possession of that north Georgia hillside. The Federals were hunkered down on the outside of the captured lunette;

Brown's Tennesseans would not be moved from their line up the hill. Sgt. Jamison of the 45th Tennessee estimated there were eight different Federal assaults. As for Brown, his staff officer Maj. Hampton J. Cheney wrote that he "did but act with his usual conspicuous gallantry and heroism, freely exposing his person where danger was thickest and by his presence and cool, calm demeanor inspired the men with courage and confidence. He was frequently urged to leave the rifle pits, and only consented when he was told that he was 'in the way.' He had not only the entire confidence but the complete devotion of his whole command." The ongoing struggle depleted the brigade's ammunition, and an "uneasy" Brown dispatched Jamison to bring up an ordnance wagon. While doing so, Jamison encountered General Johnston, who was told the brigade was "[h]olding our position firmly." Obviously before Jamison returned, Stevenson timely relieved Brown's Brigade with that of Brig. Gen. Alexander W. Reynolds so that Brown's troops could replenish their ammunition and clean their weapons, although with their blood up, the Tennesseans did not willingly give way.[18]

Events elsewhere on the field determined the outcome of this struggle. In the early afternoon, Johnston was informed that reports that the Federals were across the Oostanaula far beyond his left were false. Through Hood, Johnston ordered an attack on the Federal flank by Stewart's Division, to be supported by Stevenson and then Hindman. Unfortunately for Stewart and his men, a Federal division of the 20th Corps was in their path, and the attack became a disaster. The useless failure was compounded by the fact that Johnston learned in the meantime that the Federals were indeed crossing the river beyond his left and that the army commander had sent messengers to stop the attack. Stevenson received orders to participate in the assault, and he sent Captain George Wise of his staff to order Reynolds to attack. Reynolds reluctantly complied, and in the end, only one of his regiments, the 54th Virginia, advanced on Stewart's left. Unsupported on either side, the regiment was bloodily repulsed, and Wise wounded.[19]

Meeting with several of his generals in the waning daylight, Johnston announced his intention to retreat across the Oostanaula that night, fearing that the Army of Tennessee might be held fast at Resaca while a large flanking force operated on its line of communications. In the course of

A Military Convenience . . . in All the Hard Places

the night, the army slipped away from the unsuspecting Federals. On Brown's front, a thin line of fifty men under Lt. Col. Clack of the 3rd Tennessee was left, prepared to fight to the bitter end. Various ruses were used during the moonlit night to keep the Federals at bay, and a brief firefight ensued. Brown held back vainly waiting for Clack and his men. Insisting that an effort to rescue them be made, the brave Sgt. Jamison was dispatched, as he had "traveled the road several times today and the others have not." Feeling his way in the dark, he stealthily avoided Federals who were across the road to Dalton, and came up on the brigade's former position, not knowing if it was held by Clack or the bluecoats. Fortunately, he encountered Clack, and his last little rearguard was brought safely back to the brigade and across the Oostanaula. Van Den Corput's guns were left in Butterfield's hands.[20]

Over the next few days, Johnston groped for a suitable place for a defensive stand. Positions near Calhoun and a few miles further south at Adairsville were considered and rejected. Two roads led from Adairsville to the next possible defensive position, Cassville. Accurately predicting that Sherman would divide his force in order to use both roads, Johnston laid a trap, positioning the Army of Tennessee to strike one of Sherman's separate columns. The Confederate commander published an order to the effect that the retreat was over and the army was going to fight. In Brown's Brigade, Chaplain Deavenport wrote that the communication was "received with loud shouts." The plan fizzled when Hood, who was to launch an attack on the flank of the easternmost Federal column, discovered that a Federal force of unknown size was off to his right and rear. Still determined to fight, however, the army took a defensive position that subjected the men of Polk's corps-sized Army of Mississippi to punishing Federal artillery fire. That circumstance, plus the fact that a Federal flanking column was already across the Etowah River to the west, made it necessary to retreat once more. The incident proved to be yet another point of controversy in the postwar argument between Johnston and Hood, and doubtlessly a number of the common soldiers who were stoked up to fight were disappointed. In the 3rd Tennessee, however, Deavenport recorded that, notwithstanding the sixty miles of retreat, "there is but little demoralization in the army and the boys still have confidence in Old Joe."[21]

Johnston's next available strong defensive position was across the Etowah River at Allatoona Pass, where the Western and Atlantic Railroad passed through a range of hills through a deep cut. Sherman believed that he could outflank this position to the west, by crossing the river and advancing on Dallas, about fifteen airline miles to the southwest. After a few days to rest and replenish, Sherman's army group moved in strength across the river, and Johnston moved his army to a line stretching from Dallas back north to a small meeting house called New Hope Church. On May 25, Hood's Corps, the right of the Army of Tennessee, was deployed facing west, with Stewart's Division in the center, Hindman's on the left, and Stevenson coming into position on the right. After a long day of marching and building fortifications, Brown's Brigade was on Stevenson's left, linking to Brig. Gen. Alpheus Baker's brigade of Stewart's Division. Late that afternoon, the Federal 20th Corps launched a powerful attack on Stewart's position, which was, in that general's terms, "repulsed at every point." According to Stevenson, only a "small portion" of Brown's Brigade was engaged, although Federal fire inflicted casualties on it as well as Pettus's Brigade. The only one of Brown's regiments that appears to have been actively engaged was the 3rd Tennessee, as Deavenport recalled the unit coming under attack and driving the enemy back with "heavy loss," suffering only light casualties.[22]

Brown's men stayed in line until May 28, when Maj. Gen. Samuel G. French's Division of Polk's Army of Mississippi filed in to replace Stevenson's Division. During the change, the Federals charged the line, pushing back the Confederate skirmishers, "when to their surprise a dreadful volley was poured into them, shattering their ranks and hurling them back leaving the ground strewn with dead and wounded." French recorded that the line he took over from Stevenson was "miserable." Things became more miserable in the ensuing days, as it rained, and rained, and rained. Realizing that his move to the west had been stymied, Sherman began shifting back to the railroad. By June 8, the Federals were in possession of the railroad crossing of the Etowah and concentrated near Acworth. The Army of Tennessee was deployed to cover the roads leading to Atlanta, with its center on Pine Mountain, where Bate's Division held an advanced but precarious position. On June 14, Johnston and Hardee went to Pine Mountain to determine whether the position should be maintained, and Polk went with them to observe the ground in front of his corps. Seeing the group of rebel officers gathered, Sherman ordered a battery to open fire on them. The 5th Indiana Battery, the same guns that had served as a rallying point to blunt Stevenson's attack at Resaca exactly a month before, complied. The Hoosiers' third shot killed Leonidas Polk.[23]

On June 19, Johnston moved his army back to a line whose features included the imposing peak of Kennesaw Mountain, a few miles to the northwest of Marietta. Early on the morning of June 21, Hood's Corps marched from the right of the rebel line to the left, moving through Marietta, with the purpose of shielding the railroad from Federal forces advancing from the west. At some point prior to this, Brown came down with a "severe illness," sufficiently serious to require that he be moved to Atlanta for medical care. This short term misfortune likely saved Brown's life. On the afternoon of June 22, tentative Federal moves toward Marietta ran into Hood's skirmish line, and the one-legged corps commander decided to respond with an attack by Hindman's and Stevenson's divisions. Brown's Brigade, now under Col. Edward C. Cook, was in the front line of Stevenson's assault.[24]

The attack started badly for the men of the 3rd Tennessee. Their commander, Col. Calvin H. Walker, had his head taken off by a shot from a Federal cannon as he was preparing to go forward. Chaplain Deavenport "never saw soldiers weep so over a man." Deavenport described Walker as a tall, straight man with "long beautiful whiskers." Popular with his men, he was "wicked" and "profane" until the revivals at Dalton, when he became quietly pious. Even with that shocking death, the brigade's skirmishers advanced and pushed their Federal counterparts back. Behind them, the brigade advanced steadily, "without a waver in its ranks" under "well directed fire" from three or more Federal batteries. Three hundred yards distant, Cook ordered a charge. A correspondent wrote: "when within thirty yards of the Yankee works our little brigade found itself without supporters on right or left," Cumming's Brigade having already faltered. "[E]nfiladed on both flanks, mowed down by shot, shell and canister from twenty pieces of cannon, [the brigade was] subjected to a terrible fire of musketry in front. The smoke from the enemy's cannon enveloped a part of our line. To move forward was madness, to remain was death, but the line did remain, without flinch, until it was ordered back to a ravine, thirty or forty yards in our rear, where we remained until after dark. In that brief action, out of nine hundred, we lost two hundred and fifty as gallant men as ever defied death for the sake of liberty." The toll among the field officers of the brigade was great. Not only was Walker killed in a shocking fashion, but Cook was mortally wounded in the charge, falling into the arms of Sgt. Jamison. Col. Richard M. Saffell of the 26th Tennessee was slightly wounded, and Maj. J. P. McGuire, commanding the 32nd Tennessee in Cook's place, was also wounded. Of Brown's staff, Cheney and young Trim Brown had their horses shot, and Gid Lowe got a minie ball through his hat. Jamison deemed it "the hottest battle I was in." After laying under fire in a swampy ravine for several hours, the men were able to withdraw, presumably under the cover of darkness. Brown's impressions of the Kolb's Farm debacle are not recorded.[25]

The previous month, the Army of Tennessee gained two solid defensive victories at New Hope Church and, two days later, at Pickett's Mill. The end of June would see another such victory, as Sherman decided to abandon his flanking strategy and make a direct assault. On June 27, major attacks were made on Johnston's Kennesaw Mountain line by three Federal corps, coupled with demonstrations and a flank probe at other places. The Federals were repulsed at all points, but the probe to the rebel left was soon reinforced to the point of requiring Johnston to abandon his line, moving first back to a line of defenses around Smyrna, Georgia, and then to a second line of unique fortifications protecting an enclave on the north side of the Chattahoochee River, the last of the significant water barriers between the Yankee host and Atlanta. With his advantage in numbers, however, Sherman once again resorted to his effective flanking tactics, and on July 8, 1864, the first significant elements of his force were across that river. Johnston had no option but to retreat again, to the very doorstep of the city.[26]

Polk's demise was the first of a series of deaths and injuries in the high command of the Army of Tennessee that eventually affected Brown's prospects for promotion. A second significant casualty occurred in early July, when a mounted Thomas C. Hindman was struck in the eyes by a branch and unhorsed. Hindman's disability from this injury would linger, and eventually he would transfer. At this point, Brown was the

A Military Convenience . . . in All the Hard Places

highest ranking brigadier general in Hood's Corps, and had commanded Stevenson's Division in that officer's temporary absence for a period in June. Brown and his stout-hearted men had proven themselves in the first weeks of the campaign. They exhibited the highest morale and toughest fighting qualities of any of Stevenson's brigades, and compared favorably to any other unit in the army. Certainly, Hood was convinced. One of Hindman's brigade commanders, Brig. Gen. Arthur M. Manigault, wrote that Brown was "a favorite of Hood's." Brown was placed in command of Hindman's Division for a short period, and then shifted to command Stewart's Division on July 7, when A. P. Stewart was promoted to lieutenant general in the dead bishop's place. However, that same day, Henry D. Clayton, a brigadier junior to Brown, was promoted to major general in Stewart's place, and Brown returned to his temporary command of Hindman's Division. Stewart supported Clayton's promotion, and it could not have hurt the Alabama general's prospects that he was a part of a coterie of officers loyal to Braxton Bragg from their time at Pensacola at the start of the war. Clayton's rapid elevation, that of Brig. Gen. Edward C. Walthall, another Bragg loyalist, to command one of Polk's divisions in early June, and Bate's previous promotion caused Brown to complain to Tennessee senator Gustavus Henry, an old political ally of Neill's. Henry wrote Secretary of War Seddon that Brown was "mortified by having juniors appointed over his head" although, within the army, his promotion was "daily expected." While other lawyer-brigadiers rose in rank, Brown's signature on the anti-Bragg petition the previous October continued to be an anchor.[27]

Brown's assumption of temporary divisional command separated him from his fine brigade of Tennesseans. With their leadership gutted by the carnage at Kolb's Farm, losing Brown's experienced hand might have meant disaster for the men of the brigade. Fortunately, Col. Joseph B. Palmer of the 18th Tennessee returned in this interval, recovered sufficiently from his severe wounding at Chickamauga to assume command of the brigade as its senior colonel from July 7 onward. As events transpired, Brown would never again command what became Palmer's Brigade. While it took some time for the promotion to get through, Palmer was eventually elevated to brigadier general and commanded the brigade with courage and ability to the end of the war.[28]

With a few changes, Hindman's Division was primarily the same unit that was formed in Bragg's reorganization of the army in November 1862 as Withers's Division. By early July 1864, it was reduced to about 4,700 men. It was a veteran formation, consisting of primarily Alabama and Mississippi regiments, although it also contained a South Carolina contingent. Its men fought bravely at Murfreesboro and Chickamauga, but were caught up in the rout on Missionary Ridge, and were most recently bloodied at Kolb's Farm while advancing with Stevenson's Division. As the division served with Brown in Hood's Corps, the Tennessean likely had a degree of familiarity with its officers and men, especially the 41st Mississippi, which was part of his brigade at Perryville. The division's senior brigadier, Zachariah Deas, was out, either sick, facing a charge of drunkenness, or both, and his Alabama brigade was in command of Col. John G. Coltart, who was wounded at Shiloh and spent much of 1863 on detached duty. Its junior brigadier, William F. Tucker, was recovering from a wound inflicted at Resaca. In his place was his Mississippi brigade's senior colonel, Jacob H. Sharp, who had leveled the charge against Deas. The year before, Patton Anderson wrote that Sharp was "competent but inefficient in controlling his men and officers." The division's second Mississippi brigade, having been the recently promoted Walthall's, was also commanded by its senior colonel, Samuel Benton. Walthall recommended that another colonel, William F. Brantley, to command in his place, and at the time of Brown's assumption of command, the bureaucratic wheels were still turning on the issue. The only regular brigade commander with the division was the veteran Brig. Gen. Arthur M. Manigault of South Carolina, deemed by the departed Bishop Polk to be "a highly intelligent and competent brigade commander." Although perhaps expectant of the command himself, the Carolinian understood Brown was in line for promotion and was in any event "only too glad" Hindman was gone.[29]

Fortunately, Brown had a short period to acclimate himself to his new command, the men of which were happy to have a few quiet days, except for picket duty, in mid-July. Meanwhile, the army's long retreat from Dalton to the environs of Atlanta forced President Davis to consider the effectiveness of Johnston's management of affairs. Davis and Johnston were not friends, and the Army of Tennessee's failure to arrest Sherman's advance coupled with Johnston's call for cavalry from Mississippi that Davis could not spare brought things to the breaking point. The final straw came with the presence of Braxton Bragg, who arrived in Atlanta on July 13. In his view, Johnston was "opposed to seeking battle though willing to receive it on his own terms in his chosen position." Bragg further opined that his old enemy Hardee, the army's next ranking officer, was in favor of Johnston's "retiring policy." In Bragg's view, Hood was the best choice to replace Johnston. Davis made one last attempt to get Johnston to articulate a definite plan to defend Atlanta, and Johnston replied that his plan "must . . . depend on that of the enemy." Late on the night of July 17, Johnston was removed in favor of Hood, who was elevated to the temporary rank of full general.[30]

There is no evidence to discern Brown's position on Johnston's removal. Brown would not have been placed in temporary command of Hindman's Division without Johnston's approval. Johnston later made

John B. Hood (Credit: Library of Congress)

a favorable reference to Brown in his postwar memoirs, and in his final organization of the Army of Tennessee in 1865, out of a large collection of possible division commanders, Johnston placed Brown in command of a division. As noted above, Manigault thought Brown was a "favorite" of Hood's, and the new army commander repeatedly placed Brown in command of leaderless divisions in the coming weeks. In other words, both Johnston and Hood had reason to believe Brown was loyal to them. It was possible to be both.[31]

On July 19, less than forty-eight hours after assuming command, Hood perceived an opportunity to attack the Army of the Cumberland, Sherman's largest, as it was crossing Peachtree Creek north of Atlanta. Sherman's other two armies, the Army of the Tennessee and the one-corps Army of the Ohio, were off to the east of the city for the purpose of cutting the Georgia Railroad to Augusta. On July 20, Hood attacked Thomas's army with Hardee's Corps and Stewart's corps-sized Army of Mississippi. Hardee was not at his best, and Stewart, with the responsibility of guarding the army's left, could only employ four brigades in the attack. Because they caught the Federals essentially unawares, Stewart's men enjoyed substantial, but not decisive success. The Army of the Cumberland was not defeated.[32]

An aspect of Hardee's lack of success was the need, prior to his attack, to shift his corps a half-mile to the east. Sherman's other two armies were advancing on Atlanta from that direction along the Decatur Road. Meanwhile, Hood's old corps, temporarily under Maj. Gen. Benjamin F. Cheatham, at that time facing east, was shifted southward to block the road. Cheatham's assumption of command was the first time Brown was in a direct line of authority under "Marse Frank," although they must have been well acquainted. Through the course of the war to that point, Cheatham commanded a division largely composed of Tennessee troops, who derived a great deal of élan in that distinction. Cheatham came from a prominent Nashville family, had served in the Mexican War and prospected for gold in California, and owned a Nashville race track. He was a veteran of nearly every one of the army's battles, and at that point in the war was the army's second-ranking major general, even though he had no formal military education. While Cheatham was a veteran officer, he took command of an unfamiliar corps with two new division commanders, Clayton and Brown.[33]

A Military Convenience . . . in All the Hard Places

The failure to destroy Thomas on July 20 did not extinguish Hood's desire for a decisive blow. Receiving intelligence that the southern flank of the advancing Army of the Tennessee was in the air, Hood determined to attack once again. This time, he conceived of another Chancellorsville, where, in early May 1863, Robert E. Lee sent Lt. Gen. Thomas J. "Stonewall" Jackson's corps in a devastating assault against the flank of the Army of the Potomac. Ironically, the two Federal officers whose reputations were severely impacted by that attack, Maj. Gen. Joseph Hooker and Maj. Gen. Oliver O. Howard, were only miles away serving under Thomas. Instead of Stonewall, Hood would utilize "Old Reliable" Hardee, because his corps had not been as fully engaged on July 20 as "Old Straight" Stewart's, while Cheatham was new in corps command. All was not quiet on July 21, as Cleburne's Division was in what that commander deemed the "bitterest" fighting of his life, defending a hill from McPherson's advance. Brown's men, along with the rest of their corps and Stewart's, spent the day improving a new inner line of fortifications.[34]

Hardee's four divisions marched all night, and notwithstanding the disadvantages of tired men moving on a single road in the darkness, managed to arrive on the flank of Maj. Gen. James B. McPherson's Army of the Tennessee late on the morning of July 22. For his part, McPherson opened the day preparing to execute an order from Sherman to move to the south and east of the town to cut off a supposed Confederate retreat. When it became apparent that the Confederates were still in his front, although withdrawn from their previous works, orders were given to occupy and "reverse" the entrenchments so they faced the rebel army. The uneasy McPherson also ordered Brig. Gen. Thomas W. Sweeny's division south to a position extending east from the end of his line. Sweeny arrived just in time to engage Hardee's first line of attack, which was disorganized by the terrain, including a large mill pond in its line of advance. The irascible W. H. T. Walker was killed early in the fight, and his replacement, Brig. Gen. Hugh Mercer, was unable to provide his fiery leadership. Nonetheless, attacks by Cleburne's and Cheatham's (under Brig. Gen. George Maney) men achieved some success, and McPherson was killed.[35]

The plan for Cheatham's corps that day was to be prepared to pitch in with an attack from south to north as Hardee's assault pushed the

Federals northward. Hood concluded by 3:00 p.m. that afternoon that the opportunity would not present itself. The army commander now feared that, unless distracted, the Federals would be able to bring their full force against Hardee. He ordered Cheatham to attack the Federals in his front to divert Sherman's attention from Hardee. Those orders were altered, however, when word arrived that Hardee was in fact beginning to succeed. Cheatham's was to launch a full-fledged assault, against the line of the Federal 15th Corps.[36]

Using classic Army of Tennessee tactical doctrine, Cheatham planned to advance his divisions in an *en echelon* attack. Stevenson held the corps' right flank, and was in the closest position to actively aid Hardee. A few minutes before 4:00 p.m., the Virginian's division advanced against the Federal line, but the attack was weak and easily repulsed. The assault brigades were principally those of Reynolds and Cumming, and Brown's old brigade, then under Palmer, was either not engaged or so lightly engaged that it was not deemed to be worthy of mention in its regimental histories.[37]

Brown advanced with his division around 4:00 p.m., initially moving straight east along the railroad. All four brigades were deployed, with Manigault on the north side of the railroad with Sharp's brigade in support, and Coltart with Deas's Brigade on the south side, with Colonel Benton and Walthall's Brigade in support. Brown's orders were to advance until the enemy was encountered, "and then to attack and drive him out of his works," and hold the works "until further orders." Manigault recalled moving across some open ground, driving back an advanced line of Federals, and capturing prisoners. Most of his brigade was protected by the undulating ground. Manigault brought the brigade to a halt in a hollow in preparation for the final advance. At that point, orders arrived from Brown to delay the brigade's advance until Coltart caught up on the left. Manigault's brigade took casualties during that five minute wait, but eventually the division's front line surged forward together for the final thousand feet or so to the Federal works. The Federal fire began to take its toll, and Manigault's men started to falter, but Sharp's Mississippi men, or at least most of them, were in close support, and the rebel advance surged forward once more.[38]

A Military Convenience . . . in All the Hard Places

On the division's other axis of advance, Coltart found it hard to keep aligned on the Georgia Railroad, as "buildings, impassible fences, and slight curves of the road" resulted in the enemy being engaged about 150 yards south of the railroad. The opening of this gap with Manigault's men allowed the Federals to lash the left of the Alabama brigade with fire from the front and obliquely from its left. In the second line, Benton's men, reinforced by the 39th Alabama of Coltart's brigade, surged forward to about fifty yards from the Federal works, where they lay down under heavy fire for about ten minutes, when the order came to withdraw. A second advance was made by Coltart's men, and a lodgment made in the enemy lines for about fifteen minutes, when it was learned that the bluecoats were massing on their right flank, intending to cut them off. The line fell back under heavy fire. During the engagement, Colonel Benton was wounded twice, by a bullet in the foot and a shell fragment, and expired a few days later.[39]

The lay of the land in Manigault's line of advance was much more favorable. Earlier that day, subordinate Federal commanders manning the line in that area reported to their superiors that the railroad cut, thick undergrowth, and several buildings would help mask a rebel advance on their position. Their request to take steps to barricade the cut and remove the buildings was denied. Brown's men took advantage of that inherent weakness and used the cover presented by these features to approach the Union line. Rebel sharpshooters took possession of the upper story of a large white house near the cut and were able to fire down into the Federal entrenchments. Once in the works, the Confederates moved laterally, driving the bluecoats out. One of Sharp's men recalled that "we dashed through and over all the obstacles and mixed up with those Yankees and clubbed them with the butts of our guns until we were masters of that line of works." In the words of C. Irvine Walker of the 10th South Carolina, a "strange panic" seized the Federals and they abandoned their lines for a distance of at least half a mile. Manigault moved his men to the left, while Sharp's Mississippians occupied the line the South Carolinian's brigade originally overran. Taking stock, Manigault learned that the Federals abandoned sixteen artillery pieces, including four 20-pound Parrott guns of Capt. Francis De Gress's 1st Illinois Light Artillery.[40]

Manigault received an order to abandon the works. Whether Brown made the order on his own accord or upon direction from Cheatham is unknown. No report of the action from either Tennessean has surfaced. Perhaps in the smoke and confusion of the battle, it may have appeared that the two brigades had been repulsed. As a result, the captured works were abandoned, much to Manigault's chagrin. The Confederates moved back about a quarter mile, when Brown personally rectified the error. He rode up to the men of his former command, the 41st Mississippi, and said "41st I have seen you at Perryville. I know you can take and hold the works; the enemy have possessed them again!" The works were retaken with relative ease, and Lt. Robert M. Gill of the 41st had "the pleasure of shooting at Yankees as they ran without being shot at much." The victorious rebels soon found that their lines were subject to enfilade artillery fire. Understanding it was only a matter of time until the Federals counterattacked, Manigault sent "several messages asking for assistance, and giving notice of the condition of things." With his full division committed to the attack, and Sharp's supporting brigade already engaged in support of Manigault, Brown had no help to send.[41]

Fortunately, help was on its way. About fifteen minutes after Brown advanced, Maj. Gen. Henry D. Clayton advanced his division, the last of Cheatham's three, toward the Federal works. Clayton's orders were to "close to the right, [his] extreme right remaining fixed, and forming in two lines to begin the attack upon the enemy in [his] front and upon the left of Hindman's division, already engaged." Col. Abda Johnson, who commanded Stovall's Brigade, was to move forward to the attack, making a connection with Brown's men. Johnson later confessed he "knew nothing of the ground over which I was to move, nor of the position of the enemy or how other troops were to move or when [they would] attack." With little knowledge of the ground in front of him, Johnson led his Georgia brigade forward, first on the south, and then on the north side of the Georgia Railroad. Soon after crossing that line, Johnson met Brown, who suggested that he follow the line of the railroad forward. Clayton's other brigade, Holtzclaw's, was instructed to move on the Georgia brigade's left. While its commander, Col. Bushrod Jones of the 58th Alabama, lost sight of the Georgians, the large brick house of Troup Hurt, then occupied by Manigault's men, came into view. Jones consulted with Manigault and Sharp, and was advised to deploy his brigade to cover the rebel left. The arrival of Clayton's reinforcements was just in time for Manigault, although there was some confusion. Johnson with Stovall's men was sent to aid Sharp on the right of the penetration, while Jones's Alabamians went to the left. At Manigault's urging, some of

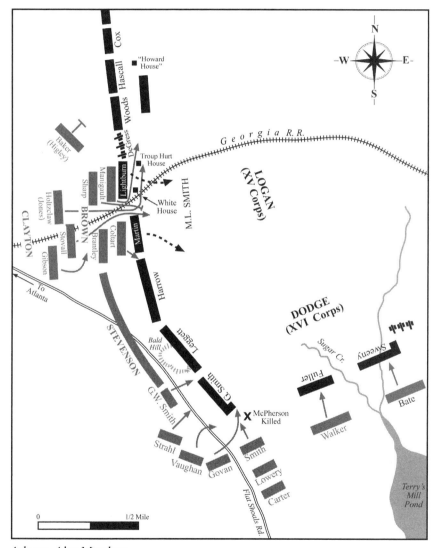

Atlanta. Alex Mendoza.

Jones's men went into the captured works, although such was not Jones's intention. Clayton ordered Baker's Brigade obliquely forward to engage Federal troops massing on the left of the penetration, and Gibson's Brigade similarly forward to support Brown on the right.[42]

Colonel Johnson reported some resistance as his men moved into the works. It is likely that they helped Sharp's men clear the previously overrun works that were temporarily abandoned by the rebels. It should be noted that historian Albert Castel has criticized Brown for *ordering* Johnson to support his division, although Johnson clearly reported he changed his front at Brown's *suggestion*, not order. According to Castel, Clayton was ordered to attack southeastwardly, essentially across Brown's rear, in the area of the bald hill, held by Harrow's division of the Federal 15th Corps. Clayton's report suggests nothing of the sort and states that he was to attack on the left of Brown's division, which is entirely consistent with the *en echelon* attack ordered by Cheatham. Further, nowhere in Clayton's report is an indication that his troops were redirected from their intended line of attack. Nonetheless, as a result of the "suggestion" reported by Johnson, Castel concluded that Brown, "as a division commander, seems to have gone beyond the limits of his capability." A much more plausible explanation for Brown's conference with Johnson was that the Tennessean was clearly aware of Manigault's and Sharp's breakthrough and suggested reinforcing success, in place of that brigade's simply groping forward and piling in behind Brown's two left brigades. Certainly, Col. Johnson, advancing blindly, was happy to get some direction.[43]

On the Federal side, troops were massing the better part of three divisions for counterattack, while the incomparable Federal artillery bombarded the rebel pocket. The bluecoat response was under the personal and energetic direction of Maj. Gen. John A. "Black Jack" Logan, now the commander of the Army of the Tennessee. In the captured works, Manigault and Sharp sent word back to Brown that they could hold their ground. But with Hardee's attack essentially defeated, the Federals were able to concentrate on Cheatham's breakthrough. From the standpoint of a South Carolinian in the front line, "the fight lasted about two and a half hours, and was very desperate." Having committed his entire division to the assault, Brown had no reinforcements to send. To the frustration of

A Military Convenience . . . in All the Hard Places

Brown's front line commanders, an order arrived to "retire quickly, as the enemy was moving in large masses on our left flank and rear, and to delay would result in the loss or capture of the forces engaged." Manigault and Sharp reluctantly retreated, and their retreat soon forced Clayton's men to withdraw as well. Manigault blamed the withdrawal on the lack of a competent commander. He seems to have been referring to Hood, making note of lack of reinforcements and overall coordination. Lt. Col. Walker of the 10th South Carolina likewise felt that, with proper support, the attack could have turned the Federal left, but that threats to both flanks with the punishing artillery fire brought about the order to retire. Walker also proudly recorded that Brown "highly complimented" Manigault's Brigade.[44]

As darkness fell on another hot Georgia day, there was still fighting on the southern end of the battlefield, but Hood's effort to emulate Chancellorsville was over. He had simply asked too much of Hardee and his men, and yet, if not for the repositioning of Sweeny's division, Hardee may have succeeded. On Cheatham's front, Stevenson's attack was nearly worthless, but Brown and Clayton, at terrible cost, had punished the 15th Corps. In Brown's division alone, casualties exceeded one thousand men. To Brown's credit, it was his division that cracked the Union line, and he was close enough to the front line to give direction. If there is fault, it perhaps came when he ordered Manigault and Sharp out of the captured trenches, but that was quickly rectified. Whether it was Brown or Cheatham or Hood who ordered the eventual retreat, there seems to be no question that the lodgment effected in the Federal line would eventually have to be abandoned, notwithstanding Manigault's difficulty with the order.[45]

While Brown was justly complimenting his men for their hard fighting, an old enemy was taking steps to remove him from command. On July 23, Braxton Bragg was at Columbus, Georgia. Whether Bragg heard something critical of Brown's performance on July 22, was concerned about the level of experienced division command in Hood's old corps, or simply was acting on his dislike of Brown, he determined to send Patton Anderson back to the army to command Hindman's Division, first merely suggesting to the authorities at Richmond that the change was expedient, and then later, "[a]fter learning the result of yesterday's operations at Atlanta," taking it on himself to order Anderson, who had a command in Florida, back to the army. The message did not reach Anderson until July 25, and he was unable to reach Atlanta until the night of July 28. That was too late, however, to relieve Brown from the fighting that occurred that day.[46]

The battle on July 22 resulted in an operational sense from Sherman's move to cut Hood's railroad connections to Augusta, Georgia, and the Confederate east. The Federal commander now determined to reorient his efforts to cut the railroads leading to Atlanta from the west. McPherson's successor, O. O. Howard, was ordered to march the Army of the Tennessee out of the entrenchments it occupied at the end of the day on July 22, all the way around the rear of the Army of the Ohio and the Army of the Cumberland, and then southward to the Lick Skillet Road, west of the city. Howard marched the night of July 26–27, and later the next day Hood learned of the move, which he was expecting. His old corps, now under Lt. Gen. Stephen D. Lee, who joined the army from a command in Mississippi, was ordered to block the move. Hood planned on having Stewart's Corps, the recently renamed Army of Mississippi, attack the flank of the Federals Hood expected Lee would stack up in front of his anticipated position.[47]

A year younger than the youthful Hood, Stephen D. Lee was a likable man who started the war with the Confederates besieging Fort Sumter. He then served as an artillery officer under his distant cousin, Robert E. Lee, in Virginia, most effectively at Second Manassas. Promoted to brigadier general, he was transferred to the army in Mississippi and, ironically, served as a commander of one of Carter Stevenson's brigades during the Vicksburg Campaign. After his exchange, he was promoted to major general and commanded the Confederate forces in Mississippi when Polk left to join the Army of Tennessee. Just the week before, Lee had launched costly and futile attacks against Federal forces at Tupelo, although that fact was not well known when he assumed his new command. While Stevenson was much more senior an officer, he had proven his mediocrity in the campaign to that point and was therefore not in the running for the command of the corps. The Army of Tennessee's two most competent senior major generals, Frank Cheatham and Patrick Cleburne, were not seriously considered, either by Hood or

Stephen D. Lee (Credit:
Library of Congress)

by the lurking Bragg. Further, Lee was a graduate of West Point, which
was a significant factor to Jefferson Davis.[48]

The movement of the two contending forces bore on the Lick Skillet
Road, which extended westerly from Atlanta. Near Ezra Church, the
Lick Skillet Road intersected a north-south road, where Hood contem-
plated that Lee would establish his blocking position to set up Stewart's
flanking attack. Unfortunately for the Confederates, Howard got an ear-
lier start than they did that day, and by late morning, the Federal 15th
Corps occupied a position on a low ridge just to the north of the Lick
Skillet Road, pushing skirmishing rebel cavalry back across the road.
Hood did not issue orders for Lee to move until 10:30 a.m. that morning.
Brown received orders to move "with the utmost dispatch" out the Lick
Skillet Road to a poor house, where he would find the cavalry division
of Brig. Gen. William H. Jackson. When Brown arrived, he found that
Jackson was being pressed and that the Federals were in a position to

interdict the road. Jackson reported that it seemed that the Federal infantry force he faced was small. Lee rode up soon afterward, and believing a quick strike would dislodge the Federals in his front, ordered Brown to attack. The order ignored Hood's injunction to not attack unless the Federals left themselves open to a counterattack, and did not give Clayton's following division time to deploy. Lee's aggressiveness and inexperience meant that Brown was to attack the bulk of the 15th Corps, on higher ground and behind improvised breastworks.[49]

Brown deployed his division from left to right, with Brantley's and then Sharp's Mississippians on the south side of the road, and the Alabama brigade, commanded that day by newly promoted Brig. Gen. George D. Johnston, across the road at a forty-five degree angle facing the Federal position. Manigault's men, who had won laurels on July 22, were kept in a reserve line. Brown's advance began not long after noon, and soon cleared the Federal skirmishers from the Lick Skillet Road, although the right brigade, Johnston's Alabamians, had some difficulty with its initial advance, encountering dense woods and several fences. In a number of places, the Federal skirmish line was itself protected with light breastworks, but Brown's massed troops overran these advanced positions.[50]

On Brown's left, Brantley attacked the 15th Corps' extreme right, and, after pushing the Federal skirmishers out of the Lick Skillet Road, flanked four Ohio regiments out of their advanced positions in front of and to the right of the main Federal line. Brantley was able to exploit a small gap in the Federal line, and for a short period almost enveloped the Ohio men, collapsed the Indiana regiment closest to the flank on the right of the brigade, and effected a lodgment on the top of the ridge held by the bluecoats. The situation provided the rebels a brief opportunity to turn the Federal right flank, but Brantley did not have enough men to exploit the breakthrough, and quick Federal reinforcements soon were there to provide the strength for a counterattack. "[B]eing greatly weakened by the killed and wounded and the innumerable cases of utter exhaustion among the best men of [his] command, as well as by the absence of a goodly number who had no legitimate excuse, [Brantley] was unable to hold the works." The brigade fell back, and then advanced again upon Brown's orders, doubtlessly issued at the instance of Lee, but again was unsuccessful. One factor that affected the performance of Brantley's men that day, as well as Brown's other brigades, was the exhaustion brought about by the combination of lack of water, a rapid march into action, and the heat. Federal soldiers suffered from heat exhaustion as well.[51]

Although Brown's orders to Brantley were to guide right, and therefore stay connected to the division line, it appears that the need to confront the advanced Ohio regiments and the terrain the Mississippians encountered caused them to separate from the other two front brigades fairly soon into the division's initial advance. Sharp and Johnston stayed connected, at least for a while, but appear to have separated as they advanced, although both commands were halted after an initial advance to reform, and Johnston ordered to move by the left flank, presumably to close up the line. Sharp's men advanced toward the Federal line and found that the right of the brigade was subject to an oblique fire from a protruding part of the Federal line, caused by the line in his front "being some distance in the rear of the works on the right and in a large hollow." The left-most regiments, the 9th Mississippi and Brown's old compatriots of the 41st, were out in front for some distance, likely benefiting from Brantley's success down the line. Finding themselves isolated, they beat a hasty retreat. When Sharp went to order the 41st to move to the right, he found it too disorganized from its withdrawal to be of any use. After retiring and reforming, a second assault was attempted, with less success, if possible, than the first. Johnston's initial advance was disrupted by "thick undergrowth" and a stout resistance from the skirmishers in his front. Moving by the left flank, probably in an effort to connect with Sharp, the line reformed and then charged. First Johnston was wounded, and then his senior colonel, and then the next senior colonel. Under the command of the next senior officer, Lt. Col. Harry T. Toulmin, the brigade hunkered down behind the advanced skirmish line, and "at this juncture" Brown "relieved it with [Manigault's] brigade."[52]

Manigault's men waited behind the other brigades of the division for about twenty minutes, hearing the sounds of the other brigades engaging the Federals. Receiving an order to advance, he moved his brigade forward to an open field. There, the brigade was halted by Lee, and Brown gave Manigault instructions to attack the Federals at the highest point of the ridge before them. Although Manigault recalled Brown stating that

Sharp had executed "a like order," Brown and officers in Johnston's brigade later wrote that Manigault was actually sent in to bolster the Alabama brigade's attack. Sharp was present, but made no remark to the contrary, and after the engagement, Manigault wondered how fellow officers could be so misleading. Manigault's men went forward, and at least portions of three of Toulmin's Alabama regiments rallied and joined the attack. Toulmin's 50th Alabama actually was able to take a section of the Federal breastworks for a short time. Manigault suffered from fire on both his flanks, as he was unsupported in his attack except by Toulmin's stalwart few, and, like Johnston's brigade, suffered particularly on the right. As his attack lost momentum, the Federals launched counterattacks on either flank, causing the line to "crumble" toward the center, "and the rest was flight and confusion," until the brigade reached its starting point.[53]

Manigault's Brigade quickly reformed, and within ten minutes went forward again, "but with like want of success." This time, it retreated further, behind a roadbed that gave the troops shelter from the storm of Federal lead showering down on his men. But soon, another order came from one of Brown's staff to attack again. A dumbfounded Manigault galloped to where Brown stood, to protest what he thought was an impossible order. It was a situation that made Manigault remember a similar protest to Patton Anderson on Missionary Ridge. The difference between Anderson and Brown, though, was that Brown was "a very different person to deal with, and in every way a better soldier and a more reasonable officer." Brown regretfully told Manigault that the order was Lee's, not his, and expressed that he did not agree. Manigault started back to his brigade, when Brown caught up to him, and, "saying that he intended to disobey General Lee's order, and would abide the consequences," countermanded the attack order. While Brown saw that Manigault's men had reached the end of their endurance that afternoon, he was obviously unhappy with their performance, writing in his report a few days later that the brigade, "behaving badly, its demoralization was so great it could not be made effective." Manigault deemed the odds so great that he could "scarcely blame either officers or men."[54]

The afternoon ended with more fruitless assaults on the Federal position, as Lee launched Clayton's Division and induced A. P. Stewart to deploy Walthall's Division against Howard, with the same results. Maj. Gen. William W. Loring's division of Stewart's Corps was then deployed as an anchor for the three engaged divisions to form on, and eventually Hood pulled them all back toward Atlanta. Losses on the Confederate side approximated 3,000 casualties, against 632 Federals. The rebel failures of the day stemmed first from a late start on a hot day. Add to that a bad combination of inexperience and aggressiveness in Lee, which led to Brown's hasty attack, and the young corps commander's reinforcement of failure thereafter. Of course, superior Federal firepower coupled with the advantages of veteran troops occupying a fortified position on high ground played a decisive part. Brown's part in this Confederate fiasco is difficult to fully evaluate, since his initial deployment of his division was under Lee's direct supervision, and it appears that that supervision remained most of the day. Brown appears to have been wounded during the struggle, necessitating a temporary absence from his command, but the sources do not indicate at what point. The division's striking power was blunted "with great slaughter" by its attack on a wide front, but whether that was Lee's or Brown's fault cannot be discerned. Lee saw fit to make "especial mention of the gallantry of . . . Brown during the engagement," while ironically, his most experienced subordinate, Manigault, admired Brown for his willingness to countermand Lee's senseless order to attack a third time. Most likely the sentiment that led Brown to disobey Lee and spare Manigault's men was reflected in a comment a postwar business associate of Brown's, Federal Maj. Gen. Grenville Dodge, heard that Brown had made—that Ezra Church was "a killing instead of a battle."[55]

That night, Patton Anderson arrived in Atlanta and issued an order assuming command of Hindman's Division. Instead of returning to his brigade, Brown was ordered to report to army headquarters. The Army of Tennessee was in need of experienced division-level officers, as there had been considerable attrition at that level in July. It took almost a month for Anderson to replace Hindman. Johnston's removal and Hood's promotion had temporarily elevated Cheatham, at least until Lee arrived. Polk's death resulted Loring's temporary and Stewart's permanent command of his corps, and Stewart's promotion in turn opened a space for Clayton. W. H. T. Walker was not replaced. His division was broken up and its brigades distributed to the other divisions of Hardee's Corps. Ezra

Church saw Stewart and his senior major general, Loring, both wounded, and Cheatham placed in temporary command of Stewart's Corps, which was resented by Stewart's senior unhurt major general, Samuel G. French, who unsuccessfully asked to be relieved.[56]

It is therefore obvious that Hood wanted to keep Brown in reserve, and once again pressed Richmond for his promotion, asking that the Tennessean be elevated to the temporary rank of major general to assume command of Loring's Division. About this time, Brown "playfully" said that he was "made a sort of military convenience in the Army of Tennessee, and was shifted around by the commanding general into all the hard places." Brown continued to have powerful Tennessee political support, and the pressing need in the army and Hood's direct request finally made the difference. Brown was appointed to the temporary rank of major general, to rank from August 4, 1864. He would eventually be confirmed in that rank by the Confederate Senate on February 20, 1865.[57]

Loring did not return to the army until September 10. Brown presumably did not take command of that division until after receiving his promotion, as he was ranked by Brig. Gen. Winfield Scott Featherston, Loring's senior brigadier. But that command did not last long. Sherman continued to sidle his lines on the west side of Atlanta, seeking to reach the railroad at East Point, about six miles southwest of the city. Maj. Gen. John M. Schofield's Army of the Ohio, soon reinforced by a corps of the Army of the Cumberland, advanced toward the junction, hindered by a command squabble, normally the province of the Army of Tennessee. The delay allowed Hood to fortify a line in their path, and on August 6 and 7, Confederate troops, primarily Bate's Division, easily repulsed the Federal advance. In a skirmish on August 10, Bate was shot through the flesh of the same leg he almost lost at Shiloh, which laid him up for several weeks. Another major general was *en route* to the army, this time Edward "Old Allegheny" Johnson, late of the Army of Northern Virginia, recently exchanged after his capture at the Battle of Spotsylvania Courthouse in May. But Johnson would not arrive for several days. Hardee asked that Brown take command of Bate's Division, which was still in position to blunt Sherman's drive to the railroad. Hood accommodated Hardee's request, and informed Richmond that Brown was placed in command of Bate's men.[58]

John C. Brown as major general (Credit: Alabama Department of Archives and History, Montgomery, Alabama)

In assuming command of Bate's Division, Brown once again found familiar troops. One of the division's units was the army's Florida Brigade, two regiments of which, the 1st and 3rd Florida, had been part of his command at Perryville. Brown's appointment was well-received by the Floridians. A captain who admired Brown encouraged the men of the brigade "to give General Brown a rousing cheer . . . reminding them of his kindness, his gentleness on the Kentucky march, how he fell wounded by our side at Perryville." While they agreed to do so, when Brown actually came around on his first inspection of the division, the jaded soldiers failed to make much of a cheer. "It was hard to say," a soldier recalled, "which of the two, the General or the Captain, we were the sorriest for." Sgt. Washington M. Ives wrote his sister a few days later and noted Brown was then in command, "and has already gained the affection of the men. Strange to say Gen. Bates possessed neither affection or respect and undoubtedly has the falsest reputation of any man I know." While the brigade was officially "Finley's Brigade," Brig. Gen. Jesse J. Finley was not yet recuperated from an injury sustained at Resaca. His senior colonel, Robert Bullock, led the brigade until the previous week, when he was wounded. At that point, the small brigade was led by Col. D. Lafayette Kenan, although Finley would return to fight at the end of the month.[59]

Brown also had past association with Brig. Gen. Robert C. Tyler's mostly Tennessee brigade, much of which had been Bate's brigade at Chickamauga. With Tyler disabled by the loss of a leg at Missionary Ridge, the unit was commanded by young Thomas Benton Smith, barely two weeks a brigadier general. The division's other two brigades were Brig. Gen. Joseph H. Lewis's famed Kentucky Orphan Brigade, and Brig. Gen. Henry R. Jackson's Georgia brigade, which had fought as part of W. H. T. Walker's division through the campaign until assigned to Bate after Walker's death. Jackson was commissioned a brigadier general early in the war, then resigned to become a major general of Georgia state troops. Finding that a dead end, he took a new commission as a Confederate brigadier in 1863 and seems to have felt he was entitled to consideration to command the division. When Brown was placed over him, Jackson wrote Bragg it was "doubtless that Genl Hood and Hardee have greater confidence in Brown than me and moreover Brown has been for some time on their list for promotion; nevertheless my position is not rendered the less irksome & awkward to me . . ." Even with the addition of a new brigade, the division had under 2,900 men.[60]

In mid-August, after spending several days bombarding Atlanta to little effect, Sherman once again decided to strike at Hood's supply lines. A cavalry raid damaged the line, but the rebels had trains chugging back into Atlanta only a couple of days later. Sherman decided that only a heavy infantry force could achieve the desired effect and devised a plan whereby six of his seven corps would move on the two rail lines that still ran into the city, the little-used Atlanta & West Point and the critical Macon & Western Railroad. Sherman's remaining corps, the 20th, would dig in at the bridgehead of the Chattahoochee. Sherman's huge strike force began a great wheeling movement on August 25, which progressed to the point of spending the day on August 29 wrecking the Atlanta & West Point. Although Hood was aware that Sherman was on the move to sever the Macon & Western, he was not sure if the attempt would be at East Point, where the two railroads joined about six miles south of Atlanta, at Rough and Ready, approximately nine miles south, or at Jonesboro, twenty-three miles south. Only late in the day on August 30, when a Federal corps had penetrated to within a mile of the Macon & Western near Jonesboro, did the Confederate commander realize his fight to save the rail link to the besieged city would be at that place.[61]

Hood already had elements of his army in Jonesboro, including Lewis's Orphan Brigade of Brown's division. Late on August 28, Brown was directed to move the remainder of the division to Rough and Ready from East Point and to prepare to repel raids from the west. But when news came near dark on August 30 of the Federal force near Jonesboro, Hardee's Corps moved on to Jonesboro. Marching at sunset, Brown's division trudged all night to Jonesboro. Lee's Corps followed, and Hood assigned command of the combined force to "Old Reliable" Hardee, with directions to attack and drive the Federal force back across the Flint River, west of Jonesboro.[62]

Fittingly, it was the Army of the Tennessee in the Federal vanguard threatening Hood's last line of supply. The main line threatening the railroad was the 15th Corps, entrenched behind breastworks, with cannon both guarding its line and menacing the railroad. Federal efficiency was juxtaposed with lack of execution on the rebel side. Hardee's Corps, led at this point by the usually efficient Cleburne, was late in arriving at Jonesboro, and Lee's Corps was not totally present until 1:30 p.m. Hardee, likely already sensing that the attack had poor prospects, requested that Hood come and take command on the field, but got no response. The Confederate plan was to attack *en echelon,* with Cleburne in command of the three divisions of Hardee's Corps to turn the Federal right. Both Confederate corps misfired, however, as Cleburne's Division, under Brig. Gen. Mark P. Lowrey, attacked Federal cavalry in a straight line ahead, rather than swinging right to attack the Federal left, while Lee jumped off too soon, with an ineffective attack resulting in the death of Brown's friend, Lt. Col. Calvin D. Clack.[63]

When it moved forward about 3:00 p.m., Brown's small division advanced with Benton Smith's (Tyler's) brigade on its right, and Jackson's brigade in the center of the front line. On the division's left marched the Florida Brigade, which that day welcomed the return of its commander, Brig. Gen. Finley, after several weeks' absence. Finley's was designated the directing brigade. Lewis's Orphans were in the second line, along with the Tennesseans of Strahl's Brigade, under Col. Andrew J. Kellar, that day under Brown's orders. Brown advanced on Lowrey's left, with Cheatham's Division, under Brig. Gen. George D. Maney, following in support. When Lowrey's line broke away, Maney moved two of his brigades into the gap between his division and Brown's. On Brown's front, the advancing brigades in the front line became separated, with a space opening between Jackson's and Smith's men. Brown ordered Jackson to reestablish a link to the right, and then to the left, and then to the right again.[64]

The attack was a failure. On Brown's right, Lee's premature attack had already played out, meaning Brown had no support on either his right or his left. Brown's men had to cross a deep gully or ravine in order to close on their entrenched and heavily armed foes. Jackson was outraged by the lack of spirit in Smith's and Finley's men, and urged his brigade forward without any support. The Floridians certainly had reason to lose spirit, as the newly arrived Finley received a wound in the foot that removed him for the remainder of the war, and Col. Kenan took a serious wound in his hand shortly thereafter. Not all of Smith's men hung back. The 20th Tennessee's colors advanced to the point where the color guard was shot down, and the regiment's commander, Maj. John Guthrie, was mortally wounded rescuing the flag. Lewis's Orphans also advanced, but were forced to jump into the gully to escape the storm of shot and shell. In the midst of the grimness of the day, a Bluegrass soldier had the one button holding his pants shot off, forcing him to shed his trousers in order to effect a retreat from the field. Others, including Sgt. Maj. Johnny Green, risked their lives to retrieve wounded comrades, a show of courage that was honored by their foes with cheers.[65]

Henry R. Jackson was not the only person who thought the Confederate infantry was listless that day. Philip D. Stephenson, a rebel artilleryman on the field, later recalled that the charge "was not to the credit of our troops." Recognizing "the venture was probably hopeless," Stephenson felt that, except for Cleburne's Division, the troops "made but little or no *real* effort to take the works!" When Hardee sought to coordinate a renewed attack with Stephen D. Lee, he determined the young corps commander's troops were too demoralized to make the effort. And while their Federal opponents observed multiple assaults by their "bold" and "gallant" foes, they noted that the usual determination of the Confederate infantry was not present. When Hood later complained of the lack of "vigor" in his men's attack, Hardee acerbically observed that it was not "surprising that troops who had for two months been hurled against breast-works only to be repulsed or to gain dear-bought and fruitless victories, should now have moved against the enemy's works with reluctance and distrust."[66]

August 31 ended with Hood ordering Lee's Corps to return to Atlanta, even while Sherman massed his corps to deal an overwhelming blow on Hardee and his remaining three divisions. After midnight on September 1, Hood was informed that Hardee failed to push the Yankees away from the railroad. With no other choice, Hood gave orders preparatory to evacuating Atlanta, leaving Hardee to screen Macon and the army's rear. Hardee's problem on September 1 was that he faced the Federals at Jonesboro with one less corps, while two Federal corps from the Army of the Cumberland joined the Army of the Tennessee on the field. Now on the defensive, Hardee moved Cleburne's Division to the right to occupy the line held by Lee's Corps, and Cheatham's Division occupied the left. Brown held the center, seeing only limited attacks from the Army of the Tennessee during the day, but with fewer troops, as Lewis's Orphans were ordered to march to the railroad to take a train back north. Once on the cars, they were told to get off, and were rushed to the Confederate right—the main Federal assault was under way.[67]

Hardee saw that his right would need reinforcement, and ordered two of Cheatham's brigades, and then the rest of that division to the right. A heavy attack by the Federal 14th Corps struck a salient held by Brig. Gen. Daniel C. Govan's Arkansas brigade. Govan's line was overwhelmed and he, along with over eight hundred of his men, were captured. Hardee skillfully used Cheatham's reinforcements and the Kentucky Orphans to restore his lines, and was able to hold out the remainder of the day. Fortunately for Brown and the rest of his small division, there was no serious attack from the Federals they had fought the day before. If there had been, it is difficult to conceive of a way Hardee and his corps would have escaped destruction.[68]

After dark, Hardee, with Brown and the rest, retreated southward. The "restless and impatient" Sherman could not sleep, and about midnight of the night of September 1–2 there were sounds of exploding shells and musketry from the direction of Atlanta, and again about 4:00 a.m. Sherman wondered whether Hood had evacuated Atlanta, or was battling the one corps he left north of the city. He got news that the former was true while organizing the pursuit of Hardee's battered corps, which turned to fight at Lovejoy's Station, approximately six miles south of Jonesboro. The strength of the rebel position gave the Federals pause, and as a result, notwithstanding the enormous disparity in numbers, only three Federal brigades went forward. Only one of the three actually attacked and was therefore easily repulsed. Having missed an opportunity to destroy an enemy in detail even greater than Bragg at McLemore's Cove almost a year before, Sherman decided to abandon the pursuit. Hood and the remainder of the army, having escaped Atlanta to the southeast, united with Hardee at Lovejoy's.[69]

Sherman's resting his army meant that Hood could do the same. In addition to the loss of morale brought about by Atlanta's fall, the Army of Tennessee was greatly diminished in men and material, and the Confederacy lost an important industrial and transportation center. While the Federals contemplated their next move, Hood shifted his troops from Lovejoy's to Palmetto, about twenty-five miles west of Atlanta on the railroad to Montgomery. It was there on September 25 that Jefferson Davis visited the Army of Tennessee for the third time, motivated, in part, by a letter from Samuel G. French that there was unrest among "several officers." Davis was already fully aware that Hardee was unhappy serving under Hood, and A. P. Stewart and other officers bluntly told the president that the army wanted Hood replaced with Johnston. That, Davis could not bring himself to do. He instead created a new "Military Division of the West," and placed Gen. Pierre G. T. Beauregard in command, ostensibly to supervise Hood and the department of Lt. Gen. Richard Taylor in Mississippi and Louisiana. To that general's immense relief, Davis authorized Hardee's transfer to command the Department of South Carolina, Georgia, and Florida.[70]

Davis's visit, Beauregard's appointment, and Hardee's relief all marked a transition between the Atlanta Campaign and the then-uncertain future that lay ahead for the Confederacy and the Army of Tennessee. For John C. Brown, the struggle for Atlanta was an opportunity to progress as a soldier, and when the balance is struck, the conclusion can only be that such was the case. On the battlefield, Brown demonstrated the ability to fight hard at Resaca and in the Battle of Atlanta. He showed admirable prudence in a bad situation at Ezra Church, and steadfastness under Hardee's command the second day at Jonesboro. Although unquestionably his temporary commands were necessitated by attrition in the army's high command, Brown's talents were recognized by Johnston, Hood, and Hardee, as was manifested by his many assignments above his rank. As a remarkable confirmation of his superiors' confidence, Brown, at one interval or another, commanded five of the Army of Tennessee's divisions that hot, bloody summer.

5

The Slaughter in
Our Ranks Was Frightful

September 1864 to May 1865

The Atlanta Campaign took a toll on the Army of Tennessee's officer corps. With Hardee's departure, only Hood remained of the army commander and three corps commanders who led the army at Resaca. Cheatham, as the senior officer in Hardee's corps, was given that command, although Loring and Cleburne also had temporarily commanded corps during the campaign. Losses during that long hot summer had occasioned myriad temporary division and brigade commands, and the effects of the attrition continued. Patton Anderson's return to the army lasted just over a month—he was shot through the mouth on August 31 at Jonesboro, and Maj. Gen. Edward Johnson was given permanent command of that division. Bate's return on October 10 restored an experienced, if not top-knotch, division commander, which would have ended Brown's temporary command. Cheatham's elevation, however, conveniently created a vacancy in the command of his division, of which Brown assumed command on October 2, 1864.[1]

Although he had only directly served with the men of Strahl's Brigade at Jonesboro, Brown doubtlessly was acquainted with many of the officers and men in the division, as three of the four brigades consisted exclusively of Tennessee troops. The senior brigadier was States Rights Gist, whose unique name reflected his fire-eating South Carolina roots. Gist and his South Carolina and Georgia troops joined the division after Walker's division was broken up in the aftermath of W. H. T. Walker's death. Next in rank was Ohio-born Brig. Gen. Otho F. Strahl, who began the war as a captain in the 4th Tennessee Regiment. Strahl assumed command of the brigade in June 1863, after its original commander, A. P. Stewart, was promoted. Brig. Gen. John C. Carter commanded the brigade that had previously been Marcus J. Wright's, the men Brown and his former brigade had helped rescue on September 19, 1863, at Chickamauga. The division's junior brigadier was Giles County native George W. Gordon, who started the war in the 11th Tennessee. All were relatively young—Gist and Strahl in their early thirties, Carter and Gordon in their late twenties, and three of the four were lawyers. Their men were proud of the division and were friendly rivals with Cleburne's Division for the reputation as the army's hardest fighting unit.[2]

Hood's plan for the month of October 1864 was to operate on the railroad in Sherman's rear, hoping to keep the bluecoats off balance sufficiently to convince the northern public that the capture of Atlanta settled nothing and that another president besides Abraham Lincoln might finally bring peace. For the first two weeks of the month, the army moved generally northward, striking the railroad at various points all the way up to above Dalton. At Dalton itself on October 13, Hood demanded the surrender of the Federal garrison, which was refused by its commander. Brown was ordered to take the Yankee fortification and "moved his division across the open fields" toward a hill that commanded the Federal position. The Federal commander lost his nerve and surrendered. Most of his men were former slaves, and the Confederates treated them with a mixture of cruelty and contempt. In a report to his superiors, the garrison commander reported seeing a number of the Confederate generals, including Hood, Cheatham, Lee, Loring, Brown, Bate, French, and Cleburne.[3]

Sherman came in pursuit. Hood thought about giving him battle near LaFayette, Georgia, in the general area of operations of the previous year, but after taking stock of his army, determined it was not in shape to fight the Federals and moved into northeastern Alabama. His eventual goal was to move the army into Middle Tennessee, and then on into Kentucky. Sherman gave up the chase and began making preparations for his eventual march to Savannah. Among other things, those preparations involved dispatching George H. Thomas and John M. Schofield, along with substantial numbers of their veteran troops, back to Middle Tennessee to confront whatever mischief Hood intended to stir up. While Hood acted with celerity in the first weeks of October, he vacillated somewhat in the next few weeks, delayed in his crossing of the Tennessee River by Union

Benjamin F. Cheatham
(Credit: Library of Congress)

fortifications at Decatur, Alabama, and logistical issues. The army did not begin its advance into the Volunteer State until November 21, from the northwestern Alabama town of Florence.[4]

The three corps of the Army of Tennessee marched north by different routes. Brown moved with Cheatham's corps through Waynesboro, over forty airline miles from Pulaski. A concentration of Federal troops in Brown's hometown caused Hood to bypass it to the west, with an intention of all three of his corps converging at Columbia, thirty-one miles to the north on the Duck River. Although Brown probably regretted not passing through his home county, it was much affected by the war. The previous winter, a Federal officer noted the "great scarcity" there. Pulaski was also a contraband center, where self-emancipated slaves gathered under the protection of the Federal garrison. A Unionist politician lectured an audience by contrasting the prewar peaceful prosperity of the county with its situation then, observing that "your courts of justice are closed, your schools and colleges converted into military hospitals . . . your farms desolated, your towns and cities depopulated, your young men and middle aged men in the army." Many had died either in battle or in "loathsome hospitals and camps," and in every church, women wear "the weeds of mourning." In addition to these distressing scenes, Brown would have found that his mother, Margaret Smith Brown, had died at age eighty-two a few days before, on November 11.[5]

Cheatham's Corps entered Maury County on November 24, and Brown and his staff stayed at farmer Nimrod Porter's house on November 25. Army headquarters was established the next day at the home of Andrew J. Polk, a brother of the slain bishop's. Cheatham's headquarters were at Hamilton Place, the home of another brother, Lucius Polk. There, on November 26, the higher ranking officers of the army passed through, including Hood, Cheatham, Brown, Bate, Walthall, as well as Governor Harris. At this point, the army was a few miles from Columbia, where the Federal force originally at Pulaski waited. The next two days, the army closed upon Columbia. Schofield, in command of the Federals, hunkered down on the north side of the Duck River opposite the town. Spurred on by a telegram from Beauregard urging quick results as Sherman was approaching the Georgia coast, and with the great flanking movements of the Army of Northern Virginia still in his mind, Hood devised a plan to cross the Duck River east of Columbia, and "go through the woods" to cut the bluecoats off from Nashville.[6]

On November 29, Hood arose at 3:00 a.m., telling Doctor Quintard that "the enemy must give me fight, or I will be at Nashville before tomorrow night." Two divisions of Lee's Corps were left to demonstrate at Columbia, while the army's remaining seven divisions crossed the Duck River three miles east of Columbia at Davis Ford. Cheatham's Corps led, with Cleburne in advance, then Bate. Brown's division was the last of the corps to cross, numbering, in the Tennessean's later estimation, no more than 2,750 men. Hood had some apprehension that the Federal troops to his west might hit his marching column from the left, so he issued two orders that would affect the division's combat effectiveness later that day. He first detached Brown's strongest brigade, Gist's, and half of his next largest brigade, Strahl's, for picket duty. Then, as the army commander wanted a supporting force for the main column, Brown was ordered to march the remaining half of his division four hundred yards to the east of the road by which the other two divisions were moving, "through

The Slaughter in Our Ranks Was Frightful

fields and woods and over rough ground, adding greatly to the fatigues of the day."[7]

On the Federal side, Forrest's effectiveness with the Federal cavalry screen deprived Schofield of solid information as to the activity to his east, although he finally obtained a better picture later the morning of November 29. Schofield also had orders from George H. Thomas to withdraw to Franklin. To execute the move, he had to consider Lee's substantial force at Columbia in the context of moving his ponderous wagon train of eight hundred vehicles and twenty thousand men north on the single road to Spring Hill. Accordingly, he dispatched Maj. Gen. David S. Stanley with the train and two divisions to Spring Hill, planning to withdraw the remainder of his force much later in the day. Around noon, just when Stanley's lead elements were hurrying into Spring Hill, Forrest and his men arrived, starting the struggle for the strategic little hamlet that would last long past the fall of darkness that late autumn day.[8]

Forrest exhibited his usual aggressiveness in his efforts to overrun the Federals and take the town, but his attack was unsuccessful. Hood arrived with the head of Cleburne's column at the crossing of Rutherford Creek, about two and a half miles south of the town, at 3:00 p.m. It was at this point that the story of Spring Hill from the Confederate side begins to fracture into a number of conflicting accounts. Cleburne was dispatched toward the town, although Hood and Cheatham later disagreed as to whether he was to take the town or just interdict the pike near there. Bate's Division crossed the creek next, and while Cheatham ordered that officer to support Cleburne, Bate reported that Hood personally ordered him to move to the turnpike and "sweep towards Columbia." The initial Confederate effort accordingly went forward in a disjointed fashion, against over six thousand Federal infantry supported by thirty-four pieces of artillery.[9]

Brown found it impracticable to effect a crossing anywhere but the ford used by Cheatham's other two divisions. His lead elements arrived at that point just as Bate's Division was preparing to cross. Brown crossed the creek around 4:00 p.m. As Cheatham had gone forward with Cleburne and Bate, Brown received his orders from Hood, who directed him to march toward the home of a Dr. Caldwell, which was almost due north of the crossing. Cheatham intercepted the column before it reached the

Caldwell place, and directed Brown to Cleburne's right, even as Cheatham heard firing from that direction. The off-road march had taken its toll, and Private Sam Watkins remembered "the men, weary and worn out, were just dragging themselves along." The column reached the Rally Hill Pike probably an hour before sunset. There, Brown "formed [his] line a speedily as worn troops could move, and, after throwing forward a skirmish line, advanced four hundred or five hundred yards."[10]

In his advance, Cleburne encountered greater resistance than was originally anticipated. Cheatham likely contemplated an attack on Stanley by his entire corps, and ordered Bate away from his mission to interdict the road from Columbia south of Spring Hill. Bate's skirmishers were just two hundred yards south of the road, and in the gathering darkness he had difficulty realigning to support Cleburne. While Bate was closing up on Cleburne's left, Brown was deploying on his right. When Brown's dispositions were complete, Cheatham ordered an advance, and then went toward the left to coordinate the attack of the other divisions. With Gist's relatively large brigade of close to 1,000 men and half of Strahl's Brigade, at least 350 men, still absent, Brown had approximately 1,400 men, deployed in accordance with Cheatham's orders to attack in two lines, leading with the right brigade. That unit was the remaining portion of Strahl's Brigade, under the command of Brown's most experienced subordinate on the field, the veteran and competent Brig. Gen. Otho F. Strahl.[11]

While much about events that night remain obscured in the murk of conflicting and often fragmentary accounts, there is no question that Brown was informed by Strahl that a Federal force of unknown size was on Strahl's right flank, "in such a position that the moment he [Strahl] swung forward to the attack, he would be exposed to a fire both on the flank and in the rear." This force was the 100th Illinois and Company F, 40th Indiana, a substantial element for the under-strength division to leave on its flank in the daylight, much less in the dark. Brown went to see for himself, and Strahl pointed out the Federal force. Brown expected that flank to be covered by Forrest's men, who had by that time departed. Without artillery or cavalry, Brown concluded he "must meet inevitable disaster if [his division] advanced on Spring Hill." Expect-

The Slaughter in Our Ranks Was Frightful

ing Brown's attack, Cheatham wondered "Why don't we hear Brown's guns?" Hood, too, expected to hear gunfire by this point, and accepted Governor Harris's offer to ride out to ascertain what was transpiring. Looking for Cheatham, Harris encountered Brown, who was just back from conferring with Strahl and his other two brigadiers and who had dispatched a staff officer to report his problem to Cheatham. Harris recalled that Brown "took me out & showed me the enemy's line extending far beyond his own right—and suggested sending another command to *his* right." Harris sent word back to Hood suggesting that Stewart's Corps should be placed on Brown's right and interdict the pike. While Harris rode to find Cheatham, Brown was confronted by some members of his division staff, who urged an attack notwithstanding the unknown Federal force that had given Brown, Strahl, and Harris pause. One officer, Captain John Ingram, who had been drinking that day, boasted he could drive the Federal troops away with Brown's escort company. Brown told Ingram to consider himself under arrest.[12]

Cheatham later wrote that when he received Brown's first report of the force on his right, he directed that Brown should "throw back his right brigade and make the attack." Neither Harris nor Maj. Joseph Vaulx Jr., afterwards the only survivor of the division's staff, mentioned this order in later accounts, however, and most significantly, neither did Brown. In fact, Brown had a discussion with his friend Brig. Gen. James R. Chalmers of the cavalry, who urged that he launch an immediate attack. Brown's response was that he had no orders, and when pressed by Chalmers, very curtly replied "I have no orders." Brown's only surviving account of the action, written in 1881, stated that Cheatham arrived just a "very few minutes" after he had dispatched his staff officer and "fully approved," as did Hood, who "directed that the attack should be delayed until the arrival of Generals Stewart and Gist, and in the meantime the whole command should be held under orders to advance at a moment's notice." J. P. Young, a participant in the battle with Forrest's troops, and the author of the first significant effort to get a handle on the events that day and evening, noted the obvious "distinct contradiction" between Cheatham and Brown, and that "here was not only the turning point of the battle, but of the campaign as well, an hour pregnant with the most fateful consequences to a nation." Though this conflict between accounts has been addressed by subsequent historians, the definitive answer continues to be elusive.[13]

Whether the order was given or not, it is unlikely that Brown's division, weakened by detachments, would have succeeded against Col. John Q. Lane's Federal brigade, which flanked the Tennessean, held higher ground, was supported by artillery, and numbered over 1,600 men, more than Brown had on the field during that critical hour. An attack by Cheatham's entire corps was called for, or alternatively, an attack by Brown's command heavily supported by Stewart's Corps, which in accordance with Harris's suggestion to Hood, was ordered to position his right across the pike beyond Spring Hill. Hood gave Stewart a guide to put his troops into the desired position, and Stewart's column of about eight thousand men marched with the guide until Stewart happened upon Forrest's headquarters. While the two conferred, Stewart was told Hood wanted Stewart to connect with Brown's right. Stewart accordingly altered his march, and coming upon Brown in the darkness, found that his fellow Tennessean's line obliqued away from the pike. Hood simply did not have an accurate concept of Brown's line. Wanting to resolve the conflicting orders, Stewart left to confer with Hood. In the meantime, Gist's brigade rejoined the division, but Brown "received no further orders that evening or during the night to advance or change [his] position."[14]

In the end, the Federals marched right by the massed Confederates. It was, in a sense, the culmination of the years of command problems, missed opportunities, and near misses that plagued the Army of Tennessee. The failure was in many ways inexplicable, and in the following years, to explain the inexplicable, legends and rumors arose claiming Hood was drugged on laudanum and Cheatham was either himself intoxicated or in the presence of a local beauty. A decade after Brown's death, S. D. Lee spread a pernicious rumor arose that Brown was drunk after imbibing on gifts of liquor received during the march, and that instead of exposing the same, Cheatham covered it up. Of course, Lee's rumor did not consider the fact that on that fateful afternoon, Brown not only encountered Cheatham, but also Chalmers, Harris, Hood, and Vaulx, in addition to Cleburne and Strahl, who did not survive the next day, and likely many other less prominent witnesses. One other major actor who had an opportunity to assess Brown's condition was present that night—A. P. Stewart. Stewart wrote several accounts of that day, and never mentioned any impairment on Brown's part. When his nephew wrote him in 1895 with news of a Dr. Mitchell apparently claiming Brown was drunk, Stewart asked him to get details from Mitchell, and wrote "What I can not understand is how the fact that B. was <u>drunk</u>, prevented Cheatham from attacking the enemy." Conceding the ambiguity of Stewart's statement ("the fact that B. was drunk"), certainly Stewart was correct that, if Cheatham had perceived the same, he should have relieved Brown and made the attack.[15]

Understandably, on the morning of November 30, Hood was chagrined that the "best move in [his] career as a soldier [came] to naught." The army resumed its march, pursuing Schofield northward toward Franklin. Brown encountered Hood, who, with the previous day's events in mind, lectured him: "when a pursuing army comes up with a retreating enemy, he must be immediately attacked. If you have a brigade in front as advance guard, order its commander to attack the enemy as soon as he comes up with him; if you have a regiment in advance, and it comes up with the enemy, give the colonel orders to attack him; If there is but a company in advance, and it overtakes the entire Yankee army, order the captain to attack it forthwith; and if anything blocks the road in front of you to-day, don't stop a minute, but turn out into the fields or woods, and move on to the front." Brown told Vaulx that Hood looking to fix blame on someone for the blunder, and was "wrathy as a rattlesnake, this morning, striking at everything."[16]

As events transpired, Hood blamed Cheatham. But as Brown rode north, Cleburne sent a message asking for a meeting. The two lawyer-soldiers had "long enjoyed very close personal relations." Brown let his column pass, and then rode off with Cleburne away from the column. Cleburne was "quite angry" and "evidently . . . deeply hurt," as he had heard from a reliable source that Hood intended to blame him for allowing the Federals to escape. Brown replied he "had heard nothing on the subject," but Cleburne felt it came from "a very reliable channel." When Brown asked Cleburne who was responsible for the failure, Cleburne "indulged in some criticisms of a command occupying a position on the left." Cleburne, as Stewart maintained years later, also told Brown the ultimate responsibility was Hood's, "as he was upon the field during the afternoon and was fully advised during the night of the movement of the enemy." At this point, the two generals were interrupted, and Cleburne promised to pick the conversation up at the "most convenient moment."[17]

Schofield got to Franklin before sunup on November 30. Leaving his subordinate, Brig. Gen. Jacob D. Cox to put his troops in a defensive position around the town and facing south, Schofield directed his personal attention to repairing the bridges across the Harpeth River that would put that river between him and Hood. The Federal defense centered on high ground near the brick home of Fountain Branch Carter, south of the town on the Columbia Pike. Two miles to the south, across intervening "gently undulating" ground, rose two hills split by the pike, Winstead Hill on the west, and Breezy Hill on the east. Cox deployed his own division on the east side of the turnpike, and placed Brig. Gen. Thomas H. Ruger's two brigade division on the west side, who built breastworks with a "formidable and fearful" abatis fashioned from a grove of locust trees and an apple orchard. The Federal fortifications left the roadbed of the pike itself unblocked. From the western boundary of the road, the Federal line ran at right angles for fifty yards, and then bent to the northwest, down the slope of the Carter hill, so that a battery could be emplaced to fire over the Federal infantry's heads. A second line, or "retrenchment," was built at Cox's direction to block the road behind the main line, which was extended by the initiative of the men of one of Ruger's brigades. Cox also placed artillery on both sides of the pike, with at least eight guns facing the approach to Ruger's position. With their work completed about noon, the doubtlessly worn out bluecoats settled down to enjoy a warm Indian summer day, anticipating that if the rebels did not interfere, they would be across the Harpeth by nightfall.[18]

John Bell Hood, however, had every intention of interfering. French's Division of Stewart's Corps led the Army of Tennessee's march to Franklin, and encountered Wagner's division drawn up on the two hills south of the town, Breezy Hill and Winstead Hill. While there was some skirmishing, French advanced a line on the flank and rear of these Federals, and they withdrew. French looked down toward the town and thought all Hood needed to do was to look at the Union positions to decline an assault. But Hood soon made the decision to attack. Though doubtless

The Slaughter in Our Ranks Was Frightful

piqued by Schofield's escape the night before, the commanding general was motivated, according to Stewart, not by his anger, but by his hope to catch the Federals in a disorganized state while crossing the river at their back.[19]

Brown had a somewhat different recollection as to Hood's reasoning. He later wrote that he, Cleburne, and Bate were summoned to a meeting with Hood, Cheatham, and Stewart. Hood remarked that the open country prevented him from turning the Federal flank without the blue-coats quickly withdrawing into Nashville. Hood stated that, "[w]hile his immediate center is very strong, his flanks are weak." Stewart would therefore attack on the extreme right, and Bate on the left. Brown re-called: "The policy of General Hood's decision was not discussed, and I cannot recollect any question propounded by him to any one present indicating a desire for an expression of opinion by anyone." Brown was ordered to form in conjunction with Cleburne, with the Tennessean on the left, and the Irishman on the right, guiding on the pike.[20]

In a speech given years after the war, Gordon stated that around 4:00 p.m., Hood and Cheatham rode up to where Brown was waiting with his brigadiers. They studied the Federal line, and Hood then ordered "Marse Frank" to make an immediate attack. Hood said "tell your officers to go with the men, to stop at nothing, and to sweep everything before them." The division accordingly advanced, in tandem with Cleburne's, "at double column with half distance" in order to easily move around obstacles such as fences and trees. As a result of obtuseness on the part of Federal division commander Brig. Gen. George Wagner, two Federal brigades of his division were in a short line about a half mile or so in front of the main line drawn on the south side of the Carter House hill. The wave of Confederate infantry deployed into line of battle about five hundred paces from that advanced position. Gordon's brigade guided on the turnpike on the right, and Gist's marched in the front line on the left of the division. The Tennessee brigades of Strahl and John C. Carter were in the second line, approximately two hundred paces behind Gordon and Gist respectively.[21]

As the rebel infantry crested a small hill before smashing into Wagner, Col. Ellison Capers of Gist's Brigade was struck with the "magnificent spectacle," "bands were playing, general and staff officers and gallant couriers were riding in front of and between the lines, 100 battle-flags were waving in the smoke of battle, and bursting shells were wreathing the air with great circles of smoke." Gordon recalled the "flying banners, beating drums, and bristling guns," and as his men prepared to rush Wagner's line, he dismounted to go forward on foot with them. Gist rode down the front of his brigade and waved his hat to his leftmost regiment, the 24th South Carolina. He, too, was forced to dismount when his horse was shot. Gist's Brigade overran the advanced Federals in their front, driving them into the locust abatis, where many were captured. The abatis proved to be a significant obstacle, but the fire of the Federals in the main line slackened while Wagner's men retreated through it, and Gist's men worked their way through as well. On Gordon's front, Wagner's advanced line delivered one volley into the tide of oncoming rebels and then broke for the rear. The pursuing Confederates shouted, "Go into the works with them! Go into the works with them!" That cry was taken up by "a thousand straining throats," and the retreating Yankees and advancing rebels ran in a bunch toward the main Federal line.[22]

During the advance, Brown and Cleburne "met several times upon the turnpike road and conferred and acted in harmony in the movement." In the rush toward the Federal line, the lead elements of the two divisions got mixed up, especially, as Gordon later recalled, when the Federals in the main line unleashed a "storm of shot and shell, canister and musketry." Brown, Gordon, and others loudly exhorted their men to follow the Federals into the works. Coupled with the shouts of the men and the pitiful sounds of the wounded and dying, it seemed to Gordon "that hell itself had exploded in our faces." Suddenly, Cleburne appeared on his horse, and almost ran Gordon down as he rode toward the Federal works. In the final advance toward the main Union line, Gordon's men mingled with those of Cleburne's left brigade, Brig. Gen. Hiram Granbury's Texans. While some of the rebels went into the Federal works, a number of others bogged down in ditch in front. Brown later wrote "the slaughter in our ranks was frightful, considering the very short time in which we were engaged." Brown ordered his two supporting brigades, Strahl's and Carter's, into the fray. In Carter's brigade, Private Sam Watkins pressed through the locusts and up to the Federal breastworks, expecting to die. On Brown's front, the fight degenerated into one long struggle

The Slaughter in Our Ranks Was Frightful

Franklin from *National Tribune.*

in turnpike. Gen. Hatch's Division was sent to Matthew's house and Gen. Croxton's Brigade to Douglas Church, on the Lewisburg pike; Hammond's Brigade, formerly commanded by Col. Capron, was sent to Triune, while Harrison's Brigade was held in reserve. Gen. Hatch found the enemy, engaged him, was pressed by a superior force, and slowly falling back, it had recrossed the river. Gen. Croxton met the rebel column advancing on the

proach close to the works before the Federal soldiers had gained the intrenchments. Some of Lane's regiments had loaded guns, and turned upon their pursuers with terrible effect.

A CRITICAL MOMENT.

The soldiers of the Twenty-third Corps, however, who occupied these works, withheld their fire as their comrades of Wagner's Division approached. This was of

Nashville, and now had beaten back the desperate assaults of the enemy with great slaughter in the battle of Franklin. Gen. Schofield knew that Gen. Hood's army was still superior in numbers to his; he therefore decided not to risk a second day's battle, when the Confederate artillery would no doubt be concentrated against his position, but to retire to Nashville, where Gen. Thomas was concentrating a large force.

BATTLEFIELD, LOOKING NORTH TOWARD FRANKLIN, FROM GEN. CHEATHAM'S HEADQUARTERS.

Lewisburg pike, was attacked by them about 10 o'clock in the morning, and kept up a skirmish until about 2 p. m, when, having repulsed the cavalry, retired before a superior force of infantry to a point two and a half miles from Franklin, when he also recrossed the river leaving the 3 Mich. Cav., Lieut.-Col. Benjamin Smith commanding, to contest the advance of the rebel infantry. Lieut.-Col. Smith remained in front of the Confederate column as it advanced on Franklin, but was finally forced to recross the river.

In the meantime the Confederate cavalry had crossed to the north side of the Harpeth for the purpose, no doubt, of cutting the Union army

great advantage to the attacking troops; they moved forward with great confidence and courage. The spirit of war seemed to rage in the blood of every officer and soldier of this Confederate column; rushed through the obstructions into the ditch, and climbed over, and pet into the Union works, musk For a time confusion reigned at the center of the Union line. of the Twenty-third Corps, crowded their places by their comrades front line, and at the same time by the enemy, who had carried works, fell back with the regiment Fourth Corps, and were purs

An account of this short campaign from Florence and Pulaski to Franklin would be incomplete without the statements of some of the commanding officers engaged. Gen. Hood, commander of the Confederate

from him by the Colonel of the same regiment (104th Ohio, Twenty-third Corps)."

Col. John Q. Lane, 97th Ohio, commanding Wagner's Second Brigade, in

"In my letter of yesterday I promise to write the particulars of the battle at this place. This I will now try to do Of course, I could not see it all, but still saw enough to give me quite a

VIEW ON THE COLUMBIA PIKE FROM NEAR THE POINT OF THE UNION ADVANCE.

his official report, in describing the retreat to the second line, says: "We had much difficulty in getting into the

idea as to what was going on. The attack commenced on our outpost about 2 o'clock on the morning of the 5th

ings there were two main ones. The turnpike from Columbia was a trunk highway, into which ran along its course lateral roads leading from all the various places in that region. It crossed the river directly in front of the town, and upon one of the old-fashioned bridges customarily used in that section of the country. About 500 yards eastward of the Columbia pike, and parallel to it ran the railroad from Nashville to Decatur. This railroad

and Hood's army to lose six Generals, men who had bravely and skilfully for the Confederate more than three years and who are a part of the legacy South now so fondly cherished mourned and children wept banks of the Cumberland to of the Gulf, on account of ons, and no hamlet was without announcement of "killed at Franklin."

courses for 1,000 yards along the bank of the river, then cut thru the southeastern end of the town and crossed the river directly under the guns of Fort Granger, which had been built during the operations of 1863.

Trouble Over Pontoons.

It had not been anyone's intention to make a stand south of the Harpeth River. If the train, as was expected, could have been gotten across the river, the troops would have followed and

The skies were as little in harmony with the awful tragedy about to be enacted as was the smiling landscape, the wide expanse of fields formed for peaceful industry and the substantial homes wherein happiness and comfort had formerly reigned. The weeping heavens had at length cleared up, the clouds rolled themselves up out of sight, and Nov. 30, 1864, was an ideal Indian Summer's day, and nowhere in the world does Indian Summer come with more delight than in Middle Tennessee.

the posts were found to be still good, and were sawed off nearly level with the water, crossbeams and planks were laid upon them, and so rapid was the work that by noon there were two good bridges over the Harpeth for the wagons and artillery, and the passage begun. The artillery of the Twenty-third Corps went over at the ford to save time, and was put in the old Fort Granger to cover the crossings and the field.

(To be continued.)

A VIEW OF FRANKLIN AND THE BATTLEGROUND FROM THE HILL WHERE THE REBELS FORMED.

across the Federal breastworks. Carter reported to Brown once by courier and another time in person, to the effect he had no support on his left. By this point, Gist was dead, shot in the chest. Even without support on the left, Carter rode forward on horseback, where he was mortally wounded by a "shot through the body." Even without their two brigadiers, the combined assault by Gist's and Carter's men forced their way into the main Federal line. While forced back, the Federals cobbled together a new line and held on.[23]

Meanwhile, Gordon, whose men were mixed in with the Texans of the now-dead Granbury, found himself pinned down in the ditch near the Carter cotton gin. The men with him wanted to surrender, but Gordon hoped to hide among the heaped up corpses and make his escape. He and a companion made the attempt, but bullets continued to fly into the ditch to the point that Gordon felt it was death to try to stay, and so he surrendered, too. Meanwhile, the supporting brigade of Otho Strahl piled into the Federal ditch almost directly facing the Carter House. There, the ditch was not only deep, but also subject to an enfilading fire from Federals across the pike. Strahl was wounded while passing rifles up to the top of the ditch, and then wounded again and finally killed while being borne from the field. His men continued to struggle into the night.[24]

Brown was mounted and supervised the desperate attack for well over an hour, until night began to fall. About the time Strahl was killed, Brown was shot in the same thigh and almost in the same location as his wound at Perryville, over two years previously. At the time of his wounding, he was attended by Maj. Vaulx and two couriers. Brown fell forward on his horse's neck, and Vaulx helped him off the horse. An ambulance was secured, and the general was taken to the rear. The wound was considered severe, but not dangerous. It was a bloody day for Brown and his men. The five general officers in the division were all wounded, captured, or killed, and the division itself suffered over a thousand casualties. Later, after the Federals moved on toward Nashville, a weeping Cheatham rode across the battlefield, grieving at the sight of the heaped up corpses of his men. The senior officer in his former division was a colonel.[25]

Chaplain Quintard saw to the burial of Cleburne, Strahl, and others at the Polk family church, St. John's Ashwood, near Columbia. He found Brown's former subordinate, Brig. Gen. A. M. Manigault, also wounded at Franklin, at nearby Hamilton Place. Later, the future bishop visited the wounded members of the 1st Tennessee Regiment at the division hospital set up in the Williamson County courthouse in Franklin on December 5, and being a medical doctor, dressed a number of wounds. The more prominent wounded were in more comfortable quarters. Quintard found John C. Carter still alive at the Harrison house a few miles south of Franklin, along with Brig. Gen. William A. Quarles and a few other officers, and frequently ministered to Carter until his death early on December 8. There is no record of Brown's care immediately after Vaulx had him removed from the battlefield, but by December 5, he was at the home of Maj. Abraham Looney on the south side of Columbia. Brown's service record reflects that as of December 13, 1864, he was on leave of absence for sixty days on a surgeon's certificate. At about this time, Neill told a newspaper editor that Brown was "rapidly recovering" from his wound.[26]

After Franklin, Hood had two choices. He could retreat back behind the Duck River and hope to winter there without interference from George Thomas's blue legions, or he could advance the tattered remnant of his army to Nashville. The latter option at least left open the chance of capturing the Tennessee capital should the Federals make an unlikely enormous mistake. With not nearly enough troops to invest the city, the Confederates occupied a thin line on its the south side, and waited in sometimes appallingly bad weather for just over two weeks for the Federals to react. Thomas attacked on December 15, forcing Hood to retire to a fallback position, which was attacked and turned on December 16. While the veteran troops of the Army of Tennessee fought bravely, their left flank was turned by overwhelming Federal forces on both days. Already gutted at Franklin, Stewart's and Cheatham's corps were the victims of these two successive days of attacks, and it fell to Stephen D. Lee's men to cover the initial phases of the Confederate retreat. The duty then fell to Cheatham, and then eventually, Forrest, who was aided by eight thin infantry brigades, including Brown's old unit under now-Brig. Gen. Joseph Palmer. The army eventually retreated south through Columbia and Pulaski to the Tennessee River. What was left of its main body crossed the river on December 25 and 26, and Hood asked to be relieved in the second week of January.[27]

When the Federal pursuit arrived in Columbia, Brown was gone from Maj. Looney's home. Although his intervening itinerary is unknown, by mid-January, he was two hundred miles to the southwest, in Columbus, Mississippi, where Bettie was able to join him. Confederate artilleryman Thomas J. Key observed that Columbus's streets "were wide and well arranged, and the buildings looked new and in good repair." While physically untouched by the war, the economic effect of the conflict weighed on the town, as Key observed that "a number of mercantile houses [were] open, but the supply of goods was not large." The physical effect of the war on the Confederacy's officer corps was illustrated by Key's encounter with three generals on crutches in one parlor in Columbus, Brown, Brig. Gen. Lucius E. Polk, and Brig. Gen. Andrew J. Vaughan Jr. In an interview with the local newspaper, Brown downplayed the Army of Tennessee's artillery losses during the Tennessee campaign.[28]

For a senior officer hoping to return to his command, Columbus made sense as a place to recuperate, so long as the Army of Tennessee, or what was left of it, remained near Tupelo. But in mid-January, President Davis ordered the stalwart few still with the colors to move east to assist Hardee, in command in South Carolina and Georgia, in his efforts to arrest Sherman's advance north from Savannah into the Carolinas. In the final extremity of the Confederacy, Davis appointed Gen. Robert E. Lee as commander of all of its armies. Stopping Sherman's advance was a concern for Lee in any event, but his promotion put it in his sphere of responsibility as well, and Lee joined many other voices in petitioning President Davis to appoint Joseph E. Johnston to command the scattered forces being gathered for that purpose. Davis finally assented, and Johnston was appointed to command "the Army of Tennessee and all troops in Department of South Carolina, Georgia and Florida." His orders were to "drive back Sherman."[29]

The Army of Tennessee traveled east by road, steamboat, and what was left of the rail system in Mississippi, Alabama, Georgia, and the Carolinas. Whether to be closer to the army as it moved east, or to make sure Bettie was left with friends, the Browns left Columbus, Mississippi, for Columbus, Georgia. While their route is unknown, travel across the tottering Confederacy, even through areas basically untouched by the war, must have been difficult. Chaplain Quintard, who made the same trip at about that time, traveled from Columbus, Mississippi, to Meridian on crowded rail cars, from there to Demopolis, Alabama, on a crowded box car where he was "vexed" with the "filthy conversation" of soldiers returning to their commands. Quintard took a train from Demopolis to Selma, Alabama, where he then took a steamboat to Montgomery, and from there by train to Columbus, Georgia. While the Browns would likely have traveled somewhat more comfortably considering the general's rank and Bettie's presence, it cannot have been an easy journey, given Brown's still unhealed wound.[30]

Brown encountered Quintard in Columbus, Georgia, on March 12, the day before he was to depart to rejoin the army somewhere in the Carolinas. Quintard recorded in his diary that Brown "made a full statement to me of his movements at Spring Hill which satisfied me fully that his skirts are all clear of even a shadow of blame. I always believed it for he is at once one of the noblest of men and most accomplished of soldiers but I was glad to have a full and frank statement from his mouth of the movements of his division at Spring Hill." As a sort of commemoration of the meeting, Quintard posted a local newspaper article in the back of his diary, recording Brown's presence in Columbus "for several days." The article stated that Brown was still on crutches from his Franklin wound, but "he has, with characteristic determination, started forward to the front." Arriving at Augusta, Georgia, near the state line with South Carolina, Brown wrote Bettie that the travel "greatly irritated" his wound. Bettie responded in a letter dated March 30 that gently chided the general that such was what she "anticipated." She regretted that her husband did not remain longer at Columbus, as she knew "very well that you were not prepared for the experiences of the journey or the campaign after joining the army." Notwithstanding Bettie's concerns, by April 1, Brown had been able to rejoin some of his troops, and arrived with them at the encampment of the Army of Tennessee at Smithfield, North Carolina.[31]

In the time it took for Brown to make his way to the army from Columbus, the scattered Confederate forces in North Carolina had finally been able to provide substantial resistance to Sherman's advance. In doing so, a number of personalities from the Army of Tennessee's past surfaced. First, Braxton Bragg, who found it "embarrassing" to serve under Johnston, combined his Department of North Carolina troops with a contingent from the Army of Tennessee under Daniel Harvey Hill, who in turn loathed Bragg. They engaged in a sharp fight with one of Sherman's columns at Wise's Forks on March 8. Then, on March 10, Joe Wheeler, leading Confederate cavalry under Lt. Gen. Wade Hampton launched a surprise attack on Sherman's cavalry at Monroe's Crossroads. At Averasboro on March 16, longtime Army of Tennessee corps commander Lt. Gen. William J. Hardee and troops pulled together from the Savannah and Charleston garrisons and other scattered commands bought Johnston an extra day or so to concentrate his forces for a strike on one of Sherman's widespread columns.[32]

That strike occurred at Bentonville on March 19. With a scant 4,500 men from the Army of Tennessee under the command of A. P. Stewart joined with the troops under Bragg and Hardee, "Old Joe" hoped to crush Maj. Gen. Henry W. Slocum's Army of Georgia, which was the new designation for the Army of Tennessee's old enemies, the Federal 14th and 20th Corps. Johnston's force exceeded 20,000 men. Even though there was initial success, the Federal host was too large to destroy. Johnston eventually retreated to Smithfield, from where he reported to Lee on March 23 that Sherman had moved on to Goldsboro to link up with Schofield, whose Army of the Ohio had been shipped to that place from Middle Tennessee. Johnston confessed that, with his small force, he could "no more than annoy" Sherman. Inferring that it was a necessity for Lee and Johnston to join, "Old Joe" left it to Lee to decide where to engage Sherman, laconically writing "I will be near him."[33]

While Sherman replenished from the Federal depots at Goldsboro, Johnston took steps to mold his army into a more cohesive force. Johnston's effort to restore morale involved formal reviews of his troops, starting with Hardee's "corps" on April 3. Brown was almost certainly present on April 4 when the commanding general reviewed the Army of Tennessee. At least in some minds, that review diminished, rather than restored, morale. For Stewart's aide, Bromfield Ridley, the sight of the army's thin ranks, just a year after the magnificent review at Dalton, "was the saddest spectacle of my life." Another blow fell over the next two days, when news of Lee's evacuation of Richmond and the Federal capture of Selma, Alabama, reached the army. While Johnston waited for the possible news of Lee's approach, he reorganized his army one final time.

The various commands that fought at Bentonville as the "Army of the South," along with the remnants of the original Army of Tennessee that had subsequently arrived, were organized into three corps under Hardee, Stewart, and Stephen D. Lee and named the Army of Tennessee. Lee's Corps was made up of divisions under Carter Stevenson and D. H. Hill. Divisions under William W. Loring, Edward C. Walthall, and James Patton Anderson were under Stewart's command, and Hardee's Corps consisted of divisions under Maj. Gen. Robert F. Hoke, Cheatham, who took command of his old division, and Brown, who was given a two-brigade division made up of "the reorganized brigades of Govan and J. A. Smith." In retaining Brown as a division commander, Johnston preferred the Tennessean to veteran and more senior division commanders such as major generals Lafayette McLaws and William B. Taliaferro from the Army of Northern Virginia, and William B. Bate and Henry D. Clayton of the old Army of Tennessee.[34]

On April 10, both armies were on the move, heading west toward Raleigh. Early the next morning, Johnston got a message from Jefferson Davis that Lee had surrendered. There would be no junction with the Army of Northern Virginia. On April 12 and 13, Johnston and Beauregard met with Davis and what was left of his cabinet at Greensboro, and received the president's reluctant consent to open negotiations with Sherman. Meanwhile, rumors began to reach the army of Lee's surrender, which, in the words of one of Brown's new command, had "a very demoralizing effect on this army." Brown's command marched through Chapel Hill and camped near Salem, west of Greensboro, on April 16, the day Johnston first met Sherman at Durham Station. There, Capt. Samuel T. Foster recorded that the men were aware talks were occurring and expected to be surrendered. On April 17, he observed that "discipline [was] very loose." The next day, the very day that Johnston and Sherman agreed to the terms of the Army of Tennessee's surrender, there was battalion drill in Brown's Division, "just to see if the men would drill."[35]

The army's surrender was not the only rumor in the camps during this interval. In their meeting, Sherman informed Johnston of President Abraham Lincoln's assassination on April 14 and his death the next morning. Sherman recalled that he "watched [Johnston] closely" and the rebel commander "did not attempt to conceal his distress." Johnston "denounced the act as a disgrace to the age, and hoped [Sherman] did not charge it to the Confederate Government." While Sherman would not put it past Jefferson Davis and others, he did not deem it possible for Johnston or Lee or any soldier to have advocated such. Johnston was not the only rebel distressed at that development. Some of the Florida troops remaining with the army heard a rumor of Lincoln's death, and seeing that Brown's tent was pitched not far from them, a group of about forty went to see if the general could confirm the rumor. Brown, still needing a cane to walk, came to the door of the tent. One of the Floridians said, "General, we hear Lincoln is dead." Brown replied, "Yes, that is the news. I believe it is true, and if true, it is the worst blow the south has received."[36]

Sherman's zeal to end the war without further bloodshed led him to agree to more generous terms than the authorities at Washington were willing to allow. The truce that accompanied the first surrender ended, and the emotions of the men swung wildly from defiance to despondence. Both sides scrambled to renegotiate, as no one intended for the war to resume. In the end, Johnston formally surrendered on the same basic terms as had Lee at Appomattox, although "Supplemental Terms" allowed the rebels amenities not provided the men of the Army of Northern Virginia. While formal surrender occurred on April 26, in case negotiations failed, the division marched another ten miles or so west. Late in the afternoon of April 27, Brown's men learned of the surrender. That day, they each received $1.25 in silver, their final payment from the Confederate treasury.[37]

Incarcerated at Fort Warren, severely wounded at Perryville and Franklin, Brown was transformed by the war from a reluctant secessionist at the time of Fort Sumter in 1861 to a last-ditch rebel in 1865. In the course of those four years, Brown learned from his experiences and became a fine soldier and competent commander. Importantly, he was recognized as such not only by his men, but by his superiors: Albert Sidney Johnston, Buckner, Stevenson, S. D. Lee, Hood, and Joseph E. Johnston. Likewise, Manigault, himself a brave and competent officer, payed tribute to Brown's qualities a soldier when subordinated to the Tennessean. That competence, combined by the attrition in the Army of Tennessee's high command, is the reason Brown rose to the rank of major general and

The Slaughter in Our Ranks Was Frightful

divisional command. Success as a division commander in the Army of Tennessee from mid-1864 forward must be downwardly defined, as there were no Confederate victories to be had in the final year of the war. Even if assigned a share of the fault for the failure at Spring Hill, Brown was arguably as successful as any other division commander in the army, a conclusion demonstrated by his role as the army's utility commander. The end of the war brought Brown's sixth (or seventh) separate division command to a conclusion, a remarkable demonstration of that utility to the army. Brown commanded Stewart's, Stevenson's, and possibly Loring's divisions for brief intervals, Hindman's, Bate's, and Cheatham's in battle in the Atlanta and Tennessee campaigns, and Cleburne's in North Carolina.[38]

But at the time of the surrender, an uncertain future loomed. Brown encountered a prominent Methodist minister, Rev. John B. McFerrin, who was present as a missionary to the army. McFerrin had a charge in Pulaski when Brown was a child. Brig. Gen. Joseph Palmer, who had what was left of Brown's old 3rd Tennessee as part of his command, attached McFerrin to his staff so that the divine might ride his horse home under the terms of the surrender. McFerrin asked Brown what he planned to do. Brown confessed that he had not made up his mind, but was considering going to Mexico. McFerrin frankly told Brown, "don't do it." Instead, Brown should "go back to Giles County where you were raised and in ten years you will be governor of Tennessee." Brown was afraid if he did that, the radical Unionist governor William G. Brownlow would have him hanged for treason. "No he won't," rejoined the other. "Do as I tell you and you will succeed." Although it was a bitter spring-time in North Carolina, as McFerrin recalled, Brown later had occasion to remember the discussion "with a laugh."[39]

6

To Liberate . . .
the True and Chivalrous Citizens

June 1865 to October 1871

Brown arrived in Nashville from North Carolina on June 6, 1865, with no more than two dollars in his pocket and "a badly damaged wardrobe." He registered with the authorities in the capital, and then went on to Pulaski. On June 13, the former rebel formally requested a pardon from Andrew Johnson, noting he had enlisted in 1861 after a call for troops from the governor of Tennessee. He executed a written oath dated June 15, in the presence of Brevet Maj. Gen. Richard W. Johnson, at the latter's headquarters in Pulaski. Johnson, an old opponent from the Army of the Cumberland, forwarded Brown's papers, noting that the "applicant is a man of influential position" and expressed the belief that Brown was sincere in his application. Another old opponent, Maj. Gen. George H. Thomas, forwarded the application with his recommendation. Within a few days, a letter went to Johnson from Bettie's aunt Sarah Polk, who noted Brown's devotion to the Union in 1861 and his willingness to be a good citizen. She made known Brown's connection to her family through Bettie, who Johnson had met. When a pardon was not promptly issued, Mrs. Polk wrote a second letter on July 28, gently prodding the president for an "early decision." At some point in the latter half of 1865, Brown journeyed to Washington and actually saw the president, "but accomplished nothing." Brown joked a few months later that he was "an unpardoned, unwashed Rebel" but was "pretty well reconstructed—all I lack is Taxation & Representation." Johnson would eventually issue a pardon, although it would not come until January 15, 1867. As events would later prove, Johnson would not forget the pardon.[1]

Most likely through the agency of Mrs. Polk, Brown's application for pardon was endorsed by Governor William G. Brownlow. An outspoken Knoxville newspaperman, Brownlow was, after Andrew Johnson, East

Tennessee's most well-known Unionist and was given the appellation "Parson" Brownlow from his previous career as a Methodist minister. Brownlow became governor when civil government was restored to Tennessee in 1865. Taking office with the new governor was a new Unionist General Assembly, which passed a measure to disfranchise almost every former Confederate in the state. Brownlow's new order was tested in the congressional elections of August 1865, and while political alliances were not yet solidified, the supporters of the governor's program of reconstruction, who came to be known as the Radicals, received only about 40 percent of the vote. The remaining representatives were Conservatives, generally described as Union men who were not inclined to be unduly punitive to the former Confederates. What was due or undue in that regard depended on the issue and the circumstance. The result demonstrated to Brownlow that a stricter control on the franchise would be required to ensure Radical control of Tennessee.[2]

On October 30, Bettie presented the general with his first child, Marie, who was, in her proud father's words, "the prettiest, sweetest, best & most promising child. . . ." Having lost everything in the war, Brown's best prospect of supporting his family was to return to Pulaski and reestablish his law practice, and by the end of 1865 he enjoyed "a large business." Like a number of his former rebel compatriots who had lost their property, he retained his professional talent and remained a natural leader of his community. Indeed, while there were financial losses among Brown's social class, the economic strata that existed in 1860 essentially remained in the years after the war. Notwithstanding the immense upheaval caused by the conflict, the pecuniary differences between Brown and the common laborer who became a private in his regiment in 1861 were not significantly different in 1865. While whites maintained their relative economic standing, Pulaski was changed in other ways. It was scarred by the fire of August 1862. There were lines thrown up by the Federal army around the place, and a fortification on a nearby hill. In early January 1866, the new *Pulaski Citizen* illustrated the most significant change when it sarcastically noted the departure of the U. S. Colored Infantry created a "solemn gloom." Likely the attitude of the county's black citizens was indeed gloomy. Legally, the condition of slavery that separated the races was no more. Nonetheless, the white residents of Middle

To Liberate . . . the True and Chivalrous Citizens

William G. Brownlow
(Credit: Library of
Congress)

Tennessee considered the freedmen their inferiors in every way, not "on a social level with the white man" and deemed "social equality a humbug and an impossibility." Such was also the case for the right to vote, although it seems to have been a given that the blacks be allowed the right to participate in the courts.[3]

Brown's position in the upper crust of white society survived the war and was no doubt enhanced by his rank and service during the conflict. He formed a partnership with former Confederate congressman James McCallum and appeared at a public meeting with the county's other "best men" to pass a resolution in favor of Andrew Johnson's reconstruction policies. His comings and goings mattered. It was news when he joined Hood, Buckner, Bate, and other former Confederates at Cheatham's wedding. Afterwards, Buckner spent some days with the Browns, receiving friends and admirers. A visitor to the town in mid-March 1866 wrote that Pulaski had "a fine court house, a wretched hotel, many handsome residences, numerous squallid [sic] huts, a cotton factory and a few very poor business houses." The white people of the county were "quiet and industrious" and "pretty tired of the war." One resident thought them to be so pacified that "a boy in blue uniform, 16 years old, could arrest and bring to the city any ten men in the county." The correspondent also painted a rosy picture as to the freedmen, noting that they were, except for a few of the aged and invalid, fully employed and were "perfectly secure in person and property." The correspondent described Brown as a "very pleasant appearing gentleman and a man of decided talent" whose law practice was having "a heavy run of business." The general was quoted as claiming to be "thoroughly reconstructed" and said that *"the rebels of the South will unite with the Democrats of the North, and rule the country."* The editor of the *Citizen,* in printing the letter, left it to the reader to determine what was untrue about the letter, although Brown's purported comment was specifically denied.[4]

For whites, genteel society slowly returned to Pulaski, notwithstanding a destructive tornado at the end of December 1865. A correspondent noted the revival of churches, the reinstitution of the courts and city government, and a "Literary League" of "principally young men who meet once a week for discussion and debate." A member was careful to point out that the League did not "consume all their time in fussing and squabbling" over current political issues such as black suffrage or the Freedmen's Bureau, but debated issues such as the advantages of a republican or monarchical form of government. Bettie helped form a chapter of the Benevolent Association through the Episcopal Church, and a society to aid the orphans of Confederate soldiers. Brown resumed his Masonic activities with Pulaski Lodge 101 and helped lead the lodge in a tribute of respect to a lost comrade, Maj. Flavel Barber, who was reburied in Pulaski in April 1866.[5]

In 1866, Pulaski became the birthplace of a far more mysterious order than the Freemasons. Six young Confederate veterans, all but one of whom served under Brown's command during the war, started a secret society, ostensibly for their mere amusement. They contrived strange titles, such as "Grand Cyclops" and "Grand Magi," donned masks and robes, prescribed an elaborate ritual, and adopted an alliterative, Greek-sounding name, the Ku Klux Klan. As notorious as the group later became, there is little or no evidence that its original intent was to organize ex-Confederate resistance. On the other hand, violence and retaliation against the freedmen and Unionists was likely never far from the minds of its founders, some of whom probably had already engaged in such. During this interval, a wartime adversary, George H. Thomas, still the commander of the Department of the Cumberland, reported that in the country districts of Tennessee, "murders robberies and outrages of all kinds being committed without any effort on the part of the civil authorities to arrest the offenders." Thomas observed that the justice system in the state, and especially in the districts outside the large cities, was particularly slanted in favor of the ex-Confederate whites, noting a sort of "freemasonry existing among rebels and rebel sympathizers." Far from being "perfectly secure in person and property," Giles County freedmen were in many cases treated as if they were still slaves, and reacted to their degradation often with fear and resentment, and their impoverished status frequently with thievery. When this factor combined with the disorderly conduct of a number of whites, often from outside the county, the native whites saw the need for an extralegal means of dealing with the threat posed to rebuilding white society. Accordingly, the sporadic acts of violence and intimidation seen since before the end of the war achieved a level of organization, by the end of 1867 or the first of 1868, as members of the Klan became regulators and vigilantes, bent on keeping blacks and Unionists in their place.[6]

Brown's role in the Klan is murky. It is logical that the founders would look to their former general for guidance. Brown's anti-Radical resistance appears much clearer on the political and legal front, as he joined with Conservatives and ex-rebels in seeking to sustain a conservative judge, who, having not vacated his office, had a replacement appointed by Governor Brownlow. Yet, it seems to be undisputed that Brown was a member of the Klan, and one source indicates he became the Grand Dragon of the Realm of Tennessee. Even if he was not, he almost certainly had a great deal of influence on the members of the original Pulaski den, and Allen W. Trelease, the author of the seminal modern history of the Klan, deemed it possible that Brown and George W. Gordon were quite significant in the reorganization of the Klan into a more formalized group.[7]

Governor Brownlow was not inclined to tolerate the rising resistance to his administration, regardless of its level of organization. In April 1866, the Radicals passed a measure that took the power of enforcing the franchise restrictions on the former Confederates from the county clerks and gave it to special registration officers who served at the pleasure of the governor. He forced the ratification of the Fourteenth Amendment through the General Assembly in July of that year, and the state's representatives were seated in Congress. The General Assembly reconvened on November 15, 1866, with the Radicals firmly in control. Governor Brownlow suggested the legislators take up the issue of black suffrage and argued that recalcitrant Conservatives, "sustained in their designs by the Acting President of the United States," were set on a state revolution. The governor accordingly asked that the legislature "authorize the enlistment of a few regiments of loyal militia . . . to suppress insurrection or protect the ballot-box." Violence in January 1867 gave new importance to the militia bill, which was passed in February 1867. Also that month, the Radicals nominated Brownlow for another term as governor and a law was passed extending the franchise to adult black males, making Tennessee the first southern state to do so. The Radicals' political clubs, known as "Union Leagues," were redirected toward the freedmen to impress them with ritual and symbolism and instruct them in Radical politics. But Conservatives claimed they constituted a "secret league" for the purpose of deluding the freedmen into voting the Radical ticket.[8]

Between Brownlow's control of the registration machinery, the existence of the Radical-aligned State Guard, and the newly enfranchised blacks, the Conservatives, with the ex-Confederates disenfranchised, faced the daunting task of gaining control of the state government in the elections of August 1867. While the Radicals told the freedmen they were responsible for emancipation, there was a genuine effort by the Conservatives to gain the black vote, and black delegates were actually invited to the Conservative convention in Nashville in April. But the Radicals were not alone in utilizing "secret leagues." In the same month the Conservatives were meeting to select West Tennessean Emerson Etheridge as their candidate for governor, the Pulaski den of the Klan called a meeting of other known Klan dens, out of which may have come some level of organization and ritual for that shadowy group. There is no evidence that

Brown was involved in that meeting, or, for that matter, that he was not. The general did not serve as a delegate to the Conservative convention.[9]

The scant record of Brown's activities during this period indicates almost no public activity of a political nature. In November 1866, he made a brief appearance at a county meeting requesting a candidate purportedly elected in a special election take his seat in the legislature. Otherwise, the news items relating to Brown concern miscellaneous civic and business activities. He paid a visit to Memphis at the end of 1866 that elicited favorable comments from the press there, and it was noted that an anonymous admirer had sent him an elegant cane of ebony and gold. A different prize manifested itself when Brown received his long-awaited pardon from Andrew Johnson in that interval. And while he had "as much business as [he] could attend to," he and McCallum suffered the misfortune of having their office burn in May 1867, although the contents were saved with the help of a number of citizens. The fire was not his only misfortune during this period, as there was a break-in at Brown's home in March 1868.[10]

Brown's ill luck was only part of the news that made the papers that spring. Klansman Frank O. McCord, the editor of the *Citizen*, kept the concept of a shadowy and mysterious Klan alive, publishing fanciful and mocking references to the organization. The paper described a parade of seventy-five Klansmen in full costume that appeared in Pulaski on June 5, 1867, in a purported "first anniversary" march. The *Citizen* reported fantastic dress, a march to the command of tooting horns, speaking in strange languages, and that the marchers "kukluxed" up First Street for some time. As intimidating as it sounds, recent scholarship has concluded that the grand meetings and parades reported during 1867 were exaggerations and lies consistent with a "broader culture of disguise, secrecy, and audacious misrepresentation." Nonetheless, Governor Brownlow was not amused by this or by the existence of other real or imagined dens in Middle and West Tennessee, regarding the group as a "secret guerilla army."[11]

Prior to the election, Brownlow deployed the State Guard in several counties to provide security for the election. A relatively small group went to Giles County, and there seems to have been little active friction between the guardsmen and the population. The disenfranchised white majority was powerless to affect the election between Brownlow and

Etheridge. Giles County had over three thousand voters prior to the war. In 1866, before the freedmen were given the vote, the eligible number was ninety-six. In 1867, there were about 2,000 eligible voters, but 1,750 of them were black. There was a large rush to the polls by the newly enfranchised blacks, and Brownlow's commissioner of registration took care to see that they had the "correct" ballots. Ultimately, Brownlow prevailed, winning the election by a vote of 74,034 to 22,550. Approximately 35,000 freedmen voted, ensuring continued Radical control. Brownlow triumphantly told the state legislature that his government was established by the "three-fold influences of time, Congressional recognition, and popular ratification," the latter by "majorities approaching to unanimity."[12]

The actual majority did not see it that way. The fact that the State Guard was organized to counter ex-Confederate lawlessness and the disfranchisement of the former rebels exacerbated the bitterness left over from the war and sullied the legitimacy of the Brownlow government. The combination of disfranchisement and the droves of former slaves organized by the Union Leagues who voted for the Radical ticket with the protection of a military force under Radical control seemed like, in the words of Andrew Johnson himself, a "despotism." Slightly over two weeks before the election, Brown responded to a letter from his former comrade, Henry D. Clayton, in a manner that reflected these very same views. Brown opened with a "rehearsed" answer relative to his business and health, and stated he had "more friends than I deserve," and a conscience that was "reasonably quiet." He then launched into a bitter complaint about "registration laws," and having "to look upon the negro as the Lord of Creation." Brown related that it was impossible to make Clayton "intelligently sensible of the degraded condition of the white man in Tennessee." The law and registration system mandated by Brownlow was made "without regard to Constitution, man or God." Brown described the practice of the local commissioner, supported by the State Guard, who registered "the faithful few of the white race, and the multitude of blacks." Doubtlessly expressing the thoughts of the bulk of former rebels, whether Klansmen or not, Brown expressed a sense of hopelessness, wondering "where is the path that leads from this anarchy, and from these abominable abuses of power—this trampling down of law and Constitution?"[13]

One answer turned out to be active resistance, which broke out in earnest in 1868. In Middle and West Tennessee, Klan and related activity burst forth, although not as openly in Giles County as in neighboring Maury, likely because a force of the State Guard remained present. The guard, however, did not stay very long, being demobilized in the aftermath of the August election. Klan outrages increased in Giles County. On January 9, 1868, a clash between blacks and whites took place in Pulaski where several blacks were injured. The "well matured and drilled" whites seemed organized and prepared for trouble, in the view of the Freedman's Bureau investigator, who reported "there is reason to believe . . . that such organization is in existence & that is called the Ku Klux Klan, having for its end the expulsion of loyal men whites and blacks from the counties of Giles & Maury and thus terrorizing similar to that which was general in this county about the breaking out of the rebellion." Disingenuously, the *Citizen* laid the blame on the freedmen. A public meeting was held in which Brown was a prominent participant, condemning "mob law" as "wrong and unwise," notwithstanding the fact that it was sometimes employed by "good patriotic and conservative men." The *Citizen*, essentially the Klan's organ in Giles County, claimed at the end of January 1868 that there had not been any Klan activity "in this locality for months." Such was not the case, as within a few days of Brown's public meeting, a group of about sixteen Klansmen attacked a white Unionist and two blacks, whipping them and threatening to kill them "because we belonged to the Union League and voted the radical ticket."[14]

Historian Allen W. Trelease concluded that at this point there seemed to be an effort by prominent citizens among the Klan leadership to rein in the more outrageous acts of violence, making a distinction, as Trelease notes, between threatening the blacks and whipping them. Controlling the rank and file Klansmen was problematic. A Giles County deputy sheriff likely exemplified their feelings against Radicals and Union Leaguers when he addressed them as "filth, more disgusting than the putrefying carcass of a Yankee-government horse that has died of the glanders" who, "along with yourselves, would make an ignorant and prejudiced race our masters." It is probable that Brown was both openly involved in this moderating effort in his capacity as a leading citizen, as he was after the January violence, and secretly involved, too, as a member of the Klan leadership, although that leadership's level of sophistication and organization was apparently more imagined than real. It may have been merely coincidental, but Brown was in Nashville in November 1867 at the St. Cloud Hotel at the same time as the Klan's purported "Grand Wizard," Nathan Bedford Forrest. He also was in Nashville on at least three other occasions between October 1867 and March 1868, which would have provided opportunities for conferring with other anti-Brownlow leaders. On the other hand, Brown's presence in the capital on at least one occasion was to chair a meeting of lawyers from all over the state to devise means of improving the legal system.[15]

Regardless of his stance on and participation in the Klan violence that erupted in 1868, Brown engaged in open political opposition to the Radicals that year. Both John C. Brown and Neill S. Brown were longtime Whigs. Like a number of other conservative ex-Whigs, they doubtlessly deemed political opposition to the Radicals more important than the label of an expired political party. In the words of East Tennessee Whig T. A. R. Nelson, alliance with the national Democrats was necessary "as there was no other organization opposed to Radicalism." Two years later, Neill explained that both the old Whig and Democratic parties as they existed in the 1850s "are extinct, and the questions which then divided them have been settled and passed away. . . . The question of slavery is forever settled, and no sane man proposes to revive it, or disturb its adjustment. This leaves no living issue between Whigs and Democrats that may prevent their joint action." Therefore, the party name "is nothing." When the anti-Radicals of Giles County met to organize on a political basis for the 1868 political season, they met as Conservatives under Brown's chairmanship, and resolved to "unite with any party who are siding to reestablish Constitutional liberty" and that "this is a 'white man's government' and all white citizens of the government are entitled to the right of suffrage." Brown and others attended the "Conservative Democratic" meeting at Nashville in June 1868.[16]

At the "Democratic State Convention," on June 9, Brown joined a group that the virulently anti-Radical Memphis *Avalanche* felt "comprised the best talent and experience in the State, contrasting remarkably with the carpet-bagging, streaked and striped, God-forsaken, mahogany-colored, startuppy Radical Conventions which have been held in the Cap-

To Liberate . . . the True and Chivalrous Citizens

itol during the past few years." Brown served on the Committee on Resolutions, which reported out a six-part resolution adopted by the convention. It asserted that while secession was dead, the larger concept of state power was not. It accepted the demise of slavery, but condemned the exclusion of white men from the government, objected to the size of the public debt and the payment of interest on that debt in gold, condemned the Radicals in general, and lauded Andrew Johnson and his defense of the Constitution "against the assaults of a revolutionary faction." Brown was later appointed to a committee to prepare an address to present the grievances of Tennesseans to the National Democratic Convention. That paper, which Brown presented at the convention on July 4, 1868, was an exhaustive indictment of the "evils" that oppressed the disenfranchised white Tennesseans. Back home in Pulaski in mid-July, Brown presided over a county meeting that "ratified" the convention's action nominating Horatio Seymour as a candidate for president against Ulysses S. Grant.[17]

Klan outrages continued into the summer of 1868 even while the Conservative leadership sought to make its voice heard. Governor Brownlow's election registrars came under attack, and the Union League in Giles and other Middle Tennessee counties was effectively eliminated by night riders. Radical politicians were assaulted. Early in the morning of June 30, a black man accused of attempted rape of two white women was lynched. He was discovered lying in the road at daylight when an omnibus ran over him on its way from the train depot. The final straw for Brownlow, however, took place in mid-June, when the Klan boarded a train "with pistols and rope in hand" looking in vain for one of his political allies, Samuel M. Arnell, who was on another train. On July 6, Brownlow called for a special session of the legislature to meet on July 28. The governor's newspaper, the Knoxville *Whig*, reported in its July 15 edition that he "daily received" letters from loyal men, such as the Radical in Bedford County who plaintively asked, "How long will the lives and property of Union men in this State be subjected to such danger?" The *Whig* replied: "Let the Legislature speak out when it meets in terms that all will understand."[18]

At this point, the state was in a "blaze of excitement." William B. Bate, then a lawyer in Nashville, was of the opinion that Brownlow's "object is to get up a fight in Tennessee so as to bring about a reaction through false sympathy and unite their already shattered lines in the Radical column of the North." The former rebels genuinely feared the restoration of the State Guard, not only because it might result in open warfare between the two factions in the state, which they thought would not turn out well for their side, but also because it would hinder the success experienced to that point in wearing down Radical political strength. The "best citizens" used their influence to rein in Klan activity, quite successfully by the time the legislature convened. The former rebel military leadership also joined to defuse the situation. A week or so before the legislature met, Brown, Cheatham, former state adjutant general W. C. Whitthorne, and others traveled to Knoxville to visit with Governor Brownlow and had a "frank" discussion about the "present threatening posture of affairs" in Middle Tennessee. According to the *Whig*, they expressed "an earnest desire to see every portion of Tennessee spared trouble and bloodshed." Brownlow must have been impressed to some extent, as his organ opined it had "no doubt they are sincere, and that their motives are good."[19]

Notwithstanding these promising developments, on July 28, Brownlow opened the special session with a strong message on events since the State Guard was demobilized earlier that year, accusing the anti-Radicals of "secretly arming themselves and perfecting a military organization known as the Ku Klux Klan, composed of ex-rebel soldiers and those who were in sympathy with them." Brownlow recommended that these organized bands "be declared outlaws by special legislation, and punished with death wherever found." Likely because of the promise of the meeting with Brownlow the week before, a number of former Confederate general officers met at Bate's law office on August 1 for the purpose of communicating to the legislature that "there is no necessity for calling out the 'Militia'" and the "evil consequences which may result from so doing." Accordingly, Brown, Forrest, Cheatham, Pillow, Bushrod Johnson, S. R. Anderson, Bate, George Maney, Gordon, William Quarles, Thomas Benton Smith, George Dibrell, and Palmer addressed a memorial to the legislature over all their signatures. In that document, the generals, a number of whom were active in opposing Brownlow, disingenuously denied a desire to subvert the state government and claimed no knowledge of any group with that goal, but stated that, if there were, "we have neither sym-

William B. Bate (Credit: Library of Congress)

pathy nor affiliation" with that group. Reflecting the "inherently desta-bilizing" effect of disfranchisement, the generals argued that if the fran-chise were restored, things would calm down. Brown, Quarles, Dibrell, Forrest, and Cheatham then went to meet with the legislature's joint Military Committee, and Brown submitted the memorial on behalf of all the generals. A legislator stated that it was Brownlow's intention to uphold the law and observed that "depredations have been committed, men have been shot or hung, others have been whipped or maltreated, and driven from their homes and families." All the generals present pro-tested as to their loyalty and those of the former Confederates they rep-resented. Brown succinctly summed matters up when he stated: "All we ask you is to give us our rights, as it is in your power to do."[20]

Brown and Gordon returned to Giles County to inform a public meet-ing about the generals' conference with the Military Committee. Keep-ing on message, they "urged upon all good citizens the necessity of living in strict subordination to the laws, and of pursuing such a course as will tend to restore perfect peace and harmony throughout the State." Not all of the generals were as circumspect, however, as Brownlow's *Knoxville Whig* commented on a much more aggressive speech Quarles gave three days later that showed "his *real* sentiments." Other Radicals observed that if the generals had the influence they inferred but had not exercised it to that point, they were as guilty as the Klan of the outrages it had perpetrated. While the special session wrangled over the severity of the counter-measures suggested, the Klan, unrestrained by their wartime leaders, engaged in further outrages, which in turn likely reinforced a report of the joint Military Committee, which detailed with specificity Klan lawlessness to that point. Complicating matters, the *Cincinnati Commercial* printed an interview with Forrest, which, while interwoven with hopes for peace, contained a veiled threat of renewed civil war.[21]

Even before the Military Committee's Klan report was printed, a joint select committee traveled to Washington to inform President Johnson of the "present condition of affairs in Tennessee." The Klan existed, they wrote, and Forrest claimed there were as many as 40,000 Klansmen in the state. They reported that the Klan dressed in "masks and ghostly uniforms," and that while "thus engaged they take out citizens and kill them—some by hanging, some by shooting, and some by the slower and more certain plan of whipping, while some are whipped not until death, but severely and disgracefully." Murders, especially of blacks, were common. Additionally, there were examples of vigilantism. It was clear that "most, if not all," of the Klan were "enemies of the government of the United States during the late civil war." Perhaps reflecting the olive branch extended by Brown and the former generals a few weeks before, Johnson was informed that "many of the 'confederate soldiers and officers' who fought gallantly during the war, disapprove of and condemn the 'Klan' and its acts of unprovoked violence." Federal troops were needed, because they would not be subject to intimidation from their fellow citizens. Indeed, the regular civil authorities in the affected counties were simply not working, either out of complicity or intimidation.[22]

Johnson was sufficiently convinced to provide the requested troops, some of which went to Giles County. Meanwhile, the special session passed a new militia law and a stringent Ku Klux Act, the latter with significant fines, jail time, and loss of voting rights. In November, the Radical's candidate, Ulysses S. Grant, won the presidential election, but the Radical vote declined by almost 18,000 statewide, a significant percentage of that—1,319 voters—from Giles County itself. It was well recognized that "in many localities the voters were intimidated and kept from the polls." Federal troops left after the election, and Klan attacks resumed. While Conservatives were doubtlessly elated with the degradation of Radical strength brought about by the Klan, lawlessness in Giles County reached the point where, on Christmas Eve 1868, Brown, Gordon, Thomas M. Jones, McCallum, and others led a public meeting condemning intrusions by mobs of vigilantes into the county jail and urging support of the civil authorities. For a while, at least, Klan activity around Pulaski waned.[23]

Yet, the new year of 1869 dawned with a spectacular Klan crime involving Giles County. Brownlow hired a Cincinnati detective, Seymour Barmore, to infiltrate the Klan in Giles County. Barmore had some success, and on January 11 he boarded a train for Nashville. Klansmen in Columbia intercepted him, and his dead body was found about six weeks later. Even before that time, Brownlow had had enough. On January 16, the House passed a bill concurring with the Senate on a bill authorizing the governor to suspend the writ of *habeas corpus* and to call out the State Guard. Four days later, the governor called for "all good and loyal citizens to enter the ranks of the State Guard," and indicated he would place certain counties under martial law, which was authorized by the legislature. In August 1868, Brown and his fellow Confederate generals believed that they had some influence over the anti-Radical resistance, but in early 1869 they struggled to maintain that influence in the rising tide of violence. In mid-January, Neill published an open letter calling on the Klan to cease its activities, expressing the view that it was hindering the state's prosperity, and urging former Confederates to look to the future.[24]

It was against this backdrop that the last round of armed conflict between the Radical state government and the Klan and other anti-Radical groups took place. On January 23, Brown, Jones, and other leading citizens of Giles County went to the capitol to assure the administration that "no militia would be needed in that county as the people were determined that the laws should be fully enforced against all offenders." Conservatives were indeed tiring of the unrestrained violence of the Klan, to the point that Forrest issued an order requiring destruction of disguises and forbidding jail incursions and acts of political intimidation. The Klan, however, was not disbanded by these reactive measures, only imperfectly restrained.[25]

As might be expected, Brownlow included Giles County in the declaration of martial law. On February 23, five companies of the State Guard occupied Pulaski, the new headquarters of a four-county "military district." The civil courts were closed, and the guard ran sweeps through the area. Then, an opportunity for a dramatic change occurred. At the height of his power in October 1867, the Parson was elected to the United States Senate seat held by David Patterson, Andrew Johnson's son-in-law, not to be vacant until early 1869. On February 25, 1869, Brownlow resigned as governor to take that seat. He was succeeded by the Speaker of the Senate, De Witt Clinton Senter. Both of the Brown brothers attended Senter's inauguration, and then General Brown and others from Giles County went to Senter to ask him to recall the militia, which had, perhaps on the strength of the late Detective Barmore's information, arrested men known to be Klansmen. Senter initially refused, but soon revoked the martial law order and restored the civil courts. The prisoners were allowed to bond out of jail, with Brown and others standing as surety, facilitating their escape. Others, including the *Citizen's* Frank McCord, left the state before they could be arrested. The paper only resumed when the danger passed.[26]

With Senter in office, the militia campaign eased to a halt. The new governor realized the futility of opposing a foe who refused to fight, especially where the local citizenry was reluctant to cooperate. Senter recalled five of the ten companies in service in April, and the remainder, including the company at Pulaski, by June. Without Brownlow's grim hand on the tiller, the Radicals were ready to steer a more moderate course. Further, the Radicals were fighting among themselves. The Radical state convention in May resulted in a split between the Brownlow-related faction, led by Senter, and an anti-Brownlow faction, led by William B. Stokes, a congressman and former Federal soldier, both of whom became Radical candidates for governor. This remarkable event was followed on

To Liberate . . . the True and Chivalrous Citizens

May 29 by a decision of the Tennessee Supreme Court striking down the 1867 franchise law that gave the governor power over voter registration. While not a sweeping decision that at the stroke of a pen enfranchised the former Confederates, it was a crack in the wall that dammed up tens of thousands of Conservative votes. Indeed, the governor continued to have power over the registrars, and as the start of the campaign against Stokes approached, the question was which, if either, would support the full franchise. Stokes spoke first, and was in favor of gradual enfranchisement of the former rebels. When Senter's turn came, he pledged to ask the legislature, if elected, to call a constitutional convention to enfranchise all adult males.[27]

Senter's control of the registrars gave him the election. The Conservatives wisely did not run a candidate, and while late in the campaign Stokes modified his position in favor of universal suffrage, the flood of ex-rebels who were allowed to vote by Senter's registrars turned the tide for Senter. Only Stokes and his supporters seem to have been disturbed that a number of the new voters were ineligible to do so under the state constitution as it then existed, and Stokes went to Washington and appealed in vain to President Grant to intervene. While the Conservatives did not run a gubernatorial candidate, their candidates for the legislature largely prevailed, winning complete control of both houses. The import of the election was reflected by the occurrence in Nashville after the polls closed. Crowds celebrated and a band played "The Bonnie Blue Flag." When the legislature met in Nashville on October 4, 1869, the Conservative comeback was well under way.[28]

Brown's status as an important Conservative leader and therefore a potential Conservative candidate became apparent in the latter part of 1869. He frequently visited Nashville, and his visits were noted in the primary Conservative organ, the Nashville *Union and American*, the offices of which he visited at least once. Obligingly, the paper printed a letter from an anonymous citizen that named prominent Conservative political leaders, including Brown and Andrew Johnson. There is reason to believe Brown and Johnson were on good terms. Brown got his pardon in 1867, and at the state Democratic convention in 1868, Brown had introduced a resolution that was highly complementary of Johnson, of which their mutual friends at the *Union and American* reminded the public in October

1869. But the return of the ex-president from Washington earlier that year introduced a new, volatile element to Tennessee politics.[29]

As historian Roger Hart observed, Senter above all others deserved the credit for "redeeming" Tennessee, but it was the Conservatives he ushered into power who became known as the state's Redeemers. Hart identified four distinct groupings among the Redeemers. The first were old Whig Unionists, such as John Baxter and John Netherland, the second being former Whigs who became Confederates, such as the two Browns, James D. Porter of Paris, and W. H. "Red" Jackson. Hart's third grouping consisted of men who united behind Johnson, a coalition of old Unionist Democrats and former rebels. As reflected by Brown's resolution the previous year, Johnson gained credibility within the Conservative coalition because of his clashes with the Radicals and efforts to lighten the effects of Reconstruction on the defeated South. The fourth group was made up of hard core secessionists, states' rights Democrats such as Isham G. Harris and William B. Bate, who lurked, at least for the time being, in the background. The preponderance of the former Whigs was marked, both in the legislature and in the Conservative leadership. For a body politic still smarting from the disruption caused by the secessionist Democrats in the preceding decade, former Whigs were thought to be a force for moderation and conservatism.[30]

Prominent historian C. Vann Woodward identified Tennessee's Redeemers as former Whigs who had little connection to the old planter aristocracy of the state, observing that "in the main they were of middle-class, industrial, capitalistic outlook." This was substantially, but not completely, true of John C. Brown. By at least 1869, Brown was indeed involved in railroad and other industrial interests. But by means of his marriage alliances with the Pointer and the Childress families, it cannot be said he had only a slight connection to the "old planter regime." Historian Roger Hart has more accurately observed that not all Tennessee Redeemers were Whig-industrialists, nor were all Whig-industrialists Redeemers. Brown and James D. Porter, who became governor in 1875, were chiefly railroad men *after* their time as Redeemer office holders. Hart appropriately observed that the Tennessee Redeemers, of whom Brown may be justly deemed the most prominent, came to power in large part based on the public's aversion to the excesses of both the Radicals and the secessionists.[31]

To Liberate . . . the True and Chivalrous Citizens

The new legislature had a prize plum to confer in October 1869, as the term of Senator Joseph M. Fowler, a Radical, was expiring. Brown's hometown *Citizen* expressed its preference for Brown, a "Hero, Patriot and Statesman." While a number of the Conservative newspapers endorsed Johnson, the former president was anathema to many Radicals and former Confederates. When the vote actually began, Johnson received the most votes, but election required a majority of both chambers combined. Etheridge, old Whig Balie Peyton, Neill, and several others got votes, with perhaps the most obscure candidate being state senator Henry Cooper, a lawyer, judge, and prewar state legislator. Henry Cooper was the brother of Edmund Cooper, whom Johnson had appointed to a position in his administration. Eventually Henry's name was withdrawn, bringing Johnson, on the last ballot of October 21, 1869, within four votes of election. That night, a collection of Johnson opponents met in a hotel room to come to an arrangement to defeat Johnson. They agreed to unite behind Henry Cooper, even though he had not been on the last ballot. Cooper won. An outraged Johnson later groused to Gideon Welles, "There never has been a greater outrage perpetrated on popular Sentiment Since the formation of the Government. Edmund Cooper's treachery on the night before the election who was elected pledged to my Support and the other votes he Carried with him for his brother conspired with the 'Radicals,' extreme 'Rebels' and the old Whigs. . . ." Johnson's allies in the press agreed with his view of "conspiracy," while the anti-Johnson Nashville *Republican Banner* noted that well-regarded public men had opposed Johnson, including Brown, Forrest, Peyton, Etheridge, and Harris. While Brown was not in the hotel meeting, he clearly worked for Johnson's defeat. Johnson was not a man to forget a slight of this nature.[32]

One other action of the new Conservative-majority legislature had a significant impact on Brown's future. On November 15, 1869, the legislature enacted a law providing for a referendum on the question of calling a constitutional convention, which was authorized by the voters on December 18, 1869. The new convention was essentially the culmination of the near decade of disruption of Tennessee's constitutional state government. In May and June 1861, under the leadership of Isham G. Harris, Tennessee's secessionists ignored constitutional niceties in ramming through the dissolution of the state's ties with the Union. At the beginning of 1865, a Unionist convention in Nashville resolved itself, with Military Governor Andrew Johnson's urging, into a constitutional convention and adopted "schedules" to the Constitution of 1834. Johnson brushed aside issues of constitutional legality as readily had his long time enemy, Harris, four years earlier. One of those schedules allowed the next legislature to establish voter qualifications, which naturally disenfranchised the former rebels. When revisited in 1869, these changes were deemed to be part of the constitution and were still in effect. The only way to relatively quickly address this issue was by means of a convention.[33]

The *Citizen* reported that a committee of citizens called upon Brown to become a candidate for the convention, based upon the general's "ability, honesty and patriotism, as well as your thorough knowledge of the wants of the people of the state . . ." Brown was willing to serve and was elected. Other prominent members of the convention included Neill, an ex-governor; James D. Porter, a staff officer of Cheatham's during the war, who would serve as governor in the future; prominent Unionist Whig John Netherland, who unsuccessfully opposed Isham G. Harris for governor in 1859; lawyer and former senator A. O. P. Nicholson, later the chief justice of the Tennessee Supreme Court; Chattanooga lawyer David M. Key, a former Confederate lieutenant colonel who would later serve as United States senator, Postmaster General, and federal judge; and fierce secessionist lawyer Joseph B. Heiskell, later the state attorney general. In the view of nineteenth-century Tennessee legal historian Joshua W. Caldwell, "[i]t was, probably, the most intellectual body of men that ever assembled in Tennessee for any purpose." Although former cavalryman General George Dibrell was a member, Brown was the highest ranking former Confederate soldier in the group. There were few Radicals, and no black delegates.[34]

While the convention was called to correct irregularity, there was an argument that it, too, was illegally approved, as all males over twenty-one, including those ostensibly disenfranchised by the 1865 schedule, were entitled to vote for it and for delegates. There was a further argument that some of the men elected to the convention were ineligible to serve under Section 3 of the Fourteenth Amendment, which disqualified large classes of former Confederates. William B. Stokes wrote a friend that he "would treat the whole thing as revolutionary and in violation of the laws of the State and the reconstruction acts of Congress." The members of the convention knew they were being watched, and the possibility of Federal intervention hung over the proceeding. Upon his election as president of the convention, Brown cautioned: "We cannot, *we must not*, be unmindful of the great changes that have impressed themselves upon our history. Let us accept the situation, and not seek to alter circumstances which have passed beyond our control."[35]

Brown's election as president was unanimous. There is no contemporary source that indicates any ulterior reason behind his election. Certainly, he was representative of the two strongest elements in the Conservative ranks in 1870, the former Confederates and the ex-Whigs. His resistance to the Radicals gave him credibility, as did his leading role in former Confederate generals' efforts to defuse a Radical military response in 1868. Some weeks before, the Nashville *Republican Banner* observed that, while Brown was "a representative man of the younger and more vigorous and progressive element of the Commonwealth, he also reflects and enjoys the confidence of its matured and experienced statesmanship. . . ." The Memphis *Avalanche* listed Brown among the luminaries of the convention, extolling him as "one of the rising men of Tennessee, destined to act a conspicuous part in the new era which is dawning." Clearly, Brown was in sympathy with and worked toward the goals of the other prominent men of the convention, including Neill, A. O. P. Nicholson, and John Netherland. Even though the Conservatives were not a true party, to the extent one existed, these men represented its moderate wing. And they had a clear goal: the convention was not called because of any widespread recognition that sweeping changes were needed in the state's fundamental law. Indeed, the final version contained few substantial departures from the Constitution of 1834. Rather, the convention was ultimately called to confirm Conservative control of the machinery of state government, cementing the *coup*, as one historian termed it, brought about by the irregular, if not blatantly illegal, votes of the former rebels to elect Senter. As legal historian Joshua W. Caldwell observed, the convention "was really a political expedient" for that purpose, as well as giving the former rebels "an opportunity to show that they accepted the results of the war."[36]

John C. Brown at the time of the Constitutional Convention (Credit: Tennessee State Library and Archives/ Courtesy of Tennessee Historical Society)

While the convention took several weeks to complete its work, the central issue was the franchise. Restoration of universal suffrage for white males was a given. The primary issue, even with the knowledge that the Radicals were ready to pounce, was whether to allow the blacks to continue to vote. As president, Brown assigned chairmanship of the Committee on Elections and Right of Suffrage to Nicholson, an old states' rights Democrat, and placed Neill on the committee. Both men were not only known statewide, but also had national reputations. Two other well-known members were Unionist A. A. Kyle and the moderate David M. Key. The committee produced both a majority and a minority report, which were debated extensively. The essence of the majority report was that no distinction as to race would be made for voter eligibility, that the issue of black suffrage should not be the subject of a separate referendum, and that the legislature might impose a poll tax as a condition of the franchise. A four-delegate minority, led by James Fentress, an "ultra, radical and rampant" Confederate veteran, and Humphrey R. Bate, a connection

To Liberate . . . the True and Chivalrous Citizens

of General Bate, held in their minority report that the blacks were "the lowest order of human beings" and not entitled to the vote, and that the "Convention should not be moved by fear of arbitrary power" in denying the vote.[37]

The convention took up the question on January 24, 1870, and from the chair, Brown observed that they had reached the "most important business of the session" and that there would be no limits on debate. In response to a jeremiad against suffrage, Neill spoke eloquently to the effect that the blacks had been promised that their right to vote would not be removed, that Tennessee intended to abide by the result of the war, and that the federal government had determined that the blacks would have these rights. Practically speaking, he contended that Tennessee needed the issue resolved and that the white majority had tens of thousands more votes in any event. If the vote were denied, the result would be a disaster, as there was an inclination in Washington to "interfere" with Tennessee. Neill did not want to "act out of fear, but of discretion." The debate went on for four days, supporters of the minority report contending that theirs was a "white man's government," supporters of suffrage more often than not conceding the purported inferiority of the blacks, but claiming fairness, past promises, the Fourteenth Amendment, and the threat of Federal interference required extending the vote. Nicholson made the last speech on January 27, and he premised it on two lines of argument. The first related to fairness. All had complained when the whites were disenfranchised and yet the minority wanted to do the same to the blacks in the new constitution. Furthermore, taxation of the blacks without representation was unjust, and they in fact had all the rights of citizens under the Fourteenth Amendment. As to the arguments relating to states' rights and the inferiority of the blacks, while Nicholson deemed them to be "great truths and principles," they were "crushed to earth" by the power of the Federal government. The convention voted the minority report down by an over 2–1 margin. A fellow delegate noted Brown was ill that afternoon, but asked for leave to record his vote on his return. The next day, Brown voted against the minority report, observing that the issue of universal suffrage had been "preached over the whole State" the previous three years and that it was a question "that should be settled finally and forever."[38]

The majority report also provided for a poll tax. Ironically, the existing constitution exempted "all free men of color" from paying a poll tax. While some saw the tax as the "best escape from unlimited negro suffrage," many saw it as simply a revenue measure. There is no question the poll tax was employed across the South to disenfranchise black voters in the last years of the nineteenth century. Notably, the only black-edited newspaper in the state, the Maryville *Republican*, had no objection to the tax. Historian Roger Hart found that delegates with more of a mercantile bent favored the tax as a revenue measure. A much more recent study, however, found that delegates from counties where blacks made up a greater proportion of potential voters were more likely to support the poll tax, and concluded that the provision was racially motivated. Both of the Brown brothers voted in favor of the tax. White opponents viewed the tax as restrictive of the franchise and discriminatory of the poor man's right to vote. Andrew Johnson made it known that he opposed the proposed constitution on this ground, and one of his primary allies, George W. Jones of Lincoln County, angrily left the convention.[39]

Nicholson predicted that the work of 1870 would have to be revisited in ten years, yet that document, which was in many particulars that of 1834, survived several decades without amendment. While there were other changes to the Constitution of 1834, the more notable were addressed to the perceived evils visited on the state by the Radicals, such as the lending of the credit of the state to private interests and the requirements for calling out the militia. The lawyers among the delegates fought for several weeks over a number of issues, and Brown joined in where he thought it appropriate, but his role as chair limited his participation in the debates. His most vociferous argument was in opposition to a schedule in the new constitution that removed all of the members of the judiciary then in office, who were mostly Radicals. Brown feared it would set a precedent for the future, when a new convention might do the very same thing, "without any reason save that these men were elected under a different party." There was no previous example, Brown argued, for such a wholesale change. Again, with the threat of Federal intervention hanging over the convention, Brown was unafraid to raise "questions of expediency and policy" when the rights of the men who followed him in the war were "imperiled." In his view, and in the view of a minority

To Liberate . . . the True and Chivalrous Citizens

of others, it might be seen as a means for intervention. Notwithstanding Brown's protest, the schedule passed.[40]

The delegates completed their work on February 23, 1870, after thirty-nine days. After offering a short amendment that was unanimously adopted, Nicholson rose and offered a resolution of thanks to Brown "for the courtesy, promptness, impartiality and ability with which he has discharged the duties of presiding officer." Brown responded with a short speech complimenting the other members, noting that the fruit of their labors "had been to liberate one hundred thousand of the true and chivalrous citizens of the State." With the exception of the departed Jones and seven Radicals, the delegates signed the document. The paper was then ceremoniously carried to the capitol. The work of the convention was done.[41]

Brown returned to his district and campaigned for the approval of the new constitution, which was ratified by a vote of 98,128 to 33,972 on March 26. While the only black-edited newspaper in the state endorsed the document, it appears a number of blacks voted against it because of the poll tax and its cementing the power of the white majority. Efforts were made to convince the authorities in Washington to intervene, and Governor Senter, alarmed by a spike in violence of a Ku-Klux nature, requested Federal troops. These efforts failed, and the threat of military reconstruction faded. Brown discharged his final duty relating to the constitutional convention on May 5, when he met with Senter and D. B. Thomas, the Speaker of the Senate, to certify the ratification vote.[42]

Old comrades, living and dead, were at the forefront that spring. On April 26, a delegation arrived in Columbia, Tennessee, to exhume Patrick Cleburne from his grave at nearby St. John's, Ashwood and return him to his adopted home in Helena, Arkansas. Local veterans organized appropriate honors, and the next day Brown rode in a dignified procession that accompanied the Irishman's remains to the train depot. Living comrades, on the other hand, were a problem. With his high public profile enhanced by his leadership at the convention, Brown was clearly a potential Conservative nominee for governor in the election to be held in November. The names most prominently mentioned with Brown included another fellow Franklin casualty, William A. Quarles, and William B. Bate, both of whom assumed prominent roles with Brown in the generals' approach to the legislature in 1868. Both were Democrats and prewar secessionists.[43]

Another candidate was Arthur S. Colyar, an old-line Whig, lawyer, mineral extraction businessman, and former Confederate congressman. Colyar wrote Andrew Johnson in May that he was conferring with a few friends on whether he should run for governor. He indicated that Bate and Brown wanted to run and would likely split a convention, in which case "Bate will out manage Brown and Brown's friends will be in bad humor." Colyar was not alone in courting the former president, as Quarles also sought his support and appears to have been more successful, as Johnson made a personal appearance with the former rebel general in Greeneville. As Bate was the "heart's best friend" of the Isham Harris wing of the prewar Democracy, Quarles courted Johnson as a counterweight.[44]

Opposition to the Radicals united old-line Whigs and Democrats of both the Unionist and secessionist stripes. The question would be whether this alliance of Redeemers could coalesce into a true political party. There is certainly evidence that some former Whigs were ready to break away in the 1869–1872 interval, but the more prominent of the former Whigs seemed ready to hold their noses and continue cooperation with the Democrats. An early test was the election of a new Supreme Court, which was to occur under the new constitution in August 1870. A Conservative nominating convention met in Nashville on July 11 and, in less than a day, nominated six candidates, which included two Unionists, two former Confederate colonels, a former Whig who served in the Provisional Army of Tennessee, and Nicholson. While there was a prevalence of prior Confederate allegiance, the equal mix of former Whigs and Democrats suggested the two factions were effectively working together.[45]

The judicial convention was carefully not styled a Democratic convention. As the summer wore on, however, the recognition that the Conservatives would have to go forward under the name of the Democratic Party began to dawn on both factions. Conservative leaders and the Conservative press emphasized it was a simply a matter of expediency, doubtless to quiet the fears of old-line Whigs about the resurrection of the "Buchanan-Breckinridge-Isham-G.-Harris-Democracy of 1860." Old Whigs such as Emerson Etheridge, W. H. Stephens, Gustavus A. Henry, and John Netherland all spoke in terms of the newly-forged alliance. Etheridge stated that there were just two parties, which were "formed immediately after the surrender in 1865. . . ." Netherland wrote: "We have now but two parties, the Radicals and their opponents—some say let the Whigs 'withdraw.' I ask where will they go? There is but one other room, and that is occupied by the Radicals. If Whigs go in that room they will sleep cold." Representing the old Democrats, Johnson also emphasized that there could only be two parties, the Democrat and Republican.[46]

Quarles reported to Johnson that he surmised that Brown and his supporters had "determined to feel their way." If they thought Brown strong enough to obtain the Conservative nomination they would go that route, and if not, "they will declare him an independent Candidate trusting to the Radical Vote." Perceiving a hope to split the Conservatives, the *Union and American* noted that certain newspapers, which were supporting Brown "because he has not the smell of the Johnson or the Harris-secession Democracy on his garments," were taking every opportunity to "injure" both sides of the old Democrats, and Brown therefore could not expect the help of either the Johnson or Harris factions if his "organs" continued. The other significant Conservative paper in Tennessee, the Memphis *Daily Appeal* agreed, observing that these few papers had the right to support Brown, "toward whom we entertain the kindest feelings, and would express no opposition to his nomination." But the "malignant old Whigs" who edited them were "doing [Brown] serious injury . . . his aspirations cannot be propitiated by [attacking] General William A. Quarles and abusing other prominent Democrats."[47]

Doubtless seeing the threat, the *Pulaski Citizen* angrily denied that Brown was considering a third party route and that he opposed a Conservative convention, trumpeting that Brown "takes a manly stand upon the platform and principles enunciated by the Democratic members of Congress. He denounces all efforts to create a third party in the State, and would scorn a nomination tendered by them." Parroting the old-line Whig narrative, Brown stated: "The great point I wish to impress upon you is, I care nothing for party names, but I am a sincere, earnest and hearty hater of Tennessee Radicalism." Neill also did his part, joining other former Whig luminaries in agreeing the old party labels were defunct. In his view, as the question of slavery was settled by the war, there were no "living issue between Whigs and Democrats that may prevent their joint action." Brown traveled about the state with the same message.[48]

As the three generals (and Colyar) maneuvered in the summer of 1870, a legal issue arose that was decidedly in Brown's favor. The Fourteenth Amendment to the United States Constitution became effective on July 28, 1868. Section 3 of the amendment provided that no one who had previously taken an oath to support the Constitution of the United States who had later been in rebellion against the government could hold state or federal office without a congressional vote to remove that "disability." While the effect of the amendment had been raised and debated in Tennessee politics in the past, it became a significant issue on May 31, 1870, when Congress passed the Enforcement Act of 1870, making the provision operative by providing a means to punish and remove officeholders who were under the disability.[49]

Bate, a prewar member of the Tennessee General Assembly and district attorney, clearly was affected by this provision, although his adherents urged otherwise. Quarles argued that a temporary appointment to replace a sick judge prior to the war did not make him the regular officeholder of that position, which meant he was not disqualified as a former "judicial officer." Although he had served as a Confederate congressman, Colyar had held no disqualifying prewar office. Brown's having held municipal office in Pulaski seems to have been of no consequence. Further, Colyar, like Brown, had received a presidential pardon from Andrew Johnson, and the unique nature of a pardon was argued by some (and confirmed some years later by the United States attorney general) to have legally made the pardoned person innocent of any offenses arising from the rebellion before the ratification of the Fourteenth Amendment. It appeared to some Conservatives that electing a person who might be challenged on the basis of Section 3 of the Fourteenth Amendment was foolishness. Although the Memphis *Daily Appeal* was a strong supporter of Bate, and to a slightly lesser extent Quarles, its editor wrote "we must commit no blunders, we must run no risks." A practical approach required Conservatives to "accept the situation" and choose the most qualified men "who are free from the disability a fiendish diabolism has thrown around our best citizens."[50]

Bate was the first to bow out. On July 27, the former general announced he was no longer a candidate, based upon the legal disability. He expressed regret that the constitutional convention had required an election in 1870 for a governor who would not take office until 1871, feeling that the disability issue might be cleared up in the interval. But, in keeping with the Conservative line that Whigs and Democrats had a strong common interest, Bate said he could not "distinguish the features of Whig and Democrat through the battle smoke of four years of strife." Quarles held on for another few weeks, but Brown's affirmative disclaimer of a third party candidacy and willingness to support a convention doubtless had an effect. The contending parties, at least in Colyar's view, appear to have reached an arrangement. Assured by both the public and likely the private pronouncements of the leaders of his core supporters, the old-line Whigs, Brown announced himself a Democrat in a letter published on August 27, 1870, holding that "no middle ground can be occupied" between the Radicals and the Democrats. The next day, Quarles withdrew, declining to "give strength" to the Radicals "by petty jealousies and personal rivalries." This meant, in the words of one Conservative West Tennessee newspaper, that there was "no division of the true men of the State. . . ."[51]

Brown was the unanimous selection of the state Democratic convention held on September 11, 1870, and accepted the nomination "to bear your standard in the great fight against Radicalism." Ten days later, the Radicals held their nominating convention, which was at least much more harmonious than the previous one. Senter was not a candidate. In the words of Judge O. P. Temple, "[t]he Democratic Party had no further use for him, and the Republicans did not forgive him for his course in 1869." Their nominee was William A. Wisener of Bedford County, an editor and lawyer who was a frequent member of the General Assembly. Wisener was a Unionist, although gleeful Democratic editors found that he had voted for a number of the secessionist measures of the 1861 General Assembly, which made them suggest that he should petition Congress for removal of his own political disability. Colyar, for the time being, went forward with his independent candidacy, with the shadowy support of Andrew Johnson, who slyly suggested Brown and his supporters had not repudiated secession.[52]

The relative lateness of the two conventions cut the campaign short. Brown announced a series of appointments in East Tennessee, inviting Wisener to attend. The general appeared at Chattanooga on October 1, but Wisener, on the basis of a misunderstanding, did not. Brown accordingly addressed Johnson's allegations of secessionism, claiming that it was a doctrine that was dead and furled with the last Confederate flag. He accused those who brought it up of wanting to divert Union men away from the anti-Radical cause. After going through his party platform, Brown claimed it contained doctrines from Andrew Jackson, Henry Clay, Stephen A. Douglas, Abraham Lincoln, and even Wisener himself. Thus, the platform was one with which all who opposed Radicalism could agree. Colyar was present and made a few remarks, promising to define his platform soon. He then announced that what he heard from Brown at Chattanooga convinced him that there was "substantially no difference in the views they entertained as to State and national policy."[53]

Wisener and Brown had their initial meeting of the campaign in Knoxville on October 6. According to the Wisener-sympathizing Knoxville *Daily Chronicle*, Brown said he was only a rebel from 1861 to 1865 and that secession was dead. He attacked the Radicals for running up the public debt, and condemned the government of the United States as a "central despotism." Wisener, said the *Chronicle*, noted that Brown had confessed to being a rebel, that he had shackled the voters with his position on the poll tax in the convention, and noted that much of the state debt related to railroads, of which Brown was a large investor. On October 11, they met again at Jonesboro, and Brown stuck to his rather ponderous review of his party's platform, pausing here and there to take a shot at Wisener or his party. The men met again at Nashville on October 23, and the *Union and American* gushed that Brown's "review of Radicalism, and especially of the record of its chosen champion, is scathing in its effect and almost leads us to regret that so benevolent looking a gentleman as Mr. Wisener should have sought such an excoriation." Subsequent debates occurred in Pulaski, Franklin, Gallatin, Winchester, Shelbyville, Murfreesboro, Humboldt, Huntington, Jackson, and Brownsville. At their last meeting in Memphis, the speeches went on for over four hours, and in the view of the reporter for the *Public Led-*

ger, were "conducted fairly, and with the civilities and politeness that belonged to politics of the old school."[54]

Brown was elected on November 8, 1870, by a vote of 78,979 to 41,500. The total vote for governor of 120,479 was significantly less than 1859's 144,113 and 1869's 175,389 (when black voters must be considered), and was even less than the approximately 132,000 votes cast in the ratification vote on the new constitution. Several factors may have played into the lower vote. The most simple was that the winner was to take office almost a year later, which likely affected enthusiasm on both sides. On the Conservative side, the uneasy alliance between Democrats and old-line Whigs likely had much to do with the tepid turnout. Future Republican gubernatorial candidate Alfred A. Freeman wrote a friend there were "thousands of honest men in Tennessee who were never Democrats at heart, men who are conservative in their feeling and have been driven to act with that party by what was regarded as the proscriptive policy of our party." These men likely had a hard time voting for a self-proclaimed Democrat. On the other hand, a number of prewar Democrats of both the secessionist and Unionist stripes could not forget Brown had been a Whig, and Neill a mainstay of that party. On the Radical side, a number of voters were likely still stinging from the bitterness of the Senter/Stokes contest.[55]

The "new" Democratic Party, made up of old-line Whigs and Democrats, secessionists and Unionists, also won a significant majority in the General Assembly, and six of the state's eight congressional seats. The resounding result made the Knoxville *Whig and Register* rhetorically wonder whether Congress could reconstruct a southern state "because it votes for the Democracy." While this was a whimsical inquiry, the fear of interference from Washington, though muted, obviously still lingered. But there appears to have been minimal stir over the result in the North. The Democratic sweep was, in the words of a Philadelphia newspaper, "anticipated." The St. Louis *Republican* said: "The people of Tennessee need not apologize for their governor-elect." Prior to the election, a Radical-leaning correspondent was quoted in a northern paper that Brown "has been mild, conciliating, just, generous and liberal, without becoming a Radical. He is a good man, in the broad meaning of the word, and if made

Governor, as he undoubtedly will be, will see that the rights of the humblest are not infringed upon."[56]

While his political endeavors garnered the most public attention, Brown had a rich personal and professional life. Two more daughters were born in these years, Daisy on April 23, 1868, and Elizabeth, who the family came to call "Birdie," on March 8, 1870. Brown continued with his law practice and obtained a large judgment for the estate of his former father-in-law, John H. Pointer, against General Gideon Pillow. He supported several community projects around Pulaski. The general continued his ascent in Masonic leadership, attaining status as a Knight Templar and Knight of Pythias. Brown's reaching the office of Most Worshipful Grand Master of the state in 1870 coincided with his gaining the leadership of the Conservative party. At some point, probably in 1869, he was offered a commission in the army of the Khedive of Egypt, and even wrote a novel, although it is lost.[57]

The governor-elect could only hope that his administration would have a better start than the conclusion, for the time being, of his life as a private citizen. The Browns had recently purchased a new home in Pulaski, but were living in their old home as tenants. On Sunday, September 10, 1871, a fire broke out and rapidly spread through the residence. There apparently was a greater loss on this occasion, as Brown some years later wrote that "most" of his "army papers" were burned. To make matters worse, Brown was struck with a sudden illness of an unspecified but very painful nature. One report indicated that the illness was brought about by the exertion and excitement of the fire. His condition deteriorated to the point a telegram was dispatched to summon Neill to his bedside. Despite that ominous sign, after a period of about ten days, Brown was reported to be recovering and was well enough to check into the Maxwell House in Nashville with his family on September 30. 1871.[58]

In reaching the governor's chair, Brown was able to capitalize on a number of advantages. He was known statewide not only as a former Confederate general, but also as a leader in the Masonic ranks. Although it is difficult to quantify, he had the advantages of family connections, not only Neill, but also the Pointers and the Childresses, the latter of which gained him the patronage of Sarah Polk. The former general had been prominent in the anti-Radical resistance, and thus the Conservative ranks,

To Liberate . . . the True and Chivalrous Citizens

but could claim he had done so not as an un-repentant secessionist, but because former Whigs who opposed disfranchisement had nowhere else to go. As is often the case, timing was important as well. His non-disqualification by the Fourteenth Amendment and the time at which the gubernatorial election in 1870 was held played a significant part in keeping his other former Confederate rivals at bay, as Bate was not loathe to note. Finally, Brown was at the right age to assert himself as one of a new generation of leaders for a redeemed, postwar state.

Although the Democrats had control of the courts and the General Assembly, Brown's assumption of the governor's chair completed the process that his predecessor, De Witt Clinton Senter, began in 1869. Brown did his part, both in the light and in the shadows, to bring things to that point. While Senter had opened the door, Brown, along with Neill, Nicholson, Netherland, and the other more moderate members of the anti-Radical coalition indeed deserved the title of Redeemers, as their recognition of what was at least minimally required by those in power in Washington helped keep Tennessee under local control. This was recognized by the editors of the Nashville *Banner* as Brown prepared to take office, and the paper quoted the governor-elect's admonition to the delegates of the constitutional convention that they should not unrealistically ignore the "great changes that have impressed themselves upon our history." The *Banner* deemed this the "spirit that will actuate the new Executive in the duties of his office, and characterize his administration. May it be attended by the happiest results to the State at large and add new laurels to the brilliant reputation which he has attained and enjoys in his private and public life, is the earnest wish of all good citizens and friends of Tennessee."[59]

7

To Improve the Present and Secure the Future

October 1871 to December 1875

The residents of Middle Tennessee saw Tuesday, October 10, 1871, open in a mixture of the unsettled and mundane. Representing the unsettled, Nashville was struck with heavy rains that morning, and it remained cloudy all day. The *Union and American* blared sensational headlines relating to the great fire then going on at Chicago, including "Sodom and Gomorrah Eclipsed" and "Hundreds Find Fiery Graves." Readers learned that an earthquake rocked the East coast, that a steamer sank at Cairo, Illinois, and that there was a race riot in Philadelphia. Representing the mundane, the chancellors of the state, trial judges with equity jurisdiction, were meeting in Nashville to establish a body of rules for practice; to the north, a good crowd braved the rain for the opening of the Robertson County Fair; to the south, work began on the new railroad depot at Pulaski.[1]

For the state's Democrats, these events, serious as some of them were, shrank in significance to their first full resumption of power since March 1862. The rain could not dampen their satisfaction when, at 11:30 a.m., the governor-elect, John Calvin Brown, accompanied by Governor Senter, Justice Peter Turney of the Supreme Court, the Speakers of both houses, former governors Neill Brown and Isham Harris, and designated members of both houses, progressed to the speaker's stand in the hall of the House of the Representatives in the capitol. After an opening prayer, a band played "Dixie." To frequent applause, outgoing Governor Senter took his leave of those assembled and expressed his hope to Brown that his "administration [would] be marked as peaceful, as prosperous and as happy as the people who elected you deserve."[2]

Brown began his speech by making reference to the desperate condition of the state brought about by its government after the termination of the war, noting the restriction of the suffrage, the expense of Brownlow's State Guard, the huge increase in the public debt, and squandering of public money by "violent partisans" and "a swarm of nomadic adventurers." Brown graciously noted, however, that Senter's two years of "wise administration," along with "conservative legislation," had done much to restore the public confidence. Restoring the public credit while relieving the public of burdensome taxation was at the forefront of his concerns, and under the new constitution, the legislature had the duty to address these issues. Brown pledged to assist the lawmakers with information, recommendations, and the execution of their legislation. While there was much work to do, there was the promise of the future:

> The bright face of hope peers out from the breaking
> clouds, and white-winged peace casts her soft shadows
> upon the rude footprints of war. With the recital of our
> wrongs let us forget them and bury forever the acrimo-
> nies they have engendered. Let us shape our policy not
> so much to criticize or justify the past as to improve the
> present and secure the future. Although success has over-
> whelmingly crowned the united effort of the people of
> Tennessee in their first political struggle after the resto-
> ration of the ballot, yet the fruits of that victory may be
> lost if we are not harmonious in sentiment and united
> in purpose.

After loud applause, Justice Turney administered the oath of office, and the band played "Hail Columbia." After a closing prayer, the band played again while Brown went to take possession of the governor's office and to receive well-wishers. The day closed with a private dinner at the Maxwell House with Senter, the Speakers, Harris, Neill, and a few other friends.[3]

Delayed by yet another illness—in this case, cholera—the new governor delivered his first message to the General Assembly two weeks later. In a businesslike fashion, he immediately launched into the issue of the state's debt. After certain credits and adjustments, Brown reported that the state had a bonded debt, with interest to January 1, 1872, of

$19,493,173.66. There was an additional "floating debt," or short-term debt, of $1,668,417.27, which the state had to immediately reduce, as well as the current expense of operating the state government of about $600,000 a year. The state was also legally required to pay notes from the Bank of Tennessee, as well as other miscellaneous costs. The greatest portion of this debt arose from both prewar and postwar state aid to railroads, which were expected to perform and pay the bonds issued by the state. Unfortunately, the destruction wrought by the war, funding failing railroads with new debt, and varying degrees of fraud and mismanagement in the immediate postwar years exacerbated the problem.[4]

Exhaustively reviewing the financial resources of the state, Brown argued that new sources of revenue were necessary, and he made several suggestions for legislation to effect the same, including new litigation taxes, taxing the execution of trustees' bonds, and taxing the bonds of local governments. Brown also suggested improvements for tax assessment and tax collection. He suggested that the legislature repeal the measure that allowed solvent railroads to pay off their debt in any state indebtedness, to avoid the possibility of "speculative transactions." As to the delinquent roads, Brown ruefully noted "[i]t will be a gratifying result when the State is entirely divorced from the railroad system." While their final sale would be at a loss, he felt it proper to acknowledge that the internal improvements achieved by the expenditure of state monies in their development were in sum beneficial.[5]

The new governor's determination to attack the debt question rang through his message. "The people are determined to preserve the honor of the State by meeting fairly all her obligations, and paying all her necessary expenses. This is their first desire, and secondary and subordinate to this, is their wish to reduce the rate of taxation." He argued, as he would many times in the future, that the question was fully discussed during the 1870 election, and "the declaration that the whole debt must be paid, met with the unqualified indorsement [sic] of the people." As events would prove, Brown made a strong state credit position the hallmark of his administration and would defend his actions in that regard to the bitter end.[6]

Neill Brown had a deep influence on his brother's political views. When Neill took office as governor in October 1847, his inaugural address called for rivers to be opened and roads constructed "to connect the markets of the world with our great interior." The elder Brown stated that "while I feel a decided zeal for all measures that may conduce to the development of the State, morally, physically, and intellectually, I have not less zeal for the preservation of the public faith. The obligations of the State are paramount, and must be promptly met, 'without sale, denial or delay.'" Repudiation, according to Neill, was "a doctrine founded in bad morals; dictated by a false and unwise policy; destructive and ruinous in its consequences; behind the present age; unworthy of the American character, and beneath the dignity of the Anglo-Saxon race." Against this ideological background, the practical argument was made that needed out-of-state capital would avoid investment in Tennessee should the state repudiate its debt. Further, as the younger Brown was to frequently advance, the fact that both parties advocated payment of the debt in the 1870 election was a clear indication that there was a wide consensus in 1871 on the wisdom of the policy.[7]

Notwithstanding this consensus, Governor Brown's initial messages on the subject were assailed from both sides. Senator Brownlow called Brown the "Rebel Governor of Tennessee" and charged that the state debt was the result of spending on the Confederate war effort. While a shrill response from the Radicals was to be expected, an otherwise friendly Democratic organ, the Memphis *Daily Appeal*, interpreted Brown's message as a call for higher taxes. Despite its disapproval, the paper gushed "the people of Tennessee will still love and cherish in their memories the gallant soldier who led their armies on so many glorious fields." A day later, though, the *Appeal* huffed that the people were not at fault for the debt and charged that "the interest of the toiling multitude be sacrificed to Governor Brown's pride of office. . . ." Other Democratic organs were quick to come to Brown's defense, the Nashville *Union and American* arguing that the burden of taxation came from the Radicals, not Brown. That paper later stated that Brown was not advocating a rise in taxes, and quoted from the *Memphis Press*: "The intimation that he has been influenced by other than the purest motives is too contemptible to call for defense at his hands, or in the press of the State." Opinion from the *Gallatin Examiner* posited, "no one on earth who knows Gov. Brown believes that he is capable of being anybody's tool, or that he would swerve a hair's breadth from what he thinks is right . . . ," and the *Columbia Herald* was quoted as stating, "The *Appeal* cannot more earnestly desire the relief of our people from the burdens of oppressive taxation than does Gov. Brown. He only wants taxation at a point that will maintain the State government and protect its credit—its financial honor and integrity."[8]

The first effort at debt reduction was unsuccessful. Brown backed a tax rate of fifty cents on each one hundred dollars' worth of taxable property, called for the resumption of interest payments as of January 1, 1874, and the issuance of new bonds to fund the principal and interest (not paid since 1868) on debt prior to that date. The tax rate climbed under the Radical regime from twenty five cents in 1865 to sixty cents in 1869, so Brown's proposal was actually a decrease. A minority report in the House Committee on Finance argued for thirty cents, although the revenue and expense numbers clearly demonstrated that without the occurrence of some very unlikely circumstances, the state would not break even. In the debate in the House, the advocates of the higher rate argued its necessity, while the advocates of the lower rate, complaining of the burden of taxation, argued its sufficiency. Eventually, the legislature adopted a compromise of forty cents. But no new bonds were authorized, and there was essentially no funding to resume interest payments.[9]

A law passed in the previous legislature liquidated whatever supervisory role the state government had in the educational process, leaving it to the counties. This was done in a fit of partisan reprisal toward the Radical Superintendent of Public Instruction rather than with any salutary intent. Brown observed that there were still "a large number of children in the State deprived of instruction in the ordinary principles of English education." In the debate, the issue of the School Fund, a recurring phantom of postwar Tennessee politics, was once more raised. Prior to the war, among the state funds deposited with the Bank of Tennessee was the School Fund, a constitutionally required fund intended to generate interest to fund the common school system. In 1861, it amounted to about a million and a half dollars. For years, the issue of the fund was a political football, one side or the other being accused of stealing the fund. Isham G. Harris, governor when the war started, was a particular target, as the fund was in a sense in his custody before the war and "missing" after the war. While Harris was the agent of the fund's demise, it was only in the sense that the fund was one of the deposits in the Bank of Tennessee when Harris strong-armed the bank into purchasing state bonds made worthless by the Confederate defeat. An effort to reestablish the fund fell short, marking the end of any legislative effort toward education for the 1871 session.[10]

Another pressing issue was the state's penal system. Brown deferred addressing the issue in his original message to the legislature, requiring some time to investigate. In the first days of November, Brown took steps to ascertain the status of the system. By way of background, beginning in 1865, the state leased the labor of convicts at the penitentiary at Nashville to small contractors, who used the labor to produce various farm machinery and implements on site at the prison. This approach was largely unsuccessful, as a fire inside the prison disrupted the contract at significant expense to the state. As a result of legislation enacted in 1870, in early 1871 many convicts were moved from the prison to the coal mines on the Cumberland Plateau in Grundy and Marion counties operated by A. S. Colyar's Tennessee Coal and Railroad Company. The free laborers objected to working with the convicts, and there was initially some unrest among both groups, but eventually production was resumed.[11]

There was doubtless a racial component to the unrest, as 496 of the state's 739 prisoners in 1871 were black, and generally black convicts were employed outside the prison in unskilled work such as mining. There was a significant labor relations consideration for the mine operators as well, as the use of the convicts' reduced labor costs in a direct sense, and also in the sense of discouraging free laborers from agitating for higher wages. From the state's standpoint, the leasing of convict labor eased the financial burden of operating the penal system at a time when money was an overarching issue. That bore great weight with the new governor. Brown acknowledged the complaints of the free laborers, but observed "while many branches of industry complain of a competition from this labor, the tax-payer is justly clamorous that it should sustain itself." To his credit, before Brown recommended a new long-term lease, he journeyed to the plateau to see how the convicts were being used in the mines and made inquiries as to the prisoners' clothing contracts, their legalities, and

To Improve the Present and Secure the Future

the "actual results" attained by employing contract labor in the mines. News of the governor's inquiries made it inside the prison walls, and he received correspondence from a prisoner complaining of "brutal" conditions there.[12]

As governor, Brown had a wide range of duties. In the first few weeks of his administration, he was inundated with hundreds of visits and petitions seeking pardons for incarcerated persons. He received numerous letters requesting appointment to jobs within his power to fill. State attorney general Joseph B. Heiskell advised him on the constitutionality of an income tax. He consulted on political issues with Democratic leaders, such as former governor Harris, Quarles, Bate, and East Tennessee Democratic newspaper editor John M. Fleming. Brown's alliance with Harris and his former rebel comrades did not insulate him from criticism in the party, some Democrats feeling "[t]he old Whig still sticks out in him." East Tennessee Democrat John Williams reported the smoldering resentment harbored by Andrew Johnson, who disliked a reference to him made by Brown in a speech in Memphis and planned a reply. An article in the unfriendly Knoxville *Weekly Chronicle* provided some detail on the issues with Johnson. During the gubernatorial campaign, Brown visited Johnson and expressed his gratitude for the pardon he received. Johnson accused Brown of taking a stand against him in the 1869 senate election, which Brown could not deny. Their parting was "cold" and they had had no contact since. The offensive reference to which Williams referred was Brown's reportedly calling Johnson a "malcontent and political harlot." Williams assured Brown that "Mr. Johnson is not a malignant man, as many suppose him to be. On the contrary, is forgiving in a high degree, and is willing to yield to others in whom he has confidence." Williams felt the former president had such confidence in former congressman George W. Jones, newspaperman John C. Burch, and Williams himself, and promised, "If you will give me all the facts of the case, I will write to him. His speech can do no good politically, as Jones suggests, but may do much harm." Brown's reply is lost, although there is no evidence Johnson was mollified.[13]

The General Assembly adjourned on December 16, 1871. It accomplished very little on the large issues facing the state, but continued the political purge of the Radicals. In light of the 1870 census, the Democrats passed a new law to apportion the state legislative districts, with one senator admitting the rank political goal to "so redistrict the state that for the next ten years not a Republican could be elected to the Legislature of Tennessee." The Democratic Nashville *Union and American* admitted that "this legislature has not, in every particular, accomplished all they aimed at, and all the people desired," but offered that the members were conscientious in making quorums, not being "dissipated" in the house or in the street, and generally showed good character while in session.[14]

Brown worked late into the night reviewing and signing bills passed by the General Assembly, and after the legislature adjourned, worked to cancel the bonds being turned in, to the point that he apologized to Gen. John C. Vaughn, the Speaker of the Senate, for not responding to his request that Brown appoint Vaughn's son-in-law as warden of the state penitentiary, confessing that "[i]t is the hardest job I ever undertook in my life." Fortunately, Brown's often uncertain health was unaffected, and he and Bettie found time to attend a lavish Christmas party at the Maxwell House. Brown's friends at the *Pulaski Citizen* observed that Brown kept his "Chesterfieldian suavity" despite his exalted status, noting that the governor "greets and is greeted by all his people with the greatest pleasure, exhibiting that inimitable consummation of urbanity peculiar to Tennessee's noblest son."[15]

Brown's senior staff as governor appears to have been solely his private secretary, John S. Wilkes, who also served as the state adjutant general. A native of Maury County, Wilkes was born in 1841 and was the son of a prominent politician. Wilkes joined Company A of the 3rd Tennessee in May 1861 and served as commissary for most of the war. After the surrender, he returned to Pulaski, read law in Brown's office, and joined Brown when he became governor. Wilkes's wartime duties made him a very competent accountant, which in turn made him a significant help to Brown in understanding and approaching the state debt situation.[16]

The operation of the new constitution made 1872 an election year for Brown's seat. Quarles, Bate, and Johnson were considered rivals. As the leading candidate, Brown was subject to calumnies from the political opposition, such as the claim from a Radical newspaper that he was shirking his duties to organize Knights of Pythias chapters all over the state, a charge the loyal *Union and American* refuted. He also kept in touch with national politics, as his friend Congressman Washington C. Whitthorne wrote from Washington that a meeting of the labor reformers in Ohio was thought in Washington to "likely to have an important influence in shaping the policy of all parties." In the same letter, Whitthorne expressed amazement that "the Women's Rights Party is coming to be regarded as an element in political calculations."[17]

An act of Congress passed February 2, 1872, required apportionment of the state as a result of the census of 1870 into nine districts. This required a special session of the legislature, which Brown called for March 12, 1872, to reapportion the state and to consider leftover issues from the regular session and fourteen new matters. Lawfully, the special session could only last twenty days, making it unlikely that much would be accomplished. The session's main business, however, was addressed. In firm control, the Democrats carved out congressional districts blatantly calculated to deprive one of East Tennessee's fiercest Radicals, Horace Maynard, of his seat.[18]

Even during the special session in March, Brown's ordinary duties continued. Accompanied by the comptroller, treasurer, and secretary of state, Brown went to Knoxville to sell delinquent railroads at public auction, his presence being necessary for quorum of commissioners. Serenaded by admirers, the governor declined to give a speech as he was in Knoxville on official business. The governor's expressed hope that he would be back to discuss political issues was seen as an indication he was going to run for reelection. Back in Nashville, a white mob attacked the jail where a "negro murderer" by the name of Jones was being held, shot the man, and then hanged him, which the police claimed they were "powerless" to prevent. The city's mayor stopped at the Maxwell House and asked Brown to help. The governor addressed the crowd and admonished them against taking the law into their own hands. Politically, he alluded to the state's recent release from Radical rule and warned: "if such scenes like these are to be enacted, in the midst of peace and omnipotence of the civil law, I warn you now that your liberty will be short lived. There will be those who desire to subject you to the will of arbitrary power. They only desire a pretext, to place you under the rule of bristling bayonets and military satraps." The mob was soothed. The *Union and American* was not able to identify any of the lynchers, although it made sure to note some were black.[19]

As the special session ended, Democratic and Conservative members of the legislature met to discuss the political outlook and endorsed Brown for another term. More endorsements appeared in the *Murfreesboro Monitor*, the *Bolivar Bulletin*, and the *Cleveland Banner*. The *Chattanooga Times* deemed such talk premature, but wrote that "Tennessee never had a better governor," while a report from upper East Tennessee indicated enthusiasm for his reelection. The *Union and American* helpfully printed all of these, and also letters from individuals supporting the governor.[20]

Brown appeared to be well on his way to a second nomination when, on April 11, his old comrade, Benjamin Franklin Cheatham, published a card announcing his candidacy for the post. Cheatham asked that the Democratic nominating convention, then set for May 9, be postponed so he could travel the state to drum up support. As an ex-Confederate general, Cheatham was well-liked, but the consensus among Conservatives was that Brown was entitled to a second term. Their two main organs, the Nashville *Union and American* and Memphis *Daily Appeal*, both came out for Brown, and the *Union and American* published endorsements from Shelbyville, Rogersville, Jonesborough, Fayetteville, and Gallatin. The *Appeal* noted the custom in the state that "faithful public servants" would be renominated for a desired second term, and that Brown had done nothing to deserve an ignominious rejection. The Jackson *Whig and Tribune* succinctly stated "the political register foots up a large balance" in the governor's favor. Brown took active steps to meet with "leaders of public opinion," and the state Democratic Executive Committee helped by denying Cheatham's request to delay the convention, although the sometimes critical *Daily Memphis Avalanche* noted that Brown had nothing to do with that decision. Getting the message, Cheatham "prudently" withdrew.[21]

On May 9, the state Democratic convention met in Nashville with two goals in mind: to defeat President Ulysses S. Grant's bid for a second term and to maintain the party's political control over Tennessee. Tennessee Democrats joined with the national party in supporting the "Liberal Republican" ticket of New York newspaperman Horace Greeley and Missouri governor B. Gratz Brown. Because of his past virulent attacks on their party, Greeley was not a popular candidate among Democrats. But the Liberal Republicans were for a relaxed policy relating to the South, including amnesty for all ex-Confederates, effective restoration of white rule, and reining in the use of Federal power to aid the freedmen. Even Andrew Johnson, not a friend of the Liberal Republicans, proclaimed he would support Greeley "without regard to former antecedents." Unanimously renominated, John C. Brown spoke of the rights deprived the "best men of the South," the threat of Federal power for the past seven years, and the hope provided by the fracture in the Republican Party. For their part, the Radicals, or more properly at this point, the Republicans, met on May 15, and endorsed the Grant ticket. It was at that time "deemed the best policy" not to contest the governor's chair, even though one speaker urged that the party "make a bold, courageous fight, and drive John C. Brown into his Ku-Klux hole at Pulaski."[22]

Later in May, word came from Washington that a bill was pending there to allow certain states supplemental representation in Congress. Because Tennessee's legislature would not meet again until early 1873, the provision allowed the state an extra seat in the House of Representatives, which would be elected at large rather than from a tenth congressional district. This obscure provision resulted in one of the most interesting years in Tennessee politics. The broad Conservative and Redeemer coalition operating under the name of the Democratic Party struggled not only with the Radicals, but within itself. Frank Cheatham and Henry S. Foote declared their candidacy, and Andrew Johnson, chafing with boredom at Greeneville, was urged to run by several friends. One of those friends was John C. Burch, who at that time sought to resolve "the misunderstanding" between the former president and Brown. Burch felt he could "safely assert that [Brown] was desirous to have you become a candidate for the state at large, & is anxious to have an adjustment of your difficulties upon terms which will be satisfactory & honorable to both." Amos Richardson of Pulaski, grateful for Johnson's assistance during the war, wrote to assure his support and to state his opinion that "Brown has no ill feelings toward you" and hoped that the "lion & the lamb could ly down together."[23]

As seen above, Brown was warned of the damage a disaffected Johnson could do to the Democratic Party. In a letter to his old comrade James Patton Anderson, Brown said he expected "lively times" relative to the congressional race, predicting: "It will be the absorbing canvass of the Summer, so far as Tennessee is concerned. I fear such a canvass will stir up bad blood and do harm. However, we can only let events take care of themselves." Resolving Johnson's hostility, however, was not the immediate problem, as Brown spent most of the summer of 1872 in bad health, suffering a strange affliction to his face. The *Union and American* reported: "His face is swollen and livid as scarcely to be recognized." Confirming the serious nature of the illness, the hometown *Pulaski Citizen* reported on July 11: "The Governor has had a very serious attack, and his friends have been very uneasy in regard to his health." While the *Citizen* reported improvement, it took a trip to Epperson Springs, northeast of Nashville in Sumner County, and more time before Brown was able to return to Nashville in mid-August "quite recovered."[24]

The business of the state continued even while the governor was indisposed, particularly its legal business. Brown hired attorney R. W. Humphreys of Clarksville to investigate and possibly settle the claims the state had with the Federal government, and initially planned to join Humphreys in Washington before his illness struck. By letter dated June 11, Humphreys made a full report on the status of the claims on both sides. Later that summer, Humphreys wrote to advise resolving a case between two railroads that hindered negotiations with the Federal government. An important case relative to the Bank of Tennessee required some legal strategy. The judge in the case had a conflict, which would require the appointment of a temporary judge, at that time usually at the instance of the local bar. Attorney General Heiskell feared that the man the bar would appoint, Cooper (probably William F. Cooper, the brother of the senator), would "do us more harm than the decision of any man I know." Heiskell recommended hiring Cooper on the case and "make him help us before some other man whose opinion who would not hurt so much." Brown agreed, and Cooper was retained.[25]

Cheatham was the front-runner for the at-large congressional slot, and sought to meet with the former president prior to the Democratic nominating convention on August 21. Johnson declined to reveal his plans to Cheatham, but denied being a candidate for office even as the convention drew near. Johnson's private secretary, E. C. Reeves, related that Johnson wanted Reeves to go to the convention and decline the nomination on

To Improve the Present and Secure the Future

Johnson's behalf, as the ex-president had a master plan for a return to the United States Senate in 1875. To Reeves's amazement, Johnson announced himself an independent candidate at a mass meeting in Nashville soon after Cheatham was nominated by the convention. Johnson and Brown's mutual friend, John C. Burch, gloomily wrote the ex-president that the division of support between Johnson and Cheatham would only help the Radicals and claimed that Johnson would only be injured by "this cast of the die," closing with an "earnest prayer" that Johnson would "not risk our all by making the race."[26]

The split in the Democracy rejuvenated Republican gubernatorial prospects. West Tennessean Alfred Ansel Freeman became the party's candidate for governor, while the Democracy's *bête noir*, Horace Maynard, ran against Cheatham and Johnson. Not surprisingly, the Republicans endorsed Grant for reelection. To compound the political pandemonium of a year that saw the Republicans split nationally and the Democrats split within the state, Arthur S. Colyar once again ran against Brown for governor as an independent candidate. Colyar's candidacy only lasted until the first week of October, when he withdrew. The virulently Republican Knoxville *Daily Chronicle* saw Johnson's candidacy as opening the door for Republicans to defeat the Redeemers who had run the state for the previous three years and to see that "ring of military and selfish politicians is *broken down.*"[27]

Brown's contest with Freeman (and, temporarily, Colyar) involved several speaking appearances across the state. The first took place at Lebanon, where the three candidates appeared before an audience of about six to seven hundred people. Brown emphasized his administration's reduction of the state debt, the size of which he blamed on the Radicals. He maintained that the state should not repudiate the debt. Brown also commented on the management of the penitentiary, which he argued was improved, and replied to charges that the convict lease was suspect. The governor deplored the status of public education in the state and thought Tennessee should get its share of the sale of public lands. Not surprisingly, he supported Greeley for president and excoriated President Grant. Brown favored political conventions and opposed a party splitting its vote, which was an oblique condemnation of Andrew Johnson's independent candidacy. Replying, Freeman argued that much of the debt was not incurred by the Radicals, but by Democrats in the years before the war. The Radicals simply followed suit. Freeman agreed with Brown on education, but disagreed on the penitentiary lease, pressing the charge that a different firm would have leased the penitentiary for more. Colyar then rose to say he was not in the race to assault Brown, "for in my heart I believe him to be an honest man." He, too, was for Greeley, and for Andrew Johnson, but warned that the opposition to Johnson was trying to dredge up the awful issues of 1861. In a short reply, Brown observed that all three candidates agreed upon state policy, and denied that he was "an advocate of the heresy of secession." Brown said he would refuse to speak of the late war and would willingly, even though a Confederate general, go and "strew flowers on Federal soldier's grave."[28]

The gubernatorial contest took back seat to the contest between Johnson, Cheatham, and Maynard. A comprehensive analysis of that race is beyond the scope of this work, but one of the constant themes of Johnson, and indeed, the Republicans, was that a "military ring" was in control of the state. Johnson reportedly blamed the ex-Confederate soldiers for his defeat in 1869 and was so motivated that he declined a purported offer from Brown and others for appointment to Senator Brownlow's seat when it came open. In an interview with a New York correspondent, Johnson made reference to this group: "There is a ring of fellows in [Nashville], such as Bate, Dick Cheatham, Quarles and the rest. They are a mutual admiration society of rebel officers, and they can talk about Chickamauga and the like, about the battles they were in and all that." The Knoxville *Daily Chronicle* gleefully included Brown in that list, even if Johnson did not. Johnson, who had already turned a cold shoulder to the efforts of mutual friends to effect a reconciliation with Brown, was a man who never forgot a slight, and the temptation to lump Brown into the "ring" must have been great. Perhaps he calculated that attacking Brown directly would cause more harm than good. Another likely consideration was that the former president's focus was on his ancient enemy, Isham G. Harris. "King Harris," as Johnson derisively called the former governor, was behind Cheatham's candidacy.[29]

The primary Democratic newspapers that supported Johnson were the Knoxville *Press and Herald*, the Nashville *Republican Banner*, and the *Daily Memphis Avalanche*. The *Herald* supported Brown, but the latter two papers reflected Johnson's muted antipathy to the governor. In early September, the *Avalanche* condemned a judicial appointment made by Brown, writing: "The revolt against partisan and ring rule, which is spreading through Tennessee like wildfire, has received much of its force form just such actions as this." The *Avalanche*'s editors, like those of the Republican Knoxville *Daily Chronicle*, made a point of noting that Brown studiously was avoiding taking a position for Cheatham or against Johnson. The *Banner*, somewhat like its man Johnson, made only slight reference to Brown, although it too spoke of the "military ring." The *Union and American* relentlessly mocked its Nashville rival for its lack of support for Brown.[30]

Brown doubtlessly preferred Cheatham. Even though he was a potential rival in April, he was the regular Democratic candidate and an old comrade. Nonetheless, it was likely Brown's consideration that attacking Johnson would do more harm than good, and perhaps the governor still held out hope that he might reconcile with the ex-president one day. Brown referred to the "military ring" only briefly and denied being part of or having sympathy with such an entity. He pointed out that he joined the army as a private and "without solicitation" was promoted. Ironically, with the exception of the rhetoric of some of the more virulent Republican newspapers, such as the Knoxville *Daily Chronicle*, there was little rancor between Brown and Freeman. The Radical Chattanooga *Herald* observed that Brown's administration, "while far from faultless, has not been provocative of bitter feelings among his opponents.—He has been as just, perhaps, as it is possible for a Bourbon Democrat to be." Brown's hometown paper, the Democratic Pulaski *Citizen,* gave Freeman credit for being "graceful and dignified" in his speech there and noted his "honesty" in discussing national politics.[31]

The campaign went on. As was usually the case during the era, the tenor of the published accounts of the candidates' speeches depended on the political leanings of the newspaper reporting the same. For example, Brown and Freeman spoke in Knoxville on October 14, and according to the Radical Knoxville *Daily Chronicle*, Freeman was "forcible and sensible." Reports from Democratic papers stated that Brown exposed Freeman's several flirtations with Conservative politics, including his votes for Etheridge in 1867 and for Seymour against Grant in 1868, constituting a "complete wiping out of Freeman." At Bristol a few days earlier, the *Chronicle* reported, Brown told "vulgar anecdotes." The *Bristol News* thought Brown the better speaker, although Freeman got credit for speaking in the "mildest and least offensive tone" heard from a Radical. Freeman tried to goad Brown into declaring his preference in the race between Johnson and Cheatham, but the governor lightly replied that it was none of Freeman's business. Crowds ranged from a "comfortably filled" courthouse in Knoxville, to "respectable sized" in Bristol, to no more than two hundred in Cleveland.[32]

Interest declined as the candidates entered West Tennessee, as the electorate tired of the contest. While there was a substantial crowd of over a thousand in Memphis, and what appears to have been a respectable crowed in Huntingdon, Brown and Freeman appeared in Bolivar and Jackson and cancelled their speeches. The crowds were respectively no more than a "corporal's guard" and "meagre." Brown continued to take credit for the reduction of the debt, called for taxing bonds in the same manner as other personal property, advocated Tennessee getting its share of Federal money for schools (to be declined, however, if it meant racially "mixed" schools), defended his stewardship of the penitentiary, and prodded Freeman on his past apostasy from Radical orthodoxy. According to the pro-Brown Memphis *Daily Appeal*, Freeman took the position that "every official act of Governor Brown was a blunder, from his inaugural address to the present moment" and "said several other things in a desultory manner." Doubtless with an eye to the at-large congressional contest, Brown warned his audience at Huntingdon of "the danger to the State of Tennessee of dividing the strength of the party among a multiplicity of candidates."[33]

Election Day, November 5, 1872, confirmed the expected results. On the national scene, Grant defeated Greeley, although the Liberal Republican carried Tennessee. Cheatham and Johnson split the Conservative vote, resulting in a plurality for Maynard that gave him the at-large seat, thereby gaining for Maynard a substantial measure of revenge for the 1871 gerrymander that deprived him of his seat in Congress. Cheatham, who became a less than enthusiastic candidate when Johnson entered the race, never again ran for public office. For his part, Johnson got the satisfaction of defeating the candidate of the secessionist wing of the Democratic Party, which was seen as the vehicle of his old enemy, Isham G. Harris. The resurgent Republicans won seven of the state's ten congressional seats. Johnson men were elected to the legislature, holding the balance of power between the regular Democrats and the Republicans in the upcoming 1873 session. As expected, Brown was reelected, 97,589 to 84,050, a majority of 13,539 votes, but considerably less than the 37,479 margin of 1870. A total of 181,539 votes were cast, an enormous increase over the 120,479 of 1870. Turnout was doubtlessly stoked by the much hotter congressional election. Johnson's disruption of the regular party and his incessant attacks on the Confederate generals likely had their effect.[34]

Having just recovered from an unspecified illness that struck at the New Year, Brown was inaugurated for the second time on January 15, 1873. While there was less fanfare than Brown's first inaugural, there was suitable dignity, with the members of the legislature in joint session and the justices of the Tennessee Supreme Court present. Brown had the satisfaction of being announced by his nephew, Neill S. Brown Jr., the Clerk of the House of Representatives. After a prayer and a band's rendition of "Hail Columbia," Brown gave a brief address that emphasized the need for the people of Tennessee, and their representatives, to strive "for the glory of a common destiny." The governor impressed on his listeners his devotion to duty and his hope that any "uncharitable or revengeful feelings . . . from the scenes of the recent canvass" be forgotten in the pursuit of the public good. Brown urged "that it is for us, in a large degree, to lay the foundation for a new greatness for Tennessee." After a concluding prayer, the band played "Sweet Spirit, Hear My Prayer," and a benediction was pronounced. The band closed with a "lively schottish." The *Union and American* observed that if there was a "citizen . . . who could point to a line or a letter" of Brown's speech that was "objectionable," then that person "will be more hypercritical than the needs of the age demand."[35]

Brown's legislative agenda was already before the lawmakers, as Wilkes had read the governor's message to the new legislature a few days before the inauguration. Although the message covered a wide range of subjects for the legislature to consider, including the prison, the criminal laws of the state, roads, and agriculture, among others, the pressing issue was once more the debt, and raising revenue to service the same and operate the state government. Brown reported that the amount of bonded debt as of July 1, 1873, was over $30 million, but with state's liens on solvent railroads and the amounts realized on the sale of delinquent railroads, the actual debt was about $21.4 million, $4 million of which was unpaid past due interest, which Brown expected to accrue at a million a year until payment was resumed. Brown stated that the question of "what shall be done with our past due coupons and bonds and the accruing interest, cannot, upon any pretext, justifiable either before the world or before the enlightened public sentiment of Tennessee, be longer postponed." Brown proposed that the bonded debt of the state, including past due coupons, be funded in a new series of forty-year bonds bearing interest at 6 percent. In addition to addressing the problem of the debt, the governor felt that the new series could be monitored to "always show precisely our bonded debt." Brown urged that the funding start in July 1874 and postulated that certain improvements in the state's system of assessment and tax collection would enable the state to pay its current expenses along with the debt.[36]

The other significant part of Brown's message concerned education. Brown reviewed the poverty of the state after the war, noting the damage created by military operations and the loss of property in slaves. These "untoward circumstances . . . paralyzed the efforts of the friends of education." Brown urged the appointment of a State Superintendent of Education, as well as an Educational Board. He recommended that funding be made available to support a system of common schools, noting that the state constitution provided for a school fund. He also recommended that the state petition the Congress of the United States for Tennessee's "proportionate share of the large public domain," ironically noting, in light of his future endeavors, that it was "being diminished every year by donations to railroads and to other corporations and to other States." Brown begged the legislature to give the issue "that attention demanded by its important influence upon the destiny of the State."[37]

Newspapers on either end of the political spectrum across the state applauded the governor's emphasis on education. Spurred by Brown's blunt message, an independent report on the deplorable state of Tennessee's schools by Joseph B. Killebrew, a petition by a committee appointed by

To Improve the Present and Secure the Future

the State Teacher's Association (of which Neill and Killebrew were members), and figures from the 1870 census that showed Tennessee was third from the bottom in the nation for "ignorance," the General Assembly got a quick start on remedial legislation. Starting on January 10, three major bills were introduced: a House version, a Senate version, and a proposal from the Teacher's Association, which sought to harmonize the other two. In the end, after several days of conference, the legislature passed a version of the Senate bill. The law provided for a State Superintendent of Public Instruction, for county superintendents, for district school boards elected locally, and for a property tax to support the schools. Further, the law set the amount of the permanent School Fund, as required by the constitution. Brown signed the bill into law on March 15, 1873, and soon thereafter nominated Col. John M. Fleming of Knoxville as the first state superintendent. The Senate overwhelmingly confirmed him. Although the new law was only a start, and much more work remained to be done in the following decades, it was recognized as the "parent act" of public education Tennessee. A generation after Brown's tenure, a historian wrote that "succeeding generations will bless his memory for his courage, constancy and exalted wisdom" in connection with the school reforms.[38]

Addressing the debt was a much more difficult issue. Little action occurred for weeks, and the state credit forces had a hard time concealing their impatience. While Brown projected confidence to an out-of-state firm, the stress connected with the legislature's sluggishness must have taken its toll on the already physically fragile governor. Around this time, a Louisville correspondent reported that Brown's "physical energies have undergone considerable change for the worse" in the preceding two years. Finally, on February 17, Senator E. A. James of Hamilton County introduced a bill that funded the debt in the way Brown requested, with forty-year bonds at 6 percent interest. Debate proceeded on the bill, and opposition appeared not only from Johnson-allied members, but also from regular Democrats and Republicans, who felt that the state simply could not pay the debt, that it burdened posterity, and that some of the debt had been illegally incurred. The James bill, amended only to ensure Confederate debt was not paid, passed the Senate in early March on a 14–10 vote.[39]

Attention then focused on the House, where much the same debate occurred. Republican L. C. Houk of Knox County argued that the debt was incurred to improve Tennessee, noting that railroads and schools and even the capitol building were constructed with the borrowed money. Like Brown, Houk focused on the honor of the state, fairness, and justice. He also met the charge that there were those who would profit by the funding with the observation that there would be those speculators who would gain by the measure's rejection. The House passed the Senate bill by a margin of 44–24. Brown had his primary legislative victory, but it was incomplete, as the assessment and revenue measures he requested were still required. With rumors of a quorum-destroying walkout in the House, and the reality of that body's inaction on the two initiatives, Brown sent the legislature a special message on March 20 predicting that the state would not be able to meet the installments of interest on the newly funded debt and the appropriations made during the current legislative session without providing for the revenue. While the assessment bill, a complex measure in eighty-two sections taxing several species of property and imposing license fees on fifty-eight occupations and businesses, was passed a couple of days later, the House simply refused to consider the revenue bill. The former law, which Brown deemed inadequate, was still in place when the legislature adjourned.[40]

The remainder of the legislative session was of little significance. Over Brown's protest that the state's revenue stream was inadequate, money was appropriated for the erection of hospitals for the insane in East and West Tennessee, which for different reasons created a source of irritation later in the governor's term. The legislature authorized repairs on the capitol and a congressional reapportionment measure that reversed the spectacular gerrymander of the previous session. Brown vetoed a few minor measures, including, on constitutional grounds, a bill that provided for local option votes on the issue of allowing liquor consumption. His allies at the Memphis *Daily Appeal* approved, observing that sobriety could not be legislated.[41]

With the legislature adjourned, Brown invited its members to an "entertainment" at Nashville's Maxwell House on March 22. The governor complimented the members for their good work in providing for the common schools, in inviting immigration, and in regulating the financial condition of the state. The event was remarkable for first the presence of, and then the toast offered by, Rep. Sampson W. Keeble, a Nashville

To Improve the Present and Secure the Future

barber who was a former slave of John Bell's son-in-law, Edwin A. Keeble. Rep. Keeble was the first black member of the legislature, and on "behalf of his race returned his thanks to the Governor for the tribute of respect and recognition of the political rights of the colored race in thus inviting him, the first colored member of a Tennessee legislature, to this banquet!" Brown's response, if any, was not recorded. As no good deed, no matter how slight, goes unpunished, the Radicals did not laud the remarkable (for the time) recognition of Keeble, but claimed Brown's courtesy toward the representative was a cynical play for the black vote.[42]

The failure to pass an improved revenue bill remained a sore spot, although the governor forged ahead with ordering the coupons for the new bonds authorized by the Funding Act. Brown's allies in the press proclaimed his policy during the legislative session as wise and non-partisan, one paper lauding Brown's "sterling worth, unflinching integrity, and sound, practical wisdom." Other papers, particularly in West Tennessee, deemed it necessary for the governor to call a special session of the legislature to repeal the Funding Act, because there was insufficient revenue to meet current expenses and appropriations. Brown was thought to be "very much demoralized over the continued opposition to the funding bill," his "pet scheme." Brown was deemed to have lost his compass, to have become a tool of "political and financial gamblers" who lured him into a "funding bog, to mire and flounder to the end of his administration." The Memphis *Daily Appeal* presciently stated that the dispute was being used to beat Brown down for the purpose of elevating Andrew Johnson over him in connection with the election for United States senator in 1875. The Nashville *Union and American*, edited by John C. Burch, a friend to both Brown and Johnson, denied that claim, blaming those who "are working simply to beat down the credit of the State that they may buy up Tennessee bonds at a low figure."[43]

At the end of April, Brown responded to the calls for a special session, publishing an open letter to the effect that he calculated that "the Assessment Act now in force will develop a largely increased amount of taxable property—ample, under the present law, to meet the necessities of the State." Brown promised, however, that "should the assessment returns disclose the fact that the revenue will not be sufficient to meet the current wants of the State after paying the interest as provided for in the

Funding Act, the General Assembly will certainly be called together in ample time to meet the emergency." The governor was in fact walking a tightrope between the anti-funders at home, who thought the law went too far, and many of the bondholders, who thought it insufficient. At least for the remainder of Brown's term, the legislature would not get another chance at the Funding Act.[44]

A seemingly innocuous event at the first of May 1873 would turn into an unexpected scandal. State comptroller W. W. Hobbs resigned on account of ill health. Brown accepted the resignation, noted that Hobbs's accounts seemed to be in order, and extended his "high personal regard" and hopes that Hobbs's health would be restored. As the legislature was not in session, Brown appointed Burch in Hobbs's place. Burch was deemed "well fitted" for the position. At the end of the month, Brown went to Atlanta for a governor's convention, which honored him by electing him its president. Reflecting perhaps on the events of nine years before, Brown "experienced emotions not felt for years," and happily noted that the presence of representatives from both sides there and the peaceful divergence of views "was the best evidence that the country was at peace." An attack of neuralgia affected Brown's eye, and he repaired to Pulaski to recover. Probably compounding his misery, a fantastic report appeared in a West Tennessee newspaper that Brown himself owned some of the state bonds that were being funded. A friendly newspaper admonished that Brown was entitled to "simple justice."[45]

Brown's continued illness delayed some of the mechanics of funding the debt. Burch urged the governor to send Wilkes on to New York "to begin the funding with the least possible delay." Eventually, even though the governor was still suffering from his affliction, Brown returned to Nashville on July 28 to begin the process. A special room was set up in the capitol for Brown, Burch, and Secretary of State Charles N. Gibbs to attend to issuing the new, green, "very handsome" bonds. Even as Brown finally began executing his most significant policy, and while he was still afflicted, the Hobbs resignation again hit the newspapers. A Radical weekly newspaper, the Nashville *Bulletin*, broke the sensational story that Hobbs resigned as comptroller in return for a payment of $12,000. Radicals charged that the office was a "glittering prize" because the fees generated by the new funding would amount to between $30,000 and

To Improve the Present and Secure the Future

$40,000. Democratic newspapers struck back, disproving the fee allegation and attacking the partiality of the *Bulletin*'s publishers.[46]

Brown, Burch, and Hobbs all published denials of the charges. Brown's response was a frosty rejoinder to the *Bulletin*'s charges, contemptuously stating that he normally would not stoop to respond. "But in the presence of a scandal so grave and so seriously calculated, if unnoticed, to affect my official and personal character, I feel that a departure from any custom hitherto is pardonable, and that the public will indulge a prompt and emphatic refutation, due alike to myself and the people of the State." He went on to claim that his only motive in appointing Burch was to put someone competent and trustworthy in the comptroller position, and that Hobbs's only motive, as he understood it, was bad health. Although Radical papers noted what they deemed inconsistencies in these denials, the loyal Democratic papers all stuck with Brown and his administration. These papers argued Brown met the charges in a "dignified, manly way." Brown, they reported, "feels keenly and views with deep regret the unjust and unprovoked war made upon him," and "defies the malice of his enemies."[47]

Eventually, Burch sued the Nashville *Banner* for defamation, and countersuits were filed in response. But the truth of the Hobbs matter did not come out until a legislative investigation in January 1875. Testimony before a special joint committee revealed a remarkable story of a physically sick, competence challenged, and morally ambivalent man. At the time of the legislative election for the comptrollership in 1873, Hobbs had a rival, John L. House. When House discerned he could not be elected, he offered to help Hobbs get elected and solicited a clerkship in the comptroller's office in return. Hobbs agreed to the clerkship, but then decided against it. To be rid of House, and, he claimed, for no corrupt reason, Hobbs paid House $3,000. This account was a sidelight to the main question of whether Hobbs received any money to resign the comptrollership. The investigation revealed the name of a banker, W. M. Duncan, who had invested heavily in Tennessee bonds, anticipating the passage of the Funding Act. Duncan felt his investment was in danger, however, when the accompanying revenue bill was not passed, especially since he deemed Hobbs to lack sufficient competence to collect the necessary revenue to protect his investment. Hearing that Hobbs was unhappy in his job, Duncan offered him $10,000 to resign, which Hobbs, under all the circumstances, felt was "not morally wrong." Importantly for Brown, the evidence gathered by the committee overwhelmingly supported the denials previously published by the governor and by Burch. Nonetheless, the affair caused a lot of talk, and as the correspondent of a Radical newspaper properly observed, the "whole transaction had a 'bad smell.'"[48]

While the truth of the matter would indeed vindicate the governor, the scandal could not have helped his neuralgic affliction, which dragged on into the autumn of 1873. Brown's correspondence from the period indicates that, even though he was occasionally well enough to visit Nashville, the "continued affliction of my eye" kept him from "attending to my correspondence." And the personal misfortune of the Hobbs scandal was only one part of the governor's cares. During this interval, Memphis suffered from a yellow fever epidemic, which resulted in about 1,500 deaths. Although there was little the state government could do in those days, Brown inquired of the city's mayor as to the situation. The fever followed on the heels of a cholera epidemic that raged across the state earlier in the year. A disaster of an additional sort occurred about this time: the financial Panic of 1873. Banks and investment houses in New York collapsed, setting off a wave of bankruptcies, a severe loss of stock values, and starting a five- or six-year economic depression. Brown deemed the situation to be of "the gravest moment." The financial crisis did not divert Brown from his purpose of executing the Funding Act. He optimistically reported to a correspondent that the process would end up saving the State a large amount of money, and he predicted "We can & will pay the interest as it matures, I think."[49]

Ultimately, the economic downturn brought about by the Panic of 1873 proved to be the undoing of Brown's primary legislative achievement. As historian Robert B. Jones observed, the Funding Act of 1873 had a chance to work in a good economic climate. Under Brown's leadership, the state forged ahead with the retirement of matured bonds, payment of interest, and issuing the new securities. But as the national (and therefore the state) economy declined, opposition to the payments started to build within the state. As a result, the Funding Act did not resolve Tennessee's debt issues. It did, however, provide Brown's political enemies

To Improve the Present and Secure the Future

with an issue with which to oppose him in the future. Brown later felt that the movement to repudiate the debt was created by Andrew Johnson "for the purpose of securing the Senatorship in 1875."[50]

All of this was in the future. Brown, Wilkes, and Burch started the new year of 1874 in New York cancelling bonds and encouraging investment in Tennessee. Showing confidence in the state's economic prospects, Tennessee's bonds were recognized on the stock exchange in the nation's financial capital. In an interview, the governor extolled his efforts toward restoring the state's credit and improving the educational system, and downplayed reports of Ku-Klux "outrages." Then, on his way back to Tennessee, the governor stopped in Washington to appear before the House Judiciary Committee on a bill to repay the state for property and railroad material seized during the war. To reinforce this show of optimism, the Nashville, Chattanooga, and St. Louis Railway Company made several large payments that reduced the state's debt by over $3 million. Brown's friends at the Memphis *Daily Appeal* avowed he "not only secured a full and fair recognition of our bonds on the stock exchange, but has thoroughly established our credit and impressed leading and influential men in New York and Washington with the importance of our State, its growth and prosperous future. He has done his duty."[51]

Resolving the dispute with the Federal government required another trip to Washington in February. Brown's visit to the capital occasioned meetings with Tennesseans and other southerners at his quarters at the Willard Hotel, one citizen writing a Memphis newspaper that Brown was in "fine health and spirits and confident of securing a satisfactory adjustment of the claims of Tennessee against the Government." A caller expressed the hope that Brown himself would one day be in Congress, and Brown responded with "a polite bow and a slight smile." He confirmed, however, that he would not again be a candidate for governor. In pressing his claims against the Federal government, Brown made sure to enlist the aid of the state congressional delegation, both Republican and Democrat. With life as a private citizen looming, Brown went to Pulaski to attend to some of his old cases in Chancery Court. Several weeks later, Brown helped organize at Pulaski and became the first president of the Tennessee River Iron and Manufacturing Company, which was formed to develop the mineral resources of that section of the state.[52]

As 1874 was an election year, the issues of who would succeed Brown as governor and Parson Brownlow as United States senator were the subject of much talk. Although Brown wrote a friend that he "would rather be a truly pious man, than be President of the United States," his potential candidacy for senator was a matter that was taken for granted, even though "no one is authorized to make the statement." There were centers of opposition, though, such as temperance adherents who objected to his veto of the liquor bill. Further, there were rumblings from West Tennessee as to the issue of funding and the debt which threatened to divide the party, and Andrew Johnson still lurked in Greeneville, with a number of zealous backers "who will never be quiet until their hero gets a place." As if to illustrate this point, newspaper articles noted that the mere fact that in 1872 Brown supported the convention process that Johnson repudiated festered among Johnson's Davidson County supporters, and resulted in a lower vote for the governor there later that year. Already there was talk as to the coming legislative election and who would pledge himself to Johnson, Brown, or another senatorial candidate.[53]

A matter that promised to be an irksome issue for the rest of Brown's term in office now began to manifest itself. At its last session, the legislature voted to establish an asylum or hospital for the insane in East and West Tennessee. Brown appointed three commissioners to recommend a location for each, and the political pressure from contending communities in already disaffected West Tennessee increased exponentially. As the section's metropolis, Memphis had a substantial claim, especially since a local facility was grossly inadequate. Brown's political friends there wrote to warn him there was "a good deal of feeling" there, M. C. Galloway of the *Appeal* quipping: "I want the Asylum located in the vicinity of Memphis so that I can have easy transit when you politicians run me crazy." Other towns were also considered. The commissioners suggested Humboldt, but after visiting the site, Brown rejected it. The Bolivar newspaper observed that if Brown had chosen Humboldt, "we shall always consider him entitled to a berth in the institution. . . ." Brown felt the constraints of the legislation, which, according to Attorney General Heiskell, left the choice of a site to the commissioners, but gave the governor the responsibility of confirming or rejecting their selection. Expressing his frustration, Brown complained to a friend in Humboldt that the asylum matter "is the most embarrassing question that has met me since I have been in office. I have been abused, and most villainously & scurrilously criticized through the press by letter, and in private circles." Already politically weak in low-tax West Tennessee, the agitation of asylum issue was not helping the governor's future prospects there.[54]

Duties of other types also required attention. In late April, Brown visited condemned criminal Bill Kelley to personally hear a request for executive clemency. While "the kind heart of Gov. Brown was touched by Kelley's appeals," the governor advised him to focus on the next life. A few days later, Brown received a report from a citizen in Smith County that Klan activities were on the rise there, and that there were "numerous threats" against African American residents. He joyfully welcomed the birth of his first and only son, John C. Brown Jr., on May 25, 1874, at the family home in Pulaski. The happy occasion was the subject of a congratulatory letter from Brown's friend Charles M. McGhee in Knoxville, laced with political advice. Apparently, the two had previously discussed the issue of Brown's candidacy for the Senate. McGhee could see reasons pro and con for a run, and felt "the state of feeling is not developed to me with sufficient clearness. I would suggest that you make the necessary preparation and await events." According to McGhee, the funding issue and the then-unanswered questions relating to Hobbs were problems. With "nothing to disguise" relating to his desire to return to the Senate, Andrew Johnson was already on the stump, staying away from the Hobbs issue, most likely because it involved his friend Burch, but hammering away on the Funding Act and the assessment law.[55]

Brown obviously made a final decision to run for senator during the mid-summer of 1874, as he took a lengthy trip to Memphis to muster support in West Tennessee at the end of July. The governor effectively started his campaign on July 21 in a speech at a Democratic meeting and barbeque at Bartlett, and addressed a sore spot among West Tennessee's whites at that time, a pending civil rights bill. Brown paternalistically stated that while "the Negro" was legally his equal, socially he was not. Brown claimed he would shed blood to vindicate black rights and denied that white Tennesseans had mistreated, robbed, or failed to be the friends of their black fellow citizens. A more comprehensive public statement of position and defense of his record appeared in the papers in the next few days, when Brown responded to a letter of inquiry signed by 172 leading citizens of Memphis relating to his position on the issues. Brown's response was that the financial measures at issue were enacted by the legislature, in more than one session, "after mature deliberation." The state's debt on January 1, 1870, was $43 million. Brown stated that more than 75 percent of that was from bonds loaned to railroad companies for construction within the state. The General Assembly passed an act, with little dissent, that allowed all railroad companies to whom bonds had been loaned to anticipate maturity of their debts and pay bonds of any series, number, or date into the treasury (with a few exceptions), not allowing the comptroller any discretion in rejecting the same. This same session directed the sale of delinquent railroads. The governor noted that, considering other miscellaneous factors, the state's debt was knocked down to $21 million after all of these measures were employed.[56]

Brown observed that both sides in the 1870 election advocated resumption of payment on the debt. The governor suggested to the legislature when he took office that interest payments resume, and that past due debt be funded with new notes. Again, there was little dispute, although no funding measure was passed. Brown wrote: "The convention that met at Nashville in May, 1872 to select a State ticket for the Democratic and Conservative voters, did me the honor of a unanimous recommendation, and without a dissenting voice, indorsed the policy of my administration in a most complimentary manner." The governor declared that there were but two ways to redeem the past due debt. Raise the money to pay it by means of taxation, or "fund" by giving new interest bearing bonds. Brown decided funding the debt was best, to avoid oppressive taxation. Accordingly, the General Assembly passed the Funding Act, and Brown felt that the anticipated recovery of property values in the state would yield sufficient funds to pay the new notes. Brown wrote that the debt was largely incurred to build the railroad system, which was key to the state's economy. Addressing the civil rights bill, Brown claimed it should be called the "social rights bill." The proposed measure would give a black man a remedy for exclusion from accommodation that a white man did not have, and therefore discriminated against whites. Further, appealing to the paternal instincts of his audience, Brown wrote that the bill would invalidate the provision in the state constitution that prohibited

To Improve the Present and Secure the Future

mixture of whites and blacks in school, complaining of the "degrada-tion" of a white child growing up "in terms of childish intimacy with the black child." Brown closed his response with the self-deprecating expression that he would not be before the people in the next election, and was therefore "animated by the single desire to promote the cause of truth."[57]

The state Democratic convention met on August 19, 1874, and nom-inated as the party's gubernatorial candidate James D. Porter, a West Tennessee lawyer and judge who was a member of the constitutional convention and served on Cheatham's staff during the war. The conven-tion then adopted a resolution endorsing Brown's administration, which friendly papers termed "no more than sheer justice" and "eminently right and proper." For strategic reasons, perhaps because Brown's incumbency as governor made him at once the strongest competitor and provided the most material for criticism, Johnson focused his criticism on Brown, while he left the other Confederate general senatorial contenders, William B. Bate and William A. Quarles, alone. The partisans of both joined in. A Shelbyville paper friendly to Johnson accused Brown's hometown *Citizen* of opposing Democratic unity. The *Citizen* rejoined that it was in fact in support of party harmony by opposing the man who ruined the Democ-racy in 1872, and that its rival's attack on Brown was simply on the basis of his prewar affiliation with the Whigs.[58]

At this critical juncture, Brown was diverted from the campaign by an ugly racial incident. In August, whites in staunchly secessionist Gibson County in West Tennessee heard "reports" that the local blacks were arming themselves for protection against the Ku Klux Klan. Inherently frayed racial relations were reportedly exacerbated by crop failures, which caused the white landowners to discharge some black workers. Sixteen blacks were arrested at Pickettsville (now Gibson) and transported to the county jail at Trenton. On August 26, a large body of armed and dis-guised white men (one of whom claimed to have been killed at Shiloh) broke into the jail, and killed or injured five or six of the prisoners. Wilkes relayed a report of the incident to the governor, who was then at Pulaski, and Brown returned to Nashville. A reporter intercepted him at the Max-well House, and showed Brown a letter from white citizens blaming the blacks and asserting the existence of an "insurrection." Brown asserted he could not call out the militia without the legislature's approval, and that he thought action by the local sheriff should suffice.[59]

The notorious Gibson County event was not the only incident of racial conflict at that time. Julia Hayden, a black schoolteacher, was murdered in Trousdale County. In Weakley County, two white men burned an African-American church, one man openly admitting that "he burned the damned church and didn't give a damn." In Smith County, citizens of Chestnut Mound wrote the governor for "advise" as "they know not in what hour at night there [*sic*] houses will be entered by a band [of] blood-thirsty men, & there [*sic*] lives taken from them." Brown met with the father and brother of the teenaged Miss Hayden, who was not a public schoolteacher but who was in Trousdale County to teach black children. While the local authorities were loath to give the crime a racial motive, her family's friends and neighbors raised a modest amount of money to add to the $500 reward offered by Brown, who assured the Haydens that "he would spare no effort to bring the perpetrators of this cruel deed to justice." Hearings were held, but no one seems to have been charged for the murder.[60]

While the Hayden murder got some national press, the affair in Gibson County created challenges for Brown on many levels. Obviously, what little racial harmony existed in the state was threatened. Prominent black citizens invited Brown, Bate, and Judge John Trimble to address a meeting of black citizens "on the condition of affairs, in view of the recent outrage at Trenton." All three declined, but Brown sent a letter that was read thanking the meeting organizers for their "pacific spirit" and promising "unceasing and vigilant efforts" to punish racial outrages. Trimble expressed hopes for peace and harmony, but Bate claimed he did not have enough facts to assign blame for the incident. Brown and Trimble received a vote of thanks, Bate did not. Elsewhere, Jefferson Davis, Isham G. Harris, and Nathan Bedford Forrest all spoke at a mass meeting in Memphis and condemned the lynching.[61]

Brown issued a proclamation on August 29 that informed the public that he would not be calling out the militia, as the criminal conduct was under the jurisdiction of the civil authorities. He deplored that the people of Tennessee "are now heralded to the world as jail-breakers and murderers, rioters and law-breakers." Revealing another great concern, Brown exhorted the people to "control evil-doers," as that would "save you from military rule, and worse, even, than that, from anarchy, and probably nothing else will." The threat that the Federal government would use the incident to impose a military occupation, which Tennessee alone among the former rebel states had avoided, loomed large. An August 31 letter to the local district attorney general reflected this primary concern: "And I scarcely have language to express my anxiety to have the guilty parties detected and brought to punishment, this is a test of the power and efficiency of the civil law, to protect society in a State where the people labor under no disabilities. If we fail in this, it will afford the most plausible pretext of bringing the military power of the General Government into requisition, of which, God knows, we have already had enough." There were those in Tennessee who wanted that to happen, the governor wrote, therefore it was important not to leave race issues to the Federal courts. "To my mind this is an important crisis, not merely for the people of Gibson county but for the State and the whole South."[62]

There were, of course, personal political considerations, as well. Newspapers in and out of Tennessee lauded Brown's initial response to the crisis, his friends at the Memphis *Daily Appeal* asserting that "Tennessee never had an abler governor than John C. Brown." One friend in West Tennessee wrote that success in arresting the murderers would "make you the coming man" and that it was a "duty" Brown "owed to our party and friends to present such a result if possible." An attorney friend, William J. Sykes, considered it debatable whether it would do any good for Brown to come to Trenton, although the local attorney general thought it would. Whether for political reasons, to build public confidence, to head off Federal intervention, or to personally make sure the utmost was done, at some point in the first week of September, Brown went to Gibson County. Brown hired additional detectives to "ferret out" the perpetrators, actually sat in with the grand jury hearing the testimony of witnesses, and gave speeches, "advising a strict enforcement of the law." He viewed the incident through a lens of paternalism toward black citizens, blaming the blacks in Pickettsville for organizing, stirred up, in his mind, by the agitation for the civil rights bill. Nonetheless, the jail-breakers were strongly condemned. Brown concluded that "[i]f wise counsels prevailed with both races, that they could and should live together in peace." The *Union and American* noted that people of both races applauded this sentiment, and Brown's action on the scene earned the admiration of an old enemy, Senator William G. Brownlow.[63]

Although the United States Attorney for the Western District of Tennessee acknowledged that Brown's efforts were "in earnest," in mid-September the federal authorities decided to exercise their jurisdiction. On September 18, Brown sent a telegram to President Grant reporting the indictments and detailing the state law under which the prosecutions would take place. Brown protested the activities of the United States Marshal and of Federal troops making arrests in the matter, reporting that "the State authorities have manifested the most earnest desire to enforce them against the guilty parties & have demonstrated by these indictments & arrests not only their disposition but ability to enforce the law & protect all citizens without regard to race color or previous condition of Servitude these efforts I can assure You will no sense be relaxed until the majesty of the law is fully vindicated." Grant replied the next day, noting the concurrent jurisdiction of the Federal courts and stating it was his "duty to enforce the acts of Congress. . . ." The investigation and prosecution thereby effectively passed out of the hands of Tennessee authorities. The Federal prosecution proceeded with a trial of fourteen defendants, with dozens others under indictment, but the intimidated witnesses to the incident begged to be excused. The jury acquitted the initial fourteen, and the remaining Federal indictments were eventually dismissed.[64]

The campaign lurked in the background. Johnson was essentially silent during September, although he granted an interview to a northern correspondent on a range of issues that were national in nature. In response to a question relative to the "recent outrages" in Tennessee, he expressed deep regret and asserted that states should afford the Federal government "no excuse or pretense for entering the states for the enforcement of law omitted to be done by the States." Brown returned to Pulaski the third week of September and, in a two-and-a-half-hour speech, addressed Johnson's lines of attack, without directly referring to the ex-president. Brown reminded his audience of his modest antecedents and denied being involved in "any rings or cliques." He further addressed claims that his advocacy of funding reflected some sort of pecuniary interest: "I have

To Improve the Present and Secure the Future

never traded in nor speculated upon your securities. I have never owned a bond or coupon of the State. I have not made one dollar out of the State, or anything connected with the State Government, or any of its institutions, and he who makes the charge, directly or by innuendo, is a liar and a slanderer." Ostensibly addressing the platforms of the two parties, he defended the Funding Act and noted that, if funding $7 million was "infamous," how would one characterize a law signed by the president in 1868 that issued $900 million in new bonds? Brown reminded his listeners that they were electing the new legislature for more than who they advocated for the open Senate seat—"capable, honest men" should be elected and counted on to do the right thing relative to the Senate seat.[65]

Johnson struck back at Shelbyville on October 6. He complained that, while the Democratic Party no longer stood for a particular set of values, he had always been a Democrat, even when he was on Lincoln's ticket. The former tailor pointed to actions he had taken in and out of office and inferred that his actions in 1872 were not against the true party, but one tainted by support of Greeley. He then turned on Brown and accused him of being "at the head of this clique that is trying to control the State." He bitterly condemned Brown for opposing him in 1869, all the while with Johnson's "pardon in his pocket." Brown, Johnson claimed, "never drew a Democratic breath in his life." Johnson denied he advocated repudiation, but then claimed taxes were too high and warned of the dangers of a "permanent debt." Johnson continued to follow his calculated strategy of attacking Brown alone while "never uttering a harsh word" against the other potential candidates, Bate, Quarles, former Confederate colonel John H. Savage, and Memphis politician William H. Stephens.[66]

Johnson's attack brought advice from Brown's friends. Attorney General Heiskell relayed his thoughts and those of Chief Justice A. O. P. Nicholson that Brown "ought in justice to yourself to make your speech over the state. The attacks on you are so bitter and persistent that they ought to be met." Accordingly, two days later at Waverly, Brown responded to Johnson, on the basis of "self-defense." While the governor was proud to be a former Whig, he argued that Johnson hardly set the standard for Democrats of the present day. Brown emphasized that the true Democrats of the day were those who wanted to rid the country of Radical rule. He attacked Johnson for various actions he took as president and denied doing anything improper in 1869, asking, "has it come to this, that an American citizen cannot decline giving his support to another for office without being hunted down and having his motives impugned? Do offices in this country belong to men, so they can have the right to demand them?" Relative to the pardon, Brown observed, "I have yet to learn that the exercise of executive clemency chains its subject to the chariot wheels of the official who dispenses it, for all time to come."[67]

It was a strange campaign. Officially, Brown was not running, but he most certainly was. Stephens was purportedly a candidate, but was thinking about moving to Colorado. Friendly newspaper editors supported Bate, but the ex-general stayed quiet and let Johnson attack the man who once temporarily commanded his division. Savage, bizarre and pugnacious, spoiled for a debate with Johnson, but was ignored. He was even unable to get a response when he accused Johnson of wanting to hang Robert E. Lee. James D. Porter, the Democrats' gubernatorial candidate, stayed away from the fight. Brown was privately assured that he "need have no fear of Porter," yet the party's candidate for governor oddly declined to defend Brown when Brown's administration was attacked by the Republican nominee, Horace Maynard. Porter justified his tactic by remarking "a man like John C. Brown, whom he had seen ride up and down the line of battle, like Henry of Navarre, needed no one to champion his administration. . . ."[68]

The final two weeks of the campaign got even nastier. Observers noted a "great deal of bitterness" on both sides, with Johnson redoubling his assault on Brown's perceived disloyalty in 1869, calling it a "foul conspiracy," and essentially an alliance with the Radicals. Brown struck back "with terrible energy," accusing Johnson of hypocrisy relating to the Funding Act, as the former president secretly advised two legislators to support the measure, while going to Nashville to have some of his own bonds funded. The governor responded to Maynard's attacks on the legislation in the same light. Indeed, Brown and his allies made the observation that Johnson and Maynard were essentially working together. Johnson in turn claimed hypocrisy on the part of Brown, who attacked

To Improve the Present and Secure the Future

his actions as president yet who, with Neill, supported the 1868 resolution in Johnson's favor. Throughout it all, Brown expressed surprise at Johnson's attacks. A friendly editor at the *Gallatin Examiner* wrote that Johnson did an "injustice" to Brown, observing that "[a]lthough rivals before the public, we know that Gov. Brown has always spoke of the ex-President in those terms that his eminence and position merit, not only during the bitter canvass of 1872, but since." In his last speech of the canvass at Memphis, Brown complained that he "had never provoked a controversy with Andrew Johnson." If Johnson had pardoned him to buy a future vote, then he had violated his trust as president. The governor said he "opposed Mr. Johnson for the Senate not through vindictive motives, but because Johnson was not his choice." Defiantly, Brown told his audience, if "anyone charged him with having been actuated by fraudulent or corrupt motives, or belonging to rings, they told a willful and malicious falsehood." The governor offered to meet such a person face to face.[69]

On November 3, Porter won by almost 50,000 votes, and the Democrats picked up five seats in Congress. The party balance in the legislature reflected the Democratic victory, as there were ninety-two Democrats and only eight Republicans. Although Porter was the winner, a Jackson newspaper deemed the result a vindication of Brown, "show[ing] the manner in which the people of Tennessee appreciate their Democratic governor, who has never, in sunshine or in storm in prosperity or in adversity been false to them." Although Brown took time to celebrate the victory with a speech to his home crowd in Pulaski, he still had weeks of duties as a lame duck. He continued to struggle with the West Tennessee asylum, making an official visit to Memphis with other state officials in November to inspect the proposed site there. Accordingly, the governor was accused by a Brownsville newspaper of planning to choose Memphis as the site to secure the votes of the Shelby County delegation, a charge Brown's friends at the *Union and American* indignantly denied. Belying Brownsville's fears, the commissioners rejected the Memphis site in December. Further illustrating that, at this point, even official duties had political consequences, Brown apparently considered a trip to Washington to try to resolve the state's claims on the Federal government, but his friend Whitthorne advised that nothing could be done before the holidays and that a trip thereafter would be "too late after-ward to do you good." If unsuccessful, Brown would suffer "an injury done where good was hoped for." After a visit by his old comrade Gen. Edward C. Walthall, Brown suffered another bout of ill health, confin-ing him to his bed in Pulaski.[70]

On January 4, 1875, the new legislature met, and a few days later Brown sent his final message. While his message related to ongoing issues, it was also a valedictory, as his leaving office marked not only a personal transition from the governorship, but the beginning of the state's transi-tion from the time of the Redeemers. The outgoing governor justifiably prided himself on his strident efforts to restore the state's credit, while acknowledging the setback dealt by the "collapse in the money centers." Nonetheless, Brown saw reason for congratulation in: "the general pros-perity of the State, the steady development of her resources, the improve-ment of her trade and commerce, the success attending her efforts to induce and encourage immigration, and, more than all, the enforcement of law and the preservation of general peace and order."[71]

For Tennessee, Brown's tenure marked a time of transition from a decade-long period of disruption marked by secession, war, reconstruc-tion, disfranchisement, violence, lawlessness, corruption, faction, eco-nomic chaos, and racial tension. Peace had returned, although the black residents of Gibson County and the family of Julia Hayden might jus-tifiably disagree. With the exception of racial issues, the great matters of the 1860s were largely over, but the mess they created was not. Brown labored long and hard within the powers granted him by the new con-stitution to clean up that mess. Brown never wavered from his honest conviction that a strong state credit policy was required, and led the state in that direction throughout his two terms. This policy in turn required additional revenue, which could only be derived from efficien-cies in government and tax collection, and ultimately economic growth, which Brown sought to foster with his educational reforms and build-ing confidence in the state's credit. Unfortunately for the state, the economic downturn brought about by the Panic of 1873 ultimately de-feated Brown's purpose. While the governor undoubtedly did not person-ally favor the equality of Tennessee's new black citizens, he recognized not only that the law required it, but that Tennessee's freedom from

Federal "interference" was best served by acknowledgment of the same. The courtesies he extended to Rep. Keeble and his efforts to respond to anti-black violence, while far less than what true equal treatment demanded, were at least steps in that direction that many others in Brown's generation would not have taken. It can be fairly said that Brown's tenure marked the beginning of a new normal for Tennessee—once again at peace after a decade of war and violence, with the majority back in control of the government, but faced with commensurate challenges and opportunities.

As discussed above, Brown did not exactly fit within C. Vann Woodward's definition of a Redeemer because of the former general's connection to the old planter aristocracy. But he clearly did have the "industrial, capitalistic outlook" that Woodward discerned. While there was a moral aspect to his views on the debt, likely instilled by Neill and other Whiggish influences earlier in Brown's life, the painful struggle for payment of the state debt had practical justification in Brown's view that out-of-state investors, whose money was needed for railroad construction and other industrial and economic endeavors, would stay away from Tennessee should there be repudiation. His public pronouncements on the issue, especially while in New York, emphasized that Tennessee's state government was a reliable partner for outside investors. Brown, like other Redeemers across the South, saw the railroads as the primary engine of economic growth for Tennessee, characterizing them in his final message as "great arteries of trade and commerce." But like the other Redeemer Democrats, he carefully moved the state away from railroad ownership. Originally enacted in late 1871 as an "experiment," the new Bureau of Agriculture was addressed "to the friends of agriculture, mining, commerce, immigration—indeed, all development of the industries and advancement of the material prosperity of the State." From the standpoint of Brown's role as a New South leader, in the final analysis, he came into office with a capitalistic and industrialist bent, he made economic development of that nature an emphasis of his administration, and he left office for endeavors that pursued the same course. As another historian of Woodward's generation, William B. Hesseltine, observed, Brown "fully illustrated the case of the lawyer turned industrial builder of the New South."[72]

Brown's contemporaries recognized the difficulties he and the state faced in 1871. An editor who was a supporter of Johnson felt it just to write that "with a bankrupt treasury and an impoverished people, [Brown's] position presented more difficult and perplexing questions to deal with than had ever before fallen on the lot of a State Executive. Our relations with the General Government were full of peril and required the most prudent and delicate handling." In the editor's view, Brown showed "enlightened wisdom" and "manly dignity" and was entitled to "a just tribute to an honest and upright Chief Executive." In extolling Brown as a "wise, safe and prudent governor," his friends at the Memphis *Daily Appeal* wrote: "He commenced his labors under the most unfavorable circumstances, but almost insurmountable obstacles have been overcome." The Memphis *Public Ledger* was somewhat lukewarm, observing little had been accomplished except the Funding Bill, but noted, "[o]f one thing we are certain: if Governor Brown has made any mistake in the administration of his office, it has been conscientiously done for what he deemed the best." The Chattanooga *Times* lauded Brown for being "able and discreet," and held "[t]hat he is honest has been proven." The Brownsville *Bee* noted the reduction of the state debt, interest payments resumed, the school reforms, and the suppression of lawlessness, reflecting the "success of the able patriotic and sensible policy adopted by him." The Nashville *Banner*, rarely a warm friend, gave Brown credit for "conscientious efforts looking to the welfare of the whole people," concluding: "A peacefully governed State, and a relatively prosperous one—considering the very hard times—tells to the credit of Governor Brown's gubernatorial career."[73]

On January 19, 1875, the day after Brown left office, the General Assembly took up the issue of the open Senate seat. While his recent incumbency gave Brown obvious advantages, the former governor had inherent weaknesses as well. The most obvious was the Funding Bill, which was never popular in West Tennessee and therefore cost him support there. The financial downturn in 1873 strengthened opposition to the state credit position, and Johnson made funding a central focus of his attacks on Brown. The Hobbs mess resurfaced when the new legislature convened, and while, as noted above, Brown was exonerated, the publicity festered during the crucial days of January 1875. Groundless claims that

To Improve the Present and Secure the Future

the Funding Bill was passed with the help of bribes also surfaced in that interval. Less obvious, but almost certainly present, was Brown's status as a former Whig, another of Johnson's points of attack. Brown made the point that there were plenty of former Whigs who now were Democrats, but the fact remained that Whigs were losing their influence in Democratic politics across the South in this period. The same Whig antecedents that helped Brown get elected governor in 1870 likely hurt him in 1875. The irony of Andrew Johnson, in many ways an unorthodox Democrat and the 1872 bolter, asserting Democratic Party purity could not have been lost on his contemporaries. Simple political jealousy doubtlessly had an effect, as well. While there was something of a tradition of former governors becoming senators, such as Johnson himself and Brownlow, there were simply a number of other aspirants. Notwithstanding Johnson's attacks on "military rings" and "cliques," the former secessionists were making a political recovery, and the ambitious Bate was in their forefront. As a final bit of irony, Johnson would use this real intra-Confederate jealousy when Forrest came to Nashville in January to advocate against Johnson. The wily ex-president recalled their prewar amity and successfully appealed to Forrest's vanity, claiming that Brown and Bate were "one horse soldiers" and "little generals" when compared to the great cavalryman.[74]

Judge Oliver P. Temple of Knoxville later wrote: "No such excitement in Senatorial contest ever occurred in the State. It was a desperate effort not only to defeat but to destroy Mr. Johnson. On the other hand he fought his enemies with all his iron will and marvelous courage." With the help of his private secretary, E. C. Reeves, who visited with every one of the incoming legislators outside of Shelby County, Johnson evaluated his opposition. Johnson told Reeves, "Brown can't be elected, but he is desperate—says I have attacked the Democratic party of which he is the head, and the party must be endorsed by my election. So Brown will not let Bate be elected; and Bate being the stronger of the two will not let Brown be elected, therefore the two will fight each other instead of fighting me; my plan is working just as I have contrived." Johnson had a hard core of support in the Shelby County delegation, in Unionist Democrats, and in the small Republican delegation, to whom he falsely promised that he would not make "personal war" on President Grant.[75]

Brown's political calculations at this stage have either been lost or else were unrecorded. He doubtless counted votes and conferred with his friends both in and out of the legislature, and early in the process was considered a "dead duck." As a correspondent of the Memphis *Public Ledger* observed, Johnson's opposition was strong enough to easily defeat him, and prevailing would require "concert of action, personal sacrifice of cherished ambition and skillful generalship." All three were lacking in the anti-Johnson camp. Isham Harris appeared on the scene, seeking, no doubt, to employ his immense political skill to provide the missing "generalship," as he hated Johnson "as the devil hates holy water." A rumor arose of an alliance between Brown and Stephens, which Brown eventually denied. Before the balloting started, Brown let a reporter know "he will never let his ambition be a cause of dissension in the Democratic party," suggesting he would withdraw if such was the case. Another rumor held that Brown's friends were advising him not to make the race. The politicians all crammed into the first two floors of Nashville's Maxwell House hotel, with Johnson, Harris, Quarles, and Porter on the first floor, and Brown, Ewing, Stephens, and Savage on the second. Embittered by the campaign, Johnson and Brown did not speak to one another. Likewise, the clashing ambitions of Brown and Bate made the old comrades "bitter and uncompromising" enemies.[76]

A simple majority of the total members of the General Assembly then voting was all that was required. Brown reached his apogee on the on the third day of voting, January 22, on the 34th ballot, with thirty-two votes, pulling his additional support from previous supporters of Bate and Stephens. It was at this point that he requested his name be withdrawn in the interest of party harmony, but almost certainly also motivated by the realization that he had reached the extent of his possible support. Brown's selfless move received approbation from many in the party. Thereafter, Bate made a run and eventually caught and passed Johnson, but could not get the necessary majority. On the 44th ballot, Bate was one vote short of the necessary majority, as only ninety-six members were voting. But Representative J. L. Orr voted for Brown on that ballot, and later claimed that the voting stopped before he could change his vote. After the 54th ballot, Speaker Lewis Bond once more nominated Brown, "for the good of the party." An uproar occurred, Bate withdrew, his supporters antagonized by Brown's seeming reappearance. A final effort was made that night to identify a candidate who could beat Johnson, which in the words of a correspondent for a Republican organ, was "a disgraceful failure." The next morning, January 26, Brown was seen on the floor "talking excitedly to the Representatives." Also seen there were Gustavus A. Henry, who was making a late run, and Isham Harris, who was doubtlessly still trying to stop Johnson. Brown obviously heard that he had no chance, as after the session started, Bond arose and stated that his renomination of Brown was not authorized, and he withdrew the same. Johnson was elected with fifty-two votes on the final ballot.[77]

Johnson later exulted that he had fought "Hood's army over again. There were many of his generals and high officers, with my pardons in their pockets, trying to beat me as they tried during the war." There was a certain ironic truth to the new senator's statement. Just as rivalries and infighting hampered the effectiveness of the Army of Tennessee over a decade before, rivalries and infighting between two of its former generals kept one of them from being elected senator in January 1875. As one observer accurately observed, "[a]ll of Brown's friends would not support Bate, all of Bate's friends would not support Brown." The Knoxville *Weekly Chronicle* gloated: "They damn Andy and the Union Democrats, and when they get tired of that the Bate men damn the Brown men and the Brown men damn the Bate men." Brown's hometown *Pulaski Citizen* published a column that downplayed the dispute between Brown and Bate, denying that Brown's motivation for withdrawing was to set up a run for senator in 1877 and noting that sowing such dissention was one of the keys of Johnson's success. Likely reflecting Brown's feelings, the *Citizen* published an observation from a correspondent of the Louisville *Courier-Journal* that, seemingly oblivious to the death of the Whig Party, men in Tennessee "sit gravely down and tell you that the Whigs of Tennessee have had all the offices since the war and it is high time the Democrats were coming in."[78]

One other parallel with the previous decade is apparent. Like slightly under a decade before, Brown returned to Pulaski in defeat. Fortunately, the town was in much better shape than in 1865 and 1866. A visitor's letter published in the *Citizen* in late 1874 noted the brisk business going on, commented on the horse trading, court business, the banks, the merchants, and the newspaper. A Nashville newspaperman observed some months later that the town exhibited "evidences of a material prosperity and refined culture." Brown and Bettie sold their home to Martin College late the previous year, and moved into an impressive home built before the war by Dr. William Batte. Brown's personal prospects were also somewhat better than in 1865, with the prestige of his former office adding to that of his status as a former Confederate general, and his reputation as a lawyer intact. Returning to his law office, Brown found it "almost constantly thronged with his many friends and admirers." Among his first engagements, Brown was named as a third arbitrator in a dispute between Tennessee railroader Sam Tate and the Louisville and Nashville Railroad, although the railroad pulled the case from arbitration before he ruled. In May, Brown and Neill were among the dignitaries who welcomed Vice President Henry Wilson to Nashville, and later that month returned to the capital "on business connected with the courts."[79]

For some years, Brown developed business interests outside his law practice and political life, and was able to more freely pursue them when out of the governor's chair. He served on the boards of banks and a mining and manufacturing concern, as a director of the Nashville and Decatur Railroad, and of a projected line from Memphis to Knoxville, locally passing from Lawrenceburg east to Pulaski. While governor, he was one of the incorporators of the Pulaski, Pisgah, and Bradshaw Turnpike Company, a turnpike from Pulaski to the Lincoln County line. Brown also bought and sold land, particularly having an eye toward court sales. As promising as these endeavors may have appeared in 1875, Brown's law practice appears to have been his main source of income. He tried a high profile case in Chancery Court in September, opposing John M. Bright, then a congressman, in a suit on behalf of an estate. The *Citizen* described it as a fight between the Nestor of the Pulaski bar (Brown) and the Ajax of Lincoln (Bright). The case was described as provoking "much intense legal scrutiny" and resulted in a judgment for Brown's client of approximately $50,000. Brown also defended an alleged counterfeiter in Federal court during this interval.[80]

Bettie easily fit back into life away from Nashville. Having started the year as the governor's wife, helping her aunt, Sarah Polk receive visitors on

New Year's, she settled back into life at Pulaski with her husband and their four children. She served as the vice president of the Reading Club, and hosted a meeting of that group. The couple hosted a much larger entertainment at their new home in October, attended by "gentlemen versed in divinity and learned in the law . . . beside a large representation of teaching talent, musical and literary, of the town." The guests enjoyed music and then "a most sumptuous collation dispensed by the gallant lord, and served with queenly grace by the fair hostess." Later, in Brown's absence, Bettie hosted a celebration for three recently married couples. The correspondent of the *Citizen* gushed that "it was a courtly scene," with "comestibles rich and rare," and that "the fair governess of the feast was more than herself."[81]

While the former governor and his wife were at home in Pulaski, Andrew Johnson reveled in his vindication and return to Washington in March 1875 for a special session of the Senate. But it was a short-lived triumph, as Tennessee's new senator suffered a stroke while visiting his daughter in late July and died on July 31. Forthwith, speculation began on who Governor Porter would appoint in Johnson's place. A few days after Johnson's death, a reporter mentioned to Porter that he had heard a dozen possible names, and Porter said "[d]ouble the number and you would have the count more nearly correct." Newspapers mentioned Brown, Bate, Quarles, Harris, and a plethora of others. Some claimed that since Johnson was from East Tennessee, his successor should come from that grand division. West Tennesseans felt it was time for one of their own to take the office. The loyal *Citizen* made it clear that Brown was its preference, but Porter appointed Chancellor David McKendree Key of Chattanooga, a friend of Brown's.[82]

As 1875 came to a close, it appeared Brown and his family were comfortably settling back into their lives in Pulaski. But opportunity knocked from out of state, and Brown, perhaps as bored with life in Pulaski as Andrew Johnson had been with that in Greeneville, seized that opportunity. As Christmas approached, it was announced in the newspapers that Brown was appointed vice president of the Texas and Pacific Railway, at a princely salary. A year that began with the disappointed prospects of a new political office ended with the promising prospects of a new field of endeavor altogether.[83]

8

So as to Confer the Greatest Blessings to the Whole South

1876–1879

The idea of a railroad to the Pacific initially surfaced in the 1830s. The 1840s saw the first efforts to have a railroad project to the west coast as Congress authorized surveys of a number of possible routes west. While the concept of a railroad to the Pacific was acknowledged by the platforms of both the Democratic and the new Republican parties in the 1850s, the rampant sectionalism of the time defeated any efforts to move forward. The secession of the southern states removed this impediment, and the Pacific Railway Act, providing for rights-of-way across public lands and government bonds for the project, was signed into law by President Abraham Lincoln on July 1, 1862.[1]

In the 1850s, the state of Texas granted numerous charters for railroads, two of which, the Southern Pacific Railroad Company and the Memphis, El Paso, and Pacific Railroad Company, were the predecessors of what eventually became the Texas and Pacific Railway Company. In 1871, Congress chartered the Texas and Pacific to build a transcontinental line generally along the 32nd parallel. The Texas legislature made a contribution in state bonds and allowed the Texas and Pacific to acquire the two previously chartered lines, with their associated land grants. Among the incorporators was Thomas Alexander Scott, the influential vice president of the Pennsylvania Railroad.[2]

Born in 1824, Scott became associated with the Pennsylvania Railroad, and by 1860, rose to the position of the company's first vice president by virtue of hard work and competence. He was not above bribery and manipulation, however. In the words of a modern historian, Scott was "impregnated with corruption." When the war came, Scott's gifts were used to help move men and material for the Union. He was commissioned a lieutenant colonel of the District of Columbia volunteers, and later was appointed Assistant Secretary of War. His path tangentially crossed John C. Brown's in 1863 when he took charge of the movement of Federal reinforcements to Chattanooga. Returning to the Pennsylvania Railroad after the war, Scott became involved in railroad schemes in the South and the West. Operating somewhat in the shadows, he built a large fortune, but in turn built business connections that were of great value to the company. By 1871, he was (briefly) the president of the Union Pacific and the president or vice president of thirty-seven other railroads.[3]

Scott gained effective control of the Texas and Pacific in 1872 and was named its president, but the practical difficulties of building a railroad through the sparsely populated southwest taxed even his considerable talents. Unable to raise much from investors, and further hindered by the 1873 financial crisis, in 1874 (the same year he finally became president of the Pennsylvania Railroad) Scott began a multi-year effort to secure a government bailout for the Texas and Pacific, which not only was resisted by competing rail enterprises, but faced growing opposition from politicians, North and South, who were weary of efforts to build private fortunes with the backing of public funds. It was in the midst of this effort that he hired John C. Brown. Brown joining Scott's effort to get public backing for a dubious railroad after years of struggling with the effect of the same in Tennessee does not seem to have created much comment, at least in Tennessee.[4]

It is unclear when Brown and Scott first became acquainted, although their names were linked in an unfavorable fashion at the start of Brown's first term as governor. Among the many ventures controlled by Scott was the Southern Railway Security Company, a holding company sponsored by the Pennsylvania Railroad chartered in March 1871 to "secure the control of such Southern railroads as may be essential to the formation of through lines" between the northeast and "the principal cities of the South." In the course of this effort, the railroads in East Tennessee became part of the system, and Scott and his compatriots set their sights on the Memphis and Charleston line. This design came at the same time as Brown's first message in October 1871 relating to requiring solvent railroads which had delayed paying the interest on bonds owing to the state to pay all accrued interest. A bill requiring payment of the interest in cash rather than in past due state bond coupons was introduced by Knoxville representative and financier Charles M. McGhee. The most indebted of the affected railroads was the Memphis and Charleston. Accordingly, a hysterical torrent of accusations against McGhee gushed from the Memphis *Daily Appeal*. The *Appeal* charged that Brown was Scott's unwitting tool in his effort to monopolize the railroads in the state. The *Appeal* was chided by the *Union and American*, which deemed the Memphis paper's demonization of Scott as the cause of high taxes as a convenient means of depressing the value of the bonds owed the state by the railroad. In the *Union and American's* view, running low-performing southern railroads with northern capital was beneficial. The Southern Railway Security Company eventually gained control of the Memphis and Charleston by means of a long-term lease, which relieved the *Appeal's* constituency of Memphis and Charleston shareholders of their fears, and opened up to the citizens of Memphis the possibility of being the focal point of a line extending westward across the continent.[5]

The use of northern capital to develop the South envisioned by the *Union and American*, however, was frustrated by the after-effects of the Panic of 1873, which substantially dried-up northern investments in the South. With Yankee dollars gone, and state treasuries such as Tennessee's burdened with debt, southerners began to look to the Federal treasury for repairs to the region's war-ravaged infrastructure, uncleared harbors, and clogged rivers. Tennesseans took this view, as well, as the *Appeal* complained about the South not getting its fair share of internal improvements. The Republican-leaning Knoxville *Whig and Chronicle* advocated for river navigation improvement in southern, and particularly East Tennessee, rivers. Brown's final legislative message in January 1875 advocated improvements of the Mississippi, Tennessee, and Cumberland Rivers, noting the monies spent on states to the north and west of Tennessee. Brown wanted "a just proportion to be applied to the same objects within our borders."[6]

Scott hired Army of the Tennessee veteran General Grenville M. Dodge as the chief engineer of the Texas and Pacific. Dodge was both a competent engineer and an effective lobbyist. Although lobbyists were certainly not new to American politics, the railroad interests of the day brought the practice to a new level, using armies of them to fight their economic battles in the political realm. When normal incentives such

Tom Scott (Credit:
Library of Congress)

as free railroad passes to the members of Congress did not work, Dodge
and Scott decided to seek the support of southern leaders, and Dodge
orchestrated an elaborate campaign to organize southern support for the
Texas and Pacific. State legislatures passed resolutions instructing their
senators and requesting their congressmen to support the Texas and Pacific. Such was the case with Tennessee, with the proviso that Memphis
be connected to the line. Newspapers across the South published articles
and opinion pieces in favor of the road. Conservatives admitted that federal funds for internal improvements "is contrary to the principles of the
old Democratic policy" but justified it by the argument that the South
should get its share of monies that other parts of the country enjoyed,
"now that the Southern states have resumed their respective membership
of the Union."[7]

Yet another means of securing southern support was to enlist the aid
of the former Confederate leaders, who retained, even in defeat, significant influence. Jefferson Davis, Alexander Stephens, P. G. T. Beauregard,

So as to Confer the Greatest Blessings to the Whole South

John B. Gordon, and others let it be known that they were in favor of the project, and in Tennessee, ex-Confederate (and former Whig) Gustavus A. Henry addressed a meeting in Clarksville that urged the Tennessee legislature to support the project. Clarksville's congressman, John D. C. Atkins, a former member of the Confederate Congress, was also known as a Scott man. It makes sense, therefore, to conclude that one reason Scott hired Brown, a Confederate major general and the first of the southern Redeemer governors, was to curry favor with the southern politicians in Congress. Mindful of southern public opinion, Scott made it known that Brown would "represent and care for the interests of the south in the [railroad's] management."[8]

As clever as Scott and Dodge were, there were two factors working against their subsidy plan. First, the scandals of the Grant administration brought a reaction from northern Democrats against raids on the Federal treasury, which of course meant that there would be no support for railroad subsidies from that quarter. Second, there was the competition. The Central Pacific Railroad, led by Collis P. Huntington, had its own scheme for the transcontinental southern route. Organizing the Southern Pacific Railroad, Huntington and his fellow Californians secured the right to extend their line to the Arizona-California border at Ft. Yuma. When a bill was introduced in 1874 authorizing a large subsidy for the Texas and Pacific, Huntington's lobbyists worked to kill the measure. From that point on, there was war between the two railroad magnates, as Scott continually sought subsidies to build his railroad to the Pacific, and Huntington sought authorization (and land grants) to extend his line east of Ft. Yuma.[9]

Brown anticipated staying in Washington most of the winter of 1876, registering at the Willard Hotel on January 6. The first session of the 44th Congress started in December 1875, and the first committee hearing on the Texas and Pacific issue came before the House Committee on Pacific Railroads on January 19, 1876. Scott and Frank S. Bond, another Texas and Pacific vice president, spoke on behalf of the Texas and Pacific, emphasizing the benefit to the South, no injury to the Federal government, and the need to foster competition. Brown appeared with them, but did not speak in this initial appearance before Congress. In response, Huntington addressed the issue of financial exposure to the government and spoke against a line to the Pacific parallel to the Southern Pacific line.[10]

A few days later, Brown made his first congressional argument before the Senate Committee on Pacific Railroads in favor of Congress's power to endorse the bonds of the Texas and Pacific, and pointed out various deficiencies in the plans of the Southern Pacific. Brown claimed that the bill had "national importance," but also afforded the South "a measure of justice and compensation." The project gave the South "every possible facility of communication, and equal, if not superior advantage, by reason of shorter distances." The Louisville *Courier Journal* reported that a senator considered Brown's argument "the ablest and most exhaustive yet delivered." Illustrating Scott's continued efforts to gain southern support, the argument was made up into pamphlet form, and distributed to newspapers in the South. In Pennsylvania, home of Scott's Pennsylvania Railroad, a newspaper reported that Brown declined "to use the lobby, or any disreputable means to carry the bill, putting it solely upon its merits as a great national work demanded by the people and for their benefit." Huntington's forces, on the other hand, were reported to be prepared to "spend a car load of money" to defeat the bill.[11]

While skirmishing with Huntington continued in Washington through the winter, Brown assumed his role as Scott's ambassador to the South. The correspondent of an Augusta newspaper reported that Brown's rooms in Washington were at the famous Willard Hotel, and became "the daily resort of able and upright southern public men, who, like himself, represent the progressive south." It was supposed that the governor's $10,000 Texas and Pacific salary would dissuade Brown from contesting for one of Tennessee's $5,000 a year Senate seats, both of which were coming open in early 1877. This would not keep the hometown *Citizen* from advocating at the end of the year that Brown be drafted for the position, noting "[i]t would be a great sacrifice to him, but he is a man who never fails in any emergency."[12]

While a Senate seat was no longer in his future, Brown kept his political connections with Tennessee alive. It is unclear whether it was for his own personal ambition or to suit Scott's purposes, if not a combination of the two. In late May, although Brown was attending to Texas and Pacific business in Texas, the state Democratic convention in Nashville elected him as a delegate at large to the national convention. Like many of the Tennessee delegation, Brown came to the convention a month later in St. Louis favoring either Governor Thomas A. Hendricks of Indiana or Union war hero Winfield Scott Hancock. Brown was a *de facto* leader of the Tennessee delegation, and when it became clear Governor Samuel J. Tilden of New York was going to be the nominee, Brown passed a resolution that Tennessee would support the nominee whoever he may be. The delegation elected him to the Committee on Resolutions, and when called on for a speech, Brown stated he had no political aspirations but would labor for the good and advancement of the party. After Tilden's nomination, Brown closed his involvement at the convention by seconding Hendricks's nomination as vice president from the floor.[13]

Having kept his political options at home open, Brown did the same with his professional situation. At the end of Brown's administration as governor, his secretary, John S. Wilkes, obtained employment as the assistant cashier of the Giles National Bank. Brown's large law practice needed tending while he was attending to Texas and Pacific matters. With a relationship of trust going back for a number of years, Brown arranged for Wilkes to take over the law office in which the former secretary had read law. Brown remained a nominal partner, but the talented Wilkes became a noted lawyer in his own right. And if matters did not work out with Scott, Brown would be able to return home and not have to start his law practice a third time.[14]

Notwithstanding the interlude in St. Louis, and a visit or two to Tennessee, most of the spring and summer of 1876 was spent on Brown's first trip to Texas on the railroad's business, both as its vice president and as a lawyer. Likely desiring to show Congress that the line was moving forward at an appropriate rate, Brown was "immediately in charge" of a concerted effort that summer to complete the line to Ft. Worth, approximately 120 miles of road from a point west of Brown's new headquarters at Marshall, Texas. But all was not business. Brown was described by a Texas paper as "fascinating in social life and an adept at winning the affections of women and the respect of men." A visit to Dallas on June 9 was announced in the city that morning, and that evening Brown was honored at a banquet with speeches and dancing organized by over a hundred former Tennesseans, many of whom were veterans of the Army of Tennessee. The familiar faces made Brown feel at home. He spoke of the struggles of the war and the men who were lost, and then turned his attention to the pursuits of peace, particularly "the great work of public improvement" in which he was engaged.[15]

Brown's executive ability brought results, as it appears that the goals for the summer were largely met, and plans were made for the next segment. News made its way back to Tennessee that Texans spoke "in the highest terms of [his] capacity and efficiency" and his "great personal popularity." Scott and his confederates obviously noticed, as Brown was reelected vice president at the annual stockholders meeting that summer and, later that year, was elected attorney for the railroad. While he was away, his fellow Democrats in Pulaski elected him a county delegate to the state guber- natorial convention in Nashville in August, which he almost certainly missed on account of railroad business in Texas. Finally, after a summer of labor, he was able to visit Pulaski briefly at the end of August, it being noted that his position with the railroad kept him "constantly busy."[16]

Brown returned to Tennessee to help campaign for the Democratic ticket in the election of 1876 and "to vote the democratic ticket straight out." Appearing with his friend Rep. W. C. Whitthorne at Pulaski, Brown gave a speech that seconded Whitthorne's charges of Republican corrup- tion in Washington. Although "quite unwell," Brown gave an "enthusi- astic speech." After voting, he went to Philadelphia, where his illness was reported to be "severe." Unfortunately, Bettie was unable to nurse to her husband, as she had to return to Tennessee to tend to two of the children, who were reported to be "very sick." Fortunately, Brown recovered and returned to Pulaski "greatly improved in health" on November 19, al- though he bore "the marks of his recent illness."[17]

As Brown recovered, the results of the presidential election of 1876 were yet unknown. The initial election returns showed Tilden safely with 184 electoral votes, one short of the number needed for election, and a comfortable majority of the popular vote. At issue were the votes in three southern states, Florida, South Carolina, and Louisiana, still under Repub- lican control. Fraud in Oregon on the part of the Democrats matched partisan rulings on the part of Republicans in the three southern states. Congress reconvened in Washington on December 4 in a foul partisan mood. Brown returned to Washington, and the struggle to subsidize the Texas and Pacific resumed in that poisonous atmosphere.[18]

In the view of prominent southern historian C. Vann Woodward, the fortunes of the Texas and Pacific and the result of the election of 1876 were linked together by the actions of a mercurial fellow Tennessean, Andrew J. Kellar. Kellar was the owner and former editor of the Memphis *Daily Avalanche* and a veteran of the Army of Tennessee who served under Brown's command in 1864. Kellar's rivals at the Memphis *Appeal* colorfully described him as "a phenomenon; he cannot be comprehended or explained. He is a political Proteus, a Sphinx, the type of versatility and mystery of all that is left to the world of the oracular and uncertain in politics and statesmanship." A prewar Douglas Democrat, Kellar styled himself an "Independent Conservative," operating both within and outside the Tennessee Democratic Party and sometimes on the fringe of the Republican Party. He was one of the earliest advocates for Brown's candidacy for governor, but became a supporter of Andrew Johnson in the 1872 congressional election and subsequently in the race for senator in 1874–75, in significant part because of Johnson's low-tax stance.[19]

While inconsistent in his politics, Kellar was consistent in his advocacy of a railroad line from Memphis to the Pacific coast and was in favor of a federal subsidy to the Texas and Pacific. And Kellar came to believe that the best prospect of achieving that was by means of Republican Rutherford B. Hayes's victory in the contested election. Support of the Texas and Pacific was only frosting on the cake; what the South really wanted was the return of home rule—white-controlled state governments. Kellar was associated with several midwestern newspaper editors, including William Henry Smith of Chicago, a very close friend of Hayes, and Henry Van Ness Boynton, a veteran of the Army of the Cumberland. In mid-December, Kellar, with Smith and other influential midwesterners, began to search for a way out of the election crisis, with Kellar focusing on breaking former Whigs away from the southern Democrats. In Hayes, they found a Republican who genuinely desired a rapprochement with the South, and who shared Kellar's goal of splitting business-minded conservatives away from the Democrats. The possibility of a split was fostered by a perception among southern Democrats that while much of the party's electoral strength came from the old

Confederacy, its northern wing was not supportive of the South's desire for federal money for internal improvements.[20]

In mid-December, Keller, Boynton, and Smith floated the concept that support for the Texas and Pacific would insure that Tom Scott and his powerful lobby would be employed on Hayes's behalf. But while his supporters were willing to take that step, it made Hayes uneasy. If a deal was made to employ Scott's influence on Hayes's behalf, it was never explicitly recorded. In late January 1877, the Congress passed a law forming a fifteen-member Electoral Commission. The fifteenth vote on the commission, Justice Joseph P. Bradley, who some years before ruled in a case in favor of the Texas and Pacific, voted with the seven Republicans to find that all of the disputed votes went to Hayes. The crisis continued, under the threat of a Democratic filibuster of the process. But a "purely political" deal crystallized, which involved the appointment of a southern cabinet member and the return of home rule in the states still run by "carpetbagger" governments. On February 20, 1877, the southern Democrats supported a vote ending the filibuster and completing the process that resulted in Hayes being inaugurated. Doubt persists as to whether the "purely political" aspects of what became known as the Compromise of 1877 were sufficient to defuse the crisis. At the time, however, it was considered an "open secret" that support for the Texas and Pacific Railway bill was part of the political and economic deal made to secure southern support for resolving the crisis in Hayes's favor.[21]

Even as deals were being made in connection with the constitutional crisis, Scott, after weeks of fruitless struggle in the congressional committees, made an arrangement with Huntington before Christmas 1876. Huntington would cease resisting Scott's subsidy, Scott would allow the western end of the line in California to be built by the Southern Pacific, Huntington would agree that that segment would be an "open highway," and Scott would support a federal subsidy for Huntington. This uneasy alliance lasted for the rest of the larger crisis, but the supporting legislation never passed, as northern Democrats blocked efforts in January and again in February. Congestion on the House calendar brought about by the electoral crisis was yet another obstacle.[22]

Kellar and his allies viewed Tennessee as the southern state where the first crack in the solid South might appear. While relations between Kellar and Brown may have cooled a bit over the state debt issue and

So as to Confer the Greatest Blessings to the Whole South

Brown's bruising fight with Andrew Johnson, they had a mutual friend in Senator David M. Key of Chattanooga. In mid-December, Key gave a speech in the Senate that called for calm in the midst of the passions brought about by the election, as in his mind the scars of the late war had yet to heal. Kellar hoped to use Key's reelection for senator in January as a test for his hoped-for new coalition in Tennessee of Republicans, Johnson-ite Democrats, Douglas Democrats from the Memphis area, and former Whigs. But as noted by historian Roger Hart, Key did not have Andrew Johnson's ability to mobilize these disparate groups. Two Senate seats were up in Tennessee in 1877, a "full" six-year term and the "short" term, electing a permanent successor to Andrew Johnson. Isham G. Harris was easily elected to the "full" term. The former governor masterfully orchestrated his return to political office in the campaign season of 1876. A staunch Bourbon Democrat, Harris likely had little sympathy for Kellar's scheme. Indeed, Harris's election signaled that the power of the Whiggish Democrats that Kellar counted on in Tennessee was past its apogee. And Key failed to defeat Brown's friend James E. Bailey, conversely indicating that the purer ex-Whigs still had substantial influence. If Key were to be part of Kellar's designs, it would have to be from a different vantage point than the Senate.[23]

Brown's role in the crisis is somewhat murky. As a Democrat, he openly supported Tilden, and in late November or early December 1876 called on the potential president and "had quite a long talk." He found Tilden had "absolute confidence that he would be inaugurated president." Yet there is reason to think that Brown's private feelings may have been conflicted. As the point man for the Texas and Pacific legislation in Washington, the deal that Kellar and his group sought to craft in connection with a Hayes victory had the promise of crowning Brown's efforts on behalf of the railroad with success. And Kellar's desire to create a new southern party based in large part on the natural interests of the ex-Whigs must have had some attraction for Brown, as it did for his friend Key, even if Kellar himself probably did not. The most direct evidence for this conclusion is Brown's later confession that he considered Hayes an honest man whose policies would restore the South and sectional harmony.[24]

Hayes indeed wanted to reconcile the South. On February 17, 1877, he wrote in his diary: "I would like to get support from the good men of the South, late Rebels. How to do it is the question. I have the best disposition toward the Southern people, Rebels and all. I could appoint a Southern Democrat in the Cabinet." Hayes went on to mention Joseph E. Johnston as a possibility. Inquiries were made, and Hayes's advisors informed him that certain southern Democrats considered Brown a desirable choice. A New Orleans newspaper reported that, on February 25, Brown was offered a cabinet position, and after considering the same a day or two, declined, stating that "he had promised the Southern people to use his best endeavors to give them a railroad to the Pacific, and that he believed he should succeed and he held the promise paramount to any political position." Indeed, Brown's high profile as the Texas and Pacific's leading lobbyist was considered a detriment by one of Hayes's advisors. Through his connections with Hayes's friends, Kellar pressed for the appointment of Key, which some thought was secured through influence wielded by his friend Brown, either by means of the Texas and Pacific connection or Brown being considered a spokesman for the South. Key had moderate views (and had suffered for them at the hands of the Tennessee Bourbons) and the advantage of being a former senator, which meant that the courtesies of that body would be extended to him in connection with confirmation. Key would eventually be appointed Postmaster General.[25]

If Brown were indeed offered the position, he had good reasons to turn it down. First, he very well may have felt obligated to complete the railroad project, an endeavor that provided him and his family a very good living and him personally with influence far beyond the state of Tennessee. Second, while claiming to avoid politics, it is reasonable to assume that it is a door that Brown wanted to leave open. Isham Harris gloated that Key politically "killed himself" by accepting Hayes's appointment, and as the Bourbons in Tennessee were gaining strength, an alliance with even a pro-southern Republican administration could prove just as politically fatal for Brown. As will be seen, Brown was sensitive to the effect cooperation with the Hayes administration might have on his *bona fides* as a Democrat.[26]

Not only did the election of 1876 create confusion as to the rightful holder of the presidency, it also resulted in the election of two competing governments in Louisiana, the Republican version headed by Governor Stephen B. Packard, a Maine-born Union veteran, and the Democratic headed by Governor Francis T. Nicholls, a war-disabled veteran of the Confederate Army of Northern Virginia. The competing systems not only resulted in a great deal of political uproar, but eventually resulted in bringing business in the great commercial center of New Orleans to a standstill. In the days and weeks after his inauguration, President Hayes received a number of appeals and petitions asking for relief. Eventually, the president determined to send an unofficial commission to Louisiana as a means of resolving the dispute in without violence and the appearance of a simple abandonment of Packard's claims, which had no chance without Federal support.[27]

The president's go-between with the Louisiana Democrats was Rep. Randall Gibson, a former Confederate general. The proposed Republican members of the commission were all moderate to conservative, and all had some sort of tie to Gibson, either through their mutual connection to Yale, Gibson's boyhood in Kentucky, or marriage. The members included Wayne MacVeagh of Pennsylvania, John Marshall Harlan of Kentucky, Joseph R. Hawley of Connecticut, and chairman Judge Charles Lawrence of Illinois. With these four Republicans, one moderate Democrat was asked to serve: Brown, who was connected to Gibson by their service in the Army of Tennessee.[28]

Having already been vetted as a possible cabinet officer, Brown was likely well known to Hayes, and was approved by Key and doubtlessly Gibson. Congress having adjourned, Brown left Washington in mid-March, 1877 and traveled home to Pulaski by way of Nashville. Surprised at his appointment, just after midnight on March 21, Brown telegraphed Key from Pulaski that he would serve "if it is believed that my co-operation will contribute anything toward a pacific solution of the troubles in Louisiana. . . ." A follow-up telegram late that afternoon asked Key for specific details. Brown explained to the *Citizen* that he did not see how a true southern man could refuse to serve in a matter so vital to the country and the South. Later, he stated that he imagined Tennessee in that condition and deemed it "moral cowardice" to decline.[29]

From Brown's point of view, service on the commission was a risky proposition. Practically speaking, he had doubts a commission of this nature would help resolve the situation, and wondered what he as a single Democrat could do with the four Republicans. Politically, the public in the South viewed this new device of a president many there deemed to have been elected by means of fraud with great skepticism. Brown's motives were questioned by those who knew he had spent much time in Washington seeking appropriations for his railroad. A Democratic organ called him a "Judas Iscariot on wheels." Even Brown's reliable friends at the *Citizen* expressed the view that Brown should stay away. "Let the radicals pick the bones of the carcass they have made, without the assistance or countenance of honest men to give their nefarious deeds the color of decency."[30]

Once his name was announced, the pressure increased, and Brown received a number of telegrams and letters urging him to decline. On March 26 he asked to withdraw, claiming a combination of delay and press of business required it. But the word came that by doing so he would "seriously embarrass" Hayes, and he got telegrams from friends in New Orleans and southern Democratic leaders encouraging him to accept, men with whom he had "stood shoulder to shoulder in battle." Further, he had built relationships with the Louisiana congressional delegation and likely considered the political advantage of pleasing them. Brown did not neglect his political flank in Tennessee, either, as he consulted with Governor Porter and others of influence, all of whom urged that he accept. Porter wrote Key on March 29, stating "Brown consulted me as to the propriety of his acceptance of the President's invitation to go to New Orleans, I urged him to go, and I trust that good will grow out of it." Caught between the pressures at home to let the Republicans stew in their juices, the issue of tarnishing his reputation as a Democrat, and the urgings from political leaders of both parties to accept, Brown agonized until March 29, when he telegraphed he would not withdraw. Kellar helpfully published a piece in the *Avalanche* reporting that Brown had spent the winter in Washington, and was "thoroughly conversant with the Southern situation and the President's views thereon."[31]

Brown knew Hawley, who was also a former major general and governor. He had met Harlan and MacVeagh once, but did not know Judge Lawrence. Even as he traveled to New Orleans late in March, all he knew of the commission was that it would not be charged with collecting evidence or reporting; it existed only for the purpose of seeking an easy and peaceable solution of the problem in Louisiana. To a reporter, Brown "frankly

So as to Confer the Greatest Blessings to the Whole South

confess[ed] that [he did] not now see how an adjustment between Nicholls and Packard can be reached" but hoped that would become clearer once he got to New Orleans.[32]

President Hayes's instructions to the commission premised its justification upon the "apparent intervention of the military power of the United States in the domestic controversies which undoubtedly divide the opinions and disturb the harmony of the people" of Louisiana. The president asked that the commission devote its "first and principal attention to a removal of the obstacles to an acknowledgment of one government. . . ." Notwithstanding the official nature of these instructions, the commissioners were understood to be unofficial "friends of the president" who could exercise some influence to facilitate an adjustment to the impasse in the Pelican State. Starting its work on April 5, 1877, the commission met with both governors, the representatives of each government, businessmen, black citizens, judges, and other groups and individuals, totaling in the hundreds. Brown later described this process as "two weeks of as hard labor as men ever performed in such business." When not meeting as a group, the commissioners would meet with Louisianans as individuals. Brown's status as a former Confederate and current Democrat was considered an advantage in dealing with Nicholls and his friends.[33]

Much of the commission's work, however, appears to have been toward hammering out a way for Nicholls to assume full control of the state in a manner that would reassure northern Republicans that the interests of their party and of the state's black citizens were not being unfairly subverted. Brown later stated that he personally went to New Orleans with a view that Nicholls led the true government, and that the commissioners had not been in the state over twenty-four hours when they all concurred in that conclusion, or at least in the conclusion that Nicholls had effective control of the state government. The focus appears to have been on achieving a concurrence in the correct and undisputed holders of the various legislative seats, which comported with the president's instructions, doubtlessly informed by Gibson or some other Louisiana insider, "to accomplish the recognition of a single legislature as the depository of the representative will of the people of Louisiana."[34]

A dispute of an uncertain nature developed that brought the commission to an impasse. Brown asked for twenty-four hours to effect a compromise, which required a private midnight meeting with his fellow ex-generals Nicholls and Gibson, in which a letter to Hayes from Nicholls was prepared that promised support of legislative resolutions that abolished race distinctions and promised a general political amnesty. Brown also suggested the Nicholls legislature pass resolutions to fracture the Packard legislature and to induce its members to join the Nicholls group, including a financial inducement of paying the *per diem* and mileage of the Packard legislators, which was later extended to the policemen and state employees loyal to Packard. This broke the impasse, and orders came from the president withdrawing the Federal troops that occupied Packard's statehouse. Lurking in the shadows was Kellar, who facilitated the transfer of funds from the New Orleans Cotton Exchange and the Louisiana State Lottery Commission to pay the deserting Packard legislators their *per diem*.[35]

With the exception of Packard and his supporters, white Louisianans were most satisfied with the result. The members of the commission were happy to achieve what even its Republican members thought was the appropriate outcome, and Hayes was pleased. Brown emerged from what could have been a potential political disaster with new laurels. A comment from a Cincinnati paper was published in the *Citizen* a few days later, observing that even Bourbon critics had to acknowledge Brown's success in Louisiana. Certainly, he received accolades from Louisiana, and it was reported that there was a "universal feeling of satisfaction" as to Brown's service and "the zeal and prudence with which he has conducted his part of this proceeding." Letters from Louisianans to connections in Tennessee stated "Brown has the credit for our salvation" and according to Brown "the merit of having contributed more than any one man in bringing about this result." The *Citizen* helpfully published these letters, including the sentiment that Brown was considered the "coming man" for the presidency in 1880.[36]

Brown and the other commissioners went to Washington to personally submit their report to President Hayes. Brown then returned to Pulaski and made plans to return to Texas for several weeks. Before his departure, he was asked to address a meeting at the courthouse in Pulaski relative to his service on the commission. Brown related the process for his difficult decision to serve, his service on the commission, and his gratification at the result. He stated he was "amused to learn he had been read out of the democratic party," and did not deny that he "admired the President's southern policy and thought it wise." Nonetheless, he counseled "strict adherence to democratic principles and a guarded organization of the party." Brown expressed his gratitude for the support he got from home, noting that he had "never deserted" his people, and regardless of the issue "he would never desert their standard or cease to labor in their interests."[37]

While Brown labored in New Orleans, Speaker of the House candidate and Ohio Republican James A. Garfield let it be known that he would be in favor of the Texas and Pacific project. With victory in Scott's grasp, the cease-fire with Huntington came to an end, and it appeared that Scott had gained the upper hand. But Congress was out of session and would not meet again until October. Brown spent the intervening time period visiting New Orleans with Bettie and traveling on behalf of the Texas and Pacific in Texas and southern California. There were trips to New York and Washington, and trips back to Pulaski, including what was doubtlessly an emotionally satisfying reunion of the 3rd Tennessee at Lynnville in Giles County. There, Brown spoke of their parting at the surrender in North Carolina, how the regiment's members, though opposed to secession, joined at the call of their state, of their steadfastness in battle, and of their faithfulness as citizens since the end of the war. The regiment's colors were displayed, which was greeted with "earnest emotion . . . on every face." Bettie was presented with a large cake with a Confederate flag and the inscription "Third Tennessee Regiment, CSA."[38]

In mid-October, the understanding forged that spring between the Republicans and the southerners that was to benefit the Texas and Pacific began to unravel. Southerners supported the reelection of Pennsylvania Democrat Samuel Randall as Speaker over Garfield. Facially, this appeared to be a favorable development for Scott and Brown, as the House Pacific Railway committee was loaded with members who supported their project. But ultimately, Randall's election was considered a breach of one of the terms of the compromise reached in March, and by the Christmas season President Hayes gave an interview indicating he was uncertain as to the wisdom of aid to the railroad, and even if that aid was forthcoming, of the amount. Hayes may also have been influenced by the size of the appropriations southern internal improvements required, and by Huntington's brazen (and illegal) construction of the Southern Pacific line across the Indian reservation at Ft. Yuma and a bridge across the Colorado River. Huntington succeeded in this *fait accompli* despite Brown's convincing the secretary of war to order the work stopped.[39]

The new year brought renewal of the struggle with Huntington, who understood it was "very much easier to stop legislation than it is to procure it." In January and February 1878, Brown appeared before first the House and then the Senate Pacific railroad committees. Brown's friend and protégé Wilkes later recalled that such appearances were for the former governor "a favorite field, calling at the same time for his extensive legal information and his sound business qualities and broad views of public policy." To the House committee, Brown argued the whole purpose of the Gadsden Treaty and Purchase was to build a southern transcontinental railroad along the 32nd parallel. He noted the inequities of the land received by the other transcontinental railroads and pointed out the strategic importance of a railroad close to Mexico and through Indian Territory. Other points were the secure position of the government's first liens on the property, the desires of the South, and the constitutional power of the government to lend aid. Brown then turned to the merits of the various bills relating to the Texas and Pacific. Addressing the opposition, Brown argued that a bill relating to a line from San Antonio linking up with Southern Pacific at El Paso had earmarks of one of Huntington's schemes "to make mischief and create diversion." He pointed out Huntington's hypocrisy in asserting in the previous Congress that the country didn't need another line between the Mississippi and the Pacific, against his current request for a subsidy to build such a road, wryly inquiring, "What new light had dawned upon the chameleon mind of this railroad magnate?" Brown also argued the debt of Huntington's other lines would keep him from building his proposed transcontinental line. A similar argument was made to the Senate committee.[40]

In an interview with the Atlanta *Daily Constitution* in February, Brown explained the benefits of a bill sponsored by former Confederate vice president and then Georgia congressman Alexander H. Stephens, which provided for one line west from the Mississippi. Brown thought it more

So as to Confer the Greatest Blessings to the Whole South

likely to pass because it meant less monetary exposure to the government. Another bill, sponsored by Tennessee representative John F. House, provided for branches to Vicksburg, Memphis, and St. Louis. Brown noted that the government guarantee sought by the Texas and Pacific was in fact not a subsidy, as transportation sold to the government would pay the interest. The guarantee was necessary for the simple purpose of being able to sell bonds at par. Brown conceded that the project would not yield a large profit, but made that a virtue, stating: "Neither Col. Scott nor his associates have gone into this enterprise for gold or glory, but with the hope of building a road that shall be of incalculable value to the southwest and the whole country." As he did in Congress, Brown turned to Huntington and argued against a projected monopoly, observing that Huntington did not have the money to build a competing line, that he just wanted to confound the Texas and Pacific. Brown concluded by stating that his prospects of success depended on the support of southerners in the Congress, noting, "Why southern congressmen should hesitate as to their duty I find it hard to guess." An editorial comment on the interview extolled "the splendid heroism [Brown] displayed on the 22nd of July, 1864, near this city" and stated "there can be no question of the great strength given to [the Texas and Pacific] measure by his name."[41]

By this time, it appeared that, notwithstanding all his efforts on the line's behalf, local considerations in the South were keeping the project from getting the full support of southern congressmen. A problem arose even in Tennessee, as in March Brown got into a squabble with the Memphis *Daily Appeal* and its correspondent in Washington over the merits of the various bills, the correspondent observing that Brown was doomed to fail. He only had about ninety votes in the House, "most, if not all of these, are due to the exertions of Governor Brown, whose personal popularity has been put forth for all it is worth—and that is a great deal. His labors to keep alive the charter and prevent a forfeiture of the franchise and privileges of the company, occupied him during many months in Texas and here; and he has given nearly a whole year to secure the passage of a bill that will enable it, with the help of the government, to complete the line through to San Diego. But all this trouble has been had for nothing." It was further noted that the House bill, which Brown seemed to be pushing at that time, did not guarantee Memphis a connection.[42]

In a reply a few days later, Brown appreciated the complimentary mention of his name, but wrote that the bill at issue left it open for Memphis to submit its claim as eastern terminus. "Believing as I do, that the completion of the Texas and Pacific line, so as to connect the Mississippi River with the Pacific coast by the most direct line, would do more than any other one enterprise could to build up the prostrate and impoverished south, I have brought to its aid every energy of my nature, and my great desire is to have the road speedily built, so as to confer the greatest blessings to the whole south." Brown stated that no one locality should be selfish as to the needs of the whole region. Responding a few days later, the correspondent noted that the bill Brown supported mentioned the 32nd parallel, basically along the line of Vicksburg, and noted that Memphis was on the 35th parallel.[43]

To further confound the proponents of the Texas and Pacific, in April, Douglas Campbell, a New York attorney representing the French bondholders of the old Memphis & El Paso, appeared before a subcommittee of the House Judiciary Committee and stated that much of the Texas and Pacific's completed line, and the whole line from Fort Worth west to El Paso, belonged to the Memphis and El Paso by its charter, that the company was an existing corporation, and that the proceedings of foreclosure and sale of its property some years before were fraudulent and void, as the proper parties were not before the court. The sale of Memphis and El Paso rights was approved by then Judge Joseph Bradley, who later was Justice Bradley of the previous year's Committee of Fifteen. There was speculation, if not suspicion, that Huntington had something to do with this new assault. Brown appeared a few days later, addressing each of Campbell's points and in the view of the *Appeal's* correspondent, "making a favorable impression on the committee, acquitting himself, I am told, with credit." He argued that the Texas and Pacific had superior title. "Governor Brown further charged that the purpose of Mr. Campbell in opening up these old Memphis and El Paso matters that had been already adjudicated by the United States court was to injure the credit of the Texas and Pacific, and delay action on the bill pending before Congress in aid of its construction. Any action on a purported lien, he stated, should be before the courts, not Congress. The subcommittee concluded the inquiry in the Texas and Pacific's favor.[44]

Huntington's line coming from the west was a real problem, and in its own way caused a split in the southern congressmen, as some thought it was better dealing with a rich capitalist with interests in the West (Huntington) than a rich one from the North (Scott). Counterattacking, in mid-May 1878, Brown argued against a bill in the Senate Committee on Military Affairs that would grant the Southern Pacific a right of way across the Ft. Yuma reservation. Brown stated the bill would infringe on rights already granted the Texas and Pacific. Brown charged that the Southern Pacific had previously argued that it already had the right of way, and now inconsistently stated that it did not, and had filed false maps with the secretary of war to back up its claim. While the committee reported favorably on the bill, the session ended in June without relief being voted to either of the competing interests. The session ended with the feeling that the Texas and Pacific was in trouble, with several factors contributing to that conclusion: Huntington coming from the west; competition between New Orleans, Vicksburg, and Memphis, which split the southern congressional vote; and a general reluctance in Congress to give more federal aid to railroads.[45]

With Congress in recess, Brown's attention shifted back to Tennessee, where the issue of the state debt continued to fester. Since 1875, the state Democratic Party was split between state credit and low-tax factions. Governor Porter won reelection in 1876 after making unpopular payments on the interest on the state debt, but then recommended in his first message to the General Assembly in January 1877 that the state seek a negotiated settlement with its creditors, a departure from the debt policy he and Brown previously pursued. A committee appointed by the legislature went to the Northeast in March 1877, and eventually a debt reduction plan whereby the state would pay the debt by issuing new thirty-year bonds that financed the debt and interest at 60 percent bearing 6 percent interest was suggested. The proposal percolated for several months, and finally in late 1877 Porter called the legislature into special session to consider the plan. Both that plan and a plan involving a 50 percent discount failed, so Porter resolved to make no further attempts until the 1878 elections.[46]

With Brown present, the state party convention was held in August, and the two factions contested the issue of who would be the Democrats' candidate for governor. The convention was held on the backdrop of a deadly yellow fever epidemic that was just beginning to ravage Memphis and West Tennessee. Eventually, Albert S. Marks, a state judge, was selected as a dark horse candidate. Back in Washington from the convention, Brown told an interviewer that Marks was a strong candidate nominated in the spirit of party harmony, and that the question had been resolved by an agreement to have the legislature devise a way for the people to vote on the issue.[47]

The year ended back in Congress with the renewal of the great struggle with Huntington. Reflecting perhaps the declining prospects of the Texas and Pacific's subsidy efforts, Scott was in Europe, trying to regain his health after a stroke in October 1878. Describing the contending parties, a reporter saw Brown as "one of the finest specimens of physical manhood and knightly courtesy to be found anywhere, and carries himself like a born leader of men. He is a big man anyway you take him, and if my opinion is worth anything the fittest leader to be found anywhere for the work he has in hand." Huntington, on the other hand, was "thoroughly equipped in all the resources and powers that underlie and win success for great enterprises." The same two great problems remained: the Southern Pacific was steadily advancing on El Paso, and despite Brown's best efforts, southern congressmen were not united in favor of the project.[48]

If there was any doubt, 1879 proved to be the year when Scott's Texas and Pacific subsidy effort ground to a halt. As early as March, the Washington correspondent of the Memphis *Daily Appeal* reported that the effort was essentially dead after four fruitless years. "But for the personal popularity of Governor John C. Brown, of this State, the hope of securing an appropriation . . . would have been abandoned long since. But the great energy and unbounded popularity of Governor Brown kept the project alive for the past two years." That conclusion likely was of little consolation to Brown, who, in addition to the frustration of years of effort, suffered that winter with an attack of "inflammatory rheumatism" and kidney disease, which was of such severity as to bring Bettie and their family doctor to Washington from Tennessee.[49]

Upon his recovery, Brown journeyed to Tennessee to take up another cause that had involved years of effort, the resolution of the state debt issue. Late into the legislative session in the first part of 1879, the General Assembly took no action on the issue. A number of the state's New York creditors banded together as the Committee on Tennessee Bondholders early in the year and offered two solutions: 60 percent of par value at 6 percent interest, or 100 percent at 4 percent interest. In late March, Brown met in Nashville with a number of like-minded state-credit Democrats, who resolved to help effect "an honorable adjustment of the debt." Eventually, the legislature passed a 50 percent par value, 5 percent interest proposal, to be ratified by the voters. Thereafter, influential men of all political stripes met and asked Brown, Porter, and others to go to New York as an unofficial citizens committee to confer with the bondholders committee to gain acceptance of the proposal. In those meetings a few weeks later, Brown and Porter were apparently successful in gaining the approval of the majority of the bondholders. But like his efforts on the Texas and Pacific, Brown's efforts in this regard were fruitless, as an apathetic Tennessee electorate rejected the proposal in August 1879. For Brown, the result of the referendum was not altogether unexpected. He told one reporter, "it would be hazardous for him to express an opinion whether or not it would ever be paid." For the state Democratic Party, the failure to unify behind this resolution foreshadowed a split that would put a Republican in the governor's office in 1880.[50]

In this interval, in Tennessee at least, Brown's name was occasionally mentioned as a candidate for vice president of the United States, or as a possible United States senator. There even was a suggestion by the Memphis *Daily Appeal* in early 1880 that Brown should run for governor of Texas, although the Austin *Weekly Democratic Statesman* contemptuously replied to the effect that the *Appeal* should give such advice when Memphis and Tennessee were in better shape than Texas. There is no evidence Brown considered such as serious talk. Although he was formerly a politician, he was still a lawyer, and 1879 saw a professional milestone as Brown was admitted to the bar of the United States Supreme Court and argued before the justices, albeit unsuccessfully, a case for the Texas and Pacific.[51]

When Brown's time as Scott's employee is considered as a whole, both successes and failures appear in the balance. On the negative side, the Texas and Pacific never got a Federal subsidy, but it was not for lack of trying. The struggle between Scott and Huntington over the Texas Pacific subsidy was marked by enormous expenditures to buy influence. If Huntington's monthly bribes during this interval were exemplified by over $10,000 in payments in March 1879, and if he was right that it cost less to hinder legislation than it did to pass it, then Scott's expenditures were undoubtedly astronomical. Scott's enterprise, whether criminal or simply corrupt, dwarfed the former governor's previous experience in breadth and scale. There is no evidence that Brown ever participated in or had knowledge of outright bribery, but neither was he blind or a fool. Brown's role as a lawyer had previously put him in the employ of criminals, so the ultimate answer was that he was first and foremost a lawyer, and the representation of corrupt characters is one of the burdens of that profession. On the positive side, Brown unquestionably grew as a lawyer, representing interests with a national scale in the courts and in Congress, and by doing so increased his own personal wealth. Moreover, even though he could have declined on the basis of absence on business, he continued to strive with his fellow Tennesseans to try to resolve the nettlesome debt issue. In his service with the Louisiana Commission, Brown used his *bona fides* as a conservative southerner to work toward the sectional reconciliation President Hayes was seeking to attain. If he retained any wartime bitterness, it never showed.[52]

The Texas and Pacific was never able to raise the money to accomplish Scott's designs, either through investment or by government aid. In November, Brown finally conceded that the effort to obtain a federal subsidy was at an end. A wild rumor in late 1879 held that Scott would revive the waning prospect of the railroad and offer the presidency of the line to Ulysses S. Grant. Brown dismissed this rumor, but hinted that management was in discussions with "outside capitalists" who would invest their money in extending the railroad. Such was indeed the case, as in December 1879, perhaps the ultimate capitalist of the day was making preparations to buy Tom Scott out of the Texas and Pacific.[53]

So as to Confer the Greatest Blessings to the Whole South

9

I Have Great Faith in the Outcome of the Texas and Pacific

1880–1889

For four years, Brown labored on behalf of Tom Scott in the name of the Texas and Pacific while Scott searched for the money required to extend the railroad westward across Texas. But as 1879 became 1880, negotiations were well under way that would result in Scott's relinquishment of control in return for the monies necessary to complete the line to El Paso. With Scott essentially disabled by the after-effects of his stroke, Brown traveled to New York to undertake the necessary negotiations with the man who would have a great influence on Brown for most of the rest of his life, Jay Gould.[1]

Like Brown, Gould was the son of a farmer. Born in 1836, he worked his way up from a fairly modest beginning in business and started investing in railroad bonds in 1857. By 1859, he was fully involved in Wall Street. Gould was a "born speculator," mastering the complex interactions of banking, currency, and the stock market. By 1867, he controlled the Erie Railroad, but was forced out by the stockholders in 1872 after, as some said, he "plundered" it. In 1869, he was involved a conspiracy to run up the price of gold, but was foiled when the United States Treasury sold a supply of gold, dropping the bottom out of the market. In 1873, he acquired control of the Union Pacific, and later the Wabash. Gould's appearance belied his wealth and power. He was "a mite of a man, dark complected, black eyed, black haired and black whiskered; . . . listless and shaken in appearance, weighing but little over 100 pounds, with no particularly intelligent expression, and in fact with hardly a manifestation of any kind of power or force in his whole showing."[2]

As the 1870s progressed, Gould added controlling interests in several western railroads, including the cornerstone of his burgeoning empire, the Missouri Pacific. By the end of 1880, he essentially controlled all but two of the railroads coming into St. Louis. And not being content with a railroad empire alone, he acquired control of the Western Union telegraph company in 1881. Notwithstanding the breadth of Gould's southwestern railroad empire, he lacked a connection to the Pacific. The only practical possibility of gaining that was the Texas and Pacific, which with heavy interest charges on its bonds, no federal aid, and no other potential investors, was ripe for acquisition.[3]

Gould was no stranger to Brown. His interest in the Union Pacific brought Gould into an uneasy alliance with Huntington to defeat Scott's efforts in Congress. Gould also had a hand in forging the temporary Scott-Gould truce in late 1876. While Gould's scheme to obtain favorable treatment for the Union Pacific was eventually fruitless, the experience and contacts he gained in this political maneuvering fostered, in the words of his modern biographer, "direct connection to the inner circle of the Republican Party." He would need that connection. In acquiring Scott's railroad, Gould acquired Scott's enemy, Huntington.[4]

The agreement that was finally hammered out by Brown and the Texas and Pacific's other vice president, Frank S. Bond, was a complicated transaction whereby Gould created a construction company that was to build the remaining line to El Paso and be compensated in first mortgage bonds and stock. At the end of two and a half years, it was anticipated Gould would own enough stock to control the election of the Texas and Pacific board of directors. It was also agreed that Scott would not resign as president until the completion of the road. With the new contract insuring the company had the means to do so, Brown was tasked with pushing that completion.[5]

The new focus on the Texas and Pacific required a change in Brown's domestic situation. Since becoming employed with the railroad, Brown maintained his home in Pulaski, and his frequent travels across the country likely made it convenient for Bettie and the children to more or less stay there. But being required to "devote his entire time" to the project, it was time to move his family to the railroad's headquarters in Marshall, Texas. Their departure was lamented in Pulaski, as Bettie and the girls were an integral part of the town's social circle. The oldest girl, Marie, known as "Miss Minnie,' was likely left to complete her curriculum at

I Have Great Faith in the Outcome of the Texas and Pacific

Jay Gould (Credit: Library of Congress)

Martin College, and later that year was dispatched to college in Georgetown, near Washington, DC. Visits to Tennessee would be short for the foreseeable future.[6]

Between the successful law practice he developed after the war and the years of lucrative salary from the railroad, Brown acquired relatively substantial wealth, to the point that in April 1880, he, Bond, and another investor bought the Dallas and Wichita line out of a court sale for $165,000, financing the purchase with a small amount of cash and a large amount of bonds. In early July, the Tennessean was in New York, calling on Democratic presidential candidate Gen. Winfield Scott Hancock with former Texas congressman John Hancock, ex-governor James W. Throckmorton of Texas, and Brown's old comrade Gen. Edward C. Walthall. In an interview, he enthusiastically reported on the Texas and Pacific's progress, the economic prospects of Texas and of Tennessee, and predicted a Hancock victory.[7]

On November 8, Scott and a group from Philadelphia embarked on a three-week tour of the Texas and Pacific and its various branch lines. Brown likely joined the party en route, and spoke on Scott's behalf when protocol required. Visits were made to multiple states, and newspaper articles noted the progress of the line and its various branches, and that approximately five thousand men were working on the line at that time. The party went to the westernmost point of the line in Callahan County, Texas, and Scott drove a ceremonial spike. While inspecting works on the Mississippi River, Brown was called on for remarks and predicted future prosperity for Louisiana and Texas. He also made a widely-reported observation that the South should concentrate on developing itself and leave national politics to the North, not so much as to show any "supine indifference," but to avoid clinging to the memories of its dead past which would keep the section from prospering.[8]

In Tennessee, the debt controversy dragged on. State-credit advocate Howell E. Jackson, an obscure state representative who was better known as the brother of former Confederate cavalryman Gen. W. H. "Red" Jackson, was elected as a compromise candidate for an open senate seat in January 1881. Later that year, a coalition of Republicans and state-credit Democrats passed a law to pay the debt at 100 percent face value with 3 percent bonds (100/3), with interest coupons receivable for taxes. This latter feature, however, resulted in the Tennessee Supreme Court's ruling that the 100/3 law was unconstitutional, as it restricted the freedom of future legislatures. Brown strongly asserted in a letter published in late 1880 his favoring "strict maintenance of the public faith," stating, "No party can maintain power and no government can prosper by ignoring this great principle." Ultimately, in 1882, "sky-blue Democrats," who favored payment of the debt, bolted the party and ran their own candidate for governor. Brown predicted that the split in the party would make Tennessee a Republican state, and blamed his old enemy Andrew Johnson, claiming that Johnson created the issue to gain the senatorship in 1874. Ultimately, another enemy of Johnson's, Isham G. Harris, and Harris's fellow Bourbon Democrats elected Gen. William B. Bate governor, successfully asserting that the party should not be split over a percentage or two, and the state debt issue was finally more or less concluded by Tennessee repudiating part of the debt.[9]

The impending takeover by Gould had no apparent effect on Brown's activities in early 1881. Brown was out and about in Texas acquiring rights of way and reported on such activities to General Dodge, now employed by Gould, in March. Scott and general superintendent George Noble resigned in April, however, and Gould and his man H. M. Hoxie assumed their roles with the railroad. This apparently occurred while Brown was on a "flying visit" to Pulaski. Bettie returned to Texas with him and made a great impression at a reception for Noble "elegantly attired in a light blue Moire antique satin with iridescent steel trimming and diamond ornaments," which was described as "the handsomest dress in the room." Perhaps Bettie and her husband were making a final statement, considering the likelihood of their departure from the scene as well.[10]

Gould, however, was very interested in Brown. According to one account, Gould was so impressed by the "discretion and frankness" with which Brown conducted negotiations on Scott's behalf that he initially determined to keep Brown in his job. In July 1881, Brown superintended a lawsuit against Huntington in Federal court in Santa Fe, New Mexico, over the issue of the Southern Pacific's building its road across the Ft. Yuma reservation. The Southern Pacific claimed its rights from a grant from the New Mexico territorial legislature, while the Texas and Pacific continued to rely on its congressional charter. Brown asked for an injunction and for acquisition of the line at an equitable price. The Dallas *Daily Herald* observed: "In Governor Brown the Texas & Pacific has an officer, not only alive to all its interests and vigilant thereof, but possessed of the highest order of intellect, as he is, and being thoroughly informed, he earnestly devotes his best endeavors to whatever he undertakes. Having superior administrative and executive ability, as he demonstrated when governor of Tennessee, of most pleasing address, quick of perception and able to take prompt advantage of circumstances, he has proven himself to be a valuable and efficient officer of the road. To him Texas and the company owes much for the rapid progress and development of this grand enterprise."[11]

At some point in the summer of 1881, Gould, seeing Brown's "strong practical sense, his broad views, his extensive legal information, his unswerving integrity and strong personal worth," offered him the job of "general solicitor" (in modern terms, general counsel) of Gould's Southwest System, a conglomeration of rail lines craftily assembled by the financier. Brown accepted. The hire was seen as yet another move by Gould to consolidate his control over his growing empire. With the job secure, Brown, Bettie, and their girls took a trip to Saratoga, New York. Some in Tennessee lamented that the former governor was not returning to the state to resume his political career. Not only was Brown not returning to Tennessee, but he was moving his business headquarters from Texas to St. Louis, the nerve center of Gould's railroad interests. Expressions of regret came not only from Texas, but from Pulaski, where Brown closed up his family residence and resigned his position on the board of Martin College. A St. Louis newspaper, however, stated that Brown "will be cordially welcomed in our midst as a citizen of great worth and influence."[12]

Over the next few years, Brown had an interesting and varied law practice. On January 18, 1882, the New Mexico suit brought the previous summer was settled by the Texas and Pacific selling its rights to the line across New Mexico, Arizona, and California to Huntington's Southern Pacific. The deal made provisions for the joint use of the track west of El Paso, although in the end the Texas and Pacific never made it that far. A scheme to extend the Texas railroad system down into Mexico eventually resulted in the former governor taking a trip across Texas and south across the border with his son and "capitalists" who were interested in a railroad project into that country. Brown exercised his new authority to appoint counsel for the system in several outlying locations. In matters of litigation, Brown appeared yet again for the Texas and Pacific in the Supreme Court of the United States. He filed an attachment in Federal court on behalf of the Missouri Pacific when the failure of a Dallas banking house threatened a loss of $83,000. When a suit was filed against Jay Gould and some associates for violation of a constitutional provision prohibiting common control of parallel railroad lines, Brown took steps to defend it and argued that the case was without merit as a mere effort to force a compromise in another matter.[13]

As in the Tom Scott days, Brown appeared before various state and federal legislative committees and regulatory commissions, but instead of arguing for subsidies, he usually argued against railroad regulation or rate cuts. A Texas lawyer termed Brown the "brains and brawn of the railroad lobby." He and Dodge corresponded on legislative policy in Congress, Dodge preferring to make a greater effort in the Senate rather than the House, "where they seem to me to be almost crazy." A serious threat materialized in 1884 when there was a legislative push to declare the land grant of the New Orleans Pacific Railway forfeit, claiming that there was no legal authorization for the original grantee, the defunct New Orleans, Baton Rouge & Vicksburg Railroad, to assign the same to the New Orleans Pacific, even though the Department of Interior and the United States attorney general assented. Dodge urged Brown to write letters to each of his friends in the House to point out the injustice of forfeiting the grant after so much effort had gone into the construction of the line. Eventually, the measure was defeated in both chambers.[14]

Brown found the time to pursue individual business opportunities. The one that secured the most publicity was an 1883 scheme to cut a ship canal 137 ½ miles across Florida, which was calculated to cut 500 miles off of the trip from New Orleans to New York by sea. A number of prominent individuals were involved, including several Tennesseans, Senator John Sherman, and fellow Civil War veterans Gov. Benjamin F. Butler of Massachusetts and Senator William Mahone of Virginia. The group elected Brown as president of the Florida Ship Canal Company, and Gen. Charles P. Stone, unfairly disgraced after the 1861 Federal disaster at Ball's Bluff, Virginia, was the chief engineer. After a rush of publicity, the project never got off the ground, as most transportation investment was still going into railroad construction. A sure sign of doom for the project was the rumor in early 1884 that Brown and his compatriots would ask for a government subsidy on the basis of coastal defense, it being noted that Brown "has had considerable experience in Government subsidies." Brown owned an interest with Congressman (and former Confederate cavalryman) George G. Dibrell, former congressman John F. House and others in the Bon Air Coal, Iron, and Lumber Company in Tennessee. And with Memphian Robert J. Looney, Brown owned the rights to a new telephone that was marketed in Texas.[15]

About this time, a newspaper article described the personalities of the various officials at Gould's headquarters in St. Louis. Brown was stated to have "a large acquaintance with public men and affairs, and is very

useful to the system in influencing and shaping national and state legislation. He is the most popular man of the syndicate, and can beat Abe.
Lincoln in telling a story." The correspondent went on to note that, at
that time, Brown was over fifty and "is a man of strong frame and much
endurance, with a great deal of intellectual vitality. As to whether or
not Governor Brown can swear, there are some very dark traditions ex-
tant, coeval with his military career, the authenticity of which, it is well,
probably not to investigate too closely. Governor Brown receives a salary of $15,000 per annum, which he spends liberally." Reflecting the last
point, perhaps, in February 1884, the Brown family passed through its
old haunts in Marshall, Texas, on the way to New Orleans to attend
Mardi Gras.[16]

The former governor also kept his connections with Tennessee, especially relating to his legacy as one of its Confederate soldiers. An appeal
in a Tennessee newspaper on behalf of a military history of Tennessee
published over the signature of Brown, Cheatham, Bate, Porter, Key, and
others asked for lists of men fallen in battle. Brown was invited to represent Tennessee at a Confederate reunion in Texas in July 1883, and as
the first colonel of the 3rd Tennessee, he attended a solemn ceremony
in Pulaski in November 1883 reinterring the remains of Lt. Col. Calvin
Clack. Addressing his former comrades and the others gathered, Brown
spoke of the past, but counseled "harmony, good will and the common
strength of a common country for the future." Brown remained popular
in his home state and was mentioned on more than one occasion by a
Tennessee newspaper as a possible candidate, either for vice president or
United States senator.[17]

The Texas and Pacific's financial condition, never good, became more
acute in 1884. Six groups of bonds totaling over $40 million were issued
by the company since 1875. The dire situation was no secret, and Brown
found it necessary to deny a rumor that the company was going into
receivership. To give the creditors a measure of control, the board was
reorganized late that year to include seats representing the bondholders,
with Gould's men holding the remaining seats. Brown retained his seat
on the board as one of Gould's representatives. Eventually, in the spring
of 1885, the new board appointed a committee to examine the condition
of the line, report on its business, and suggest a plan to restore finances.

Unfortunately, the party's special train collided with another train as it went around a sharp bend. Two men were mangled and killed and Brown suffered a dislocated shoulder.[18]

Brown's injury was not the only difficulty he experienced in 1885. First, in March of that year, the Gould system suffered labor troubles. Gould's aggressive expansion created competition with other western railroads. Cut-throat competition that required rate-cutting and the expenses of expansion created financial pressure on the railroads to cut costs, which naturally included wages. Labor, which was at a premium in the years prior to 1884, was now in surplus, which gave the railroad employees less power over their wages and working conditions. A reduction of 10 percent occurred in October 1884, and another of 5 percent occurred in February 1885. The first backlash occurred in March 1885, when, in a series of purportedly spontaneous work stoppages, a strike of railroad workers on the Gould system occurred. The workers' plight coupled with Gould's reputation made other workers and the public in general sympathetic to the strikers, and the Union Pacific's Knights of Labor sent an organizer.[19]

The Knights of Labor were first organized in 1869 in Philadelphia. Unlike today's labor unions, the Knights strove to represent all types of labor in all endeavors, skilled and unskilled. There was a sort of mystical ritual drawn from its founder's religious background, and the ritual was passed on by word of mouth. Membership was open to all wage earners, except doctors, lawyers, bankers, and liquor salesmen. The goals of the order were vague, although, like all labor organizations, it sought to achieve higher wages and better working conditions, as well as the abolition of prison and child labor, and progressive for the time, equal pay for the sexes. Arbitration was preferred to strikes, although strikes were conceded to sometimes be necessary, especially since, as a practical matter, arbitration required that both sides be willing to arbitrate. The head of the order was the Grand Master Workman, who in 1885 was Terence V. Powderly.[20]

The strike was resolved between March 12 and 16, 1885. On March 12, a committee of strikers and citizens in Sedalia, Missouri, adopted a resolution to the effect that the company should reinstate the striking workers, and that effective on April 1, the wage rates would revert to those paid the previous September, that no wage reduction should occur for at least a year, that no one would be discharged for participating in the strike, and that overtime should be paid at time and a half. Bearing the endorsement of various state officials, this agreement was reduced to writing by R. S. Hayes, the Missouri Pacific's first vice president, on March 15, 1885, thereby becoming the "Hayes Agreement." The strikers accepted the settlement on March 16. As noted by a congressional committee, "[t]hroughout the entire time the strike was conducted in the most orderly manner and the final settlement, though an apparent victory for the striking employees, was in no sense unfair or unjust to the railroad company." As Brown was the Gould system's counsel, it is easy to credit Brown's claim to a member of the Knights that he had written the Hayes Agreement, or was its "founder."[21]

Brown's second oldest daughter, Daisy, suffered from consumption, as tuberculosis was then known. As 1885 wore on, she weakened, rallying at one point or another, the last to the extent that she was able to visit her mother's family in Murfreesboro in the first part of that summer. Himself suffering with the dislocated shoulder, Brown spent time with the girl, and when she made a comment as to how he worked with his injured arm, Brown tenderly said he would work on his hands and knees if it would restore her health. Unfortunately, her condition worsened, and Daisy expired on August 10 at the age of seventeen. Brown was present at her death, supported by his friend, Bishop Quintard.[22]

Personal tragedy notwithstanding, the conundrum of the Texas and Pacific remained. In September, the inspection tour resumed. Brown and others went over the entire line, and estimates were made as to what it would cost to put the road in a "fair condition." Considering the road's floating indebtedness (short term debt continually renewed) and its earnings, it became clear to the committee that the company could no longer pay interest. The road needed improvement, also, as only 400 of its 1,487 miles had steel rails. The board took all of this into account and concluded that it would have to suspend debt payments. The Texas and Pacific also owed its big sister in the Gould system, the Missouri Pacific, approximately $1,250,000.[23]

Cleverly, the debt owed the Missouri Pacific was used as a basis to seek a court-supervised receivership of the Texas and Pacific, in order to keep third parties from dismembering the road, as separate mortgages were held on each of its three individual divisions. On December 15, 1885, Gould's Missouri Pacific Railway Company filed suit in a Louisiana Federal court against Gould's Texas and Pacific, setting forth these and other facts, asserting that foreclosure of the mortgages on the three divisions would result in separate trustees for each, preventing the road from being operated as a whole, and stating that if the monies were instead used to put the deteriorating road in "first class condition," it "would, without doubt, have an earning capacity and a traffic that would enable said company to pay off its entire floating indebtedness, and at the same time meet the fixed charges created by its mortgages without difficulty. . . ."[24]

Late on December 16, 1885, United States circuit judge Don A. Pardee entered an order granting the receivership and appointing Brown and Lionel A. Sheldon as receivers. Slightly younger than Brown, Sheldon was a "man of fine physique and marked ability." He was a New York-born, Oberlin-educated Ohio lawyer who joined the Federal army during the Civil War, and as a result of service in the region, settled in New Orleans, where he practiced law, including about three years in partnership with Judge Pardee. He later served as a Republican congressman from Louisiana, and as territorial governor of New Mexico until earlier in 1885. While Judge Pardee saw the need for the receivership, skeptics charged that the deteriorated condition of the Texas and Pacific was part of a deliberate policy by Gould to depress the value of the road so that the bondholders and other creditors could be defrauded. They charged that Brown, as Gould's creature, would "proceed to gobble up the Texas and Pacific Railroad in the approved style of the receiver for his boss." Needing trusted assistance in his new role, Brown summoned his friend, John S. Wilkes, from Pulaski to act as the railroad's treasurer.[25]

While Sheldon took a trip to St. Louis to get oriented, Brown took immediate control of the situation. From New Orleans on the night of December 16, 1885, he telegraphed all the officers and agents of the Texas and Pacific and announced the appointment of the receivers and their assumption of control over its business and property. Judge Pardee asked that he "go immediately over the line" to keep the road's business from being hindered, and to make sure that the employees were paid. Brown arrived in Marshall the afternoon of the next day. While in the machine shops there, he was met with a committee wanting to know if the receivers would comply with the Hayes Agreement with the Knights of Labor. After explaining that he had just been appointed and that things were a bit chaotic, Brown replied that the receivers were not bound by the agreement, but were under the orders of the court. The committee then asked if the receivers would ratify the agreement, and Brown stated that while he could not do so, he would say that employees would not be removed without cause and in all respects be treated fairly and would not have their wages diminished. After a discussion as to whether all cars and engines would be rebuilt in the company's shops, Brown indicated that the receivers would do so as best they could. The group seemed to be satisfied with the discussion. Brown then saw to paying the workers and went on to Dallas that night, established an office there, and announced no changes would be made in employment except as necessity demanded.[26]

Doubtlessly believing that the Texas and Pacific's business was under control, Brown departed for Tennessee for the happy event of daughter Marie's marriage at age twenty to thirty-two-year-old congressman Benton McMillin on January 5, 1886. Although born in Kentucky, McMillin made his home in Carthage and was serving his fourth term as representative of Tennessee's Fourth District. The marriage occurred in the family's home in Pulaski and was presided over by Bishop Quintard, which made some recall the marriage of Marie's parents in 1864. Still in mourning, the family remembered Daisy with a portrait in the corner and a basket of flowers. Marie had "attained a brilliancy of mind and womanly beauty that won a host of admirers, and made her a central attraction in the social concourse." The couple left for Washington that afternoon after a stop to decorate Daisy's grave with some of the bridal flowers. They would in due time present Governor and Mrs. Brown their first grandson, named Brown McMillin.[27]

Business demanded that the remainder of the Brown family depart for New Orleans the day after the nuptials. Brown appeared before Judge Pardee on January 9, as lawyers representing creditors other than the Missouri Pacific petitioned that their clients be made parties to the case, and also to ask the judge to add another receiver, based in New York. The court declined to do so, noting that the business of the railroad required the receivers to live along its line. By January 24, Brown was in St. Louis, meeting with some newly-appointed Texas and Pacific officials. Brown noted the need of new rails and ties and said that the entire income of the road would be devoted to that purpose. In a letter to Dodge a few days earlier, Brown wrote: "I have great faith in the outcome of the Texas and Pacific, and I assure you that so far as within me lies, I shall contribute everything I have to bring it out of its present difficulties."[28]

More family obligations soon required a return to Tennessee. Neill Brown died early in the morning of January 30, 1886, after a period of "feebleness" lasting some months. For the last few years of his life, he served for a time as a trustee of the state insane asylum and supported the state-credit "sky-blue" faction of the Democratic Party in 1882, remaining active in the state party. Otherwise, he made a few occasional ceremonial appearances. Prior to his own passing, Neill suffered the death of two of his sons, J. Trim Brown, his brother's former staff officer, in 1878, and another who was killed at work in New Mexico in 1881.[29]

During the ten days Brown was away from the railroad, the first indications of unresolved labor issues arose. Although Gould was on a cruise at the time of the previous year's strike, he personally met with Powderly and his executive board in August 1885 and helped resolve a pending strike on the Wabash line. This was interpreted as a virtual capitulation on Gould's part and made Powderly's board much more aggressive. Likely, some of that aggression also came from the fact that not all of the Wabash strikers regained their jobs. Indeed, evidence exists that in several ways in several locations, the Missouri Pacific and its associated railroads violated the Hayes Agreement even as new grievances arose. On January 10, 1886, delegates from the local assemblies of the Knights met in St. Louis and approved resolutions that led the executive committee of their district assembly to believe it had the right to call a strike on its own.[30]

The first ripple toward a new labor difficulty arose while Brown was in Tennessee in connection with his brother's death. The Knights at Marshall presented a seven-point proposal similar in many respects to the matters raised by the committee at Marshall in December. Brown and Sheldon "carefully" reviewed the document, and Brown replied on February 4, reminding them of the December conversation that made it clear that the receivers were not bound by any old agreements, that court approval was necessary for new agreements, but that the receivers "shall endeavor to do full justice to all employees of the receivers, and shall endeavor by all proper means to retain their confidence and promote their interests in every way consistent with the best interest of the property we represent." As Brown later related, the agreement, in the receivers' view, "would virtually relegate their authority to the Knights of Labor."[31]

Brown was known to the Knights as a powerful voice in Gould's circle. The receivers' rejection of the proposal was interpreted by some as the first move to use the receivership to undermine their position. A *causus belli* arose on February 17, 1886, when C. A. Hall, a Knight who was employed in the Marshall shops, was terminated. Until February 24, the receivers and their management had no inkling there was trouble afoot. On that date, a Knight at Marshall wired George Noble, who the receivers had hired as their general agent for Texas, asking him to come to Marshall to "settle trouble in the shops." Noble inquired and got no information of such trouble. Meanwhile, Sheldon traveled through Marshall, where he was met at the shop by Martin Irons, chairman of the Knights executive board, who it was noted was not an employee of the receivers. Sheldon was in a hurry to get to Dallas, and in any event needed to confer with Brown, who was then sick in bed and "too ill to do business." Irons then sent a communication dated the next day, February 28, saying that a strike was imminent. No response was made because the receivers did not recognize his authority to negotiate and because there was no intimation of trouble in the shops.[32]

At 3:00 p.m. on March 1, Texas and Pacific workers at Marshall and Big Spring Creek walked out "to a man," starting, in the words of an investigating congressional committee, "the greatest railroad strike in the history of the United States." Brown believed that the majority of the workers had no real grievance and did not leave the shop on their own accord. He published an order on the evening of March 1, notifying the strikers that if they returned by 10:00 a.m. on March 4, they would retain their employment, and if not, they would be "absolutely discharged." The Knights chose to escalate matters by expanding the strike to the Missouri Pacific. The strike was expanded for two reasons: it gave the Knights the opportunity to address grievances across the Gould system, and the Texas and Pacific strikers could not carry on alone.[33]

I Have Great Faith in the Outcome of the Texas and Pacific

Within the narrower context of the Texas and Pacific, the receivers stood fast on the powers conferred by the court. A committee of concerned citizens in Marshall sought to mediate the dispute and asked for a meeting prior to the March 4 deadline. Brown replied that the deadline was "inflexible," stating: "We have paid the men promptly the same wages they have received for the past year without a murmur from them. We have not changed the manner nor hours of work, and in no way, as we are aware, have we done the men the slightest injustice . . . [n]otwithstanding this, they left the shops without the slightest cause. . . ." After a further attempt early on March 4, which Brown again rebuffed, the committee made one last effort to set up a meeting, saying the men would return to work if Brown would agree to confer with them. Brown replied that in general the receivers would be glad to do so, but that workers who had been replaced would not be rehired. At this point, the committee gave up.[34]

When the House Select Committee on Existing Labor Troubles examined Brown later in the spring, the former governor was questioned quite closely on the strike. Brown denied that he had any "feeling" against the labor organization and stated that, from the start, he did not discriminate against anyone who wanted to return to work "because he was a member of any organization, or not a member of any organization, for all should be put on the same footing." Brown denied objecting to labor organizations in general, testifying, "I should be pleased to see all labor organized on what I conceive to be a proper plan." Brown's concern was that the Knights, a "secret organization," was undertaking to speak for men who were not among their members. But he would confer with any committee from any labor organization composed of the company's employees. When asked if he opposed arbitration with labor organizations, Brown agreed with the concept, but noted that the labor organizations were "unfair" to railroads, in that they wanted thirty days' notice prior to a discharge or reduction in force, yet workers could "quit without notice at the blowing of a whistle, leaving your trains on a side-track, and your shops unprotected."[35]

Already, there were incidents of violence, as masked men took possession of trains, uncoupled cars, and disabled engines, either by removing important parts or "killing" the engine, which meant extinguishing their fires and emptying them of water. Generally, only the trackmen, yardmen, and men in the shops and freight warehouses were the strikers. Engineers, firemen, conductors, and trainmen generally did not participate. In Brown's view, these employees and the line's passengers, as well as the physical facilities at Marshall, Texarkana, Fort Worth, and three other locations, were in danger. Bridges were burned, and rails and switches were displaced, and Brown received reports of "violent men assembled in large multitudes." Brown acted decisively to invoke legal process, applying with Judge Pardee's approval to the various local Federal courts for protection. Writs of assistance were issued to Federal marshals, and warrants for arrest issued. Brown was careful to relate to the committee that he often conferred with the marshals, that while he wanted the writs "vigorously enforced," mobs broken up, and the railroad's property protected, the receivers "were especially desirous that no man should be hurt, and that only the flagrantly lawless or violent men should be arrested or imprisoned."[36]

On March 8, while Brown and Sheldon moved to suppress the strike, it became general across the system. Both Gould and Powderly were surprised, and Powderly likely more discomfited than Gould, who during most of the strike was on a cruise in the West Indies, leaving Hoxie in charge of the system. Faced with violence, Hoxie also went to the courts for protection and, by the third week of March, was well on the way to defeating the strike. Powderly, on the other hand, doubtlessly seeking to gain control of Irons at the source of the strike, sent Brown a telegram on March 11 asking for arbitration "to settle the difficulties with the Texas and Pacific employees." Brown replied the same day, pointing out that the railroad had no problem with its existing employees, only its former employees, those who were seeking to impair the operations of the road by violence and intimidation. And, in a supplemental reply, Brown helpfully pointed out that the court was open for any party to air grievances against the receivers. When questioned by the congressional committee, Brown noted that arbitration and conferring were two different concepts. He defended his decision to turn down Powderly's request, saying he thought it would at that point in time do no good, as the strike was then ten days old, acts of violence had occurred, replacement workers had been hired, and the marshals were deployed. Brown added that, if he thought some good would come of it, "I would not have delayed to avail myself of it, for no one deprecated the strike more than I did."[37]

Although violence continued into April, the strike was effectively defeated by the end of March. Gould declared it at an end on April 6, and the Knights belatedly did so on May 4. The fragmentation of leadership in the Knights was a serious impediment to the success of the strike. Further, unlike the 1885 strike, the 1886 strike's acts of violence deprived the Knights of a great deal of public sympathy, although a newspaper in Irons's hometown of Sedalia, Missouri, mocked Brown's invitation of a meeting of the governors similar to 1885, noting that the strikers said "their future action depends on whether Mr. Brown imprisons, shoots or simply deposes the governors." More seriously, Brown was hanged in effigy on at least one occasion in March, and the congressional committee heard testimony from a witness who stated a striker said the killing of Brown "would be a good thing." There is no direct evidence of the effect on Brown's health or the feelings of his family, but the enormous strain of the strike shortened the life of Gould's confidant Hoxie.[38]

Brown's appearance before a subcommittee of the House Select Committee occurred in May. In addition to his view of circumstances as recounted above, Brown was also asked about the use of convict and Chinese labor on the Texas and Pacific. He denied Congress's power to regulate the rates and wages on the railroads, pointing out the difference between a railroad built on land the owner was compensated for and a steamboat plying the waters, which are public. The friendly Fort Worth *Daily Gazette* thought Brown's argument "an ingenious one," which would survive a test in the Supreme Court. When asked about government ownership of the railroads, Brown replied: "I think the fewer business interests the Government has the better for the Government and the people and the business to be subserved by it." Brown's attitude as a railroad lawyer in 1886 was little different than his viewpoint as governor in 1871.[39]

Even in the midst of the strike, the issues relating to the reorganization of the Texas and Pacific went on. On two occasions in March, Grenville Dodge wrote to warn of various actions of the bondholders as to the three divisions of the railroad that he deemed detrimental to the whole, especially relating to the Eastern Division. Dodge hoped that Judge Pardee's trip along the line would enable him to "see the exact position of it and act upon his own judgment." In early April, Dodge wrote again, noting that the bondholders committee met on April 23, some bondholders "demanding hatred and hammer for their bonds." These matters dragged on into the summer, as individual committees floated various plans. A committee looking out for Gould's interests was headed by former general Isaac Wistar and a group of Philadelphians, and proposed to redeem the railroad's debt to the Missouri Pacific by issuing a quantity of Texas and Pacific stock conveniently sufficient to give Gould control. Brown's Knoxville friend Charles M. McGhee was a member of a committee based in New York holding Rio Division bonds, and Brown wrote McGhee expressing the hope that the conflicting interests would be harmonized "so as to furnish us the means to place the property in better condition." Brown thought Wistar was someone that McGhee would find to be a reasonable man, and complained that members of the Rio Division committee knew nothing "about the condition of the property."[40]

Brown's wish for "harmony" among the competing interests was realized, at least to the extent that the competing committees created a compromise group representing a broader set of interests than Gould's. The new committee included Wistar, McGhee, Robert Fleming, a British investor, and a few others. There were many knotty questions to resolve, including the operation of the railroad during reorganization, and the future of the company once the receivership was over. Brown had an ally in McGhee, stemming from their long and friendly relations, and in this period Brown and Wistar were on good terms, as well. Wistar seems to have had something to do with Brown's appointment as receiver, and indicated to Brown that he would be the president of the railroad once it came out of the reorganization.[41]

Back in Tennessee in November 1886, Brown got up from a sick bed to speak at a political rally in Pulaski, prior to the gubernatorial election that selected Democrat Bob Taylor over his Republican brother Alf in the celebrated "War of the Roses." He was met with a large crowd and applause so loud that it was several minutes before he could begin his talk, which was an endorsement of his party's platform. He recalled associations with his fellow veterans, the struggle with the Radicals to regain control of the state government, and then commented on the political issues of the day. Happily, during this two-week visit, the family was vis-

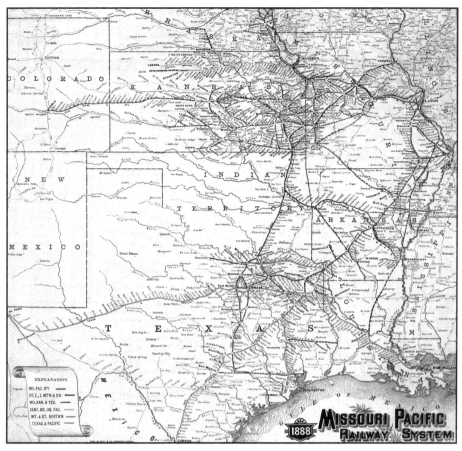

Missouri Pacific System, 1888 (Credit: Kansas State Historical Society)

ited by Minnie and McMillin. Both Brown and McMillin were among a list of dark horse candidates for an upcoming Senate vacancy, but the Bourbon candidate, outgoing governor Bate, was elected.[42]

Brown's receiver work continued on into 1887. At the first of the year, the huge improvements done under the receivers' care were noted in a Galveston newspaper. "The enormous amount of work done by Governor Brown since he has taken charge of the road is said by well-posted railroad men to be without a precedent among railroad enterprises. He is regarded as the coming railroad man in the South and Southwest and as the only man who can and does checkmate Jay Gould in his efforts to grasp men as he has some of their enterprises and use them to his own purposes." A month later, Brown predicted that the road would be taken out of the receivership within a year. Indicating the influence and prestige Brown had accumulated, the Tennessean was elected the chairman of a large meeting of Western and Pacific railway managers in Chicago called to resist the enactment of an interstate commerce law.[43]

A number of powerful men had substantial money at stake in the results of the receivership. A common criticism, therefore, was that the receivers were spending too much money to get the railroad back in shape. Brown acknowledged that the "expenses are still heavy, but I am examining minutely into all Departments with a view of reducing it everywhere that it is possible to do so, and think we will be able to make a material reduction in the current expenses." Expensive though it was, the work continued, to the point that the road was advertised for sale to occur in early November. That October, Brown reported the road was in a "good and very safe condition," noting the improvements to the road and the purchase of new equipment. On November 7 and 8, Brown rode a special train across a large portion of the railroad, arriving in Marshall with representatives of the railroad and various creditors for the sale of the Texas portion of the line. The Texas line was sold to a "purchasing committee" represented by Wistar, for a total of $10,000,000. Thereafter, Wistar and his "committee" went to New Orleans and purchased the "New Orleans Pacific" and the terminal and other properties for a total of $5,000,000. It was, as matters turned out, accurately speculated that Brown would end up leading the reorganized railroad, which brought smiles from the employees at the railroad's offices. To pave the way for Brown's ascendancy, Sheldon resigned effective December 1, 1887, after Gould paid him off. Wistar characterized Sheldon, put in place by his former law partner Judge Pardee, as "a low political adventurer, without property, credit, veracity or character."[44]

With the end of the receivership anticipated, personal tragedy struck again. Since her marriage, Minnie spent most of her time with McMillin in Washington. But in October of that year, she came home to Pulaski in feeble health. Nonetheless, her death on December 7 was unexpected, and Bishop Quintard and other clerics were there to comfort the family and conduct the burial service. With McMillin frequently in Washington, it appears that Brown and Bettie took on the responsibility of raising their grandson, Brown. The next week, the new Memorial Church of the Messiah was dedicated in Pulaski, made possible by a large gift from Brown. Originally intended as a memorial to Daisy, Quintard consecrated the building in memory of both departed girls.[45]

Brown and Fleming came to develop a feeling of mutual antipathy, which Brown was too politic to admit to McGhee but that Fleming openly acknowledged. Fleming became a constant critic, one to whom Brown, at least initially, gave "little weight" to because of the Englishman's lack of "experience in the details of railway affairs." Brown reported to McGhee that "some of Mr. Fleming's positions were so absurd, and so utterly contradictory to what I told him, that I did become irritated—not in the way of feeling unkindly towards him, but in the sense of compelling me to defend myself . . . I intended merely to be frank and positive." In the sense of all humans are imperfect, Brown admitted to mistakes, but invited comparisons to the prices paid by the neighboring railroads, where he felt he compared favorably. Fleming's railroad ignorance kept him from taking into account the "dead haul" costs of the railroad (cars returning empty) while transporting construction materials the rebuilding required. Brown emphasized that he had "cut down everything to a minimum" to meet the wishes of the committee. In turn, Fleming complained, "Brown has really no idea of economy."[46]

In February 1888, the sales of November were "set aside by all the parties in interest," likely because they did not sufficiently resolve the claims of the bondholders. New bonds and stock certificates were issued, thus bringing down the fixed charges against the company's property. These and business dealings with mortgage trustees, internally with the Missouri Pacific as to the money owed it, and other difficulties were resolved by May, with Gould quietly buying up large amounts of Texas and Pacific stock. Wistar and his committee procured an agreement from Gould that Brown would be named the reorganized company's president, which occurred in May. George Gould, Jay's son, was appointed its vice president. This ran counter to the expectations of some that Brown would eventually end up going back to his position as general solicitor for the Gould system, a position that was not offered. As Brown now stood for management with some independence of Gould, the financier became hostile, in McGhee's view, because Brown "failed to go back to his old place and had set himself up against his wishes." Gould also planned to install George as president of the railroad. And even the group that wanted more independence continued to hector Brown over expenses, to the point that an exasperated Brown told McGhee, "if the people who own the property, including yourself, believe that my administration is too extravagant, or otherwise unsatisfactory, I am ready at any moment to step down and out." That time had not yet come, and Brown's faithful service to the company, regardless of who controlled it, could not be denied. The Texas and Pacific named its new transfer steamer traversing the Mississippi River at New Orleans the *Governor John C. Brown*.[47]

The Tennessee Democratic convention elected Brown a delegate to the national convention, with a platform that called for the renomination of Grover Cleveland. The year ended with Cleveland unexpectedly defeated for reelection. In New York that December, Brown "talked freely" of the election, saying that Cleveland was "the best President the country has ever had since Washington and Lincoln." Brown blamed money "poured into the rural districts" for Benjamin Harrison's victory. Knowing Harrison, Brown said that "he means to work for the best interests of the government," which would be a disappointment to the worst element of the Republican Party. Brown went on to predict, however, that Harrison would not do as well as Cleveland did.[48]

On October 26, 1888, Judge Pardee signed an order discharging Brown from his receivership of the Texas and Pacific effective October 31. Brown as receiver was directed to deliver to the company all "property, funds and assets" of the company and to account for its funds since June 1, 1888, his accounts previous to that date having been previously approved. Within a few months, Gould was able to drop his secretive control of the company and elect a board of directors that dropped the representatives of the bondholders. At that meeting, Brown, who was reelected president, reported to the board that his efforts in the Texas state capital of Austin to pass a railroad commission bill were likely successful.[49]

Notwithstanding his reelection as president, which undoubtedly was for public appearances, Brown's tenure at the Texas and Pacific was effectively over. The failure of the Texas cotton crop in the fall of 1888 resulted in lost revenue, which in turn adversely affected the price of the road's securities. With Gould back in control, McGhee and the others realized that their hopes for an entity with some independence from the

I Have Great Faith in the Outcome of the Texas and Pacific

financier were at an end, and they began positioning themselves to protect their investment in the reorganized company. One of McGhee's correspondents deemed Brown a "fool" who did not have "enough sense to steal." While he would not have agreed, McGhee wondered if it were a mistake to put Brown in the presidency over Gould's objections. Loyal, it seems, almost to the end, McGhee urged consideration of leaving Brown as president and putting operations in the hands of an experienced railroad man, leaving him to attend to "legal, political and financial requirements" of the road.[50]

At the first of 1888, Brown suffered a "hemorrhage of the stomach," perhaps brought on by the constant stress of his job and the pain of the loss of his two girls. Through the years, his health was occasionally doubtful. Its precarious nature, doubtlessly along with the even more doubtful situation with the railroad, made him think of permanently returning to Tennessee. On April 1, 1889, an opportunity to do so arose: he was elected a director and president of the Tennessee Coal, Iron & Railroad Company, which had recently changed ownership. Started as the Sewanee Mining Company, it assumed its name under Brown's old political rival Arthur S. Colyar. With extensive holdings in Tennessee and Alabama, it was one of the largest coal and iron companies in the world. Brown and his family would occupy an "elegant" home in Nashville.[51]

Returning to Dallas, Brown was initially in "excellent health and buoyant spirits." He sent his resignation in to Gould, effective May 1, if not sooner. Keeping up appearances, Brown said there was no friction with the Texas and Pacific people; the main consideration was to get back home to Tennessee for personal and social reasons. He said that for the entire time he was in Texas, his family was with him only a portion of the time, and that he always had maintained his domicile and voted in Pulaski. Also, he expected that the duties of his new job would be much lighter than those with the Texas and Pacific. During his return trip to Texas Brown's apparent good health soon disappeared, as the stomach hemorrhage returned for ten days.[52]

Thus ended Brown's career in the transcontinental railroad business. Historian Richard White has observed that the transcontinentals were not "businesses devoted to the efficient sale of transportation but rather as corporate containers for financial manipulation and political networking."

The fact that the best-known biography of Jay Gould mentions Brown but once indicates where the former governor stood in the larger picture of Gould's enterprises. While his prominence enabled Brown to be a significant cog in Scott's, and to a lesser extent, even Gould's political network, increasing distance in time from his having held office and distance in space from Tennessee led the former governor to fall back on his two greatest strengths—executive ability and legal expertise. Those talents made Brown a great deal of money when he suited the plans of the financiers who employed him. But men like Jay Gould could employ any number of people with those talents. Notwithstanding his years of effort on behalf of Scott, Gould, and the Texas and Pacific, when Brown no longer suited Gould's plans, he was cast aside.[53]

Texans expressed their regret. A writer for the Fort Worth *Daily Gazette* wrote that Brown had been a factor in the progress of Texas during his time there. "Of the man himself, it is difficult to speak in exaggerated terms . . . As an executive officer of vast interests, he has few equals. Clear of judgment, firm of resolution, swift and steady in execution, he has never been known to fail or falter in the consummation of any design." A writer for another paper asked a slightly less complimentary question, yet one that demonstrated Brown's effectiveness: "What will the railroads do for some one to lobby their measures through the legislature when Brown is gone? Will they ever find one that will fill the bill as well? We think not." The locomotive engineers at Marshall passed a resolution in Brown's honor, and the mayor of Dallas, along with officers and employees, traveled to Tennessee in July to present Brown with a silver service. The mayor invited Brown to return to Dallas to give a speech on "Railroad Day" at the state fair.[54]

As July became August, Brown and his family vacationed at Cape May, New Jersey. Leaving his family on the coast, Brown returned to Nashville "much improved." On August 12, Brown took a trip to Birmingham, Alabama, on company business, and then returned to Nashville. From there, he went to Red Boiling Springs, a mineral springs resort in Macon County, northeast of Nashville, for reasons of health, indicating that he was not "much improved." He developed a slight complaint with hemorrhaging, but it worsened to the point that on August 16, he telegraphed Bettie's brother, John W. Childress, to come at once. Brown's previous experiences

I Have Great Faith in the Outcome of the Texas and Pacific

with the condition must have been serious, because he told a friend, "If this keeps up, we know what must happen." Brown continued to have hemorrhages and understood that he would not survive. When his attending physician told him he was in a precarious condition, he remarked "I know it." Childress asked him if he wanted to speak about business matters, Brown stated that his affairs were in order. Brown remained conscious until a few minutes before his end and died at 2:00 a.m. on August 17, 1889.[55]

A telegram was sent to the family, still on the Atlantic coast. McMillin responded, indicating that they would leave the next day. A special train went to the station nearest to Red Boiling Springs with friends and delegations of Confederate veterans to escort the body to Nashville. On August 20, a funeral train departed for Pulaski, with Birdie, John C. Brown Jr., McMillin, Quintard, Childress, and others in the family car. Other cars transported dignitaries such as Senator Bate, former Governor Albert Marks, Chief Justice Peter Turney, members of the Masonic order, and officials of the Gould System. Bettie stayed home on the orders of her physician, as he felt she could not "undergo the excitement and fatigue of the trip." When the train reached Pulaski, it was met with "an immense concourse of citizens." Services took place at the Episcopal Church, conducted by Quintard and the Rev. D. L. Wilson of the Presbyterian Church. Brown's pallbearers were veterans of the 3rd Tennessee. After a Masonic graveside service, Brown was laid to rest in the family plot at Maplewood Cemetery near Marie and Daisy.[56]

Many tributes were published. From Republican-leaning Knoxville, the *Journal* observed that Brown "met his republican friends with the same hearty grasp of the hand as he did his democratic friends, and no one felt any reserve in his magnetic presence." From Memphis, the *Avalanche* said Brown's death left Tennessee "grievously bereft." The former governor "was to her a true and loyal son; in his hands her honor was safe and her interests were jealously guarded." The Lebanon *Democrat* stated Brown "was the purest of American statesmen; a firm friend of his native State, in peace as well as in war; a business man of unimpaired integrity, and an honor alike to the State of his birth and the nation he loved so well." The Huntington *Republican* said: "Tennessee has never had a son more devoted to her interests or with more capacity to serve her." From Bolivar, the *Bulletin* extolled: "Not since John Sevier has the State had so distinguished a Governor." The Giles County *Democrat* said Brown prepared for his death with a "stainless and useful life," the Pulaski *Citizen* that Brown had "no superior in the true elements of manhood." Perhaps most succinctly, Brown's friends at the Fort Worth *Gazette* wrote: "Governor Brown was a great man, and had achieved a more varied success and distinction than the majority of great men. . . ."[57]

In the decades Bettie survived the general, she split her residential time between the fine, well-furnished new house she and her husband were to occupy together in Nashville and their home in Pulaski, which still stands as "Colonial Hall." Like many other wives and daughters of Confederate veterans, Bettie joined the Daughters of the Confederacy, whose stated goal was to "foster a proper respect for and pride in [the Confederacy's] glorious war history." Bettie was briefly the president of the national organization of the United Daughters of the Confederacy (and the first president of the organization under that name), and was also a prominent member of the Daughters of the American Revolution. She traveled to the Charleston Exposition in 1902 and once more visited Fort Sumter. During World War I, she was, in her son's words, an "ardent war worker." A few years before her death on March 1, 1919, at age seventy-seven, a newspaper article noted that "[h]er interest in all matters pertaining to the Confederacy knows no abatement. . . ."[58]

Of Brown's children, only Elizabeth ("Birdie") and John C. Brown Jr. survived the general, along with his young grandson, Brown McMillin. In 1896, Birdie married John C. Burch Jr., the son of Brown's friend of the same name, the former editor and state comptroller. On May 18, 1898, Birdie bore Burch a son, John C. Brown Burch. Sadly, Birdie, the last of the three Brown girls, died at age thirty-four on August 31, 1904. John C. Brown Jr. practiced law for a number of years and was twice married and divorced, but had no children. He died in Nashville on December 1, 1936, at age sixty-one. Brown McMillin died childless in 1912.[59]

As had Benton McMillin, John C. Burch remarried and eventually moved his with his son and new wife to Memphis. John C. Brown Burch attended the University of the South, and in later life was prominent in that institution's alumni affairs. He became an investment broker and died in 1977. Through him, John C. Brown and Elizabeth Childress Brown have living descendants.[60]

In 1891, Bettie had a magnificent monument erected over her husband's grave. The monument is "a life-size statue of Gov. Brown executed in Italy, made of the finest Italian marble, set on a handsome base." Clad in his Confederate uniform, the marble Brown faces southward, fixing its stone gaze on the land and people for whom he fought for much of his life. The four sides of the base respectively state Brown's name and lifespan, his status as a leading Mason, his career as a soldier, and his legal, political, and business pursuits. It was a full and useful life, the broad range of which Bettie tried to capture on the four panels of the monument. Not able to do her husband full justice on so small a canvas, she compensated there by succinctly summing up John Calvin Brown's short but full sixty-two years: "[h]e was successful in every undertaking and faithful to every trust."[61]

Certainly, on the level of personal attainment, Brown's life was a success. He was an accomplished lawyer through most of his career. A dedicated Mason, he rose to the office of Grand Master of Tennessee the year he was elected governor. He enlisted in 1861 as a private and mustered out in 1865 as a major general. With other Conservatives, he set out after the war to restore the franchise and majority rule and ended up as president of the constitutional convention that made that possible. A defeated rebel in 1865, he was elected governor five years later. Starting his work life as a teacher, he supported education as a private citizen in Pulaski and as the governor of Tennessee. After his time as governor, Brown became a trusted lieutenant and lawyer to two of the great financial barons of the latter half of the nineteenth century and was also trusted by the president of the United States to defuse the tense final stages of Reconstruction in Louisiana. In the last ten years of his life, Brown became known as a vigorous and effective railroad executive and lawyer, and attained a significant level of influence as such in Congress, the state legislatures, and the courts. His solid grasp of the powers granted him as receiver helped break the railroad strike in 1886. As a citizen of Pulaski, as a soldier and an officer, as governor, and as an advocate of the Texas and Pacific, Brown fared well in the court of public opinion, being generally

Elizabeth Childress Brown (Credit: Tennessee State Library and Archives)

well-liked and respected. His efforts as a lawyer and in business made him, for the time, a relatively wealthy man. And finally, he was fortunate in his marriages, marrying into two prominent families and fathering four children.

But many of those successes must be qualified, because few were full. It is a curious fact of Brown's life that he often struggled in losing causes. He lost as a Unionist in 1861 when he fought to keep Tennessee in the Union. Notwithstanding his brave and effective service and honorable wounds, his service as a soldier was also marked with the defeat of the Confederacy. His time as governor was in many ways consumed by the debt controversy, which remained unresolved when he left office in 1875. Notwithstanding his political success to that point, Brown's bid to become senator in 1875 was a bitter defeat, brought about by the enmity and ambition of Andrew Johnson and the jealousy of William B. Bate. On behalf of Tom Scott, Brown was unable to overcome the hostile political climate and obtain federal subsidies for the Texas and Pacific. Brown began his efforts for that railroad with a vision of it terminating within view of the blue waters of the Pacific Ocean, and ended them with it not extending outside the state of Texas. Indeed, another nominal success, Brown's becoming president of the Texas and Pacific, was ultimately an empty attainment when he lost his usefulness to Jay Gould. And sadly, even his personal life had its reverses, as he lost two of his beloved daughters before his often perilous health caused an early death, a death that cut short the promise of years of usefulness to the Volunteer State as railroad industrialist and elder statesman.

Viewed from a twenty-first-century perspective, John Calvin Brown is best known for his time as a rebel. In the course of the Civil War, eight Tennesseans served at the rank of major general or higher. Of those eight, Brown was the most junior, being the last to attain that rank. Yet, with the exception of Alexander P. Stewart, who became a corps commander, and Patrick Cleburne, who it is widely thought should have been, Brown had a wartime record that compares favorably to any other infantry major general, Tennessean or otherwise, in the Army of Tennessee, although the standard of performance for officers in that ill-starred host is relatively low. For that reason alone, Brown is a significant figure in Tennessee's military history.

Brown is much less well known for his time as a railroader. While significant for his efforts on Scott's behalf in the halls of Congress, and for his assistance in defeating the railroad strike against Gould's system in 1886, Brown never was much more than a tool to be used by the enormously rich and often corrupt men he served. Even his role in the momentous events of 1877 in Washington and Louisiana likely came about as a result of his connection to Scott. That is not to say his service was not honorable, or that he did not advance the development of the rail line placed in his care when given an opportunity to do so, or that his professional attainments were not such as to be envied by any lawyer of his time or, indeed, our own. By means of his time as governor and his service to the Confederacy, he was recognized, by Tom Scott at least, as a man of influence in the South, but by the time Brown passed into the service of Jay Gould, his competence as a lawyer and knowledge of railroad matters seems to have mattered the most. And in the end, Jay Gould had the means to hire any number of competent and experienced railroad lawyers, or for that matter, ex-generals or politicians.

Brown merits much more attention for his role as the most important of Tennessee's Redeemers in the transformational decade from 1866 to 1875. It can be fairly concluded that Brown stands with William G. Brownlow, D. W. C. Senter, and Andrew Johnson as the most significant Tennesseans of that period. Each led, or at least represented, a faction of the still reforming body politic of the state during that critical ten years: Brownlow the Radicals, Senter the more conservative former Whig Unionists, Johnson old Unionist Democrats, and Brown the former Confederates, especially those of Whig antecedents who often reluctantly joined the Confederacy. Oddly, by the end of that period, all of them had passed their political apogee, with Brownlow, Senter, and Brown out of office, and Johnson removed by death. They would be supplanted by what came to be known as the Bourbon Democrats, who were led by Isham Harris with the aid of William B. Bate. The Bourbons led a Democratic Party that Brown played a large role in consolidating, defining, and bringing to power in 1870.

Brown's role with the Ku Klux Klan will likely never be defined, but there is little question he was a significant leader in the anti-Radical resistance in the fluid period from 1867 to 1869. That leadership was somewhat formalized in 1868 when he joined the other former Confederate generals in their approach to the legislature. While others, such as Neill Brown, A. O. P. Nicholson, and John Netherland, appeared to be leaders of the Constitutional Convention of 1870, Brown's unanimous choice as president of the convention marked him for the future, and he joined them in formulating a new constitution which, in the words of a prominent Tennessee constitutional scholar, sent a message that Tennessee Conservatives "accepted the results of the war." Of course, regaining power from the Radicals, whether by legal, illegal, or extra-legal means, made it much easier to accept those results.[62]

The final chapter of Brown's role in this ten years of change occurred during his three years plus as governor, as he struggled with the state's enormous debt and worked on education and other reforms. More importantly, given the irregularity of the Brownlow years and the sense that the Senter governorship was more properly an interregnum between Radical and Conservative/Democratic administrations, Brown's ultimate gift to the people of Tennessee as their governor was to return Tennessee to a state of normalcy. The issues facing the governor and the state were those of peace, not of widespread violence or civil war. Normalcy had to be defined in a new matrix, given the great changes that had occurred since 1861, but for that to occur, the majority of the people had to have an element of confidence in the state government as those matters were addressed. Even though there were those who thought Brown's approach to the debt or other issues was wrong, the general feeling, reflected by the newspapers of the time, was that Brown had honestly and conscientiously confronted the state's issues. Brown recognized this in his final address as governor, stating that while he "may not at all times have met public expectation, I have earnestly and faithfully desired, above all other considerations, to promote the general welfare."[63]

Brown's lack of longevity, his defeat in 1875 for the seat in the United States Senate, his years away from the state working for Scott and Gould, his Whig-to-Democrat politics, his politically expensive struggle against the state debt, his late promotion in a defeated army, and his shadowy role with the Ku Klux Klan all work against his being remembered in our time as a great Tennessean. His Volunteer State contemporaries would have disagreed. At his death, they remembered "a soldier, a lawyer, a statesman and an organizer and operator of railroad systems" who, "called to the office of governor at a time so trying, when it was necessary to rehabilitate the state, both politically and financially . . . proved himself 'one man picked out of ten thousand,' and by his extraordinary efficiency and wisdom earned the lasting gratitude and admiration of the people."[64]

I Have Great Faith in the Outcome of the Texas and Pacific

Notes

Abbreviations Used in Notes

JCB	John C. Brown
CCNMP	Chickamauga and Chattanooga National Military Park
NARA	National Archives and Records Administration, Washington, DC
OR	*War of the Rebellion: A Compilation of the Official Records of the Union and Confederate Armies,* 128 vols. (Washington, DC: US Government Printing Office, 1880–1901). OR citations are to Series I unless otherwise noted and take the following form: volume number (part number, where applicable), page number(s).
ORS	Janet B. Hewett, Noah A. Trudeau, and Bryce A. Suderow, eds., *Supplement to the Official Records of the Union and Confederate Armies* (Wilmington, NC: Broadfoot Publishing Co., 1994–2004).
PAJ	LeRoy P. Graf, Ralph W. Haskins, and Paul H. Bergeron, eds., *The Papers of Andrew Johnson,* 16 vols. (Knoxville: University of Tennessee Press, 1967–2000).
PJD	Lynda Lasswell Crist, Mary Seaton Dix, Kenneth H. Williams, Peggy L. Dillard, and Barbara J. Rozek, eds., *The Papers of Jefferson Davis,* 12 vols. to date (Baton Rouge: Louisiana State University Press, 1971–2008).
TSLA	Tennessee State Library and Archives, Nashville

Preface

1. See Thomas L. Connelly, *Army of the Heartland* (Baton Rouge: Louisiana State Univ. Press, 1967), x–xii; Richard M. McMurry, *Two Great Rebel Armies* (Chapel Hill: Univ. of North Carolina Press, 1989), 5–9.

2. See Roger L. Hart, *Redeemers, Bourbons & Populists: Tennessee 1870–1896* (Baton Rouge: Louisiana State Univ. Press, 1975); Robert B. Jones, *Tennessee at the Crossroads: The State Debt Controversy, 1870–1883* (Knoxville: Univ. of Tennessee Press, 1977).

3. The continued viability of Woodward's thesis in that regard is discussed in Chapter 7.

4. The legend of his family's destruction of Brown's papers appears to stem from a 1908 article indicating that Brown wrote an account explaining his role in the November 29, 1864, missed opportunity at Spring Hill, Tennessee, that was "not accessible to the public." J. P. Young, "Hood's Failure at Spring Hill," *Confederate Veteran* 16 (1908): 30, 36.

5. "Governor Brown Dead," *Fort Worth Weekly Gazette*, August 22, 1889.

1. Desires the Perpetuity and Integrity of Our Union

1. "The Late Maj. F. C. Barber," *Pulaski Citizen*, April 13, 1866; "Bearing them Back," *Pulaski Citizen*, January 25, 1867; "Religion in the Army of Tennessee," *Pulaski Citizen*, July 3, 1868; "Walker, Clack and Barber," *Pulaski Citizen*, April 20, 1866; "The Dread Alternative," *Memphis Public Ledger*, November 21, 1883; 1860 United States Federal Census, Giles County, Tennessee.

2. "The Dread Alternative," *Memphis Public Ledger*, November 21, 1883.

3. Joshua W. Caldwell, *Sketches of the Bench and Bar of Tennessee* (Knoxville: Ogden Brothers and Co., 1898), 291; James McCallum, *A Brief Sketch of the Settlement and Early History of Giles County, Tennessee* (Pulaski: Pulaski Citizen, 1928), 40; "Ex-Gov. John C. Brown," *Nashville Evening Herald*, August 17, 1889; George W. Newman, *Brown Family Timeline: 1745–1919* (n.p., 2001), 2–5; Ancestry.com, *U.S., Sons of the American Revolution Membership Applications, 1889–1970* [online database] (Provo, UT: Ancestry.com Operations, Inc., 2011), applications filed by John C. Brown Jr., March 11, 1903, and William S. Tyson, May 25, 1928 (accessed September 13, 2013); "Cemetery Near Bryson," Giles County Miscellaneous Records, Mf no. 499, TSLA. Angus is deemed only a "possible" veteran because there is scant evidence of his service.

4. McCallum, *Early History of Giles County*, 9–10, 13, 17–18, 40, 43, 63–64; Robert H. White, *Messages of the Governors of Tennessee* (Nashville: Tennessee Historical Commission, 1957), 4:176.

5. Caldwell, *Sketches*, 291, 362; William S. Speer, *Sketches of Prominent Tennesseans* (Nashville: Albert B. Tavel, 1888), 9; Karl F. Kaestle, *Pillars of the Republic: Common Schools and American Society, 1780–1860* (New York: Hill and Wang, 1983), 193–94; 1840 United States Federal Census, Giles County, Tennessee; Edward A. McMillin to David A. Smith, 10 March 1862, in *Letters Received by the Office of the Adjutant General, Main Series, 1861–1870*, M-619, NARA; Newman, *Brown Family Timeline*, 7.

6. White, *Messages*, 4:176–77; Caldwell, *Sketches*, 362–63.

7. Robert E. Corlew, *Tennessee: A Short History*, 2nd ed. (Knoxville: Univ. of Tennessee Press, 1981), 187–95; Jonathan M. Atkins, *Parties, Politics and the*

Sectional Conflict in Tennessee, 1832–1861 (Knoxville: Univ. of Tennessee Press, 1997), 81–146; Joseph O. Baylen, "A Tennessee Politician in Imperial Russia, 1850–1853," *Tennessee Historical Quarterly* 14 (1955): 227–30.

8. "Graveyard, Home All that Mark Site of Century-Old Jackson College," *Nashville Tennessean*, June 18, 1933; Jackson College catalog, 1845–1846, Box 1, Folder 20, Joseph Branch O'Bryan Papers, TSLA. Worthy of mention, but considered untrustworthy, is an account whereby John attended a barbeque in 1844 at Andrew Jackson's home, the Hermitage. Old Hickory exhorted: "'We have restored the government to sound principles and extended the area of our institutions to the Rio Grande! Now for Oregon and Fifty-four-forty!' 'Or fight!' added young John Calvin Brown, then a boy of seventeen, in the audience; afterward governor of Tennessee. General Jackson spied the boy and laughed. 'Yes, Johnny,' he said, 'if we have to. I've fought some battles for the Southwest end of this Union and, old as I am, I reckon there's one more left in me for its northwest end if need be.'" Augustus C. Buell, *History of Andrew Jackson: Pioneer, Patriot, Soldier, Politician and President* (New York: Charles Scribner's Sons, 1904), 2:381. See Milton W. Hamilton, "Augustus C. Buell: Fraudulent Historian," *Pennsylvania Magazine of History and Biography* 80 (October 1956): 478. It indeed seems unlikely that the younger brother of a prominent Whig would be at the described event.

9. Lawrence O'Bryan to "Friend William," 21 November 1845, Box 1, Folder 11, Joseph Branch O'Bryan Papers, TSLA.

10. McCallum, *Early History of Giles County*, 104–6; "Wurtemburg Academy," *Pulaski Western Star*, June 14, 1849; "Examinations at Wurtemburg Academy," *Pulaski Gazette*, June 13, 1851.

11. "Ex-Gov. John C. Brown," *Nashville Evening Herald*, August 17, 1889; "A Sketch of the Deceased," *Nashville Daily American*, August 18, 1889; "The State Mourns," *Giles County Democrat*, August 21, 1889; "Sketches of the Bench and Bar of Tennessee," *Nashville American*, September 20, 1897; White, *Messages*, 4:178–80; Baylen, "A Tennessee Politician," 229; Clara M. Parker, *Giles County, Tennessee Will Abstracts, 1815–1900* (n.p., 1988), 11; "Administrator's Notice," *Pulaski Western Star*, June 14, 1849. Born in 1762, Hugh Brown served during the Revolution and as an Indian fighter, and moved to Maury County with his brother, Rev. Duncan Brown, a cousin with the same name as John's father. Newman, *Brown Family Timeline*, 19; 1850 United States Federal Census, Maury County, Tennessee; Ancestry.com, *U.S., Sons of the American Revolution Membership Applications, 1889–1970* [online database], application of William L. Granbery, November 23, 1923 (accessed September 15, 2013).

12. JCB to "Dear Brother," 15 January 1849, 19 January 1849, 31 January 1849; Thomas D. Eldridge to Neill S. Brown, 7 January 1849, 19 January 1849, all in Box 1, Folder 5, Neill S. Brown Governor's Papers, TSLA.

13. White, *Messages*, 4: 194–97, 213.

14. Ibid., 200–16, 221–41; 247–53.

15. Ibid., 265–70, 279–82.

16. Baylen, "A Tennessee Politician," 228, 230–52.

17. Caldwell, *Sketches*, 291–92; Advertisement for Walker & Brown, *Pulaski Western Star*, August 1, 1850; 1860 United States Federal Census, Giles County, Tennessee; "General John C. Brown," *Confederate Veteran* 3 (August 1895): 242; *A. C. Esselman v. W. P. Brown*, 34 Tenn. 303 (1854); "Valuable Land for Sale," *Pulaski Western Star*, March 7, 1850; "Insurance," *Pulaski Gazette*, April 30, 1852; Advertisement for Protection Insurance Company, *Pulaski Gazette*, October 1, 1852; "Mr. Editor," and "Public Meeting," *Pulaski Western Star*, July 18, 1850; "Monday morning at 11 o'clock," *Pulaski Gazette*, July 9, 1852; "At a meeting of the Whigs," *Pulaski Gazette*, June 11, 1852; "Elections," *Pulaski Western Star*, December 20, 1850; "Florence Rail Road Convention," *Pulaski Gazette*, May 14, 1852; "Railroad Meeting," *Pulaski Gazette*, June 11, 1852; "Pursuant to a Resolution," *Nashville Union and American*, January 15, 1854.

18. "Married," *Pulaski Western Star*, November 8, 1850; 1840, 1850, 1860 United States Federal Census, Giles County, Tennessee; Margaret Butler, *Legacy: Early Families of Giles County* (n.p., 1991), 62; Stephen V. Ash, *Middle Tennessee Society Transformed, 1860–1870* (Knoxville: Univ. of Tennessee Press, 2006), 10–11, 44; W. Thomas Cardin, "History of Pisgah," in *Flournoy Rivers' Manuscripts and History of Pisgah*, Clara M. Parker and Edward Jackson White, comp. (Pulaski, Tenn., n.d.), 20; Tennessee Biographical Questionnaire re: John C. Brown, MS-485, TSLA; McMillin to Smith, 10 March 1862; John C. Brown grave monument, Maplewood Cemetery, Pulaski. Ann's middle name appears in a family Bible noted in the John Henry Pointer family tree on Ancestry.com (viewed September 28, 2013).

19. Corlew, *Tennessee: A Short History*, 272–75; Paul H. Bergeron, Stephen V. Ash, and Jeanette Keith, *Tennesseans and Their History* (Knoxville: Univ. of Tennessee Press, 1999), 105–6; Lewright B. Sikes, "Gustavus Adolphus Henry: Champion of Lost Causes," *Tennessee Historical Quarterly* 50 (Fall 1991): 173, 180; Atkins, *Parties, Politics*, 170 (quote), 181–2; "The Last and Worst Gerrymander," *Nashville Daily American*, January 22, 1852.

20. Atkins, *Parties, Politics*, 195–201; W. Darrell Overdyke, *The Know-Nothing Party in the South* (Baton Rouge: Louisiana State Univ. Press, 1950), 48–50. William James Cooper, *The South and the Politics of Slavery, 1828–1856* (Baton

Rouge: Louisiana State Univ. Press, 1978), 364–65; "Amongst the Delegates," *Nashville Union and American*, June 15, 1855; "Grand American Rally," *Daily Nashville True Whig*, July 16, 1855; "Ex-Gov. Neill S. Brown," *Nashville Daily Patriot*, December 10, 1855.

21. "The Ratification Meeting on Monday Night," *Nashville Daily Patriot*, March 5, 1856; "Letter of Ex-Gov. Neill S. Brown Accepting the Post of Elector for the State at Large," *Nashville Daily Patriot*, June 19, 1856; Atkins, *Parties, Politics*, 198–201, 204–11; "Brown and Harris in Weakly," *Nashville Daily Patriot*, September 13, 1856; "From the Western District," *Nashville Daily Patriot*, September 23, 1856; "The Canvass," *Nashville Union and American*, September 23, 1856; Sam Davis Elliott, *Isham G. Harris of Tennessee: Confederate Governor and United States Senator* (Baton Rouge: Louisiana State Univ. Press, 2010), 34–35, 39–40.

22. Anne H. Hopkins and William Lyons, *Tennessee Votes, 1799–1976* (Knoxville: Univ. of Tennessee Bureau of Public Administration, 1978); Cardin, "History of Pisgah," 20.

23. Nelle Roller Cohen, *Pulaski History, 1809–1850: The Beginning, The Building, The Development, The Institutions, And the People of the Town of Pulaski, Tennessee*, (n. p. 1951), Eighth Installment; Tennessee Biographical Questionnaire re: John C. Brown, MS-485, TSLA (a document filled out by John C. Brown Jr. in 1922 indicates John was mayor in 1851, which seems too soon); Robert M. McBride and Dan M. Robison, *Biographical Directory of the Tennessee General Assembly* (Nashville: Tennessee Historical Commission, 1975), 1:86; "Legislature of Tennessee," *Daily Nashville Patriot*, October 9, 1857.

24. Ann E. Brown grave monument, Maplewood Cemetery, Pulaski; Butler, *Legacy*, 62; Passport Applications, 1795–1905, RG 59, M-1372, NARA; "Passengers Sailed," *New York Herald-Tribune*, October 4, 1858; "Ex-Gov. John C. Brown," *Nashville Evening Herald*, August 17, 1889; "Sketches of the Bench and Bar of Tennessee," *Nashville American*, September 20, 1897; "My Father's Centennial," *Pulaski Citizen*, January 5, 1927; "Tennesseans in Rome" *Nashville Union and American*, June 9, 1859, "Tribute of Respect," *Pulaski Citizen*, January 6, 1860.

25. Corlew, *Tennessee: A Short History*, 282; Atkins, *Parties, Politics*, 215–17, 220; William W. Freehling, *The Road to Disunion: Secessionists Triumphant, 1854–1861* (New York: Oxford Univ. Press, 2007), 220–21; James M. McPherson, *Battle Cry of Freedom: The Civil War Era* (New York: Oxford Univ. Press, 1988), 210–11; Daniel W. Crofts, *Reluctant Confederates: Upper South Unionists in the Secession Crisis* (Chapel Hill: Univ. of North Carolina Press, 1989), 70–72.

26. Newman, *Brown Family Timeline*, 20; Atkins, *Parties, Politics*, 225–26; "Opposition State Convention," *Daily Nashville Patriot*, February 23, 1860; Murat

Halstead, *Caucuses of 1860. A History of the National Political Conventions of the Current Presidential Campaign: Being a Complete Record of the Business of all the Conventions: with Sketches of Distinguished Men in Attendance Upon Them, and Descriptions of the Most Characteristic Scenes and Memorable Events* (Columbus: Follett, Foster and Company, 1860), 104–20.

27. Freehling, *The Road to Disunion*, 288–322; Mary Emily Robertson Campbell, *The Attitude of Tennesseans Toward the Union, 1847–1861* (New York: Vantage Press, 1961), 105–24.

28. "Letter of W. P. Kendrick of Wayne," *Daily Nashville Patriot*, June 13, 1860; "The Constitutional Union Convention," *Daily Nashville Patriot*, July 11, 1860; "Correspondence of the Banner," *Nashville Republican Banner*, July 10, 1860; Masthead, *Daily Nashville Patriot*, July 13, 1860; "Political Discussion," *Pulaski Citizen*, August 10, 1860; "Reports of the Canvass," *Nashville Republican Banner*, August 11, 1860; *Rhodes v. State*, 41 Tenn. 351 (1860).

29. "Cox, Nicholas Nicholls," *Biographical Directory of the United States Congress, 1774–Present*, http://bioguide.congress.gov (accessed September 30, 2013); "The Canvass," *Nashville Union and American*, September 11, 1860; "Our Correspondence," *Daily Nashville Patriot*, September 4, 1860; "The 7th District," *Daily Nashville Patriot*, September 28, 1860; "Brown and Cox in Perry County," *Daily Nashville Patriot*, October 20, 1860; "Seventh Congressional District," *Nashville Republican Banner*, October 3, 1860.

30. Atkins, *Parties, Politics*, 226–35; "Vote of Tennessee," *Daily Nashville Patriot*, November 27, 1860; Campbell, *The Attitude of Tennesseans*, 135–45.

31. White, *Messages*, 255–69, 271.

32. Crofts, *Reluctant Confederates*, 102, 104–6. Crofts divides conditional Unionists into more complex subgroups.

33. Campbell, *The Attitude of Tennesseans*, 171–72, 174; Atkins, *Parties, Politics*, 236, 242; "State Convention," *Daily Nashville Patriot*, February 1, 1861; "Public Meeting in Giles—Nomination of Delegates to the State Convention," *Nashville Union and American*, January 30, 1861.

34. Campbell, *The Attitude of Tennesseans*, 175–76, 182–85; "Election Returns," *Nashville Union and American*, February 19, 1861; Secretary of State Election Returns (State, County and Local) , RG 87, Election Returns—Statewide General Elections, 1861, Roll 1861-1, Tenn. Governor, Congress, & Ratification of CSA Constitution, TSLA; Neill S. Brown to Andrew Johnson, 17 February 1861, PAJ 4:500 ; OR, Series IV, 1:179–81; Atkins, *Parties, Politics*, 242–43; "County Union Meetings—Giles County" and "Fort Sumter Attacked," *Nashville Republican Banner*, April 13, 1861.

35. Crofts, *Reluctant Confederates*, 324, 338; Neill S. Brown to Andrew Johnson, 17 February 1861; Oliver P. Temple, *East Tennessee and the Civil War* (1899;

reprint, Freeport, NY: Books for Libraries Press, 1971), 228–30, 236–38; "Letter from Ex-Gov. Neill S. Brown," *Nashville Republican Banner*, May 1, 1861.

36. "Position of Hon. John C. Brown," *Nashville Republican Banner*, October 7, 1870; Mrs. James K. Polk to Andrew Johnson, 30 June 1865, Case Files of Applications from Former Confederates for Presidential Pardons, 1865–67, RG 94, M-1003, NARA; Crofts, *Reluctant Confederates*, 47, 342–45; McMillin to David A. Smith, 10 March 1862, NARA; "The Dread Alternative," *Memphis Public Ledger*, November 21, 1883; "Flying Artillery of Giles County," *Nashville Republican Banner*, April 27, 1861.

2. Fellow Victims of the Fatal Blunder

1. White, *Messages*, 5:289–94; Elliott, *Isham G. Harris*, 70–72; see also Sam D. Elliott, "Tennessee's Declaration of Independence: Armed Revolt and the Constitutional Right of Revolution," *Tennessee Bar Journal* 44 (December 2008): 25.

2. Roll of Third Tennessee Regiment, Confederate States of America Collection, 1850–1876, David M. Rubenstein Rare Book and Manuscript Library, Duke University; Tennessee Civil War Centennial Commission, *Tennesseans in the Civil War* (1964; reprint, Knoxville: Univ. of Tennessee Press, 2000), 181; "Tennessee Militia—Officers," *Nashville Republican Banner*, May 10, 1861; "Army Appointments," *Nashville Republican Banner*, May 11, 1861; N. F. Cheairs, *I'll Sting if I Can: The Life and Prison Letters of Major N. F. Cheairs, C. S. A.*, ed. Nathaniel Cheairs Hughes Jr. (Signal Mountain: Mountain Press, 1998), 47; 1860 United States Federal Census, Giles County; "Camp Cheatham" and "General Orders," *Nashville Daily Patriot*, May 21, 1861.

3. Louis Adams Diary, Giles County Miscellaneous, MF 499, TSLA; Roll of Third Tennessee Regiment, Rubenstein Library, Duke Univ.; "First Regiment flag," *Nashville Union and American*, June 4, 1861; Cheairs, *I'll Sting if I Can*, 47.

4. Roll of Third Tennessee Regiment, Rubenstein Library, Duke Univ.; John Berrian Lindsley, ed., *The Military Annals of Tennessee: Confederate* (1886; reprint, Wilmington, NC: Broadfoot Publishing Company, 1995), 176; "From Camp Trousdale," *Nashville Union and American*, August 1, 1861; OR 52(2):122–23; Samuel H. Stout, "Some Facts of the History of the Organization of Medical Service of the Confederate Armies and Hospitals," in *The Southern Practitioner* (Nashville, TN: Jno. Rundle and Sons, 1901), 23:584–85.

5. Elliott, *Isham G. Harris*, 75, 86–87; Thomas L. Connelly, *Army of the Heartland: The Army of Tennessee, 1861–1862* (Baton Rouge: Louisiana State Univ. Press, 1967), 52–53, 64–65.

6. OR 4:407–8 and 52(2):149, 151; Adams Diary, TSLA; Roll of Third Tennessee Regiment, Rubenstein Library, Duke Univ.

7. Connelly, *Army of the Heartland*, 67–71; OR 4:478.

8. William Preston Johnston, *The Life of Gen. Albert Sidney Johnston* (New York: D. Appleton and Co., 1878), 358–59.

9. OR 4:484, 7:853; McBride and Robison, *Biographical Directory*, 1:161, 567; Tennessee Civil War Centennial Commission, *Tennesseans in the Civil War*, 1:212, 242.

10. Connelly, *Army of the Heartland*, 73–85, 105–6; Edward C. Bearss, "The Construction of Fort Henry and Fort Donelson," *West Tennessee Historical Society Papers* 21 (1967): 64–65; Benjamin Franklin Cooling, *Forts Henry and Donelson: The Key to the Confederate Heartland* (Knoxville: Univ. of Tennessee Press, 1987), 44, 58–62, 84.

11. Bearss, "The Construction of Fort Henry and Fort Donelson," 25–28; Cooling, *Forts Henry and Donelson,* 65–71, 81; OR 7:840–41.

12. Adams Diary, TSLA; Roll of Third Tennessee Regiment, Rubenstein Library, Duke Univ.; Thomas Hopkins Deavenport diary, Civil War Collection, TSLA; "Donelson," *Pulaski Citizen*, October 15, 1887; Connelly, *Army of the Heartland*, 97–99; OR 7:844–45; St. John R. Liddell, *Liddell's Record*, ed. Nathaniel Cheairs Hughes Jr. (1985; reprint, Baton Rouge: Louisiana State Univ. Press, 1997), 39–45.

13. Cooling, *Forts Henry and Donelson,* 78–79, 88–111; Connelly, *Army of the Heartland*, 107; Timothy B. Smith, *Grant Invades Tennessee: The 1862 Battles for Forts Henry and Donelson* (Lawrence: Univ. Press of Kansas, 2016), 70–128.

14. OR 7:130–31; Connelly, *Army of the Heartland*, 112–13; Cooling, *Forts Henry and Donelson*, 128–29; Ezra Warner, *Generals in Gray* (Baton Rouge: Louisiana State Univ. Press, 1959), 89–90, 241; Nathaniel Cheairs Hughes Jr. and Roy P. Stonesifer Jr., *The Life and Wars of Gideon J. Pillow* (1993; reprint, Knoxville: Univ. of Tennessee Press, 2011), 7–16, 39–104, 162, 172–73.

15. Johnston, *Albert Sidney Johnston*, 433, 491; Charles P. Roland, "Albert Sidney Johnston and the Loss of Forts Henry and Donelson," *Journal of Southern History* 23 (February 1957): 45, 62; "Donelson," *Pulaski Citizen*, October 15, 1887; Deavenport diary, TSLA; Adams diary, TSLA; Roll of Third Tennessee Regiment, Rubenstein Library, Duke Univ. See also OR 7:346, 349. Brown noted in his report that the brigade reached the fort on February 9 and 10, but the preponderance of the evidence indicates February 8.

16. Roll of Third Tennessee Regiment, Rubenstein Library, Duke Univ.; "Donelson"; Deavenport diary, TSLA; OR 7:329, 346, 349.

17. OR 7:328–29; Cheairs, *I'll Sting If I Can*, 47; Cooling, *Forts Henry and Donelson*, 131–34; Hughes and Stonesifer, *Gideon J. Pillow*, 216–17; Johnston,

Albert Sidney Johnston, 436–48; Roland, "Albert Sidney Johnston and the Loss of Forts Henry and Donelson," 62.

18. OR 7:347, 352; Cooling, *Forts Henry and Donelson,* 140–46; Flavel C. Barber, *Holding the Line: The Third Tennessee Infantry, 1861–1864,* ed. Robert H. Ferrell (Kent, OH: Kent State Univ. Press, 1994), 18–19.

19. Deavenport diary, TSLA; Adams diary, TSLA; Cooling, *Forts Henry and Donelson,* 148–60; OR 7:330; Smith, *Grant Invades Tennessee,* 244–54; "Donelson"; Barber, *Holding the Line,* 20–21. As historian Timothy Smith pointed out to the author, the shots probably did not hit near Brown's lines, but even distant explosions could have resulted in this incident. Ned bore the last name Brown, suggesting he was owned by Brown or a member of his family. His other slave, Major, had the last name of Pointer, indicating that the man was provided by his wife's family. The two did not get along until Brown and one of his officers loaded blank pistols and set up a "duel" between the two, the perceived mutual danger of which ended their quarrel. "Donelson."

20. Hughes and Stonesifer, *The Life and Wars of Gideon J. Pillow,* 222–24; Cooling, *Forts Henry and Donelson,* 164–65; OR 7:347.

21. OR 7:331, 347; Adams diary, TSLA.

22. Cooling, *Forts Henry and Donelson,* 167–76; Smith, *Grant Invades Tennessee,* 261–62, 268–97; OR 7: 330, 344–45, 347, 350, 352, 356.

23. OR 7:196–97, 210, 331, 345, 348, 350, 352; Adams diary, TSLA; "Donelson."

24. OR 7:178–79, 195–96, 208–9, 331–32, 348, 350, 352–53, 356; Cooling, *Forts Henry and Donelson,* 172; Smith, *Grant Invades Tennessee,* 299–301; Deavenport diary, TSLA.

25. OR 7:332, 348; Barber, *Holding the Line,* 26–28; Cooling, *Forts Henry and Donelson,* 176; James Jobe, "Forts Henry and Donelson: Disastrous And Almost Without Remedy," *Blue & Gray Magazine* 28, no. 4 (2011): 6, 46–47; Kendall D. Gott, *Where the South Lost the War: An Analysis of the Fort Henry–Fort Donelson Campaign, February 1862* (Mechanicsburg, PA: Stackpole, 2003), 211–15. The author is indebted to historian Timothy Smith for sharing his analysis of this confusing series of events prior to the publication of his book.

26. Cooling, *Forts Henry and Donelson,* 180–83; Hughes and Stonesifer, *Gideon J. Pillow,* 229–32; OR 7:348; "Donelson"; Cheairs, *I'll Sting If I Can,* 22–23.

27. Cooling, *Forts Henry and Donelson,* 170, 183–88; Smith, *Grant Invades Tennessee,* 338–47; OR 7:333, 348–49, 350–51, 357; Cheairs, *I'll Sting If I Can,* 22–23; Barber, *Holding the Line,* 30.

28. OR 7:333, 349, 354; Cheairs, *I'll Sting If I Can,* 24–25; Barber, *Holding the Line,* 31.

29. Cooling, *Forts Henry and Donelson,* 200–204; Hughes and Stonesifer, *Gideon J. Pillow,* 232–38; Connelly, *Army of the Heartland,* 123–25; Edward A. McMillin

to David A. Smith, 10 March 1862, NARA; John S. Wilkes, "Third Tennessee Infantry," in Lindsley, ed., *Military Annals*, 180.

30. Cheairs, *I'll Sting If I Can*, 24–25; Cooling, *Forts Henry and Donelson*, 208–11.

31. Barber, *Holding the Line*, 32; Cooling, *Forts Henry and Donelson*, 213–14; Deavenport diary, TSLA; Adams diary, TSLA; Roll of Third Tennessee Regiment, Rubenstein Library, Duke Univ.; "Grant at Donelson," *National Tribune*, December 12, 1889.

32. OR 7:336; Cheairs, *I'll Sting If I Can*, 33; Cooling, *Forts Henry and Donelson*, 178–80.

33. Deavenport diary, TSLA; Barber, *Holding the Line*, 35–37; OR Series II, 3:269; "Donelson"; Herschel Gower and Jack Allen, eds., *Pen and Sword: The Life and Journals of Randal W. McGavock* (Nashville: Tennessee Historical Commission, 1959), 597.

34. Gower and Allen, eds., *Pen and Sword*, 595–97; Barber, *Holding the Line*, 37–39.

35. Barber, *Holding the Line*, 39; Gower and Allen, eds., *Pen and Sword*, 598–601.

36. Minor H. McLain, "The Military Prison at Fort Warren," in *Civil War Prisons*, ed. William B. Hesseltine (Kent, OH: Kent State Univ. Press, 1972), 32, 34, 41–43; Gower and Allen, eds., *Pen and Sword*, 601, 633, 647, 653; Cheairs, *I'll Sting If I Can*, 59–60, 64; OR Series II, 3:837–38.

37. OR Series II, 3:280, 327; Warner, *Generals in Gray*, 123, 227–28; Edward A. McMillin to David A. Smith, 10 March 1862, Smith to Lincoln, 14 March 1862, and Hay endorsement, 19 March 1862, all in Letters Received by the Office of the Adjutant General, Main Series, 1861–1870, M-619, NARA; Gower and Allen, eds., *Pen and Sword*, 625.

38. Gower and Allen, eds., *Pen and Sword*, 610–11; OR 52(2):158–63, 229; Walter T. Durham, *Nashville: The Occupied City* (1985; reprint, Knoxville: Univ. of Tennessee Press, 2008), 38, 148, 159; PAJ 5:365–66

39. Durham, *Nashville: The Occupied City*, 154; "Unionism in Tennessee," *New York Times*, June 9, 1862; PAJ 5: 440–41; Gower and Allen, eds., *Pen and Sword*, 633, 635, 638. On June 21, Neill gave a pro-Union speech at Pulaski, but begged off on account of illness on July 4. PAJ 5:496, 540n1.

40. Durham, *Nashville: The Occupied City*, 74; Gower and Allen, eds., *Pen and Sword*, 648–49.

41. Cheairs, *I'll Sting If I Can*, 62, 66, 68, 75; Gower and Allen, eds., *Pen and Sword*, 608, 644–45.

42. Cheairs, *I'll Sting If I Can*, 46–47; Gov. John C. Brown Autograph Album, Confederate Collection, TSLA; General Joseph B. Palmer Autograph Album, Mf no. 1977, TSLA. The "Ditch digging Genrl" was doubtlessly Pillow.

43. Gower and Allen, eds., *Pen and Sword*, 653, 658–62; Cheairs, *I'll Sting If I Can*, 95; OR Series II, 4:445; Tennessee Civil War Centennial Commission, *Tennesseans in the Civil War*, 181.

44. Barber, *Holding the Line*, 67; Wilkes, "Third Tennessee Infantry," 180; John C. Brown Compiled Service Record, Compiled Service Records of Confederate General and Staff Officers and Non-regimental Enlisted Men, M-331, NARA. Brown's service record indicates his date of appointment to his new rank was September 30, 1862, which seems late.

45. Herman Hattaway and Archer Jones, *How the North Won: A Military History of the Civil War* (Urbana: Univ. of Illinois Press, 1983), 156–218; Earl J. Hess, *Banners to the Breeze: The Kentucky Campaign, Corinth, and Stones River* (Lincoln: Univ. of Nebraska Press, 2000), 1–23; Gerald J. Prokopowicz, "Last Chance for a Short War: Don Carlos Buell and the Chattanooga Campaign of 1862," in *Gateway to the Confederacy: New Perspectives on the Chickamauga and Chattanooga Campaigns, 1862–1863*, eds. Evan C. Jones and Wiley Sword (Baton Rouge: Louisiana State Univ. Press, 2014), 36–59.

46. Connelly, *Army of the Heartland*, 193–98, 205–9; Hess, *Banners to the Breeze*, 22–25; Kenneth W. Noe, *Perryville: This Grand Havoc of Battle* (Lexington: Univ. Press of Kentucky, 2001), 34–41, 58; McPherson, *Battle Cry of Freedom*, 512–17.

47. Hess, *Banners to the Breeze*, 20; Noe, *Perryville*, 55–57; OR 16(2):759, 761, 766, 775; "Sketch of General Anderson," J. Patton Anderson Papers, University of Florida Smathers Libraries, Special and Area Studies Collections, P.K. Yonge Library of Florida History; Larry Rayburn, "'Wherever the Fight Is Thickest': General James Patton Anderson of Florida," *The Florida Historical Quarterly* 60, no. 3 (January 1982): 313–22.

48. OR 16(2):763; Tennessee Civil War Centennial Commission, *Tennesseans in the Civil War*, 1:213, 242; David W. Hartman, comp., *Biographical Rosters of Florida's Confederate and Union Soldiers, 1861–1865* (Wilmington, NC: Broadfoot, 1995), 1:82, 260; Warner, *Generals in Gray*, 217–18, 311; George C. Bittle, "Fighting Men View the Western War, 1862–1864," *Florida Historical Quarterly* 47 (July 1968): 25–27; Jonathan C. Sheppard, *By the Noble Daring of Her Sons: The Florida Brigade of the Army of Tennessee* (Tuscaloosa: Univ. of Alabama Press, 2012), 78; George Winston Martin, *"I Will Give Them One More Shot": Ramsey's 1st Regiment Georgia Volunteers* (Macon: Mercer Univ. Press, 2010), 219, 226; Noe, *Perryville*, 371.

49. Sheppard, *By the Noble Daring of Her Sons*, 78–81; David J. Coles, "Ancient City Defenders: The St. Augustine Blues," in *Civil War Times in St. Augustine*, ed. Jacqueline K. Fretwell (St. Augustine, FL: St. Augustine Historical Society,

1988), 81, 83; Connelly, *Army of the Heartland*, 224–26; Noe, *Perryville*, 64–66; Hughes, *Hardee*, 121.

50. Noe, *Perryville*, 66–71, 98–99; Connelly, *Army of the Heartland*, 226–30; Coles, "Ancient City Defenders," 84.

51. Larry J. Daniel, *Days of Glory: The Army of the Cumberland, 1861–1865* (Baton Rouge: Louisiana State Univ. Press, 2004), 131–37, 141–42; Nathaniel Cheairs Hughes Jr. and Gordon D. Whitney, *Jefferson Davis in Blue: The Life of Sherman's Relentless Warrior* (Baton Rouge: Louisiana State Univ. Press, 2002), 104–16.

52. Hess, *Banners to the Breeze*, 81–85; Connelly, *Army of the Heartland*, 241–47; David Urquhart, "Bragg's Advance and Retreat," in *Battles and Leaders of the Civil War*, ed. Robert Underwood Johnson and Clarence Clough Buel (1884–1887; reprint, New York: Thomas Youseloff, 1956) 3:602; James Lee McDonough, *War In Kentucky: From Shiloh to Perryville* (Knoxville: Univ. of Tennessee Press, 1994), 197–200; Noe, *Perryville*, 89–95, 124–133; Liddell, *Liddell's Record*, 86–87.

53. Joseph Wheeler, "Bragg's Invasion of Kentucky," in *Battles and Leaders of the Civil War* 3:14–15; Liddell, *Liddell's Record*, 88; OR 16(1):1120; Noe, *Perryville*, 136–41, 170–72; Sheppard, *By the Noble Daring of Her Sons*, 85; Connelly, *Army of the Heartland*, 258–63.

54. OR 16(1):1024–25, 1087, 1120; Noe, *Perryville*, 171, 214.

55. Sheppard, *By the Noble Daring of Her Sons*, 85–86; Noe, *Perryville*, 172, 175–80, 193–213, 219–226; David R. Logsdon, ed., *Eyewitnesses at the Battle of Perryville* (Nashville: Kettle Mills Press, 2007), 7–16; Connelly, *Army of the Heartland*, 263; OR 16(1):1121; ORS 2:279–81; Robert S. Cameron, *Staff Ride Handbook for the Battle of Perryville* (Fort Leavenworth, KS: Combat Studies Institute Press, 2005), 159.

56. Noe, *Perryville*, 238–39. As Noe observes, there is no source indicating if Brown got orders to attack, and if so, from whom, although an earlier monograph on the battle indicates it was Hardee. Kenneth A. Hafendorfer, *Perryville: Battle for Kentucky* (Louisville: KH Press, 1991), 248. It is even possible that Bragg himself ordered the attack. See Sheppard, *By the Noble Daring of Her Sons*, 86. Insofar as Anderson was on the left, as there is no indication Brown was under Buckner's orders, and as it seems unlikely that Bragg was ordering individual brigades about, it is probable that the order, if one came at all, came from Hardee. OR 16(1):1121.

57. Coles, "Ancient City Defenders," 86; Noe, *Perryville*, 238–41; Logsdon, *Eyewitnesses at the Battle of Perryville*, 44–45; W. C. Hearn, "Forty-First Mississippi Regiment—A Lost Sword," *Confederate Veteran* 6 (April 1898): 152; Joseph Palmer to J. S. Montgomery, 28 October 1862 [published in

Macon Daily Telegraph, November 18, 1862], ORS 2:665–67; David Logsdon, "Middle Tennessee Eyewitnesses to the Civil War," http://www .midtneyewewitnesses.com/eyewitness-book-series/perryville/confederates (accessed June 22, 2014).

58. Noe, *Perryville*, 239–41; Logsdon, *Eyewitnesses at the Battle of Perryville*, 44–45; "Brig. Gen. Brown," *Knoxville Register*, October 21, 1862; "A Sketch of the Deceased," *Nashville Daily American*, August 18, 1889; "Ex-Gov. John C. Brown," *(Nashville) Evening Herald*, August 17, 1889.

59. Noe, *Perryville*, 240–41, 263, 266, 268–69, 371; Logsdon, *Eyewitnesses at the Battle of Perryville*, 46–47, 49. Neill's son James Trimble Brown was on the staff as an aide de camp at this juncture, not as ordnance officer.

60. Connelly, *Army of the Heartland*, 265–66; Noe, *Perryville*, 313–15; Sheppard, *By the Noble Daring of Her Sons*, 90; Hess, *Banners to the Breeze*, 110.

61. Cameron, *Handbook for the Battle of Perryville*, 59; H. H. Cunningham, *Doctors in Gray: The Confederate Medical Service* (Baton Rouge: Louisiana State Univ. Press, 1958), 116–22; Hess, *Banners to the Breeze*, 111–13; "Brig. Gen. Brown," *Knoxville Register*, October 21, 1862.

62. Special Order 33, Department No. 2, November 9, 1862, John C. Brown Compiled Service Record, NARA; William R. Snell, ed., *Myra Inman: A Diary of the Civil War in East Tennessee* (Macon, GA: Mercer Univ. Press, 2000), 177, 203 (the 1860 Census for neighboring Hamilton County, shows Anna Bradshaw, age 40, married to a J. N.? Bradshaw, a minister, with a six year old son named "Jimmy"); Hess, *Banners to the Breeze*, 116, 120.

63. OR 20(2):411, 447–48, 456; Tennessee Civil War Centennial Commission, *Tennesseans in the Civil War*, 1:228–29, 232–33, 273–75.

64. B. F. Carter to Cynthia Carter, 4 January 1863, Pope-Carter Family Papers, Perkins Library, Duke Univ. (this letter indicates part of Brown's convalescence may have been in Pulaski); "Ex-Gov. John C. Brown," *Nashville Evening Herald*, August 17, 1889; "A Sketch of the Deceased," *Nashville Daily American*, August 18, 1889; Steven Woodworth, *Jefferson Davis and His Generals: The Failure of Confederate Command in the West* (Lawrence: Univ. Press of Kansas, 1990), 182–83, 186–87; James Lee McDonough, *Stones River: Bloody Winter in Tennessee* (Knoxville: Univ. of Tennessee Press, 1980), 33, 36–37, 46–47, 51–52; Stanley Horn, *The Army of Tennessee* (1941; reprint, Wilmington, NC: Broadfoot Publishing, 1987), 195–96. Stevenson's departure obviated a need for a third corps, and Kirby Smith returned to East Tennessee.

65. Hess, *Banners to the Breeze*, 177–78; Daniel, *Days of Glory*, 181–90; Larry J. Daniel, *Battle of Stones River: The Forgotten Conflict Between the Confederate Army of Tennessee and the Union Army of the Cumberland* (Baton Rouge: Louisiana State Univ. Press, 2012), 31–38, 40–48, 64–68; OR 20(1):664.

66. Horn, *Army of Tennessee*, 200–205; Daniel, *Battle of Stones River*, 166–68; Peter Cozzens, *No Better Place to Die: The Battle of Stones River* (Urbana: Univ. of Illinois Press, 1990), 164–66; OR 20(1):678, 804–5.

67. Daniel, *Battle of Stones River*, 171–75, 180–81; Cozzens, *No Better Place to Die*, 174–75, 178–96.

68. Daniel, *Battle of Stones River*, 183–95; Cozzens, *No Better Place to Die*, 183–96; Hughes and Stonesifer, *Gideon J. Pillow*, 253–58. Pillow's biographers do not credit the cowardice story.

69. Daniel, *Battle of Stones River*, 198–99; Grady McWhiney, *Braxton Bragg and Confederate Defeat* (Tuscaloosa: Univ. of Alabama Press, 1969), 370–73; Woodworth, *Jefferson Davis and His Generals*, 194–98; "General Bragg," *Winchester Daily Bulletin*, January 11, 1863; Thomas L. Connelly, *Autumn of Glory: The Army of Tennessee, 1862–1865* (Baton Rouge: Louisiana State Univ. Press, 1971), 69–92; Noe, *Perryville*, 339; Liddell, *Liddell's Record*, 116–17 ("Bragg's manner made him malignant enemies and indifferent, callous friends.").

3. Boys, Them Damn Yanks Can't Whip You

1. B. Frank Carter to Cynthia Carter, 15 January 1863, Pope-Carter Papers, Perkins Library, Duke Univ.; Special Order 27, Hardee's Corps, January 16, 1863, JCB Compiled Service Record, NARA; Hughes and Stonesifer, *Gideon J. Pillow*, 260–65; Earl J. Hess, *The Civil War in the West: Victory and Defeat from the Appalachians to the Mississippi* (Chapel Hill: Univ. of North Carolina Press, 2012) 180; Connelly, *Autumn of Glory*, 109, 115–16; "Review of General Hardee's Troops at Tullahoma," *Winchester Daily Bulletin*, March 21, 1863.

2. OR 23(2):619; Lucy Virginia French Diary, February 1, 1863, TSLA (according to census records, Mary Armstrong would have been no more than eighteen at the time); R. Lockwood Tower, ed., *A Carolinian Goes to War: The Civil War Narrative of Arthur Middleton Manigault* (Columbia: Univ. of South Carolina Press, 1983), 72; G. W. Dillon Diary, TSLA; "Review of General Hardee's Troops at Tullahoma," *Winchester Daily Bulletin*, March 21, 1863; William Lee White and Charles Denny Runion, eds., *Great Things are Expected of Us: The Letters of Col. C. Irvine Walker, 10th South Carolina Infantry, C. S. A.* (Knoxville: Univ. of Tennessee Press, 2009), 52; Hughes, *General William J. Hardee*, 154–55; Connelly, *Autumn of Glory*, 120–21; OR 23(2):780–85, 787–91, 847.

3. OR 24(1):191–94; 23(2):849, 851, 867–68; Sam D. Elliott, *Soldier of Tennessee: General Alexander P. Stewart and the Civil War in the West* (Baton Rouge: Louisiana State Univ. Press, 1999), 85–86.

4. Elliott, *Isham G. Harris*, 140–42, 214; "The Governorship of Tennessee," *Memphis Daily Appeal*, April 9, 1863; "Next Governor," *Fayetteville Observer*, May 7, 1863; "We have recently received communications," *Chattanooga Daily Rebel*, June 13, 1863; "The Convention," *Chattanooga Daily Rebel*, June 19, 1863; "Tennessee State Convention," *Chattanooga Daily Rebel*, June 21, 1863.

5. OR 23(1):386–89, 291–93, 23(2):482, 886; "Battle at Knoxville—Defeat of the Yankee Raiders," *Chattanooga Daily Rebel*, June 21, 1863; Robert Tracy McKenzie, *Lincolnites and Rebels: A Divided Town in the American Civil War* (New York: Oxford Univ. Press, 2006), 146–47; Henry Downs Jamison Jr. and Marguerite Jamison McTigue, comps., *Letters and Recollections of a Confederate Soldier, 1860–1865* (n. p., 1964), 65; B. Frank Carter to Cynthia Carter, 20 June 1863, Pope-Carter Papers, Perkins Library, Duke Univ.; G. W. Dillon Diary, TSLA; Snell, ed., *Myra Inman*, 203. The 45th Tennessee, and possibly the 26th, did not make the trip.

6. Daniel, *Days of Glory*, 257–69; Elliott, *Soldier of Tennessee*, 95–98; G. W. Dillon Diary, TSLA.

7. Connelly, *Autumn of Glory*, 126–34; Steven E. Woodworth, *Six Armies in Tennessee: The Chickamauga and Chattanooga Campaigns* (Lincoln: Univ. of Nebraska Press, 1998), 30–45; Michael R. Bradley, *Tullahoma: The 1863 Campaign for Control of Middle Tennessee* (Shippensburg, PA: Burd Street Press, 2000), 74–89; Sam D. Elliott, ed., *Doctor Quintard: Chaplain C. S. A. and Second Bishop of Tennessee* (Baton Rouge: Louisiana State Univ. Press, 2003), 76.

8. Connelly, *Autumn of Glory*, 139–48; Elliott, *Soldier of Tennessee*, 111–13; G. W. Dillon Diary, TSLA; Hughes, *General William J. Hardee*, 158–60; "Special Army Correspondence," *Knoxville Register*, July 26, 1863; Jamison and McTigue, eds., *Letters and Recollections*, 69; Larry J. Daniel, *Soldiering in the Army of Tennessee: A Portrait of Life in a Confederate Army* (Chapel Hill: Univ. of North Carolina Press, 1991), 130–31.

9. Elliott, ed., *Doctor Quintard*, 81–82; Craig R. Symonds, *Stonewall of the West: Patrick Cleburne and the Civil War* (Lawrence: Univ. Press of Kansas, 1997), 135; Roger Q. Mills to J. P. Douglas, 10 January 1901, in "Concerning Re-Enlistment at Dalton," *Confederate Veteran* 9 (January 1901): 13; *Constitution of the Comrades of the Southern Cross* (Macon, GA: Burke, Boykin and Company, 1863); OR Series IV, 2:670–71.

10. "Hon. Neill S. Brown," *Chattanooga Daily Rebel*, July 14, 1863; David McCallie, ed., *THM: A Memoir* (Bloomington, IN.: WestBow Press, 2011), 61; Special Orders, Stewart's Division, Army of Tennessee, John C. Brown Compiled Service Record, NARA; OR 23(2):954, 959.

11. Peter Cozzens, *This Terrible Sound: The Battle of Chickamauga* (Urbana: Univ. of Illinois Press, 1992), 23–26, 31–32; David A. Powell, *The Chickamauga Campaign: A Mad Irregular Battle: From the Crossing of the Tennessee River Through the Second Day, August 22–September 19, 1863* (El Dorado Hills, CA: Savas Beatie, 2014), 69; William Glenn Robertson, "The Chickamauga Campaign: The Fall of Chattanooga," *Blue & Gray Magazine* 23 (Fall 2006): 7–13.

12. OR 30(4):554, 566, 570, 578, 583–84, 586–87; Robertson, "The Fall of Chattanooga," 19–23; Powell, *A Mad Irregular Battle*, 82–83; Cozzens, *This Terrible Sound*, 49.

13. OR 30(4): 590, 597, 599, 610–11; Robertson, "The Fall of Chattanooga," 43–50; Powell, *A Mad Irregular Battle*, 101–9; Cozzens, *This Terrible Sound*, 53–63; Steven E. Woodworth, "'In Their Dreams': Braxton Bragg, Thomas C. Hindman, and the Abortive Attack in McLemore's Cove," in *The Chickamauga Campaign*, ed. Steven E. Woodworth (Carbondale: Southern Illinois Univ. Press, 2010), 52–53.

14. William Glenn Robertson, "The Chickamauga Campaign: McLemore's Cove: Rosecrans' Gamble, Bragg's Lost Opportunity," *Blue & Gray Magazine* 23 (Spring 2007): 14–16, 19–20; Powell, *A Mad Irregular Battle*, 112–22; Woodworth, "'In Their Dreams,'" 54–55.

15. Robertson, "McLemore's Cove: Rosecrans' Gamble, Bragg's Lost Opportunity," 42–46; Powell, *A Mad Irregular Battle*, 142–59; Woodworth, "'In Their Dreams,'" 61–65; J. P. Anderson to Etta Anderson, 5 October 1863, J. Patton Anderson Papers, Younge Library, University of Florida.

16. Powell, *A Mad Irregular Battle*, 161–62; Milton P. Jarnigan Reminiscences, 20th Tennessee File, CCNMP; Judith Lee Hallock, *Braxton Bragg and Confederate Defeat*, vol. 2 (Tuscaloosa: Univ. of Alabama Press, 1991), 59–61; Elliott, *Soldier of Tennessee*, 117–19; Woodworth, "'In Their Dreams,'" 66.

17. Woodworth, *Six Armies in Tennessee*, 76–84.

18. OR 30(2):361; Bromfield Ridley, *Battles and Sketches of the Army of Tennessee* (1906; reprint, Dayton, OH: Morningside Bookshop, 1995), 208–10, 312–13; N. J. Hampton, *An Eyewitness to the Dark Days of 1861–65 or, A Private Soldier's Adventures and Hardships During the War* (Nashville: N. J. Hampton, 1898), 29.

19. OR 30(1):248–49; William Glenn Robertson, "The Chickamauga Campaign: The Armies Collide: Bragg Forces His Way Across Chickamauga Creek," *Blue & Gray Magazine* 24 (Fall 2007): 6, 48–50; William Glenn Robertson, "The Chickamauga Campaign: The Battle of Chickamauga Day 1, September 19, 1863," *Blue & Gray Magazine* 24 (Spring 2008): 8, 20–21; Woodworth, *Six Armies in Tennessee*, 84.

20. Woodworth, *Six Armies in Tennessee*, 86–89; Powell, *A Mad Irregular Battle*, 288–394; Cozzens, *This Terrible Sound*, 121–82; Robertson, "The Battle of Chickamauga Day 1," 8, 20–26, 40–41; OR 30(2): 361; Ridley, *Battles and Sketches*, 219.

21. Raymond S. Eresman, "Union and Confederate Infantry Doctrine in the Battle of Chickamauga" (master's thesis, U. S. Army Command and General Staff College, 1991), 59; Luke J. Barnett III, "Alexander P Stewart and the Tactical Employment of His Division at Chickamauga" (master's thesis, U. S. Army Command and General Staff College, 1989), 94, 108–11; Lee White, "A. P. Stewart at Chickamauga," in *The Chickamauga Campaign*, ed. Woodworth, 91–93; OR 30(2): 361–2, 401; Powell, *A Mad Irregular Battle*, 405–9; Ridley, *Battles and Sketches*, 220.

22. OR 30(2):370–371, 375–6, 378, 380–83; Powell, *A Mad Irregular Battle*, 411–19; David S. Bodenhamer Sketch, Civil War Collection, TSLA; Robertson, "The Battle of Chickamauga Day 1," 42; T. L. Corn, "Brown's Brigade at Chickamauga," *Confederate Veteran* 21 (March 1913): 124; Gustavus W. Dyer and John Trotwood Moore, comps., *Tennessee Civil War Veterans Questionnaires* (Easley, SC: Southern Historical Press, 1985), 2:566 (T. J. Corn [Corn's spelling has been corrected]); Barnett, "Alexander P Stewart and the Tactical Employment of His Division at Chickamauga," 97–100; Lindsley, *Military Annals*, 474.

23. OR 30(2):372, 376; Lindsley, *Military Annals*, 363–64.

24. Powell, *A Mad Irregular Battle*, 414–17, 419; OR 30(2):371, 375, 378, 380; Brown's Brigade marker, September 19, 1863, 2:30 p.m., CCNMP.

25. OR 30(2):362, 371, 383; White, "A. P. Stewart at Chickamauga," 95–99; Robertson, "The Battle of Chickamauga Day 1," 43–44; Ridley, *Battles and Sketches*, 220; Powell, *A Mad Irregular Battle*, 563–64; D. Augustus Dickert, *History of Kershaw's Brigade with Complete Roll of Companies, Biographical Sketches, Incidents, Anecdotes, Etc.* (Newberry, SC: E. H. Aull Company, 1899), 268; David A. Powell and David A. Friedrichs, *The Maps of Chickamauga* (New York: Savas-Beatie, 2009), 123, 125, 127, 137.

26. Barnett, "Alexander P Stewart and the Tactical Employment of His Division at Chickamauga," 111–12; White, "A. P. Stewart at Chickamauga," 98–99; Powell, *A Mad Irregular Battle*, 541; Glenn Tucker, *Chickamauga: Bloody Battle in the West* (1961; reprint, Dayton, OH: Morningside, 1981), 152–63; Robertson, "The Battle of Chickamauga Day 1," 41–44; Eresman, "Union and Confederate Infantry Doctrine in the Battle of Chickamauga," 59.

27. OR 30(2):371, 373; Jamison and McTigue, eds., *Letters and Recollections*, 163; Corn, "Brown's Brigade at Chickamauga," 124; Lindsley, ed., *Military Annals*, 475.

28. Robertson, "The Battle of Chickamauga Day 1," 47–50, 52.

29. Ridley, *Battles and Sketches*, 222; OR 30(2):363, 371–72; Powell and Friedrichs, *The Maps of Chickamauga*, 142–43.

30. William Glenn Robertson, "A Tale of Two Orders: Chickamauga, September 20, 1863," in *Gateway to the Confederacy*, ed. Jones and Sword, 131–42; William Glenn Robertson, "The Chickamauga Campaign: Day 2, September 20, 1863," *Blue & Gray Magazine* 25 (Summer 2008): 9, 19–24; David A. Powell, *The Chickamauga Campaign: Glory or the Grave: The Breakthrough, the Union Collapse and the Defense of Horseshoe Ridge, September 20, 1863* (El Dorado Hills, CA: Savas Beatie, 2015), 74–103, 125–33, 160–61; OR 30(2): 363–4.

31. Robertson, "The Chickamauga Campaign: Day 2, September 20, 1863," 22–24; Powell and Friedrichs, *The Maps of Chickamauga*, 147, 160–61; Powell, *Glory or the Grave*, 161–64; OR 30(2):372.

32. Powell and Friedrichs, *The Maps of Chickamauga*, 160–61; OR 30(2):372 375–81; Ridley, *Battles and Sketches*, 225; Bodenhamer Sketch, TSLA; Powell, *Glory or the Grave*, 165–68.

33. OR 30(2): 364, 367, 372, 379. Writing in 1913, T. J. Corn of the 26th Tennessee stated that Brown was unhorsed by grapeshot on September 19, but the lack of a contemporary account of the same, coupled with the passage of time, makes it likely he was referring to Brown's wound on September 20. Corn, "Brown's Brigade at Chickamauga," 124.

34. OR 30(2):364; Robertson, "The Chickamauga Campaign: Day 2, September 20, 1863," 24–28, 40–49.

35. B. F. Carter to Cynthia Carter, 28(?) September 1863, Pope-Carter Papers, Perkins Library, Duke Univ.; Connelly, *Autumn of Glory*, 230–34; Woodworth, *Six Armies in Tennessee*, 132–33; Earl J. Hess, *Braxton Bragg: The Most Hated Man of the Confederacy*, (Chapel Hill: Univ. of North Carolina Press, 2016), 171-74.

36. OR 30(2):24, 367, 370, 373–74; Elizabeth Childress Brown, Tennessee Death Records, 1908–1959, roll no. 95, TSLA; "Maj. John W. Childress," *Nashville Daily American*, October 9, 1884; J. W. Childress to Andrew Johnson, 23 June 1865, Case Files of Applications from Former Confederates for Presidential Pardons, 1865–67, M1003, NARA; William S. Speer, *Sketches of Prominent Tennesseans*, 26–27; Tennessee Biographical Questionnaire re: Mrs. John C. Brown, MS-485, TSLA.

37. "A Society Event of the Civil War," *Nashville Tennessean*, May 4, 1913; Annie Somers Gilchrist, *Some Representative Women of Tennessee* (Nashville: McQuiddy Printing Company, 1902) 12.

38. Hallock, *Braxton Bragg and Confederate Defeat*, 2: 89–90, 95–98; Woodworth, *Six Armies in Tennessee*, 138–39; David A. Powell, *The Chickamauga*

Campaign: Barren Victory: The Retreat into Chattanooga, the Confederate Pursuit, and the Aftermath of the Battle, September 21 to October 20, 1863, (El Dorado Hills, CA: Savas Beatie, 2016), 110-12; Petition to Davis, October 4, 1863, Simon Bolivar Buckner Collection, Huntington Library, San Marino, Calif.; Connelly, *Autumn of Glory*, 235–38; Liddell, *Liddell's Record*, 151; Petition to Davis, October 4, 1863, Item 3172, Collection 169, Confederate States Army Papers, Georgia Historical Society (A. P. Stewart's copy); Craig L. Symonds, "War and Politics: Jefferson Davis Visits the Army of Tennessee," in *Gateway to the Confederacy*, 161–65; Hal Bridges, *Lee's Maverick General: Daniel Harvey Hill* (New York: McGraw-Hill, 1961), 237; OR 30(4):742–43; William W. Mackall to wife, 5 October 1863, W. W. Mackall Papers, Southern Historical Collection, University of North Carolina: Hess, *Braxton Bragg*, 137, 178-79. Brown's quote was part of a response to an inquiry from Longstreet in 1888. Then, Brown's recollection of the identity of the signers was hazy, and he "[did] not care to name any of the officers, unless [he could] name them all." He recalled that William B. Bate and Edward C. Walthall did not sign, and was unsure about Stewart. JCB to J. Longstreet, 14 April 1888, James Longstreet Papers, Perkins Library, Duke Univ. (typescript in Chickamauga Chattanooga National Military Park library).

39. OR 52(2):538; Symonds, "War and Politics: Jefferson Davis Visits the Army of Tennessee," 169–75; Hallock, *Braxton Bragg and Confederate Defeat*, 99–100; Woodworth, *Jefferson Davis and His Generals*, 242–43; Connelly, *Autumn of Glory*, 245–46.

40. Wiley Sword, *Mountains Touched With Fire: Chattanooga Besieged, 1863* (New York: St. Martin's Press, 1995), 43–45, 96–111; Peter Cozzens, *The Shipwreck of their Hopes: The Battles for Chattanooga* (Urbana: Univ. of Illinois Press, 1994) 29–31; John C. Oeffinger, ed., *A Soldier's General: The Civil War Letters of Major General Lafayette McLaws* (Chapel Hill: Univ. of North Carolina Press, 2002), 206; G. W. Dillon Diary, TSLA.

41. Woodworth, *Six Armies in Tennessee*, 146–69; Hess, *The Civil War in the West*, 193–96; Evan C. Jones, "A 'Malignant Vindictiveness': The Rivalry Between Grant and Rosecrans," in *Gateway to the Confederacy*, 199–202.

42. Alexander Mendoza, *Confederate Struggle for Command: General James Longstreet and the First Corps in the West* (College Station: Texas A&M Univ. Press, 2008), 102–14; Woodworth, *Six Armies in Tennessee*, 174–78; McMurry, *Two Great Rebel Armies*, 135–36; OR 52(2):557; Connelly, *Autumn of Glory*, 232, 261–62; Horn, *Army of Tennessee*, 296; Elliott, *Soldier of Tennessee*, 140. Compare the organization of the army at the end of October 1863 with that of November 20, 1863. OR 31(2):618, 31(3):659.

43. OR 31(1):8–10, 31(3):685–86; Connelly, *Autumn of Glory*, 250–51; Elliott, *Soldier of Tennessee*, 140; Warner, *Generals in Gray*, 66, 238–39, 292–93;

Larry Gordon, *The Last Confederate General: John C. Vaughn and his East Tennessee Cavalry* (Minneapolis: Zenith Press, 2009), 78–80.

44. OR 31(2): 662, 667; 31(3):685; 32(2):506; Lindsley, *Military Annals*, 177–79.

45. "Lookout Mountain and Vicinity," *Athens (Georgia) Southern Banner*, November 25, 1863.

46. Bodenhamer Sketch, TSLA; OR 30(1):246; 31(3):695, 699; 31(2):718.

47. JCB to G. L. Gillespie, 14 November 1863, and JCB to Stevenson, 17 November 1863, both in Stevenson Papers, Museum of the Confederacy (MOC); G. W. Dillon Diary, TSLA; OR 31(3):700–2.

48. Liddell, *Liddell's Record*, 158–60; JCB to Stevenson, 17 November 1863, Stevenson Papers, MOC; OR 31(2):630, 31 (3):710.

49. William T. Sherman, *Memoirs of Gen. W. T. Sherman* (New York: Charles L. Webster and Company, 1891) 1:391; OR 31(2):585–89, 630–31, 668–71; Bodenhamer Sketch, TSLA; JCB to J. J. Reeve, 21 November 1863, Stevenson Papers, MOC.

50. OR 31(2):672, 674, 723; JCB to J. J. Reeve, 23 November 1863, Stevenson Papers, MOC; Cozzens, *Shipwreck of Their Hopes*, 137–41; Connelly, *Autumn of Glory*, 272.

51. Ulysses S. Grant, *Personal Memoirs of U. S. Grant* (New York: Charles L. Webster and Company, 1886), 2:56–57; OR 31(2):29–33, 718, 725; Cozzens, *Shipwreck of Their Hopes*, 159–63.

52. Sword, *Mountains Touched With Fire*, 207–12.

53. OR 31(2):719–30.

54. OR 31(2): 725–29; Cozzens, *Shipwreck of Their Hopes*, 184.

55. OR 31(2):726, 729–30, 733.

56. Connelly, *Autumn of Glory*, 273; OR 31(2): 726; Bodenhamer Sketch, TSLA.

57. Sword, *Mountains Touched With Fire*, 233–36, 242; John R. Lundberg, "Baptizing the Hills and Valleys: Cleburne's Defense of Tunnel Hill," in *The Chattanooga Campaign*, ed. Steven E. Woodworth and Charles D. Grear (Carbondale: Southern Illinois Univ. Press, 2012), 71–75; Hamilton County, Tennessee GIS data.

58. OR 31(2):726–27, 730, 749; Cozzens, *Shipwreck of Their Hopes*, 211–12; "Battle of Chattanooga," *Athens (Georgia) Southern Banner*, December 16, 1863; "The Federal Account," *Memphis Daily Appeal*, December 23, 1863.

59. Steven E. Woodworth, *Nothing But Victory: The Army of the Tennessee, 1861–1865* (New York: Alfred A. Knopf, 2005), 471–75; Sword, *Mountains Touched With Fire*, 243–47; OR 31(2):633, 726–7, 730; "The Federal Account."

60. OR 31(2):360, 633, 727, 735.

61. Woodworth, *Nothing But Victory*, 472–77; Sword, *Mountains Touched With Fire*, 251–54; Cozzens, *Shipwreck of Their Hopes*, 220–32; OR 31(2):727; Jamison and McTigue, eds., *Letters and Recollections*, 165.

62. Sword, *Mountains Touched With Fire*, 254–58; G. W. Dillon Diary, TSLA; OR 31(2):729.

63. Woodworth, *Six Armies in Tennessee*, 198–202; Hughes, *General William J. Hardee*, 175–77; OR 31(2):727, 729, 738; Bodenhamer Sketch, TSLA; G. W. Dillon Diary, TSLA.

64. Connelly, *Autumn of Glory*, 276–78, 284–87; Hughes, *General William J. Hardee*, 183–86; Richard M. McMurry, *Atlanta 1864: Last Chance for the Confederacy* (Lincoln: Univ. of Nebraska Press, 2000), 10–11; Mary Boykin Chesnut, *A Diary from Dixie*, ed. Ben Ames Williams (Boston: Harvard Univ. Press, 1949) 317.

65. Barber, *Holding the Line*, 148, 150–51; B. F. Carter to Cynthia Carter, 3 December 1863, Pope-Carter Papers, Perkins Library, Duke Univ.; Connelly, *Autumn of Glory*, 291; G. W. Dillon Diary, TSLA.

66. "Confederate States Congress," *The (Richmond) Daily Dispatch*, December 30, 1863; Wiley Sword, "'Our Fireside in Ruins': Consequences of the 1863 Chattanooga Campaign," in *Gateway to the Confederacy*, ed. Jones and Sword, 231–32, 241–43; Liddell, *Liddell's Record*, 120; Symonds, *Stonewall of the West*, 183–86.

67. OR 52(2):586, 595–96, 598, 606–7; Symonds, *Stonewall of the West*, 186–91; Bruce Levine, *Confederate Emancipation: Southern Plans to Free and Arm Slaves During the Civil War* (New York: Oxford Univ. Press, 2006) 25–29; Connelly, *Autumn of Glory*, 318–21; Diane Neal and Thomas W. Kremm, *The Lion of the South: General Thomas C. Hindman* (Macon, GA: Mercer Univ. Press, 1993), 37–38, 188–90; Russell K. Brown, *To the Manner Born: The Life of General William H. T. Walker* (Athens: Univ. of Georgia Press, 1994), 194–203; Elliott, *Soldier of Tennessee*, 167–68; Thomas Robeson Hay, "The South and the Arming of the Slaves," *The Mississippi Valley Historical Review* 6 (June 1919): 34, 39–48; Sword, "'Our Fireside in Ruins,'" 232–36.

68. Symonds, *Stonewall of the West*, 190–91; Hay, "The South and the Arming of the Slaves," 48; Levine, *Confederate Emancipation*, 17; Campbell Brown, *Campbell Brown's Civil War: With Ewell and the Army of Northern Virginia*, ed. Terry L. Jones (Baton Rouge: Louisiana State Univ. Press, 2001), 11–12, 318–20.

69. Martha Abernathy, *The Civil War Diary of Martha Abernathy, Wife of Dr. Charles C. Abernathy of Pulaski, Tennessee*, ed. Elizabeth Paisley Dargan (Beltsville, MD: Professional Printing, 1994), 55; Levine, *Confederate Emancipation*, 102–3; Connelly, *Army of the Heartland*, 320–321.

70. Barber, *Holding the Line*, 152; Charles G. Rogers Compiled Service Record, General and Staff Officers, and Non- Regimental Enlisted Men, M-331, NARA; Connelly, *Army of the Heartland*, 292–94.

4. A Military Convenience . . . in All the Hard Places

1. Historian Steven Woodworth has theorized that these were two of the three strikes against Cleburne in early 1864, along with foreign birth. Woodworth, *Jefferson Davis and His Generals*, 262–63.
2. OR 31(3):833, 32(2):660, 669, 742, 805–6, 811; J. Patton Anderson Compiled Service Record, M-331, NARA; Landon C. Hayes and G. A. Henry to Jefferson Davis, 15 February 1864, and Memorandum, J. Davis to Secretary of War, 23 February 1864, both in William B. Bate Compiled Service Record, M-331, NARA; C. Stevenson to S. Cooper, 2 February 1864, W. J. Hardee endorsement, 12 February 1864, John Bell to J. A. Campbell, 22 February 1864, I. G. Harris to J. Seddon, 24 February 1864, Bromfield Ridley to G. A. Henry, 14 March 1864, G. A. Henry to Sec. of War, 28 March 1864, and Jno. B. Johnson et. al. to G. A. Henry, 8 March 1864, all in John C. Brown Compiled Service Record, M-331, NARA; J. Patton Anderson, "Sketch of General Anderson's Life" and Braxton Bragg to Anderson, 28 February 1864, both in J. Patton Anderson Papers, Younge Library, University of Florida; Dianne Neal and Kremm, *Lion of the South: General Thomas B. Hindman,* Hindman, 191–92.
3. Buck T. Foster, *Sherman's Mississippi Campaign* (Tuscaloosa: Univ. of Alabama Press, 2006), 14–32; Connelly, *Autumn of Glory*, 369; OR 32(1): 127–29, 32(2):198–99, 644, 670.
4. Barber, *Holding the Line*, 155–59; Keith S. Bohannon, "'Witness the Redemption of the Army': Reenlistments in the Confederate Army of Tennessee, January–March, 1864," in *Inside the Confederate Nation: Essays in Honor of Emory M. Thomas*, ed. Lesley J. Gordon and John C. Inscoe (Baton Rouge: Louisiana State Univ. Press, 2005), 111–27.
5. Barber, *Holding the Line*, 160–61; OR 32(1): 127–29; Jamison and McTigue, eds., *Letters and Recollections*, 168; B. F. Carter to wife, 21 February 1864, Pope-Carter Papers, Perkins Library, Duke Univ.; Elliott, ed., *Doctor Quintard*, 117. A number of refugee Confederate Tennesseans, especially East Tennesseans, moved to Georgia during the war. Griffin appears to have been a place where quite a number of Middle Tennesseans gathered. There were several army hospitals there, a branch of the Bank of Tennessee, and eventually one of the state's Confederate newspapers, the *Rebel*. In his letter recommending Brown's promotion, noted above, John Bell wrote from Griffin. Todd Groce, *Mountain Rebels: East Tennessee Confederates and the Civil War, 1860–1870*

(Knoxville: Univ. of Tennessee Press, 1999), 121–23; *Daily Chattanooga (Griffin) Rebel*, June 27, 1864; John Bell to J. A. Campbell, 22 February 1864, John C. Brown Compiled Service Record, M-331, NARA.

6. Foster, *Sherman's Mississippi Campaign*, 106–19; "A Society Event of the Civil War," *Nashville Tennessean*, May 4, 1913; Elliott, ed., *Doctor Quintard*, 118; "War and Matrimony," *Richmond Daily Dispatch*, April 2, 1864.

7. Albert Castel, *Decision in the West: The Atlanta Campaign of 1864* (Lawrence: Univ. Press of Kansas, 1992), 54; OR 32(1): 417–84; 32(2):799, 803, 805; Barber, *Holding the Line*, 162–63.

8. Barber, *Holding the Line*, 164; "A Society Event of the Civil War"; OR 35(1): 195–99; Warner, *Generals in Gray*, 81–82; "Interesting from Charleston," *San Francisco Daily Evening Bulletin*, March 3, 1864; E. Milby Burton, *The Siege of Charleston* (Columbia: Univ. of South Carolina Press, 1970), 183–210; JCB to J. J. Reeve, 22 March 1864, Stevenson Papers, MOC.

9. G. Clinton Prim Jr., "Born Again in the Trenches: Revivals in the Army of Tennessee," *Tennessee Historical Quarterly* 43 (Fall 1984): 250, 265 ("greatest revival"); Barber, *Holding the Line*, 167–68, 173–75; Jamison and McTigue, eds., *Letters and Recollections*, 91; Deavenport Diary, TSLA; "Religion in the Army of Tennessee," *Pulaski Citizen*, July 3, 1868; Derrell C. Roberts, *The Gray Winter of 1864 in Dalton* (Dalton, GA: Whitfield-Murray County Historical Society, 1991), 48–49, 59–64; "Reminiscences—Mother of the Confederacy," *Confederate Veteran* 2 (April 1894): 108; Thos. B. Osborne to Julia Osborne, 22 April 1864, Thomas Osborne Papers, Eastern Kentucky University Archives, Richmond, KY.

10. Castel, *Decision in the West*, 119; McMurry *Atlanta 1864*, 42–43, 58–59; William T. Sherman, *Home Letters of General Sherman*, ed. M. A. DeWolf Howe (New York: Charles Scribner's Sons, 1909), 292.

11. George Wise Diary, North New Jersey History and Genealogy Center, Morristown and Morris Township Library; Barber, *Holding the Line*, 179–84; Deavenport Diary, TSLA; OR 38(1):367–68, 38(3):811; Jamison and McTigue, eds., *Letters and Recollections*, 168.

12. Castel, *Decision in the West*, 140–51; "Letter from the Army," *Memphis (Atlanta) Daily Appeal*, May 25, 1864; Barber, *Holding the Line*, 183–86; McMurry, *Atlanta 1864*, 63–68; George Wise Diary, North New Jersey History and Genealogy Center; "Distances on the Georgia State Road," *Richmond Daily Dispatch*, June 1, 1864.

13. "Letter from the Army"; "From the Front," *Memphis (Atlanta) Daily Appeal*, May 24, 1864; Hampton, *An Eyewitness to the Dark Days of 1861–1865*, 44–46; Lindsley, ed., *Military Annals*, 478.

14. OR 38(3):645–47; Joseph E. Johnston, *Narrative of Military Operations Directed During the Late War Between the States* (New York: D. Appleton and

Company, 1874), 305, 309–10; Philip L. Secrist, *The Battle of Resaca* (Macon, GA: Mercer Univ. Press, 1998) 17–28; 156–63.

15. Johnston, *Narrative of Military Operations*, 310–11; OR 38(1): 221, 241, 38(3): 812; "Letter from the Army"; Lindsley, ed., *Military Annals*, 478–79; Castel, *Decision in the West*, 164–65; Secrist, *The Battle of Resaca*, 35–37; Hampton, *An Eyewitness to the Dark Days of 1861–1865*, 46; George Wise Diary, North New Jersey History and Genealogy Center. Shortly after Brown's death, S. C. Bowers, a veteran of the 18th, recalled an episode when before an assault was made on a ridge, the division commander told Brown that if any of his men should falter in the assault, he should shoot them down. Brown indignantly replied: "I am commanding Tennesseans and neither pistols nor bayonets are necessary to keep their faces to the front." Brown's remark was felt to have inspired the subsequent successful assault. There is no indication as to when this remark was made, but, if true, it seems most likely to have occurred at this point. See "The Late John C. Brown," *Nashville Daily American*, September 5, 1889.

16. OR 38(1):221, 488–89, 38(2):85–86, 38(3):812; Castel, *Decision in the West*, 165–66; Deavenport Diary, TSLA; "Letter from the Army"; Johnston, *Narrative of Military Operations*, 311–12.

17. Johnston, *Narrative of Military Operations*, 312–13; OR 38(2):322–23, 38(3):812; "Letter from the Army"; John B. Hood, *Advance and Retreat* (1879; reprint, Edison, NJ: Blue and Gray Press, 1985), 96; Lindsley, *Military Annals*, 479; Deavenport Diary, TSLA.

18. Secrist, *The Battle of Resaca*, 52–56; OR 38(2):341, 352, 360, 365–66, 371–72, 38(3):812–13; Castel, *Decision in the West*, 174–75; Lindsley, *Military Annals*, 479–80; "Letter from the Army"; Jamison and McTigue, eds., *Letters and Recollections*, 169; Deavenport Diary, TSLA; McMurry, *Atlanta 1864*, 71–72.

19. Castel, *Decision in the West*, 175–78; Johnston, *Narrative of Military Operations*, 313–14; OR 38(3):813; George Wise Diary, North New Jersey History and Genealogy Center; McMurry, *Atlanta 1864*, 72.

20. Castel, *Decision in the West*, 179–81; "Letter from the Army"; Jamison and McTigue, eds., *Letters and Recollections*, 169–70.

21. McMurry, *Atlanta, 1864*, 75–84; Deavenport Diary, TSLA. For the controversy, see Johnston, *Narrative of Military Operations*, 319–25; Hood, *Advance and Retreat*, 99–116; Stephen M. Hood, ed., *The Lost Papers of Confederate General John Bell Hood* (El Dorado Hills, CA: Savas Beatie, 2015) 81–99.

22. OR 38(3):813, 818; Deavenport Diary, TSLA; Jamison and McTigue, eds., *Letters and Recollections of a Confederate Soldier*, 171; Castel, *Decision in the West*, 209–26; McMurry, *Atlanta 1864*, 85–89; Lindsley, *Military Annals*, 179; Ridley, *Battles and Sketches*, 303–5; Sam Davis Elliott, "'I Regard Maj. Gen. Stewart as the Best Qualified of the Maj. Gens. of this Army': Alexander P.

Stewart and His Division in the First Phase of the Atlanta Campaign," in *Confederate Generals in the Western Theater: Essays on America's Civil War,* ed. Lawrence L. Hewitt and Arthur W. Bergeron (Knoxville: Univ. of Tennessee Press, 2010), 146–48.

23. Deavenport Diary, TSLA; Samuel G. French, *Two Wars: An Autobiography of Gen. Samuel G. French* (Nashville: Confederate Veteran, 1901), 199–202; Johnston, *Narrative of Military Operations,* 336–38; McMurry, *Atlanta 1864,* 100–103; Earl J. Hess, *Kennesaw Mountain: Sherman, Johnston and the Atlanta Campaign* (Chapel Hill: Univ. of North Carolina Press, 2013), 6–10.

24. Hess, *Kennesaw Mountain,* 15–25, 34–38; "A Victory Which was Never Won; Orders on the Death of Gen. Polk," *New York Times,* July 17, 1864.

25. Deavenport Diary, TSLA; "Religion in the Army of Tennessee"; "A Victory Which was Never Won; Orders on the Death of Gen. Polk"; "How a Rebel Brigade was Smashed," *Boston Herald,* July 21, 1864; "News from Rebel Sources," *Louisville Daily Journal,* July 7, 1864; "Death of Col. Ed. C. Cook of the Thirty-Second Tennessee," *Daily Chattanooga (Griffin) Rebel,* June 29, 1864; "From Georgia—The Battle of Kennesaw Mountain," *Richmond Daily Dispatch,* July 4, 1864; Jamison and McTigue, eds., *Letters and Recollections,* 171–72; Lindsley, ed., *Military Annals,* 480; OR 38(3):814–15.

26. Hess, *Kennesaw Mountain,* 62–63, 71–142; McMurry, *Atlanta 1864,* 108–10, 113–18; Robert D. Jenkins Sr., *To the Gates of Atlanta: From Kennesaw Mountain to Peach Tree Creek, 1–19 July 1864* (Macon, GA: Mercer Univ. Press, 2015), 13–120.

27. Manigault, *A Carolinian Goes to War,* 195, 214; Neal and Kremm, *Lion of the South,* 196–7; H. D. Clayton to wife, 7 June 1864 (Stewart recommended promotion), Henry D. Clayton Papers, W.S. Hoole Special Collections Library, University of Alabama; Elliott, *Soldier of Tennessee,* 194; OR 38(3):641, 813, 38(4):748, 761, 769, 38(5):868; Warner, *Generals in Gray,* 52–53, 325–26; Steven H. Newton, *Lost for the Cause: The Confederate Army in 1864* (Boston: DaCapo Press, 2000), 124; Hallock, *Braxton Bragg and Confederate Defeat,* 2:269; PJD 10:506, 525, 529; G. A. Henry to J. Seddon, 7 August 1864, M437, Letters Received by Confederate States Secretary of War, NARA.

28. J. B. Palmer Compiled Service Record, M-268, NARA; OR 38(5):957, 39(3):871; Warner, *Generals in Gray,* 227–28; Lindsley, *Military Annals,* 364–70.

29. OR 38(3):656, 679, 38(5):179, 953; Zachariah C. Deas Compiled Service Record, M-331, NARA; John G. Coltart Compiled Service Record, M-311, NARA; Jacob H. Sharp Compiled Service Record, M-269, NARA; Samuel Benton Compiled Service Record, M-269, NARA; Warner, *Generals in Gray,* 210–11; Manigault, *A Carolinian Goes to War,* 195; A. M. Manigault Compiled Service Record, M-331, NARA. Historian Gary Ecelbarger erroneously asserts in his book on the Battle of Ezra Church that Brown was promoted

from colonel over Manigault to be placed in command of the division. Actually, Brown ranked Manigault as a brigadier general by several months. Gary Ecelbarger, *Slaughter at the Chapel: The Battle of Ezra Church. 1864,* (Norman: Univ. of Oklahoma Press, 2016), 75–76.

30. White and Runion, eds., *Great Things are Expected of Us: The Letters of Colonel C. Irvine Walker, 10th South Carolina Infantry, C. S. A.,* 130; Manigault, *A Carolinian Goes to War,* 198; McMurry, *Atlanta 1864,* 131–40; OR 38(5): 883, 39(2):712–14; Connelly, *Autumn of Glory,* 365–72, 386–90, 410–22. Connelly, at 420–21, notes that Bragg's long letter of July 15 may not have actually reached Davis by the time the decision was made to relieve Johnston, but that Bragg made his sentiments known in telegraphic messages.

31. Johnston, *Narrative of Military Operations,* 306; OR 47(1):1061; Manigault, *A Carolinian Goes to War,* 195. For the reaction of much of the army's high command, see Castel, *Decision in the West,* 364.

32. Castel, *Decision in the West,* 366–67, 369–85; Larry J. Daniel, *Days of Glory: The Army of the Cumberland, 1861–1865* (Baton Rouge: Louisiana State Univ. Press, 2004), 411–14; Woodworth, *Nothing But Victory,* 530; Hughes, *Hardee,* 221–27; Elliott, *Soldier of Tennessee,* 204–9. A recent treatment of the battle is Robert D. Jenkins Sr., *The Battle of Peach Tree Creek: Hood's First Sortie, 20 July 1864* (Macon, GA: Mercer Univ. Press, 2014).

33. Castel, *Decision in the West,* 371; Christopher Losson, *Tennessee's Forgotten Warriors: Frank Cheatham and his Confederate Division* (Knoxville: Univ. of Tennessee Press, 1989) 2–27, 133–35; Warner, *Generals in Gray,* 47–48, 193–94.

34. Hood, *Advance and Retreat,* 173–78; Steven Davis, "Hood and the Battles for Atlanta," in Theodore P. Savas and David A. Woodbury, eds., *The Campaign for Atlanta & Sherman's March to the Sea,* vol. 1 (Campbell, CA: Savas Woodbury, 1992), 64–66; Irving A. Buck, *Cleburne and His Command* (1908; reprint, Wilmington, NC: Broadfoot, 1987), 233; Castel, *Decision in the West,* 385–89.

35. Gary Ecelbarger, *The Day Dixie Died: The Battle of Atlanta* (New York: St. Martin's Press, 2010), 55–69, 70–147; Woodworth, *Nothing But Victory,* 540–43; Castel, *Decision in the West,* 395–404; Hughes, *Hardee,* 229–31.

36. Ecelbarger, *The Day Dixie Died,* 56, 149–51; Woodworth, *Nothing But Victory,* 542, 563; Castel, *Decision in the West,* 405.

37. Castel, *Decision in the West,* 405; Losson, *Tennessee's Forgotten Warriors,* 181; Ecelbarger, *The Day Dixie Died,* 141–54; Lindsley, ed., *Military Annals,* 179, 364, 480–81.

38. Manigault, *A Carolinian Goes to War,* 226–27; White and Runion, eds., *Great Things Are Expected of Us,* 131–32; "John Calhoun Higdon-Experiences and Life During the Civil War," 3rd Tennessee File, Chickamauga and

Chattanooga National Military Park (Higdon wrote that a third of Sharps's men refused to go forward); Ecelbarger, *The Day Dixie Died*, 155–58; Bell I. Wiley, "A Story of 3 Southern Officers," *Civil War Times Illustrated* 3 (April 1964): 33.

39. OR 38(3):778–79; E. T. Sykes, "Walthall's Brigade, A Cursory Sketch With Personal Experiences of Walthall's Brigade, Army of Tennessee, 1862–1865," in *Publications of the Mississippi Historical Society*, ed. Dunbar Rowland (Jackson: Mississippi Historical Society, 1916), 1:575–76; Ecelbarger, *The Day Dixie Died*, 163, 169.

40. Woodworth, *Nothing But Victory*, 542, 563; Castel, *Decision in the West*, 406; Ecelbarger, *The Day Dixie Died*, 164; OR 38(3):246, 251, 787, "John Calhoun Higdon-Experiences and Life During the Civil War"; "Manigault at Atlanta," *Anderson (SC) Intelligencer*, July 6, 1882; Manigault, *A Carolinian Goes to War*, 227–28; White and Runion, eds., *Great Things Are Expected of Us*, 131–33.

41. Manigault, *A Carolinian Goes to War*, 228; Wiley, "A Story of 3 Southern Officers," 33; Castel, *Decision in the West*, 405–6.

42. OR 38(3):819–20; ORS 7:118–19, 121–22, 127.

43. ORS 7:127; OR 38(3):819–20; Castel, *Decision in the West*, 407–8.

44. Woodworth, *Nothing But Victory*, 565–67; Manigault, *A Carolinian Goes to War*, 229; OR 38(3):631; White and Runion, eds., *Great Things Are Expected of Us*, 132; Ecelbarger, *The Day Dixie Died*, 179–90.

45. Ecelbarger, *The Day Dixie Died*, 208–15; Castel, *Decision in the West*, 411–14; Losson, *Tennessee's Forgotten Warriors*, 182; Stephen Davis, *Atlanta Will Fall: Sherman, Joe Johnston, and the Yankee Heavy Battalions* (Wilmington, DE: SR Books, 2001) 138–48.

46. OR 38(5):904; James Patton Anderson, "Autobiography of Gen. Patton Anderson, CSA," 24 SHSP 57, 69, 71 (1896).

47. McMurry, *Atlanta 1864*, 155–57; Castel, *Decision in the West*, 416–18, 422–26.

48. Bruce S. Allardice, "It Was Perfect Murder: Stephen D. Lee at Ezra Church," in *Confederate Generals in the Western Theater*, ed. Lawrence Lee Hewitt and Arthur W. Bergeron (Knoxville: Univ. of Tennessee Press, 2011), 221–25; Woodworth, *Jefferson Davis and His Generals*, 262, 285.

49. Earl J. Hess, The *Battle of Ezra Church and the Struggle for Atlanta* (Chapel Hill: Univ. of North Carolina Press, 2015), 40–56, 78–79, 81; Ecelbarger, *Slaughter at the Chapel*, 60-70; OR 38(3):762, 767, 799; Allardice, "It Was Perfect Murder," 228–29.

50. Hess, The *Battle of Ezra Church*, 59, 73–74, 78–80; OR 38(3): 767, 776, 789, 799.

51. OR 38(3):189, 222–23, 785–86, 799–800, 802–8; Hess, *The Battle of Ezra Church*, 58–72, 156; Ecelbarger, *Slaughter at the Chapel*, 91-100.

52. OR 38(3): 768, 776–71, 789–94; Hess, *The Battle of Ezra Church*, 73–93; Ecelbarger, *Slaughter at the Chapel*, 78-88.

53. Manigault, *A Carolinian Goes to War*, 232–34; OR 38(3):768, 776, 781–2; Hess, *The Battle of Ezra Church*, 86–91, 110–11; Ecelbarger, *Slaughter at the Chapel*, 102-107.

54. Manigault, *A Carolinian Goes to War*, 234–5; OR 38(3):782, 768.

55. Hess, *The Battle of Ezra Church*, 145–77; OR 38(3):765, 767–8; Butler, "The Life of John C. Brown," 21; Manigault, *A Carolinian Goes to War*, 234–5.

56. OR 38(3):769, 926, 38(5):907; French, *Two Wars*, 219–20.

57. OR 38(5):924–25; J. P. Young, "Hood's Failure at Spring Hill," *Confederate Veteran* 16 (January 1908): 25, 36; G. A. Henry to J. Seddon, 7 August 1864, M437, Letters Received by Confederate States Secretary of War, NARA; John C. Brown Compiled Service Record, NARA; *Journal of the Congress of the Confederate States of America, 1861–1865* (Washington, DC: Government Printing Office, 1904–1905) 4:581. Having heard that Stewart and Loring were wounded, Bragg urged that Maj. Gen. Franklin Gardner, recently exchanged from imprisonment after his capture at Port Hudson, Louisiana, in 1863, should be sent to the army. OR 38(5):948.

58. French, *Two Wars*, 222; Warner, *Generals in Gray*, 86; McMurry, *Atlanta 1864*, 161–62; OR 38(3):690, 38(5):953, 955–56, 983; W. B. Bate to Braxton Bragg, 23 August 1864, Braxton Bragg Papers, Western Reserve Historical Society, Cleveland, Ohio.

59. Sheppard, *By the Noble Daring of Her Sons*, 190–95; John L. McKinnon, *History of Walton County* (Atlanta: Byrd Printing Company, 1911) 296–97; Washington Ives to Sister Katie, 21 August 1864, Washington A. Ives Papers, Florida State Library.

60. Warner, *Generals in Gray*, 149–50, 186, 284, 312; OR 38(3):662, 681; H. R. Jackson (?) to Braxton Bragg, 11 August 1864, Braxton Bragg Papers, Western Reserve Historical Society, Cleveland, Ohio (context of unsigned letter indicates author was Jackson); see also Zack C. Watters, ed., "Lines of Battle: Maj. Gen. William B. Bate's Partial Reports of the Atlanta Campaign," in *The Campaign for Atlanta & Sherman's March to the Sea*, (Campbell, CA: Savas Woodbury, 1992) 1:169–76; Castel, *Decision in the West*, 459.

61. McMurry, *Atlanta 1864*, 164–72; Connelly, *Autumn of Glory*, 461;

62. OR 38(3):693–94, 38(5):998, 1006; Connelly, *Autumn of Glory*, 462; Castel, *Decision in the West*, 496; Sheppard, *By the Noble Daring of Her Sons*, 195.

63. Woodworth, *Nothing But Victory*, 580–81; Thomas E. Schott, "Lieutenant General William J. Hardee, the Historians, and the Atlanta Campaign," in *Confederate Generals in the Western Theater*, vol. 2, ed. Lawrence Lee Hewitt and Arthur W. Bergeron Jr. (Knoxville: Univ. of Tennessee Press, 2010), 177;

Hughes, *General William J. Hardee*, 236; OR 38(3):700, 727; Castel, *Decision in the West*, 500–503; Lindsley, ed., *Military Annals*, 179.

64. OR 38(3):708; ORS 7:104; Sheppard, *By the Noble Daring of Her Sons*, 196.

65. OR 38(3):700–701, 709; Castel, *Decision in the West*, 502–3; "From the Augusta Constitutionalist, The Fall of Atlanta," *Wilmington Journal*, September 15, 1864; Sheppard, *By the Noble Daring of Her Sons*, 196; "Flag of the 20th Tennessee," *Confederate Veteran* 2 (April 1894): 118; Ed Porter Thompson, *History of the Orphan Brigade* (Louisville, KY: Lewis N. Thompson, 1898), 273; A. D. Kirwan, ed., *Johnny Green of the Orphan Brigade: The Journal of a Confederate Soldier* (Lexington: Univ. of Kentucky Press, 1956), 154–56.

66. ORS 7:104; Philip D. Stephenson, *The Civil War Memoir of Philip Dangerfield Stephenson, D.D.*, ed. Nathaniel Cheairs Hughes Jr. (Conway: Univ. of Central Arkansas Press,1995), 232; OR 38(3):700–2; Woodworth, *Nothing But Victory*, 581.

67. Castel, *Decision in the West*, 505, 509–11; McMurry, *Atlanta 1864*, 174–75; Kirwan, ed., *Johnny Green of the Orphan Brigade*, 157–58.

68. OR 38(3):728–29; Hughes, *Hardee*, 239–40; Schott, "Hardee, the Historians and the Atlanta Campaign," 179; Hughes and Whitney, *Jefferson Davis in Blue*, 279–85; Castel, *Decision in the West*, 520–21.

69. William T. Sherman, *Memoirs of General William T. Sherman* (New York: D. Appleton and Company, 1876), 2:107–9; Castel, *Decision in the West*, 530–32.

70. Connelly, *Autumn of Glory*, 467–72, 477; Horn, *The Army of Tennessee*, 368–74; Alexander P. Stewart, "The Army of Tennessee: A Sketch," in *Military Annals of Tennessee*, 97, 103; Hughes, *General William J. Hardee*, 244–49.

5. The Slaughter in Our Ranks Was Frightful

1. Losson, *Tennessee's Forgotten Warriors*, 195–99; OR 38(5):1013, 1016, 39(1):826, OR 45(1):733; John C. Brown Compiled Service Record, NARA.

2. Losson, *Tennessee's Forgotten Warriors*, 196–98.

3. Anne J. Bailey, *The Chessboard of War: Sherman and Hood in the Autumn Campaigns of 1864* (Lincoln: Univ. of Nebraska Press, 2000), 26–28, 42–43; OR 39(1):722–23, 45(1):733–34; Stephenson, *The Civil War Memoir of Philip Daingerfield Stephenson, DD*, 255.

4. OR 45(1):669; Connelly, *Autumn of Glory*, 481–90; Bailey, *The Chessboard of War*, 42–47, 71–75.

5. Bailey, *The Chessboard of War*, 75–77; Ash, *Middle Tennessee Society Transformed*, 90; "The Union Meeting in Giles County," *Nashville Daily Union*, March 3, 1864; Newman, *Brown Family Timeline*, 6.

6. Jill K. Garrett and Marise P. Lightfoot, *The Civil War in Maury County, Tennessee* (Columbia, TN, 1966), 169; Elliott, ed., *Doctor Quintard, Chaplain C. S. A. and Second Bishop of Tennessee*, 94, 182, 185; OR 45(1):670, 730–31; Bailey, *The Chessboard of War*, 80–81.

7. Elliott, ed., *Doctor Quintard, Chaplain C. S. A. and Second Bishop of Tennessee*, 185; Young, "Hood's Failure at Spring Hill," 26; Benjamin F. Cheatham, "The Lost Opportunity at Spring Hill, Tenn.—General Cheatham's Reply to General Hood," *Southern Historical Society Papers* 9 (October, November, and December, 1881): 524, 537.

8. Donald B. Connelly, *John M. Schofield and the Politics of Generalship* (Chapel Hill: Univ. of North Carolina Press, 2006), 126–27; Jamie Gillum, *Twenty-five Hours to Tragedy: The Battle of Spring Hill and Operations on November 29, 1864, Precursor to the Battle of Franklin* (Spring Hill, TN, 2014), 78–86; Young, "Hood's Failure at Spring Hill," 30.

9. Wiley Sword, *The Confederacy's Last Hurrah: Spring Hill, Franklin and Nashville* (1992; reprint, Lawrence: Univ. Press of Kansas, 1993), 120–26; Young, "Hood's Failure at Spring Hill," 30–31; James Lee McDonough, *Nashville: The Western Confederacy's Final Gamble* (Knoxville: Univ. of Tennessee Press, 2004) 61–64; Losson, *Tennessee's Forgotten Warriors*, 204; Eric A. Jacobson and Richard A. Rupp, *For Cause and for Country* (Franklin, TN: O'More Publishing, 2007), 98-102; Cheatham, "The Lost Opportunity at Spring Hill, Tenn.," 539–40.

10. Cheatham, "The Lost Opportunity at Spring Hill, Tenn.," 525, 537–38; Gillum, *Twenty-Five Hours to Tragedy*, 156–63, 260; Sam R. Watkins, *Co. Aytch: A Side Show of the Big Show* (New York: Collier Books, 1962), 231.

11. Gillum, *Twenty-Five Hours to Tragedy*, 261–4, 282; H. M. Field, *Bright Skies and Dark Shadows* (New York: Charles Scribner's Sons, 1890), 215; Young, "Hood's Failure at Spring Hill," 35. Gillum at p. 288 estimates the division had 1,600 men at the time it deployed to attack, but if Gist is conservatively estimated at 1,000 and Strahl at 700 (extrapolated from post-Franklin numbers at OR 45(1):680), using Brown's 2,750 figure for November 29, 1,400 seems to be a more reasonable estimate.

12. OR 45(1):255; Field, *Bright Skies and Dark Shadows,* 215–16; Jones, ed., *Campbell Brown's Civil War*, 165; Cheatham, "The Lost Opportunity at Spring Hill, Tenn.," 538; Young, "Hood's Failure at Spring Hill," 34–35. An 1884 letter from Lane to Col. Ellison Capers of Gist's brigade states that at some point only 500 men were between Spring Hill and the Confederates, but it is impossible to reconcile that with Lane's more detailed report of December 7, 1864. See Walter B. Capers, *The Soldier-Bishop, Ellison Capers* (New York: Neale Publishing, 1912), 112–13.

13. Cheatham, "The Lost Opportunity at Spring Hill, Tenn.," 538; Jacobson and Rupp, *For Cause and for Country*, 128–30; Field, *Bright Skies and Dark Shadows*, 215–16; Jones, ed., *Campbell Brown's Civil War*, 165. See Horn, *The Army of Tennessee*, 388; McDonough, *Nashville*, 66 ("some misunderstanding of orders—or a pronounced case of stubbornness"). Cheatham's narrative indicates he intended a massed attack against Spring Hill by his whole corps. If such were the case, then Cleburne and Bate were not ready to advance at the point in time Brown was purportedly ordered forward.

14. OR 45(1):255, 712; Cheatham, "The Lost Opportunity at Spring Hill, Tenn.," 538. There is more to the Spring Hill story, but the other details do not relate to Brown. The author has addressed the affair from Stewart's and Harris's standpoint in earlier works. The most recent of Hood's biographies relies on at least double, if not triple hearsay to the effect that S. D. Lee, who was not present, wrote Hood in 1875 that Stewart heard that Cheatham and Cleburne were to blame because they did not want to fight a night engagement. Stephen M. Hood, *John Bell Hood: The Rise, Fall and Resurrection of a Confederate General* (El Dorado Hills, CA: Savas Beatie, 2013), 123.

15. Hood, *John Bell Hood*, 116; Losson, *Tennessee's Forgotten Warriors*, 209–12; James W. Ratchford, *Memoirs of a Confederate Staff Officer: From Bethel to Bentonville*, ed. Evelyn Ratchford Sieburg and James E. Hanson II (Shippensburg, PA: White Mane Books, 1998) 61–62; "A Stirring Day on Franklin Field," *Augusta (Ga.) Chronicle*, November 10, 1903; White and Runion, eds., *Great Things are Expected of Us*, 148 (contains a contemporary [December 1864] statement of Cheatham covering for one of his division commanders, "a close personal friend."); A. P. Stewart to "My Dear Nephew" [Wharton Jones], 29 April 1895 (Stewart's letter was provided to the author in 1999 in connection with a symposium on Spring Hill, but with no attribution as to its source).

16. Hood, *Advance and Retreat*, 290; Field, *Bright Skies and Dark Shadows*, 219.

17. Hood, *Advance and Retreat*, 289–90; Losson, *Tennessee's Forgotten Warriors*, 215; Cheatham, "The Lost Opportunity at Spring Hill, Tenn.," 538–39.

18. Connelly, *John M. Schofield and the Politics of Generalship*, 133–34; Jacobson and Rupp, *For Cause and For Country*, 185–87, 204; Jacob D. Cox, *The Battle of Franklin, Tennessee, November 30, 1864: A Monograph* (New York: Charles Scribner's Sons, 1897), 37–41, 46, 48, 51–56, 58, 62–63; OR 45(1):348, 737.

19. French, *Two Wars*, 292–94; John P. Hickman letter, *Confederate Veteran* 22 (January 1914): 15; Hood, *John Bell Hood*, 142–58; Jacobson and Rupp, *For Cause and For Country*, 237–42; Losson, *Tennessee's Forgotten Warriors*, 218. Hood later wrote that Cleburne went into battle with enthusiasm, but it is doubtful that such an experienced soldier did not foresee the approaching

disaster. Another witness, Brig. Gen. Daniel C. Govan, wrote Cleburne was "despondent" over the prospect of the attack. Hood, *Advance and Retreat*, 294; Buck, *Cleburne and His Command*, 290.

20. James D. Porter, *Confederate Military History—Tennessee* (1899; reprint, Wilmington, NC: Broadfoot Publishing Company, 1987), 10:156–57.

21. "Confederate Monument at Franklin," *Confederate Veteran* 8 (January 1900): 5, 6–7; OR 45(1):736; Cox, *The Battle of Franklin, Tennessee*, 73.

22. OR 45(1):737; "Confederate Monument at Franklin," 6–7.

23. Porter, *Confederate Military History—Tennessee*, 10:157; "Confederate Monument at Franklin," 7–8; Losson, *Tennessee's Forgotten Warriors*, 220–21; Watkins, *Co. Aytch*, 234–35; Lindsley, ed. *Military Annals*, 301; OR 45(1):737; Elliott, ed., *Doctor Quintard*, 191; Jacobson and Rupp, *For Cause and For Country*, 314, 349–51.

24. Jacobson and Rupp, *For Cause and For Country,* 307–8, 351–54; Ridley, *Battles and Sketches*, 425.

25. Porter, *Confederate Military History—Tennessee*, 10:157; "A Sketch of the Deceased," *Nashville Daily American*, August 11, 1889; "Ex-Governor Neal [*sic*] S. Brown," *Macon Daily Telegraph*, December 19, 1864; "Disastrous Campaign in Tennessee," *Confederate Veteran* 12 (July 1904): 340–41; Field, *Bright Skies and Dark Shadows*, 239; Sword, *The Confederacy's Last Hurrah*, 237–38; Losson, *Tennessee's Forgotten Warriors*, 226–27; Jacobson and Rupp, *For Cause and For Country*, 408–9, 416; Connelly, *Autumn of Glory*, 506.

26. Elliott, ed., *Doctor Quintard*, 187–94; Garrett and Lightfoot, *The Civil War in Maury County, Tennessee*, 170; John C. Brown Compiled Service Record, NARA; "Ex-Governor Neal [*sic*] S. Brown," *Macon Daily Telegraph*, December 19, 1864.

27. Sword, *The Confederacy's Last Hurrah*, 300–422; Hood, *John Bell Hood*, 177–78; McDonough, *Nashville,* 113–274; Horn, *The Army of Tennessee*, 406–21; OR 45(1):655, 711, 724; see generally Stanley F. Horn, *The Decisive Battle of Nashville* (1956; reprint, Baton Rouge: Louisiana State Univ. Press, 1991).

28. Wirt A. Cate, ed., *Two Soldiers: The Campaign Diaries of Thomas J. Key C.S.A. and Robert J. Campbell U.S.A.* (Chapel Hill: Univ. of North Carolina Press, 1938), 178–79; Elliott, ed., *Doctor Quintard*, 218; "Gen. John C. Brown of the Army of Tennessee," *Macon Daily Telegraph*, January 20, 1865.

29. Connelly, *Autumn of Glory*, 512–22; OR 47(2):1247; Nathaniel Cheairs Hughes Jr., *Bentonville: The Final Battle of Sherman and Johnston* (Chapel Hill: Univ. of North Carolina Press, 1996) 21–24.

30. Jill K. Garrett, ed., *Confederate Diary of Robert D. Smith* (Columbia, TN: Sparkman Chapter, UDC, 1997), 166–74; Ridley, *Battles and Sketches*, 455; Elliott, ed., *Doctor Quintard*, 231–32, 234, 241–45.

31. Elliott, ed., *Doctor Quintard,* 247; Charles Todd Quintard Diary, entry for May 25, 1865, Charles T. Quintard Collection, University of the South; "Bettie" to JCB, 30 March 1864[5], John C. Brown Compiled Service Record, NARA; Ridley, *Battles and Sketches,* 455; Mark L. Bradley, *This Astounding Close: The Road to Bennett Place* (Chapel Hill: Univ. of North Carolina Press, 2000), 58–64.

32. Hughes, *Bentonville,* 14–15, 21–29; Bradley, *This Astounding Close,* 12–15; OR 47(1):1130; Mark A. Smith and Wade Sokolosky, *"No Such Army Since the Days of Julius Caesar": Sherman's Carolinas Campaign from Fayetteville to Averasboro* (Fort Mitchell, KY: Ironclad Publishing, 2005), 124–29.

33. Connelly, *Autumn of Glory,* 525–28; Mark L. Bradley, *Last Stand in the Carolinas: The Battle of Bentonville* (Campbell, CA: Savas Woodbury, 1996), 165–400; Hughes, *Bentonville,* 46–211; Bradley, *This Astounding Close,* 17–25; OR 45(2):1453–54.

34. Ridley, *Battles and Sketches,* 455–56; Bradley, *This Astounding Close,* 66–69, 80; OR 47(3):773–74. That Johnston would have dropped McLaws and Taliaferro, who fell out of favor in Lee's army, is no surprise. While the reason for Clayton's exclusion is unknown, Bate's performance in the 1864 Tennessee campaign had been criticized in some quarters. See Elliott, ed., *Doctor Quintard,* 199–200.

35. Bradley, *This Astounding Close,* 81–90, 135–43; Ridley, *Battles and Sketches* 457; Samuel T. Foster, *One of Cleburne's Command: The Civil War Reminiscences and Diary of Capt. Samuel T. Foster, Granbury's Texas Brigade, CSA,* ed. Norman T. Brown (Austin: Univ. of Texas Press, 1980), 163–65; Buck, *Cleburne and His Command,* 306. Near the end of his classic history of the Army of Tennessee, Thomas Lawrence Connelly wrote: "For all its troubles and defeats, the army possessed a greatness deep in the ranks—at Greensboro, while Johnston surrendered nearby to Sherman, General John C. Brown drilled his division." Connelly, *Autumn of Glory,* 535.

36. Sherman, *Memoirs of General William T. Sherman,* 2:349; "President Lincoln's Death: How the News Was Received in Johnston's Army," *Atlanta Journal,* November 23, 1901.

37. Bradley, *This Astounding Close,* 206–26; Foster, *One of Cleburne's Command,* 166–69. Brown kept a silver dollar out of his share, and it was later displayed at an exposition in Nashville. "Relics at the Centennial Exposition," *Confederate Veteran* 5 (November 1897): 562.

38. Brown's grave monument indicates he was wounded at Fort Donelson, Perryville, Chickamauga, Atlanta, and Franklin. The wounds at Donelson and Atlanta (Ezra Church) must have been minor, as the author has been unable to locate any primary account of the same.

39. "Soldier and Preacher," *Pulaski Citizen*, September 5, 1889; Oscar Penn Fitzgerald, *John B. McFerrin: A Biography* (Nashville: Publishing House of the M. E. Church, 1888), 99–100, 130, 272, 283–84.

6. To Liberate . . . the True and Chivalrous Citizens

1. JCB to S. B. Buckner, December 17, 1865, Simon Bolivar Buckner Papers, Huntington Library, San Marino, California; "Letter from Giles County, Tennessee," *Pulaski Citizen*, March 30, 1866; "By Telegraph," *Janesville (Wisconsin) Gazette*, June 15, 1865; JCB to A. Johnson, 13 June 1865, John C. Brown Amnesty Oath, 15 June 1865, R. W. Johnson endorsement, 15 June 1865, George H. Thomas endorsement, 22 June 1865, Sarah C. Polk to A. Johnson, 30 June 1865, Sarah C. Polk to A. Johnson, 28 July 1865, W. G. Brownlow to A. Johnson, 23 November 1865, and jacket endorsement, 15 January 1867, all in Case Files of Applications from Former Confederates for Presidential Pardons ("Amnesty Papers"), 1865–67, Records of the Adjutant General's Office, 1780s–1917, RG 94, Publication M1003, NARA. Brown's application for pardon, and the supporting correspondence from Sarah Polk, adopted two common themes of higher-ranking Confederates seeking pardon. Brown noted that he followed his state, and Mrs. Polk pointed out that Brown was a Unionist to (almost) the bitter end. See Kathleen R. Zebley, "Rebel Salvation: The Story of Confederate Pardons" (PhD diss., University of Tennessee, 1998), 70.

2. E. Merton Coulter, *William G. Brownlow: Fighting Parson of the Southern Highlands* (1937; reprint, Knoxville: Univ. of Tennessee Press, 1999), 6–34, 134–206, 259–77; Paul H. Bergeron, *Andrew Johnson's Civil War and Reconstruction* (Knoxville: Univ. of Tennessee Press, 2011), 48–57; James Welch Patton, *Unionism and Reconstruction in Tennessee, 1860–1869* (1934; reprint, Gloucester, MA: Peter Smith, 1966), 75–77, 114; Thomas B. Alexander, *Political Reconstruction in Tennessee* (Nashville: Vanderbilt Univ. Press, 1950), 92–93, 97–99.

3. Marie Brown tombstone, Maplewood Cemetery, Pulaski; JCB to Buckner, 17 December 1865, Huntington Library; Ash, *Middle Tennessee Society Transformed*, 192–93, 227–28; Robert Tracy McKenzie, *One South, or Many?: Plantation Belt and Upcountry in Civil War Era Tennessee* (New York: Cambridge Univ. Press, 1994), 98–101, 116, 119; OR 49(2): 979; "Evacuated," *Pulaski Citizen*, January 19, 1866; "Prospectus," *Pulaski Citizen*, January 5, 1866; Alexander, *Political Reconstruction in Tennessee*, 100–1.

4. Ash, *Middle Tennessee Society Transformed*, 227–33; "The Confederate Gen. Ewell and lady and Gen. John C. Brown, also of the late Confederate army, were in Nashville last week," *New Orleans Times-Picayune*, December 5, 1865;

"Tennessee," *New York Times*, March 17, 1866; "Gen. S. B. Buckner," *Pulaski Citizen*, March 30, 1866; "Letter from Giles County, Tennessee," *Pulaski Citizen*, March 30, 1866. Brown's legal business in this period was of the varied nature required of a small town practice. See *Abernathy v. Black*, 42 Tenn. 314 (1865); *Farquharson v. McDonald*, 49 Tenn. 404 (1871); *Williamson v. Anthony*, 51 Tenn. 78 (1871); "An Interesting Trial," *Pulaski Citizen*, April 20, 1866; *Ayers v. State*, 45 Tenn. 26 (1867); *Fulton v. Davidson*, 50 Tenn. 614 (1871); Elizabeth W. White, comp., *Giles County Chancery Court Extracts* (n. p., 1990), 4:1.

5. "A Delayed Letter from a Lady Correspondent at Pulaski," *Nashville Union and American*, January 4, 1866; "Reconstruction in Giles County," *Nashville Republican Banner*, December 24, 1865; Advertisement for Brown & McCallum and "A Destructive Tornado," *Pulaski Citizen*, January 5, 1866; "The Pulaski Literary League," *Pulaski Citizen*, February 23, 1866; Ash, *Middle Tennessee Society Transformed*, 230; "Crippled Confederates," *Pulaski Citizen*, April 13, 1866; "The Educational Meeting Last Week," *Pulaski Citizen*, November 23, 1866; "Meeting of Physicians," *Pulaski Citizen*, February 7, 1867; "Organization of Giles County Orphan Society," *Pulaski Citizen*, February 8, 1867; "Giles County Agricultural and Mechanical Society," *Pulaski Citizen*, May 10, 1867; "Giles College," *Pulaski Citizen*, October 26, 1866; "College Meeting last Monday," *Pulaski Citizen*, November 9, 1866; "A Delightful Hop," *Pulaski Citizen*, September 27, 1867; "General John C. Brown," *Confederate Veteran* 3 (August 1895): 242; "The Late Maj. F. C. Barber," *Pulaski Citizen*, April 13, 1866; "Tribute of Respect," *Pulaski Citizen*, April 20, 1866.

6. Susan Lawrence Davis, *Authentic History of the Ku Klux Klan, 1865–1877* (New York: Susan Lawrence Davis, 1924), 6–22; Compiled Service Records of Lester and McCord, Compiled Service Records of Confederate Soldiers Who Served in Organizations from the State of Tennessee, M-268, NARA; Allen W. Trelease, *White Terror: The Ku Klux Klan Conspiracy and Southern Reconstruction* (New York: Harper and Row, 1971) 3–14; "Letter from Giles County, Tennessee"; United States Congress, *House Executive Documents, Report of the Secretary of War* (1867), 182–3; Ash, *Middle Tennessee Society Transformed*, 202–5; Ben H. Severance, *Tennessee's Radical Army: The State Guard and Its Role in Reconstruction, 1867–1869* (Knoxville: Univ. of Tennessee Press, 2005) 9; Mark W. Summers, *A Dangerous Stir: Fear, Paranoia and the Making of Reconstruction* (Chapel Hill: Univ. of North Carolina Press, 2009), 253; Elaine Frantz Parsons, *Ku-Klux: The Birth of the Klan During Reconstruction* (Chapel Hill: Univ. of North Carolina Press, 2015), 28–36, 44–67. See also Thomas B. Alexander, "Kukluxism in Tennessee, 1865–1869," *Tennessee Historical Quarterly* 8 (September 1949): 195–219; Eric Foner, *Reconstruction: America's Unfinished Revolution, 1863–1877* (1988; updated ed., New York: Harper and Row, 2014), 342–43; Edward John Harcourt, "Who Were the

Palefaces? New Perspectives on the Tennessee Ku Klux," *Civil War History* 51 (March 2005): 23–66. Harcourt acknowledges Trelease's impressive research, but extrapolates from the formation of the Pale Faces in nearby Maury County in January 1868 that the initial formation of the Pulaski Klan two years before was not as benign as traditionally indicated. Although conceding that the evidence is "scant and unreliable," the most recent scholarly treatment of the Pulaski Klan concurs with Trelease that the original intent of the group was not for the purpose of carrying out racial violence. Instead, the founders had the goal of "unifying and invigorating demoralized southern society." Parsons, *Ku-Klux*, 32, 35–36.

7. Severance, *Tennessee's Radical Army*, 9; "The Chancellorship in this District— Maj. Noah's Card," *Nashville Union and American*, August 25, 1866; "Good Thing Spoiled," *Memphis Public Ledger*, September 7, 1866; Davis, *Authentic History*, 21–22; John C. Lester and David L. Wilson, *Ku Klux Klan: Its Origin, Growth, and Disbandment*, intro. and notes by Walter J. Fleming (1884; reprint, New York: Neale Publishing Co., 1905), 26; Trelease, *White Terror*, 13–14. Historian Stanley Horn wrote that Gordon was the Grand Dragon of Tennessee. Stanley F. Horn, *Invisible Empire: The Story of the Ku Klux Klan, 1866–1871* (Cambridge: Riverside Press, 1939), 113. The closest Horn comes to naming Brown as a member is in a list of thirteen Confederate generals, "four of them high officials in the Ku Klux Klan." *Invisible Empire*, 113. Pulaski historian and Brown biographer Margaret Butler concluded, on much the same grounds discussed above, that Brown was a Klan member. Butler, *The Life of John C. Brown*, 29.

8. Eugene G. Feistman, "Radical Disfranchisement and the Restoration of Tennessee, 1865–1866," *Tennessee Historical Quarterly* 12 (June 1953): 135, 144–45; Alexander, *Political Reconstruction in Tennessee*, 105–112, 119–21, 142–46; Bergeron, *Andrew Johnson's Civil War and Reconstruction*, 114–17; Corlew, *Tennessee: A Short History*, 333–34; White, *Messages of the Governors of Tennessee*, 5:530–35, 551–53; Severance, *Tennessee's Radical Army*, 1, 17–21; Bergeron, Ash, and Keith, *Tennesseans and Their History*, 166; "Radical Leagues," *Nashville Union and Dispatch*, October 30, 1866; "Union Leagues in the South," *Nashville Union and Dispatch*, January 31, 1867; Foner, *Reconstruction*, 283; "Proscription," *Pulaski Citizen*, July 19, 1867.

9. Trelease, *White Terror*, 11–16; Lonnie E. Maness, "Henry Emerson Etheridge and the Gubernatorial Election of 1867: A Study in Futility," *West Tennessee Historical Society Papers* 47 (1993): 37–47.

10. "County Meeting last Monday" and "College Meeting Last Monday," *Pulaski Citizen*, November 9, 1866; "Giles College," *Pulaski Citizen*, October 26, 1866; "Coal Oil," *Fayetteville Observer*, January 31, 1867; "Elder Peter Lowry has met with good success in Giles," *Nashville Union and Dispatch*, May 11,

1867; "Gen. John C. Brown," *Pulaski Citizen*, January 4, 1867; "Well Caned," *Pulaski Citizen*, January 18, 1867; "Pardoned," *Pulaski Citizen*, February 1, 1867; "Fire," *Pulaski Citizen*, May 17, 1867; "Gen. Brown and McCallum and Maj. T. M. Jones tender their grateful thanks," *Pulaski Citizen*, May 17, 1867; JCB to Henry D. Clayton, 15 July 1867, Hoole Special Collections Library, Univ. of Alabama; *Memphis Daily Avalanche*, March 8, 1868.

11. "Kuklux Klan," *Pulaski Citizen*, April 5, 12, 19, 26 and May 3, 1867; "KuKlux Klan. Grand Demonstration Wednesday Night," *Pulaski Citizen*, June 7, 1867; Parsons, *Ku-Klux*, 44–53 (quote on 53); Severance, *Tennessee's Radical Army*, 88.

12. Severance, *Tennessee's Radical Army*, 92–93; JCB to Clayton, 15 July 1867, Hoole Special Collections Library, Univ. of Alabama; "List of Voters in Giles County," *Pulaski Citizen*, October 26, 1866; "What Does It Mean," *Pulaski Citizen*, March 29, 1867; "The Election," *Pulaski Citizen*, August 2, 1867; Alexander, *Political Reconstruction in Tennessee*, 155; White, *Messages*, 5: 571–73.

13. Foner, *Reconstruction*, 215; Patton, *Unionism and Reconstruction*, 179–80; Derek W. Frisby, "A Victory Spoiled: West Tennessee Unionists during Reconstruction," in *The Great Task Remaining Before Us: Reconstruction as America's Continuing Civil War*, ed. Paul A. Cimbala and Randall M Miller (New York: Fordham Univ. Press, 2010), 20; "President Johnson's Impression of Affairs in Tennessee," *Pulaski Citizen*, July 12, 1867; Severance, *Tennessee's Radical Army*, 10–11; JCB to Clayton, 15 July 1867, Univ. of Alabama.

14. Parsons, *Ku-Klux*, 57, 63, 67; Severance, *Tennessee's Radical Army*, 150–51, 168–69, 174; Trelease, *White Terror*, 24–25; Alexander, *Political Reconstruction in Tennessee*, 180–82; "Unfortunate Affray," *Pulaski Citizen*, January 9, 1868; "Ku-Klux Klan, *Pulaski Citizen*, January 31, 1868; Report of Michael Walsh, January 11, 1868, Affidavit of Frank Dickerson, January 14, 1868, Reports of Outrages, Riots, and Murders Affidavits Relating to Outrages, Mar. 1866–Aug. 1868, M-999, NARA.

15. Trelease, *White Terror*, 33–34, 40–41; "To the People of Giles County," *Pulaski Citizen*, January 31, 1868; Parsons, *Ku-Klux*, 157; Foner, *Reconstruction*, 425; "Personal," *Nashville Union and Dispatch*, November 19, 1867; "Personal," *Nashville Union and Dispatch* January 31, 1868; "Personal," *Nashville Union and Dispatch*, March 5, 1868; "Convention of Lawyers," *Memphis Public Ledger*, October 30, 1867.

16. Thomas B. Alexander, "Persistent Whiggery in the Confederate South, 1860–1877," *Journal of Southern History* 27 (August 1961): 305, 318; "Gov. Neill S. Brown" *Nashville Union and American*, August 16, 1870; "County Convention," *Pulaski Citizen*, June 5, 1868.

17. "Convention," *Daily Memphis Avalanche*, June 10, 1868; "The Democratic State Convention," *Nashville Union and Dispatch*, June 10, 1868; "Our

Grievances," *Nashville Republican Banner*, July 12, 1868, "Old Giles," *Nashville Republican Banner* July 23, 1868.

18. Severance, *Tennessee's Radical Army*, 176–78, 180; "Summary Justice," *Pulaski Citizen*, July 3, 1868; White, *Messages*, 5:608–14; Kathleen R. Zebley, "Unconditional Unionist: Samuel Mayes Arnell and Reconstruction in Tennessee," in *Tennessee History: The Land, the People and the Culture*, ed. Carroll Van West (Knoxville: Univ. of Tennessee Press, 1998), 190–94; "Kuklux Operations," *Knoxville Whig*, July 15, 1868.

19. W. B. Bate to M. W. Cluskey, 31 July 1868, Box 1, Folder 7, Michael Walsh Cluskey Papers, Western Kentucky Univ. (hereafter cited as Cluskey Papers); Trelease, *White Terror*, 44–45; "The Situation," *Knoxville Whig*, July 29, 1868.

20. White, *Messages*, 5:609–14; Bate to Cluskey, 31 July 1868, Cluskey Papers; "Peace," *Nashville Union and Dispatch*, August 2, 1868; Mark W. Summers, *The Ordeal of the Reunion: A New History of Reconstruction* (Chapel Hill: Univ. of North Carolina Press, 2014), 161("inherently destabilizing").

21. "The Confederate Generals Indorsed by Giles County," *Nashville Union and Dispatch*, August 6, 1868; "Thirteen Rebel Generals," *Knoxville Whig*, August 12, 1868; Horn, *Invisible Empire*, 104; William E. Hardy, "'Fare well to all Radicals': Redeeming Tennessee, 1869–1870" (PhD diss., University of Tennessee, 2013), 25–26n15, 29–35; "The Mask Lifted—Brownlow's Statements as to the Ku Klux Klan Sustained—Forrest Convicts Himself," *Knoxville Whig*, September 16, 1868; Patton, *Unionism and Reconstruction*, 195; Severance, *Tennessee's Radical Army*, 150–51. Newspaper reports such as that appearing in the *Commercial* themselves had an effect, as attention from politicians and the press gave Klansmen more incentive to commit violence. Parsons, *Ku-Klux*, 148–49.

22. "The Tennessee Troubles," *Knoxville Whig*, September 23, 1868; Patton, *Unionism and Reconstruction*, 196–98.

23. "Federal Troops Come to Tennessee," *Knoxville Whig*, September 16, 1868; Severance, *Tennessee's Radical Army*, 185, 187–89, 241–42; Trelease, *White Terror*, 45–46, 179; Patton, *Unionism and Reconstruction in Tennessee, 1860–1869*, 196–98; "The Result in Tennessee," *Knoxville Whig*, November 11, 1868; Hardy, "Fare well to all Radicals," 53; Foner, *Reconstruction*, 342–43; "Giles County," *Nashville Union and American*, December 29, 1868; "Mob Law Reprobated," *Nashville Republican Banner*, December 29, 1868.

24. Trelease, *White Terror*, 178; "Martial Law," *Nashville Union and American*, January 18, 1869; White, *Messages*, 650; Hardy, "Fare well to all Radicals," 54, 62–64.

25. "Martial Law," *Memphis Daily Appeal*, January 28, 1869; Severance, *Tennessee's Radical Army*, 197–98; Trelease, *White Terror*, 179–80.

26. Severance, *Tennessee's Radical Army*, 206–8, 214–25; White, *Messages*, 5:591–94; Corlew, *Tennessee: A Short History*, 342–43; "Gov. Senter," *Nashville Union and American*, February 26, 1869; Trelease, *White Terror*, 182–83.

27. Trelease, *White Terror*, 182; Severance, *Tennessee's Radical Army*, 216–25; Hardy, "Fare well to all Radicals," 106–45.

28. Corlew, *Tennessee: A Short History*, 344; White, *Messages*, 6: 23–33; Alexander, *Political Reconstruction in Tennessee*, 215–26; Summers, *The Ordeal of the Reunion*, 162–63; Robert B. Jones, "The Press in the Election," *Tennessee Historical Quarterly* 65 (Winter 2006/7): 320, 335–37.

29. "Personal," *Nashville Union and American*, February 19, 1869, July 10, 1869, August 24, 1869, October 6, 1869, October 19, 1869; "Anonymous," *Nashville Union and American,* September 19, 1869; "Andrew Johnson," *Nashville Union and American,* October 5, 1869; Hardy, "Fare Well to all Radicals," 88–102; Robert B. Jones and Mark E. Byrnes, "'Rebels Never Forgive': Former President Andrew Johnson and the Senate Election of 1869," *Tennessee Historical Quarterly* 66 (Fall 2007): 250, 251–57.

30. Hart, *Redeemers, Bourbons and Populists* (Baton Rouge: Louisiana State Univ. Press, 1975), 1–2; C. Vann Woodward, *The Origins of the New South* (Baton Rouge: Louisiana State Univ. Press, 1951), 1–3; Jones and Byrnes, "'Rebels Never Forgive,'" 252–53, 257; Thomas B. Alexander, "Whiggery and Reconstruction in Tennessee," *Journal of Southern History* 16 (1950): 291, 301–3; Michael Perman, *The Road to Redemption: Southern Politics, 1869–1879* (Chapel Hill: Univ. of North Carolina Press, 1984), 88.

31. Woodward, *The Origins of the New South*, 20 (quotes); "Pulaski Manufacturing Company," *Pulaski Citizen*, April 9, 1869; "Pulaski Savings Bank," *Pulaski Citizen*, April 30, 1869; "Nashville and Decatur Railroad," *Nashville Union and American*, November 10, 1869; Hart, *Redeemers, Bourbons and Populists*, 25–27.

32. Jones and Byrnes, "'Rebels Never Forgive,'" 257, 262–3; "United States Senator," *Pulaski Citizen*, September 10, 1869; White, *Messages*, 6:51–2; A. Johnson to Welles, 8 December 1869, PAJ 16: 146; "We are not going to quarrel," *Pulaski Citizen*, November 12, 1874.

33. *Journal of the Proceedings of the Convention of Delegates Elected by the People of Tennessee to Amend, Revise, or to Reform or Make a New Constitution for the State* (Nashville: Jones, Purvis and Co., 1870), 3–4 (hereafter cited as *Convention Journal*); Elliott, *Isham G. Harris*, 71–73; Bergeron, *Andrew Johnson's Civil War and Reconstruction*, 55–56; Corlew, *Tennessee: A Short History*, 322–23; White, *Messages*, 5:389–90, 6:52; John C. Burch to A. Johnson, 9 March 1870, PAJ 16: 175.

34. "A Call Upon General Brown to Become a Candidate for the Convention" and "Our Representative," *Pulaski Citizen*, November 26, 1869; "Our

Flotarial Representative," *Pulaski Citizen*, December 3, 1869; "The Convention," *Pulaski Citizen*, December 24, 1869; Joshua R. Caldwell, *Studies in the Constitutional History of Tennessee*, 2d ed. (Cincinnati: Robert Clarke, 1907), 298–99; Alexander, *Political Reconstruction in Tennessee*, 230–33.

35. "The Efforts to 'Legalize' Tennessee," *Fayetteville Observer*, January 6, 1870; "Who May be Members of a State Convention?" *Memphis Daily Appeal*, October 3, 1869; "How Tennessee is Misrepresented," *Nashville Union and American*, January 5, 1870; "Invoking Federal Interference," *Nashville Union and American,*, January 8, 1870; Hart, *Redeemers, Bourbons and Populists*, 2–3; *Convention Journal*, 8; "The Convention," *Nashville Union and American,* January 11, 1870.

36. "Old Giles," *Nashville Republican Banner*, November 28, 1869; "We have not yet seen," *Daily Memphis Avalanche*, December 26, 1869; Hart, *Redeemers, Bourbons and Populists*, 2–10; Wallace McClure, "The Development of the Tennessee Constitution," *Tennessee Historical Magazine* 1 (December 1915): 292, 310; William H. Combs, "An Unamended State Constitution: The Tennessee Constitution of 1870," *The American Political Science Review* 32 (June 1938): 514, 515; Caldwell, *Studies in the Constitutional History*, 296.

37. *Convention Journal*, 42, 92, 97–98; "Constitutional Convention," *Memphis Daily Appeal*, January 15, 1870; Alexander, *Political Reconstruction in Tennessee*, 230–33; "A set of twelve young men," *Daily Memphis Avalanche*, December 12, 1869.

38. "The Convention," *Nashville Union and American*, January 25, 26, 27, 28, and 29, 1870.

39. Article IV, Section 1, Constitution of 1834; "Restriction of Suffrage by the Convention," *Memphis Public Ledger*, January 12, 1870; Hart, *Redeemers, Bourbons and Populists*, 4–6; Frank B. Williams Jr., "The Poll Tax as a Suffrage Requirement in the South, 1870–1901," *Journal of Southern History* 18 (November 1952):469, 472–83; Hardy, "Fare Well to all Radicals," 214–20; *Convention Journal*, 293–97; Caldwell, *Studies in the Constitutional History*, 315–17; A. Johnson to George H. Nixon, 4 March 1870, PAJ 16: 171–73 John C. Burch to A. Johnson, 9 March 1870, PAJ 16:, 174–75.

40. Caldwell, *Studies in the Constitutional History*, 300, 324–25; "The Convention," *Nashville Union and American*, February 5 and 6, 1870; "The Convention," *Nashville Republican Banner*, February 24, 1870; *Convention Journal*, 253–54; 438–39, see also 195–96, 200–01, 205–6, 235, 248–49, 266, 284, 289–90, 292–97, 300–1, 308–9, 324–28, 332–33, 350, 357–59, 361–66, 376–77.

41. *Convention Journal*, 405–8; "The Convention," *Nashville Union and American*, February 24, 1870.

42. "Communication," *Pulaski Citizen*, March 4, 1870; "The New Constitu-
tion," *Pulaski Citizen*, March 11, 1870; "Public Speaking," *Pulaski Citizen*,
March 18, 1870; "Lincoln," *Nashville Union and American*, March 19, 1870;
Alexander, *Political Reconstruction in Tennessee*, 233–37; "The Constitutional
Convention," *Nashville Republican Banner*, February 22, 1870; Corlew, *Ten-
nessee: A Short History*, 351; Hart, *Redeemers, Bourbons and Populists*, 8–9;
"The Reconstruction Committee" and "Troops for Tennessee Refused," *Wash-
ington Evening Star*, March 26, 1870; "Governor Senter was rather on the
see-saw," *Washington Evening Star*, April 11, 1870; "The Case of Tennessee,"
Washington Evening Star, April 12, 1870; *Convention Journal*, 443; "Free
Again," *Memphis Daily Appeal,* May 9, 1879.

43. "Gen. P. C. [*sic*] Cleburne . . . Arkansas," *Columbia Herald*, April 29, 1870;
"Gen. Wm. A. Quarles," *Memphis Daily Appeal*, June 4, 1870; "The presence
in Memphis of General John C. Brown," *Memphis Sunday Appeal*, June 20,
1870; "Personal," *Memphis Public Ledger*, June 24, 1860; "Proceedings of
the Anti-Coercion and Southern Rights Convention," *Nashville Union and
American*, February 1, 1861 (Quarles); "Democratic Rally," *Nashville Union
and American*, October 28, 1860 (Bate).

44. McBride and Robison, *Biographical Directory*, 2:181–83; A. Colyar to
A. Johnson, 19 May 1870, PAJ 16: 189 W. A. Quarles to A. Johnson, 21 July
1870, PAJ 16: 201–3; Letters, Carter's Depot, *Knoxville Weekly Chronicle*, July 20,
1870; "To all the extent of our power," *Memphis Daily Appeal*, July 7, 1870.

45. Alexander, "Whiggery and Reconstruction in Tennessee," 301–5; Hart, *Redeemers, Bourbons and Populists*, 8–9; "Judicial Convention," *Nashville Union
and American*, July 12, 1870; Sam D. Elliott, "When the United States Attorney Sued to Remove Half the Tennessee Supreme Court: The Quo Warranto
Cases of 1870," *Tennessee Bar Journal* 49 (August 2013): 20, 24.

46. "Judicial Convention," *Nashville Union and American*, July 12, 1870; "The
Lebanon Herald and the Democracy," *Nashville Union and American*, July 23,
1870; "Letter of Col. Stephens to Old Line Whigs," *Nashville Union and
American*, August 4, 1870; "Political," *Memphis Daily Appeal*, August 12,
1870; "Em. Etheridge," *Memphis Daily Appeal*, August 15, 1870; "From Hon.
G. A. Henry," *Memphis Daily Appeal*, August 18, 1870; "Andrew Johnson's
Mass Meeting," *Knoxville Weekly Chronicle*, July 27, 1870.

47. W. A. Quarles to A. Johnson, 21 July 1870, PAJ 16: 201; "Gubernatorial"
Nashville Union and American, August 9, 1870; "These columns abundantly
attest," *Memphis Daily Appeal*, August 13, 1870.

48. "General Brown," "Name the Paper," and "Stop the Lie!" *Pulaski Citizen*,
August 12, 1870; "Gov. Neill S. Brown," *Nashville Union and American*, August 16, 1870; "Our Next Governor," *Pulaski Citizen*, August 5, 1870; "The

Shelbyville Rescue and Our Record," "Nothing in a Name," *Pulaski Citizen*, August 19, 1870; "GEN. J.C. BROWN who is a prominent candidate for Governor," *Clarksville Chronicle*, August 20, 1870; "Conservative Demonstration," *Knoxville Weekly Chronicle*, August 17, 1870; "Gen. John C. Brown," *Memphis Public Ledger*, July 19, 1870.

49. Elliott, "When the United States Attorney," 22–24.

50. McBride and Robison, *Biographical Directory*, 1:34, 2:181–83; "A newspaper editor has certain duties to perform," *Memphis Daily Appeal*, July 21, 1870; Endorsement indicating Colyar pardon, September 22, 1865, Case Files of Applications from Former Confederates for Presidential Pardons ("Amnesty Papers"), 1865–67, Records of the Adjutant General's Office, 1780s–1917, RG 94, Publication M1003, NARA; Elliott, "When the United States Attorney," 24; "Political Disabilities," *Nashville Union and American*, August 18, 1870; "To all the extent of our power," *Memphis Daily Appeal*, July 7, 1870.

51. "Political," *Memphis Sunday Appeal*, August 7, 1870; A. S. Colyar to A. Johnson, 30 August 1870, PAJ 16: 209; "General John C. Brown," *Memphis Daily Appeal*, August 27, 1870; "Encouraging Prospects for Harmony," *Nashville Union and American,* September 2, 1870.

52. White, *Messages*, 6:122–32; Temple, *Notable Men of Tennessee*, 184; McBride and Robison, *Biographical Directory*, 813–14; "Record of the Radical Candidate for Governor" and "Mr. Wisener's Disabilities," *Nashville Union and American*, September 24, 1870; Hart, *Redeemers, Bourbons and Populists*, 11; "Secession in Tennessee," *Sweetwater Enterprise*, September 29, 1870; "Speech at Gallatin, Tennessee," September 17, 1870, PAJ 16: 209, 214.

53. "The Gubernatorial Canvass," *Nashville Union and American*, September 25, 1870; "Telegraphic," *Nashville Union and American*, October 2, 1870 (supplement); "Chattanooga," *Nashville Republican Banner*, September 2, 1870; "Gen. Brown's Speech," *Memphis Public Ledger*, October 4, 1870; "Withdrawal of Col. Colyar," *Nashville Union and American*, October 4, 1870; A. S. Colyar to A. Johnson, 5 October 1870, PAJ 16: 216–17.

54. "The Gubernatorial Canvass," *Knoxville Daily Chronicle*, October 7, 1870; "Telegraphic," *Nashville Union and American*, October 12, 1870; "Gubernatorial Canvass," *Nashville Union and American*, October 23, 1870; "Gubernatorial Canvass," *Nashville Union and American*, October 25, 1870; "Gubernatorial Canvass," *Nashville Union and American*, October 30, 1870; "Telegraphic" and "Gubernatorial Canvass," *Nashville Union and American*, November 2, 1870; "Brevities," *Memphis Public Ledger*, November 2, 1870; "Speaking Saturday," *Memphis Public Ledger*, November 7, 1870.

55. White, *Messages*, 6:30 (table); Hardy, "Fare Well to all Radicals," 240 (quote).

56. "Telegraphic," *Nashville Union and American*, November 9, 1870; White, *Messages*, 6:132–35; Hart, *Redeemers, Bourbons and Populists*, 12–13; "The *Knoxville Whig and Register*," *Nashville Union and American*, November 15, 1870; "The Elections," *Philadelphia Evening Telegraph*, November 9, 1870; "New Governor of Tennessee," *Nashville Union and American*, November 26, 1870 (quoting St. Louis *Republican*); "The Democrats of Tennessee," *New Hampshire Patriot*, September 28, 1870.

57. Daisy Brown grave marker, Maplewood Cemetery, Pulaski; "Mrs. Elizabeth Brown Burch," *Confederate Veteran* 12 (October 1904): 498; "The Pulaski Library Association," *Pulaski Citizen*, March 26, 1869; "Blood Horse Association," *Pulaski Citizen*, April 2, 1869; "Tennessee Biographical Questionnaire re: John C. Brown," MS-485, TSLA. Many of these interesting details come from the questionnaire, which was filled out by Brown's son after his death. No other primary source speaks of his novel or the Khedive. For the conclusion that the offer from the Khedive came in 1869, see John Dunn, "'An American Fracas in Egypt': The Butler Affair of 1872," *Journal of the American Research Center in Egypt* 42 (2005/2006): 153, 154–55; John C. Brown grave marker, Maplewood Cemetery, Pulaski; "F & AM," *Nashville Union and American*, October 8, 1869; "Masonic," *Nashville Union and American*, November 18, 1870; "The Banner on Saturday says," *Memphis Public Ledger*, February 20, 1871; "Personal Intelligence," *Columbia Herald*, June 30, 1871; *Mitchell v. Wade*, 39 Ark. 377 (1882); "Nashville and Decatur Railroad," *Nashville Union and American*, May 6, 1871; "Personal," *Nashville Union and American*, November 16, 1870, "The City," *Nashville Union and American*, November 18, 1870; "State News," *Nashville Union and American*, December 11, 1870; "A Terrible Conflagration," *Pulaski Citizen*, August 24, 1871; "Knights Templar," *Nashville Union and American*, May 14, 1871; "Brevities," *Memphis Public Ledger*, May 31, 1871.

58. "Fire" and "Illness of General Brown," *Pulaski Citizen*, September 14, 1871; "Governor Brown's Residence Destroyed by Fire," *Knoxville Daily Chronicle*, September 14, 1871; JCB to James Longstreet, 14 April 1888, Perkins Library, Duke Univ.; "Illness of Gen. John C. Brown," *Nashville Union and American*, September 15, 1870; "Condition of Gov. John C. Brown," *Nashville Union and American*, September 16, 1871; "Personal," *Nashville Union and American*, October 1, 1871; "General Brown," *Nashville Republican Banner*, September 17, 1871; "General Brown Out of Danger," *Nashville Union and American*, September 20, 1871; "Gov. Brown Sick," *Galveston Daily News*, September 19, 1871.

59. "Governor John C. Brown," *Nashville Republican Banner*, October 1, 1871.

7. To Improve the Present and Secure the Future

1. "Dies Irea!," "Earthquake," "Cairo," and "Philadelphia," *Nashville Union and American*, October 10, 1871; "River News," "The Chancellors in Convention," "Robertson County Fair," and "Tennessee News," *Nashville Union and American*, October 11, 1871.
2. "Inauguration," *Nashville Union and American*, October 11, 1871.
3. Ibid.
4. "Gov. Brown Unwell," *Pulaski Citizen*, October 19, 1871; White, *Messages*, 6:140–4; "Where We Stand," *Nashville Union and American*, July 28, 1874; Robert B. Jones, *Tennessee at the Crossroads: The State Debt Controversy, 1870–1883* (Knoxville: Univ. of Tennessee Press, 1977), 4–14; Foner, *Reconstruction*, 379–80.
5. White, *Messages*, 6:145–52.
6. Ibid., 142; "Brown," *Memphis Daily Appeal*, October 31, 1874; "Washington," *Boston Daily Advertiser*, December 28, 1880.
7. Atkins, *Parties, Politics and the Sectional Conflict in Tennessee*, 98–110; White, *Messages*, 4:180–86, 6:142; "The Governor's Policy," *Nashville Union and American*, November 3, 1871; "Where We Stand."
8. "A Card from Senator Brownlow," *Knoxville Weekly Chronicle*, October 18, 1871; "The Governor's Message," *Memphis Daily Appeal*, October 25, 1871; "Governor Brown a Repudiator," *Memphis Daily Appeal*, October 26, 1871; "The Governor's Message," *Nashville Union and American*, October 27, 1871; "The Governor's Policy," *Nashville Union and American*, November 3, 1871; "Governor Brown's Position," *Nashville Union and American*, November 11, 1871; "State Finances and Gov. Brown," *Nashville Union and American*, November 12, 1871; "Gov. Brown and Taxes," and "To This Complexion Has the *Appeal* Come at Last," *Nashville Union and American*, November 14, 1871.
9. Jones, *Tennessee at the Crossroads*, 9, 21–22; "The Governor's Policy," *Nashville Union and American*, November 3, 1871; "Gov. Brown and the Minority," *Nashville Union and American*, November 5, 1871; "Tennessee Legislature," *Nashville Union and American*, November 17, 1871; "The Legislature—the Tax," *Jackson Whig and Tribune*, November 25, 1871; "Taxation for the Next Year," *Memphis Daily Appeal*, December 16, 1871; Butler, "The Life of John C. Brown," 90–92.
10. White, *Messages*, 6:66–69, 154–55, 173–79; Butler, "The Life of John C. Brown," 75–78; Elliott, *Isham G. Harris of Tennessee*, 213–14.
11. White, *Messages*, 6:160–63, 166; Karin A. Shapiro, *A New South Rebellion: The Battle against Convict Labor in the Tennessee Coalfields, 1871–1896* (Chapel Hill: Univ. of North Carolina Press, 1998), 48–49; "Gone to Prepare the Way, *Nashville Union and American*, January 14, 1871; "All Quiet Again," *Nashville*

Union and American, January 22, 1871; "The Sewanee coal miners," *Knoxville Daily Chronicle*, January 21, 1871; "The Coal Miners' Strike," *Winchester Home Journal*, January 26, 1871.

12. White, *Messages of the Governors of Tennessee*, 6:166–67; Shapiro, *A New South Rebellion*, 48–58; Connie L. Lester, *Up from the Mudsills of Hell: The Farmers' Alliance, Populism, and Progressive Agriculture in Tennessee, 1870–1915* (Athens: Univ. of Georgia Press, 2006), 173–74; "The Sewanee Coal Mines," *Nashville Union and American*, November 5, 1871; JCB to T. A. Atchison, et al., 6 November 1871, W. —— to JCB, 8 November 1871, JCB to John Porterfield, 29 November 1871, and "Louisiana Tiger" to JCB, 21, 28 November 1871, all in John C. Brown Governor's Papers, TSLA.

13. "Over one hundred persons," *Pulaski Citizen*, October 26, 1871; "Pardoned," *Nashville Union and American*, November 1, 1871; A. S. Colyar to JCB, 19 August 1871, A. O. P. Nicholson to JCB, 1 September 1871, James D. Porter to JCB, 12 October 1871, J. D. C. Atkins to JCB, 19 December 1871, Don Cameron to JCB, 20 December 1871, John M. Bright to JCB, 17 January 1872, J. Heiskell to JCB, 13 December 1871, and John Williams to JCB, n.d. (probably November 1871), all in John C. Brown Governor's Papers, TSLA; "The Ex-President and Gov. Brown," *Knoxville Weekly Chronicle*, December 13, 1871; "The Democracy In Tact," *Pulaski Citizen*, November 9, 1871; "Our Nashville Letter," *Knoxville Daily Chronicle*, December 15, 1871; McBride and Robison, *Biographical Directory*, 1:101, 413. The author's review of published accounts of Brown's speeches at the end of the 1870 campaign finds no reference to Johnson as a "malcontent and a political harlot." A report of Brown's last speech at Memphis indicates that he only mentioned Johnson in passing, as one of the Tennesseans who recognized that the states were sovereign under the Constitution. "Speaking Saturday," *Memphis Public Ledger*, November 7, 1870.

14. White, *Messages of the Governors of Tennessee*, 6:180; Butler, "The Life of John C. Brown," 50; "At the Capitol," *Fayetteville Observer*, December 14, 1871; "County Lines," *Nashville Union and American*, December 15, 1871; "The Black Flag Raised," *Knoxville Weekly Chronicle*, December 20, 1871; "The General Assembly," *Nashville Union and American*, December 16, 1871.

15. "Executive Labors," *Pulaski Citizen*, December 21, 1871; John C. Vaughn to JCB, 16 December 1871, and JCB to John C. Vaughn, 29 December 1871, both in John C. Brown Governor's Papers, TSLA; "The Christmas Season," *Nashville Union and American*, December 16, 1871; "Clishmaclaver," *Pulaski Citizen*, November 23, 1871.

16. "Executive Labors"; "Judge John S. Wilkes," *Confederate Veteran* 16 (March 1908): 106; B. L. Wilkes and John S. Wilkes Compiled Service Records, NARA;

"Ex-Adjutant General Wilkes," *Memphis Daily Appeal*, January 21, 1875; "Capt. Jno. Wilkes," *Pulaski Citizen*, December 10, 1874.

17. "The Shelbyville Commercial favors the re-election of Governor Brown." *Nashville Union and American*, January 20, 1872; "Personal," *Memphis Daily Appeal*, February 10, 1872; "For Governor," *Knoxville Daily Chronicle*, February 27, 1872; "The Pulaski Citizen," *Nashville Union and American*, March 2, 1872; "The Murfreesboro News," *Jackson Whig and Tribune*, March 9, 1872; "The Next Governor," *Jackson Whig and Tribune*, March 16, 1872; "Gov. Brown," *Nashville Union and American*, January 7, 1872; "Radical Misrepresentation," *Nashville Union and American*, March 7, 1872; W. C. Whitthorne to JCB, 16 February 1872, John C. Brown Governor's Papers, TSLA.

18. White, *Messages*, 6:180–200, 214, 225; Butler, "The Life of John C. Brown," 53–55.

19. "Personal," *Nashville Union and American*, March 19, 1872; "Personal," *Memphis Daily Appeal*, March 25, 1872; "A Night of Excitement," *Nashville Union and American*, March 26, 1872.

20. "The Legislative Banquet at the Maxwell," *Nashville Union and American*, March 29, 1872; "Meeting at the Capitol," *Nashville Union and American*, March 28, 1872; "The Next Governor," *Nashville Union and American*, March 22, 1872; "Personal," *Nashville Union and American*, March 19, 1872 (quoting *Chattanooga Times*); "The State Convention," *Nashville Union and American*, March 30, 1872; "Spirit of the Press," *Nashville Union and American*, April 3, 1872 (quoting *Chattanooga Times*); "Our Next Governor," and "The Voice of the People," *Nashville Union and American*, April 6, 1872; "Letters from the People," *Nashville Union and American*, April 10, 1872.

21. "Spirit of the Press," *Nashville Union and American*, April 12, 1872; "State Politics," *Nashville Union and American*, April 13, 1872; "State Politics," *Nashville Union and American*, April 16, 1872; "Gubernatorial," *Nashville Union and American*, April 16, 1872; "State Politics," *Nashville Union and American*, April 20, 1872; "State Politics," *Nashville Union and American*, April 23, 1872; "State Politics," *Nashville Union and American*, April 27, 1872; "The Political Outlook" and "State Politics," *Nashville Union and American*, April 27, 1872; "State Convention," *Jackson Whig and Tribune*, April 27, 1872; "The Gubernatorial Contest," *Memphis Daily Appeal*, April 28, 1872; "General B.F. Cheatham" *Daily Memphis Avalanche*, May 1, 1872; White, *Messages*, 6: 217–20.

22. White, *Messages*, 6:220–25; Andrew L. Slap, *The Doom of Reconstruction: the Liberal Republicans in the Civil War Era* (New York: Fordham Univ. Press, 2006), 92–93, 189; "Speech at Knoxville, Tennessee," August 10, 1872, PAJ 16: 337–38; Jean Edward Smith, *Grant* (New York: Simon and Schuster, 2001), 548–51; "Democratic State Convention," *Nashville Union and Ameri-*

can, May 10, 1872; "State Politics," *Daily Memphis Avalanche*, May 10, 1872; "John C. Brown," *Pulaski Citizen*, May 16, 1872; "The Radical Convention," *Nashville Union and American*, May 16, 1872.

23. "Congressional," *Nashville Union and American*, May 22, 1872; Act of May 30, 1872, *United States Statutes at Large*, vol. XVII, chap. 239, 192 (1873); "A Tenth Member," *Memphis Public Ledger*, May 25, 1872; "Cheatham-Johnson-Foote," *Memphis Daily Appeal*, May 25, 1872; "New Advertisements,"*Nashville Union and American*, June 1, 1872; Trefousse, *Andrew Johnson*, 360–611; J. C. Burch to Johnson, 22 May 1872, T. W. Bullock to Johnson, 24 May 1872, J. C. Burch to Johnson, 25 May 1872, R. K. Byrd to Johnson, 29 May 1872, and A. R. Richardson to Johnson, 29 May 1872, all in PAJ 16: 303–7.

24. John Williams to JCB, n.d. (probably November 1871), JCB to J. Wilkes, 18 June 1872, and JCB to Charlton, 9 September 1872, all in John C. Brown Governor's Papers, TSLA; JCB to J. Patton Anderson, 1 June 1872, James Patton Anderson Papers, Younge Library, Univ. of Florida; "Personal," *Nashville Union and American*, June 6, 1872; "Health of Gov. Brown," *Nashville Union and American*, July 9, 1872; "Gov. Brown," *Pulaski Citizen and Press*, July 11, 1872; "State News," *Jackson Whig and Tribune*, July 27, 1872; "Personal," *Nashville Union and American*, August 3, 1872; "Personal," *Memphis Daily Appeal*, August 16, 1872.

25. JCB to R. W. Humphreys, 22 May 1872, R. W. Humphreys to JCB, 11 June 1872, R. W. Humphreys to JCB, 29 August 1872, J. Heiskell to JCB, 13 July 1872, and JCB to Heiskell, 22 August 1872, all in John C. Brown Governor's Papers, TSLA.

26. Losson, *Tennessee's Forgotten Warriors*, 258–59; "Speech at Knoxville, Tennessee," August 10, 1872, PAJ 16: 331 Lloyd Paul Stryker, *Andrew Johnson: A Study in Courage* (New York: Macmillan, 1929), 831–32; White, *Messages*, 6:232–39; Interview with *Cincinnati Commercial* Correspondent, August 20, 1872, PAJ 16: 340–42 John C. Burch to Johnson, 25 August 1872, PAJ 16:348–49

27. "The John C. Brown Democracy," *Knoxville Daily Chronicle*, August 13, 1872; White, *Messages*, 6:241–47; McBride and Robison, *Biographical Directory*, 2:309; "Independent Candidate for Governor," *Nashville Union and American*, August 31, 1872; "An Independent Played Out," *Memphis Daily Appeal*, October 8, 1872; "Our Opportunity," *Knoxville Daily Chronicle*, August 27, 1872.

28. "Gubernatorial Canvass," *Pulaski Citizen*, September 12, 1872; "The Gubernatorial Race," *Nashville Union and American*, September 18, 1872.

29. "From the Capital," *Knoxville Daily Chronicle*, September 20, 1872; White, *Messages*, 6:255–66; "Interview with New York Herald Correspondent," September 27, 1872, PAJ 16: 377–79; "Tennessee Politics," *Daily Memphis*

Avalanche, August 26, 1872; "That Military Ring," *Knoxville Daily Chronicle*, September 22, 1872; William R. Sevier to Johnson, 24 September 1872, PAJ 16: 376–77; Elliott, *Isham G. Harris*, 210–11; "The Giants at Tullahoma," *Knoxville Daily Chronicle*, November 3, 1872.

30. White, *Messages*, 6:277–78; "The Situation," *Memphis Public Ledger*, November 1, 1872; "Who are the strongest advocates of Democratic disorganization in Tennessee?" and "It is a reasonable conjecture," *Nashville Union and American*, October 31, 1872; "Governor Brown," *Daily Memphis Avalanche*, September 4, 1872; "Governor John C. Brown" *Daily Memphis Avalanche*, September 10, 1872; "Did you say the *Banner*," *Nashville Union and American*, October 25, 1872; "The Gubernatorial Canvass," *Knoxville Daily Chronicle*, October 15, 1872; "The *Banner* and Mr. Johnson," *Nashville Union and American*, October 29, 1872; "Strange Company for a Democrat," *Nashville Union and American*, October 31, 1872.

31. "Gov. Brown in Marshall," *Nashville Union and American*, September 5, 1872; "The Situation in the State," *Fayetteville Observer*, September 19, 1872. Brown was no Bourbon Democrat in the sense of Isham Harris.

32. "The Gubernatorial Debate" and "The Gubernatorial Canvass," *Knoxville Daily Chronicle*," October 15, 1872; "Jno. C. Brown at Knoxville," *Nashville Union and American*, October 15, 1872; "The Canvass," *Nashville Union and American*, October 18, 1872; "The Gubernatorial Discussion," *Bristol News*, October 15, 1872; "Letter from Cleveland," *Knoxville Daily Chronicle*, October 9, 1872.

33. "Gubernatorial," *Memphis Daily Appeal*, October 22, 1872; "Failed," *Bolivar Bulletin*, November 1, 1872; "Candidates for Governor," *Jackson Whig and Tribune*, November 2, 1872, "The Gubernatorial Canvass," *Nashville Union and American*, November 2, 1872.

34. White, *Messages*, 6:279–86; Losson, *Tennessee's Forgotten Warriors*, 260–61; A. Johnson Jr. to A. Johnson, 10 November 1872, L. C. Houk to A. Johnson, 21 November 1872, R. Bennett to A. Johnson, 17 December 1872, and A. Colyar to A. Johnson, 21 January 1873, all in PAJ 16: 400, 407, 412–13, 418; Hart, *Redeemers, Bourbons and Populists*, 17; "The Next Governor," *Memphis Public Ledger*, January 27, 1874; "The Election," *Nashville Union and American*, November 27, 1872.

35. "Personal," *Pulaski Citizen and Press*, January 2, 1873; White, *Messages*, 6:316–19; "Inauguration Ceremonies" and "The Governor's Inaugural," *Nashville Union and American,* January 19, 1873.

36. "Personal," *Pulaski Citizen and Press*, January 2, 1873; "Tennessee," *Memphis Daily Appeal*, January 10, 1873; White, *Messages*, 6:290–1; Jones, *Tennessee at the Crossroads*, 23–24.

37. White, *Messages*, 6:299–302.

38. "The Governor's Message," *Knoxville Daily Chronicle*, January 12, 1873; "Ignorance in Tennessee," *Memphis Daily Appeal*, January 12, 1873; White, *Messages*, 6:326–39; Butler, "The Life of John C. Brown," 80–84; Corlew, *Tennessee: A Short History*, 396; John Trotwood Moore and Austin Foster, *Tennessee, The Volunteer State: 1769–1923* (Chicago: S. J. Clarke, 1923), 556.

39. White, *Messages*, 6:320–21; Jones, *Tennessee at the Crossroads*, 23–28; "Governor Brown," *Pulaski Citizen and Press*, January 23, 1873.

40. Jones, *Tennessee at the Crossroads*, 26–39; "Judge Houk's Speech" and "Speech of Judge Houk," *Nashville Union and American*, March 18, 1873; "Speech of Judge Houk," *Nashville Union and American*, March 19, 1873; White, *Messages*, 6:322–26; "Legislative," *Nashville Union and American*, March 23, 1873; "The Funding Bill," *Jackson Whig and Tribune*, March 29, 1873.

41. White, *Messages*, 6:338, 360 (quotes), 339–62; "The Tippling Bill," *Memphis Public Ledger*, March 26, 1873; "Governor Brown's Veto Message," *Memphis Daily Appeal*, March 27, 1873.

42. JCB to Lacy, 21 March 1873, letterbook, John C. Brown Governor's Papers, TSLA; "The Governor's Banquet," *Nashville Union and American*, March 23, 1873; McBride and Robison, *Biographical Directory*, 2:484–5; Corlew, *Tennessee: A Short History*, 363–4; "The contrast between Tennessee and Kentucky Democracy," *Knoxville Weekly Chronicle*, May 21, 1873.

43. JCB to American Bank Note Company, 14 February 1873, letterbook, John C. Brown Governor's Papers, TSLA; "Governor Brown's Veto Message," *Memphis Daily Appeal*, March 27, 1873; "The Louisville Commercial's Nashville correspondent says," *Pulaski Citizen*, April 3, 1873; "For sterling worth," *Clarksville Weekly Chronicle*, April 5, 1873; "Will an Extra Session be Called?" *Memphis Public Ledger*, March 28, 1873; "A Governor Demoralized," *Jackson Whig and Tribune*, April 5, 1873; "Voice of the Press," *Memphis Public Ledger*, April 7, 1873; "The Extra Session," *Memphis Public Ledger*, April 9, 1873; "The *Avalanche* Gets After the Funders," *Bolivar Bulletin*, April 25, 1873; "The Next Gubernatorial Race," *Knoxville Weekly Chronicle*, April 30, 1873; "The Compound Interest Bosh," *Nashville Union and American*, May 1, 1873.

44. "Important Document," *Memphis Public Ledger*, May 1, 1873; Jones, *Tennessee at the Crossroads*, 29–30.

45. "The Comptrollership," *Nashville Union and American*, May 6, 1873; JCB to Hobbs, 1 May 1874, letterbook, John C. Brown Governor's Papers, TSLA; "The New State Comptroller," *Memphis Daily Appeal*, May 2, 1873; "Gov. Brown at the Convention," *Pulaski Citizen*, May 29, 1873; "Local News," *Pulaski Citizen*, June 26, 1873; "We regret to learn that Governor Brown" *Jackson Whig and Tribune*, July 5, 1873; "Is it Possible?—Let Him Speak," *Bolivar Bulletin*, June 27, 1873; "Gov. Jno. C. Brown," *Nashville Union and American*, June 28, 1873.

46. "We find in a special," *Memphis Daily Appeal*, July 25, 1873; John C. Burch to JCB, 28 June 1873, John C. Brown Governor's Papers, TSLA; "Personal," *Nashville Union and American*, July 29, 1873; "Finance and Trade," *Memphis Daily Appeal*, August 1, 1873; "Sale of the Comptroller's Office," *Nashville Union and American*, August 8, 1873; "The 'Burch' Applied," *Memphis Daily Appeal*, August 10, 1873; "Sale of the Comptroller's Office," *Nashville Union and American*, August 15, 1873; "About the Sale of the Comptroller's Office," *Knoxville Weekly Chronicle*, August 20, 1873; "The Radical War on State Officers," *Nashville Union and American*, August 21, 1873; "A Pretty Story Spoiled," *Nashville Union and American*, August 21, 1873; "Bargain and Sale," *Nashville Union and American*, August 17, 1873; "The Comptrollership," *Memphis Daily Appeal*, August 20, 1873; "Bargain and Corruption," *Pulaski Citizen*, August 21, 1873.

47. "Bargain and Sale," *Nashville Union and American*, August 17, 1873; "The Comptrollership," *Memphis Daily Appeal*, August 20, 1873; "Veto of the Tippling Bill," *Knoxville Weekly Chronicle*, August 27, 1873; "The Rebound," *Nashville Union and American*, August 24, 1873; "The Bargain and Sale Story, *Nashville Union and American*, August 23, 1873; "Governor John C. Brown," *Memphis Daily Appeal*, August 28, 1873; "The Radical War on State Officers," *Nashville Union and American*, August 29, 1873.

48. "The Libel Suits," *Nashville Union and American*, June 21, 1874; "Those Libel Suits," *Nashville Union and American*, June 23, 1874; "Light at Last," *Nashville Union and American*, January 22, 1875; W. H. Morrow to A. Johnson, 12 August 1873, PAJ 16: 433; "From Nashville," *Knoxville Weekly Chronicle*, January 27, 1875.

49. "State News," *Jackson Whig and Tribune*, August 23, 1873; JCB to J. May?, 8 October 1873, letterbook, and JCB to I. G. Harris, 22 October 1873, letterbook, both in John C. Brown Governor's Papers, TSLA; John H. Erskine, "A Report on Yellow Fever As It Appeared in Memphis, Tennessee in 1873," in *Public Health Papers and Reports* (Memphis: American Public Health Association, 1873), 385, 389; United States Surgeon General's Office, *Cholera Epidemic of 1873 in the United States* (Washington, DC: Government Printing Office, 1875), 135; "There's a Cry from Macedonia," *Nashville Union and American*, October 7, 1873; Quentin R. Scrabec Jr., *The 100 Most Significant Events in American Business: An Encyclopedia* (Santa Barbara, CA: ABC-CLIO, 2012), 69–72; JCB to F. Snipes, 22? November 1873, letterbook, John C. Brown Governor's Papers, TSLA; Jones, *Tennessee at the Crossroads*, 33–34.

50. Jones, *Tennessee at the Crossroads*, 32–38; Corlew, *Tennessee: A Short History*, 357–58; "Ex-Gov. Brown on the Tennessee Situation," *Nashville Daily American*, February 21, 1882.

51. "Tennessee's Debt," *Memphis Daily Appeal*, January 10, 1874; "Personal," *Nashville Union and American*, January 6, 1874; "Southern News," *Memphis Daily Appeal*, January 12, 1874; "Tennessee Finances," *Memphis Public Ledger*, January 21, 1874; "Southern News," *Memphis Daily Appeal*, January 17, 1874; "Governor Brown," *Memphis Daily Appeal*, January 20, 1874.

52. "Gov. Brown," *Pulaski Citizen*, February 19, 1874; "Memphis and Knoxville Railroad—Cheering Prospects," *Memphis Daily Appeal*, February 17, 1874; "By the Way—No. IV," *Memphis Public Ledger*, March 5, 1874; JCB to W. C. Whitthorne, 22 March 1874, letterbook, John C. Brown Governor's Papers, TSLA; "Returned," *Nashville Union and American*, March 3, 1874; "Giles County," *Nashville Union and American*, March 8, 1874; "A Step in the Right Direction," *Nashville Union and American*, June 23, 1874.

53. JCB to A. Bright, Brownsville, 7 February 1874, letterbook, John C. Brown Governor's Papers, TSLA; "Shelby's Organization," *Nashville Union and American*, February 18, 1874; "Oliver," *Pulaski Citizen*, March 26, 1874; "Ye Anti-Funders," *Nashville Union and American*, February 19, 1874; "The Fight Going On," *Knoxville Weekly Chronicle*, March 11, 1874; "Political Gossip," *Nashville Union and American*, March 4, 1874; A. Johnson to John P. White, 30 January 1874, PAJ 16: 510–12; "How the Land Lies in this County," *Nashville Union and American*, June 26, 1874; "The Important Question for Tennessee," *Nashville Union and American*, March 31, 1874.

54. Linda T. Austin, "Escape from the Asylum: The End of Local Care of the Mentally Ill in Memphis and Shelby County," *Tennessee Historical Quarterly* 72 (Spring 2013): 50–53; M. C. Gallaway to JCB, 8 April 1874, R. J. Chester to JCB, 9 April 1874, D. D. Saunders to JCB, 26 April 1874, J. W. Pettigrew to JCB, 5 May 1874, W. A. Thompson, MD, Humboldt, to JCB, 6 May 1874, J. Heiskell to JCB, n.d., JCB to G. Day, 21 May 1874, letterbook, and M. C. Galloway to JCB, 6 June 1874, all in John C. Brown Governor's Papers, TSLA; "West Tennessee Insane Asylum," *Memphis Public Ledger*, May 13, 1874; "Fighting for a Site," *Nashville Union and American*, May 7, 1874; "Humboldt," *Memphis Public Ledger*, May 7, 1874; "Ledger Lines," *Memphis Public Ledger*, July 21, 1874; "State Politics in Memphis," *Memphis Public Ledger*, May 15, 1874; Thomas Logwood to A. Johnson, 30 April 1874, PAJ 16: 538–40.

55. "No Hope," *Nashville Union and American*, May 1, 1874; James Murphy to JCB, 7 May 1874, and C. M. McGhee to JCB, 9 June 1874, both in John C. Brown Governor's Papers, TSLA; Ancestry.com, *U. S., Sons of the American Revolution Membership Applications, 1889–1970* [online database] (Provo, UT: Ancestry.com Operations, Inc. 2011), application filed by John C. Brown Jr., March 11, 1903 (accessed September 13, 2013); "Interview with *Nashville Republican Banner* Reporter," April 30, 1874, and "Speech at Memphis,

Tennessee, May 16, 1875 A. Johnson to Richard M. Edwards, 20 July 1874, PAJ 16: 533–37, 540–57, 576–77.

56. "Bartlett," *Memphis Daily Appeal*, July 22, 1874; "Where We Stand," *Nashville Union and American*, July 28, 1874.

57. "Where We Stand," *Nashville Union and American*, July 28, 1874.

58. White, *Messages*, 6:395–97; "The State Convention," *Pulaski Citizen*, August 20, 1874; "The Glorious Work of Yesterday," *Nashville Union and American*, August 20, 1874; "Governor Brown," *Athens Post*, August 28, 1874; "The Shelbyville *Commercial*," *Pulaski Citizen*, August 6, 1874; Trefousse, *Andrew Johnson: A Biography*, 370; Stryker, *Andrew Johnson: A Study in Courage*, 833.

59. "Lynch Law" and "Gibson County," *Nashville Union and American*, August 27, 1874; "Gibson County," *Memphis Daily Appeal*, August 28, 1874; Margaret Vandiver, *Lethal Punishment: Lynchings and Legal Executions in the South* (New Brunswick, NJ: Rutgers Univ. Press, 2006), 34–35.

60. "Gibson County," *Nashville Union and American*, August 27, 1874; Statement of George A. Henderson, September 1, 1874, Statement of Andrew Seagroves, September 3, 1874, and James and Rob McKinney to JCB, 7 September 1874, all in John C. Brown Governor's Papers, TSLA; "Julia Hayden's Murder," *Nashville Union and American*, September 2, 1874; "A Mystery Still," *Nashville Union and American*, September 11, 1874.

61. "Tennessee Troubles," *New York Tribune*, October 27, 1874; "Let Us Have Peace," *Nashville Union and American*, August 28, 1874; "Mass-Meeting," *Memphis Daily Appeal*, August 29, 1874.

62. "Governor's Proclamation," *Pulaski Citizen*, September 3, 1874; Vandiver, *Lethal Punishment*, 37; "Gibson County's Lynchers," *Milan Exchange*, September 10, 1874.

63. "Governor John C. Brown," *Memphis Daily Appeal*, August 30, 1874; "Notwithstanding its Civil Rights predilection," *Nashville Union and American*, September 1, 1874 (reprint from *New York Tribune*); W. W. McDowell to JCB, 4 September 1874, and William J. Sykes to JCB, 4 September 1874, both in John C. Brown Governor's Papers, TSLA; "Jackson," *Nashville Union and American*, September 9, 1874; "Gibson County," *Memphis Daily Appeal*, September 9, 1874; "Memphis," *Nashville Union and American*, September 10, 1874; "Trenton Notes," *Milan Exchange*, September 10, 1874; "Gibson County," *Nashville Union and American*, September 11, 1874; "Brownlow," *Nashville Union and American*, September 17, 1874; "Senator Brownlow," *Nashville Union and American*, September 20, 1874.

64. "Notwithstanding the prompt action of Governor Brown of Tennessee," *Nashville Union and American*, September 12, 1874; "Federal Interference in Tennessee," *Nashville Union and American*, September 13, 1874; "Personal," *Nashville Union and American*, September 18, 1874; "Brown to Brownlow,"

Clarksville Weekly Chronicle, October 3, 1874; "Gov. Brown," *Nashville Union and American,* September 22, 1874. "Gov. Brown," *Pulaski Citizen,* September 24, 1874; JCB to U. S. Grant, 18 September 1874, and U. S. Grant to JCB, 19 September 1874, both in John Y. Simon, ed., *The Papers of Ulysses S. Grant,* vol. 25 (Carbondale: Southern Illinois University Press, 2003), 228–29; "Hands Off!" *Nashville Union and American,* September 19, 1874; "Washington," *Nashville Union and American,* September 20, 1874; "Still Harping, etc.," *Memphis Daily Appeal,* October 13, 1874; "Washington," *Nashville Union and American,* October 13, 1874; Vandiver, *Lethal Punishment,* 37–38. Klan activity continued in Smith County into October. See James and Rob McKinney to JCB, 7 September 1874; Judge S. M. Fite to JCB, 8 September 1874, George H. Morgan to JCB, 9 September 1874, John W. Carr to JCB, 12 September 1874, George H. Morgan to JCB, 27 October 1874; and J. H. Corder to JCB, 28 October 1874, all in John C. Brown Governor's Papers, TSLA.

65. "Interview with New York Herald Correspondent," September 18, 1874, PAJ 16: 581–84; "Gov. Brown," *Nashville Union and American,* September 22, 1874; "Gov. Brown," *Pulaski Citizen,* September 24, 1874; "Columbia," *Nashville Union and American,* October 3, 1874; "The Governor," *Nashville Union and American*; Hart, *Redeemers, Bourbons and Populists,* 20.

66. "Speech at Shelbyville, Tennessee," PAJ 16: 586–99; "On the Warpath," *Nashville Union and American,* October 7, 1874; Trefousse, *Andrew Johnson,* 370; Stryker, *Andrew Johnson,* 833; "Dresden," *Nashville Union and American,* October 13, 1874.

67. J. Heiskell to JCB, [?] October 1874, John C. Brown Governor's Papers, TSLA; "Brown and Johnson," *Nashville Union and American,* October 10, 1874; "Dresden," *Nashville Union and American,* October 13, 1874.

68. "Tennessee," *Memphis Daily Appeal,* October 7, 1874; "An Office for Somebody," *Memphis Public Ledger,* September 30, 1874; "General Bate for United States Senator," *Memphis Daily Appeal,* October 2, 1874; "The Senatorial Fight," *Nashville Union and American,* October 11, 1874; J. Heiskell to JCB, [?] October 1874, John C. Brown Governor's Papers, TSLA; "Repartee," *Memphis Daily Appeal,* October 16, 1874; "The following are the closing remarks," *Clarksville Weekly Chronicle,* October 17, 1874.

69. "Nashville," *Memphis Daily Appeal,* October 14, 1874; "Chattanooga," *Nashville Union and American,* October 29, 1874; "Andy Johnson," *Memphis Daily Appeal,* October 18, 1874; "Governor Brown," *Memphis Daily Appeal,* October 30, 1874; "Brown," *Memphis Daily Appeal,* October 31, 1874; "Maynard a funder," *Nashville Union and American,* October 27, 1874; "The gubernatorial candidates," *Nashville Union and American,* October 24, 1874; "Columbia," *Nashville Union and American,* October 14, 1874; "Springfield," *Nashville Union and American,* October 16, 1874; "It Was the Same," *Memphis Public*

Ledger, December 22, 1874; "Family Jars," *Nashville Union and American*, October 11, 1874.

70. White, *Messages*, 6:407–8; "The Democratic Jubilee," *Nashville Union and American*, November 6, 1874; "Review of Governor John C. Brown's Administration," *Jackson Whig and Tribune*, November 28, 1874; I. G. Harris to JCB, 30 September 1874, I. G. Harris to JCB, 30 September 1874, M. C. Galloway to JCB, 9 November 1874, and W. C. Whitthorne to JCB, 13 December 1874, all in John C. Brown Governor's Papers, TSLA; "The Insane Asylum," *Memphis Daily Appeal*, November 24, 1874; "Ledger Lines," *Memphis Public Ledger*, November 24, 1874; "Brownsville's Back Up," *Nashville Union and American*, December 1, 1874; "Wouldn't Do," *Nashville Union and American*, December 11, 1874; "Personal," *Nashville Union and American*, December 1, 1874; "The Grundy Co. Murderers," *Memphis Public Ledger*, December 9, 1874.

71. White, *Messages*, 6:362–93.

72. Edward L. Ayers, *The Promise of the New South: Life after Reconstruction* (New York: Oxford Univ. Press, 1993), 9; White, *Messages*, 6: 384, 391; William B. Hesseltine, *Confederate Leaders in the New South* (Baton Rouge: Louisiana State Univ. Press, 1950), 199–222.

73. "Gov. Brown's Message," *Pulaski Citizen*, January 21, 1875; "Governor John C. Brown's Message," *Memphis Daily Appeal*, January 8, 1875; "Governor Brown's Message," *Memphis Public Ledger*, January 9, 1875; "The retiring governor" and "If Gov. Brown," *Pulaski Citizen*, January 28, 1875; "Gov. Jno. C. Brown," *Pulaski Citizen*, February 25, 1875.

74. "Senatorial Siftings," *Nashville Union and American*, December 24, 1874; Jones, *Tennessee at the Crossroads*, 32–45; Moore and Foster, *Tennessee, The Volunteer State*, 556; "Brown," *Memphis Daily Appeal*, October 31, 1874; Alexander, "Persistent Whiggery in the Confederate South," 322–24; "The United States Senatorship," *Nashville Union and American*, October 8, 1874; "The Senatorship," *Memphis Daily Appeal*, December 31, 1874; Hart, *Redeemers, Bourbons and Populists*, 23; Temple, *Notable Men of Tennessee*, 440–41; "The Senatorial Fight," *Memphis Public Ledger*, January 22, 1875.

75. Temple, *Notable Men of Tennessee*, 440–43; Trefousse, *Andrew Johnson*, 370–71; Stryker, *Andrew Johnson*, 833. Interestingly, two years earlier, a correspondent from Greeneville wrote to warn Brown not to appoint Reeves as judge, as he was "utterly incompetent." Felix A. Reeve to JCB, 22 January 1873, John C. Brown Governor's Papers, TSLA.

76. "Nashville," *Memphis Public Ledger*, January 2, 1875; "From Nashville" and "Nashville," *Knoxville Weekly Chronicle*, January 27, 1875; "Nashville," *Memphis Daily Appeal*, January 5, 1875; "Nashville," *Memphis Daily Appeal*, January 13, 1875, "Nashville," *Memphis Daily Appeal*, January 19, 1875; "The Senatorial Fight," *Memphis Public Ledger*, January 22, 1875.

77. White, *Messages*, 6:409–11; "Gov. John C. Brown's Withdrawal," *Nashville Union and American,* January 24, 1875; "Nashville," *Memphis Daily Appeal*, January 24, 1874; "Letters From Nashville," *Knoxville Weekly Chronicle*, January 27, 1875; "Letter From Nashville," *Knoxville Weekly Chronicle*, February 3, 1875. There is currently no detailed study of this election from Bate's perspective. See William M. Chesney, "The Public Career of William B. Bate" (master's thesis, University of Tennessee, 1951), 35–36.

78. "Interview with New York Tribune Correspondent," PAJ 16: 706; "Letter From Nashville" and "The Bourbon Rebel," *Knoxville Weekly Chronicle*, February 3, 1875; "Gov. Brown and Gen. Bate," *Pulaski Citizen*, February 3, 1875.

79. "Letter from Pulaski," *Pulaski Citizen*, December 31, 1874; "Dr. Munsey," *Nashville Union and American*, May 18, 1875; "Martin College," *Pulaski Citizen*, November 12, 1874; "Governor John C. Brown House," Tennessee Historical Commission marker, Pulaski, Tennessee; "Mrs. General Brown," *Pulaski Citizen*, September 16, 1875; "Gov. Jno. C. Brown," *Pulaski Citizen*, February 25, 1875; "Abortive Arbitration," *Milan Exchange*, March 18, 1875; "At Nashville," *Memphis Daily Appeal*, May 8, 1875; "Vice President Wilson," *Nashville Union and American*, May 8, 1875; "Personal," *Nashville Union and American*, May 20, 1875.

80. "Report of Condition," *Pulaski Citizen*, January 7, 1876; "Nashville and Decatur Railroad," *Pulaski Citizen*, November 12, 1869; "The Tennessee River Iron and Manufacturing Company," *Pulaski Citizen*, June 25, 1874; "Memphis and Knoxville," *Memphis Daily Appeal*, June 8, 1875; "Nashville and Decatur Road," *Nashville Union and American*, November 11, 1874; Elizabeth W. White, comp., *Giles County Chancery Court Extracts* (n. p., 1990), 4:76, 147; "Large Land Sale," *Pulaski Citizen*, November 25, 1875; "Brown and Bright," *Pulaski Citizen*, September 30, 1875; "A Heavy Suit Determined," *Pulaski Citizen*, December 2, 1875; "The Counterfeiters," *Pulaski Citizen*, October 28, 1875; "Counterfeiters," *Memphis Daily Appeal*, September 12, 1875.

81. "New Year's Calls," *Nashville Union and American*, January 1, 1875; "Mrs. Gen. Brown" and "The Reading Club," *Pulaski Citizen*, November 11, 1875; "There was an elegant entertainment," *Pulaski Citizen*, October 7, 1875; "Reception at Gen. Brown's," *Pulaski Citizen*, December 9, 1875.

82. Trefousse, *Andrew Johnson*, 373–77; PAJ 16: 775; "The Senatorship," *Morristown Gazette*, August 11, 1875; "The Senatorial Succession," *Nashville Union and American*, August 7, 1875; "The Senatorship," *Memphis Daily Appeal*, August 12, 1875; "We have had very little to say," *Pulaski Citizen*, August 19, 1875; David M. Abshire, *The South Rejects a Prophet: The Life of Senator D. M. Key 1824–1900* (New York: Praeger, 1967), 65, 72.

83. "It has been announced," *Pulaski Citizen*, December 23, 1875.

8. So as to Confer the Greatest Blessings to the Whole South

1. Richard White, *Railroaded: The Transcontinentals and the Making of Modern America* (New York: W. W. Norton and Co., 2011), 17; John Debo Galloway, *The First Transcontinental Railroad: Central Pacific, Union Pacific* (New York: Simmons-Boardman, 1950), 27–40, 49–51, 60–62.

2. Texas and Pacific Railway, *From Ox-Teams to Eagles: A History of the Texas and Pacific Railway* (Dallas: Texas and Pacific Railway, 1946), 1–5; White, *Railroaded*, 94 ("impregnated"); Albert J. Churella, *The Pennsylvania Railroad,* vol. 1, *Building an Empire, 1846–1917* (Philadelphia: Univ. of Pennsylvania Press, 2012), 420.

3. "A Railroad Prince Dead," *New York Times*, May 22, 1881; White, *Railroaded*, 4–5; T. Loyd Benson and Trina Rossman, "Re-Assessing Tom Scott, the 'Railroad Prince,'" http://eweb.furman.edu/~benson/col-tom.html (accessed July 21, 2013); Churella, *The Pennsylvania Railroad,* 406; "C. M. McGhee and Tom Scott," *Memphis Daily Appeal*, October 25, 1871.

4. Churella, *The Pennsylvania Railroad*, 421–22; White, *Railroaded*, 94, 105–9, 118–33; Mark W. Summers, *Railroads, Reconstruction, and the Gospel of Prosperity: Aid under the Radical Republicans, 1865–1867* (Princeton: Princeton Univ. Press, 1984), 172–73.

5. Churella, *The Pennsylvania Railroad*, 438–441; White, *Messages*, 6:151–52; "C. H. McGhee and Tom Scott" and "Our Railroads," *Memphis Daily Appeal*, October 25, 1871; "Governor Brown a Repudiator," *Memphis Daily Appeal*, October 26, 1871; "Tom Scott and Taxes," *Nashville Union and American*, November 8, 1871; "Northern Capital," *Nashville Union and American,* January 25, 1872; "The Railroad Lease," *Nashville Union and American*, February 25, 1872; "Let Us Have Peace," *Memphis Daily Appeal*, December 13, 1871; "The Press and Tom Scott," *Memphis Daily Appeal*, January 25, 1872; William Joseph MacArthur Jr., "Charles McClung McGhee, Southern Financier," (PhD diss., Univ. of Tennessee, 1975), 75–79. As it turned out, the Southern Railway Security Company was unsuccessful in its effort to gain effective control of all southern lines, and that failure, coupled with the Panic of 1873, resulted in its collapse. Churella, *The Pennsylvania Railroad*, 441–42; Summers, *Railroads, Reconstruction*, 176–77.

6. C. Vann Woodward, *Reunion and Reaction: The Compromise of 1877 and the End of Reconstruction* (Boston: Little, Brown and Company, 1951; New York: Oxford Univ. Press, 1991), 54–63; "State Debts—North Carolina," *Memphis Daily Appeal*, January 31, 1874; "We do not know anything," *Knoxville Whig and Chronicle*, December 8, 1875; White, *Messages*, 6:385.

7. White, *Railroaded*, 30–31, 102–109; Scott R. Nelson, *Iron Confederacies: Southern Railways, Klan Violence, and Reconstruction* (Chapel Hill: Univ. of North

Carolina Press, 1999), 77–81; Woodward, *Reunion and Reaction*, 72–81; "The Legislature," *Pulaski Citizen*, February 18, 1875; "The refusal of the House," *Nashville Union and American*, February 23, 1875; "The Texas Pacific," *Nashville Union and American*, January 12, 1875; "The Texas Pacific Railroad," *Memphis Daily Appeal*, December 6, 1874.

8. Woodward, *Reunion and Reaction*, 79–80, 94; Nelson, *Iron Confederacies*, 94; "The Texas Pacific," *Nashville Union and American*, January 12, 1875; "The Texas and Pacific," *Atlanta Daily Constitution*, January 7, 1876.

9. Woodward, *Reunion and Reaction*, 60–62, 81–84; Cerinda W. Evans, *Collis Potter Huntington* (Newport News, VA: The Mariner's Museum, 1954), 1:252–53.

10. "The Nashville American says," *Galveston Daily News*, December 30, 1875; "Personal," *Washington National Republican*, January 6, 1876; "Ex-Gov. Jno. C. Brown," *Pulaski Citizen*, January 7, 1876; "Capital Topics," *Washington National Republican*, January 20, 1876; "Col Scott on the Ground," *New York Tribune*, January 20, 1876; "The Pacific Railroad Committee," *Washington Evening Star*, January 20, 1876.

11. "Washington," *(Philadelphia) North American and United States Gazette*, February 8, 1876; "Courier-Journal special," *Memphis Public Ledger*, February 9, 1876; "Texas and Pacific Railroad," *Pulaski Citizen*, February 17, 1876; "We have received in pamphlet form," *Memphis Daily Appeal,* February 16, 1876; "Texas and Pacific Railroad," *The (Bloomsburg, Pa.) Columbian*, February 11, 1876.

12. "The Senate Committee on Railways" and "The Enemies of the Texas and Pacific," *Washington National Republican*, March 25, 1876; "The Augusta (Ga.) Chronicle," *Daily Arkansas Gazette*, February 15, 1876; "The Washington correspondent," *Memphis Public Ledger*, January 25, 1876; "Ex-Gov. Isham G. Harris," *Pulaski Citizen*, December 14, 1876.

13. "Fort Worth," *Galveston Daily News*, May 28, 1876; "The State Convention," *Memphis Public Ledger*, June 1, 1876; "Political," *Memphis Daily Appeal*, June 1, 1876; "Tennessee at St. Louis," *Memphis Public Ledger*, June 24, 1876; "St. Louis," *Memphis Daily Appeal*, June 27, 1876; "Well Done," *Memphis Daily Appeal*, June 30, 1876; "Tennessee and Gov. Hendricks," *Bolivar Bulletin*, July 13, 1876.

14. "Brown and Wilkes," *Pulaski Citizen*, January 20, 1876; "A Panoramic View of Pulaski," *Pulaski Citizen*, March 1, 1883; "Judge John S. Wilkes," *Confederate Veteran* 16 (March 1908): 136.

15. "We learn from the Nashville American," *Memphis Public Ledger*, April 27, 1876; "Fort Worth," *Galveston Daily News*, May 28, 1876; "Governor Porter of Tennessee" and "Ex-Governor John C. Brown," *Austin Weekly Democratic Statesman*, April 13, 1876; "Railroad Building in Texas," *Galveston Daily News*,

June 11, 1876; "Current Dots," *Pulaski Citizen*, June 6, 1876; Philip Lindsley, *A History of Greater Dallas and Vicinity* (Chicago: Lewis Publishing Company, 1909), 1:113–14; "Gov. Jno. C. Brown," *Pulaski Citizen*, June 22, 1876.

16. "The Trans-Continental," *Galveston Daily News*, August 12, 1876; "Railroad News," *Galveston Daily News*, September 2, 1876; "Texas papers and correspondents," *Pulaski Citizen*, August 24, 1876; "At the annual meeting," *Memphis Public Ledger*, August 14, 1876; "Ex-Gov. Jno. C. Brown," *Pulaski Citizen*, November 2, 1876; "Monday's Convention," *Pulaski Citizen*, July 6, 1876; "Ex-Governor John C. Brown," *Memphis Daily Appeal*, September 7, 1876.

17. "Gov. Brown is coming all the way from Philadelphia," *Pulaski Citizen*, October 19, 1876; "Pulaski," *Nashville Daily American*, October 18, 1876; "The American of yesterday," *Memphis Public Ledger*, November 11, 1876; "Gov. Jno. C. Brown," *Pulaski Citizen*, November 23, 1876.

18. Woodward, *Reunion and Reaction*, 17–21; "Texas Pacific Railroad," *Washington National Republican*, December 21, 1876; "Capital Notes," *Washington National Republican*, December 22, 1876; "The Texas Pacific," *Washington National Republican*, December 23, 1876.

19. Woodward, *Reunion and Reaction*, 27–28; Grady Tollison, "Andrew J. Kellar, Memphis Republican," *West Tennessee Historical Society Papers* 16 (1962): 29; "Colonel A. J. Kellar's Address," *Memphis Daily Appeal*, September 1, 1872; "Appointing Partisans to the Bench," *Knoxville Chronicle*, September 11, 1872; Hart, *Redeemers, Bourbons and Populists*, 15–22; Jones, *Tennessee at the Crossroads*, 107; Kellar to A. Johnson, 14 November 1874, PAJ 16: 619–20.

20. Tollison, "Andrew J. Kellar, Memphis Republican," 51–53; Woodward, *Reunion and Reaction*, 23–26, 29, 47; Foner, *Reconstruction*, 578; Ari Hoogenboom, *Rutherford B. Hayes: Warrior and President* (Lawrence: Univ. Press of Kansas, 1995), 282–88; Rutherford B. Hayes, *Diary and Letters of Rutherford Birchard Hayes, Nineteenth President of the United States*, ed. Charles Richard Williams (Columbus: The Ohio State Archeological Society, 1922–1926) 3:364.

21. Hoogenboom, *Rutherford B. Hayes*, 283, 288; Foner, *Reconstruction*, 578–79; White, *Railroaded*, 126–27; Woodward, *Reunion and Reaction*, 65–66, 116–21, 149–84, 207–9; see also "The Foster-Matthews Bargain," *Atlanta Daily Constitution*, March 31, 1877.

22. White, *Railroaded*, 124–25; Woodward, *Reunion and Reaction*, 113–16, 126–35, 174–77.

23. Woodward, *Reunion and Reaction*, 31–32, 49, 169–70; Abshire, *The South Rejects a Prophet*, 112–19, 123, 125–26; Elliott, *Isham G. Harris*, 220–28; Hart, *Redeemers, Bourbons and Populists*, 24n30. Abshire suggested that Brown worked for Key against Bailey, which Hart deemed unlikely. Brown and Bailey were confined at Fort Warren together in 1862.

24. "Tilden's Confidence," *Atlanta Daily Constitution*, December 3, 1876; Woodward, *Reunion and Reaction*, 36–49; 168–69; "Ex-Gov. Brown," *Pulaski Citizen*, May 3, 1877. Several aspects of Woodward's thesis relative to the Compromise of 1877 have been attacked in the over fifty years since *Reunion and Reaction* appeared. See White, *Railroaded*, 127 (the decisiveness of Scott's influence on Hayes's emerging as president has been "discredited"); Michael Les Benedict, "Southern Democrats in the Crisis of 1876–1877: A Reconsideration of Reunion and Reaction," *The Journal of Southern History* 46 (November 1980): 489, 494 (Woodward "greatly overestimated" both the role southerners played in moderating Democratic opposition to Hayes and the part the railroad played in influencing the southerners); Allan Peskin, "Was There a Compromise of 1877?" *The Journal of American History* 60 (June 1973): 63–75 (the fact that few of the components of the purported deal came to fruition shows there was no agreement). But see C. Vann Woodward, "Yes, There Was a Compromise of 1877," *The Journal of American History* 60 (June 1973): 215–23. As historian Mark Summers recently wrote, *Reunion and Reaction* is "so well written, it deserves to be right." Summers, *The Ordeal of the Reunion*, 452n26.

25. Hayes, *Diary and Letters of Rutherford Birchard Hayes*, 416–17; Woodward, *Reunion and Reaction*, 169; "Washington," *Memphis Daily Appeal*, October 10, 1877 ; "The Texas-Pacific Subsidy," *Bangor Daily Whig and Courier*, April 14, 1877; "Hayes and His Cabinet," *Bolivar Bulletin*, April 19, 1877; Ben Perley Poore, *Perley's Reminiscences of Sixty Years in the National Metropolis* (Philadelphia: Hubbard Brothers, 1886), 2:341; "State News," *Milan Exchange*, March 22, 1877; Abshire, *The South Rejects a Prophet*, 145–52.

26. "Ex-Gov. Brown," *Pulaski Citizen*, May 3, 1877; Abshire, *The South Rejects a Prophet*, 195.

27. Edwin Erle Sparks, *National Development, 1877–1885* (New York: Harper and Brothers, 1907), 89–92; Garnie W. McGinty, *Louisiana Redeemed: The Overthrow of Carpet-Bag Rule 1876–1880* (1941; reprint. Gretna, LA: Firebird Press, 1999), 116–17; "Anarchy in Louisiana," *New York Times*, April 13, 1877; Mary Gorton McBride, *Randall Lee Gibson of Louisiana: Confederate General and New South Reformer* (Baton Rouge: Louisiana State Univ. Press, 2007), 166–67.

28. McBride, *Gibson*, 168; Sparks, *National Development*, 91; "The President" *Ouachita (Monroe, La.) Telegraph*, April 6, 1877.

29. Abshire, *The South Rejects a Prophet*, 161; JCB to Key, 21 March 1877 (at 12:40 a.m.), and JCB to Key, 21 March 1877 (at 5:40 p.m.), both in David M. Key Papers, Chattanooga Public Library (hereafter cited as Key Papers); *Pulaski Citizen*, March 22, 1877; "The Louisiana Commission," *New York Times*, March 23, 1877; "Ex-Gov. Brown," *Pulaski Citizen*, May 3, 1877; "Gov.

Jno. C. Brown," *Pulaski Citizen*, March 29, 1877. Oddly, Brown denied his original acceptance in an interview with the *Atlanta Constitution* a few days later. "Louisiana's Jury," *Atlanta Constitution*, March 31, 1877; "Ex-Gov. Brown," *Pulaski Citizen*, May 3, 1877.

30. "Ex-Gov. Brown"; "Louisiana's Jury"; "The Louisiana Commission," *Richland (Rayville, La.) Beacon*, March 31, 1877; "The new Louisiana Commission is determined," *Fayetteville Observer*, April 5, 1877; "The Louisiana Commission," *Atlanta Constitution*, March 29, 1877; "A party organ," *Austin Weekly Democratic Statesman*, March 29, 1877; "Gov. Jno. C. Brown," *Pulaski Citizen*, March 29, 1877.

31. "Ex-Gov. Brown"; "Louisiana's Jury"; Porter to Key, 29 March 1877, Key Papers; "The Pulaski Citizen," *Pulaski Citizen*, April 5, 1877; "Ex-Gov. John C. Brown," *Cincinnati Daily Gazette*, March 30, 1877.

32. "Louisiana's Jury."

33. Executive Doc. No. 97, "Commission Sent by the President to Louisiana in April, 1877," *Index to the Executive Documents of the House of Representatives For the Second Session of the Forty-Fifth Congress, 1877–78,* vol. 17 (Washington, DC: Government Printing Office, 1878), 2–3; "Their Scope and Duty," *Atlanta Constitution*, April 4, 1877; McGinty, *Louisiana Redeemed*, 118; "The Louisiana Commission," *Washington National Republican*, April 3, 1877; "Louisiana Commission," *Washington National Republican*, April 10, 1877; "The Commission at Work," *Washington National Republican*, April 13, 1877; "The Fortunate Five," *Atlanta Constitution*, April 24, 1877; "Louisiana's Jury."

34. "The Fortunate Five"; "Ex-Gov. Brown"; "Their Scope and Duty"; Ex. Doc. 97, p. 3.

35. "Ex-Gov. Brown"; "Under Brown's Eye," *Atlanta Constitution*, April 20, 1877; "The Thieves' Quarrel," *Atlanta Constitution*, April 21, 1877; "Louisiana," *Atlanta Constitution*, April 22, 1877; Ex. Doc. 97, pp. 4–15; Woodward, *Reunion and Reaction*, 219–20.

36. "Louisiana"; "The Fortunate Five"; "Changed Their Tune," *Pulaski Citizen*, May 10, 1877; "Ex-Gov. John C. Brown," *Pulaski Citizen*, May 3, 1877.

37. "Order Out of Chaos," *Washington National Republican*, April 26, 1877; "Ex-Gov. Brown."

38. Woodward, *Reunion and Reaction*, 222–24; *New York Herald-Tribune*, June 11, 1877, and September 20, 1877; "Houston Local Items," *Galveston Daily News*, May 11, 1877; "The State Capital," *Galveston Daily News*, May 13, 1877; "Vice-President John C. Brown," *Galveston Daily News*, August 30, 1877; "Pulaski Pickings," *Nashville Daily American*, June 14, 1877; "Ex-Governor John C. Brown," *Memphis Public Ledger*, October 2, 1877; "Lynnville," *Memphis Public Ledger*, October 4, 1877; "Down in Dixie," *Atlanta Daily Constitution*, October 7, 1877.

39. Woodward, *Reunion and Reaction*, 230–35; Evans, *Collis Potter Huntington*, 1:261–62; "A Chance," *Memphis Daily Appeal*, October 5, 1877.

40. White, *Railroaded*, 120–21 (Huntington quote); Caldwell, *Sketches of the Bench and Bar*, 294; "Aid for Pacific Railroads," *New York Times*, January 27, 1878; John C. Brown, *Argument of John C. Brown, Vice President Texas and Pacific Railway Company before House Committee on Pacific Railroads, January 25, 1878, in Behalf of the Texas and Pacific Railway Company* (Washington: Thomas McGill and Co., 1878); "The Federal Focus," *Atlanta Daily Constitution*, February 23, 1878; "Governor John C. Brown," *Memphis Daily Appeal*, February 27, 1878.

41. "Texas and Pacific Railway" and "Governor John C. Brown," Atlanta *Daily Constitution*, February 19, 1878.

42. "Our Capital Letter," *Memphis Daily Appeal*, March 8, 1878.

43. "Ex-Gov. Brown," *Memphis Daily Appeal*, March 12, 1878; "Our Capital Letter," *Memphis Daily Appeal*, March 19, 1878.

44. "Our Capital Letter," *Memphis Daily Appeal*, April 17, 1878; "The Texas and Pacific Railroad," *New York Times*, April 19, 1878; "Our Capital Letter," *Memphis Daily Appeal*, April 23, 1878; "Our Capital Letter," *Memphis Daily Appeal*, May 11, 1878; "Still on the Boards," *Daily Arkansas Gazette*, May 17, 1878; "Uncle Daniel Drew," *(Macon)Georgia Weekly Telegraph*, May 21, 1878.

45. "The Work of Congress," *Washington Post*, May 15, 1878; "Telegraphic Items from Washington," *San Francisco Daily Evening Bulletin*, June 10, 1878; "What the Texas Pacific Wants, *San Francisco Daily Evening Bulletin*, June 20, 1878; "Washington Correspondence," *Georgia Weekly Telegraph*, May 21, 1878.

46. Jones, *Tennessee at the Crossroads*, 85–96; Hart, *Redeemers, Bourbons and Populists*, 28–30.

47. "Tennessee All Right," *Washington Post*, August 19, 1878. As the epidemic spread, Brown was noted to have made a contribution to the Howard Association, which was succoring the yellow fever victims. "Increasing and Spreading," *Memphis Daily Appeal*, October 17, 1878.

48. Churella, *The Pennsylvania Railroad*, 1:425; "Editorial Correspondence," *Georgia Weekly Telegraph*, December 17, 1878.

49. "Southern Pacific Railroad—Governor John C. Brown," *Memphis Daily Appeal*, March 12, 1879; "The Texas and Pacific," *Washington Post*, February 21, 1879; "Editorial Correspondence," *Georgia Weekly Telegraph and Georgia Journal & Messenger*, February 18, 1879.

50. Jones, *Tennessee at the Crossroads*, 99–105; Hart, *Redeemers, Bourbons and Populists*, 40–48; "The State Capital," *Memphis Daily Appeal*, March 29, 1879; "State Credit," *Memphis Daily Appeal*, April 5, 1879; "The Tennessee Committee in Conference with Leading Bankers," *Milan Exchange*, April 24, 1879;

"The Debt of Tennessee," *New York Times*, April 19, 1879; "The Debt of Tennessee," *Memphis Public Ledger*, April 25, 1879; "Political Opinions," *Washington Post*, August 16, 1879.

51. "Southern Pacific Railroad—Governor John C. Brown," *Memphis Daily Appeal*, March 12, 1879; "Over the State," *Milan Exchange*, October 2, 1879; "Ex-Governor John C. Brown," *Memphis Public Ledger*, January 12, 1881; *(Austin) Weekly Democratic Statesman*, March 25, 1880; "The Courts," *Washington Post*, March 7, 1879; *Hough v. Railway Company*, 100 U. S. 213 (1879).

52. White, *Railroaded*, 127–28.

53. "Ex-Governor Brown," *Memphis Daily Appeal*, November 12, 1879; "Brown," *Memphis Daily Appeal*, November 28, 1879; Julius Grodinsky, *Jay Gould, His Business Career, 1867–1892* (Philadelphia: Univ. of Pennsylvania Press, 1957), 253–56; "Through to California," *Austin Weekly Democratic Statesman*, December 25, 1879.

9. I Have Great Faith in the Outcome of the Texas and Pacific

1. "Jay Gould's Syndicate," *New York Sun,* December 16, 1879; John Thomas Scharf, *History of Saint Louis City and County From the Earliest Periods to the Present Day, Including Biographical Sketches of Representative Men* (Philadelphia: Louis H. Evarts and Co., 1883), 2:1178.

2. "Jay Gould is Dead," *New York Evening World*, December 2, 1892; Maury Klein, *The Life and Legend of Jay Gould* (Baltimore: Johns Hopkins Univ. Press, 1986), 15–17, 49–115, 137–75, 493; Grodinsky, *Jay Gould*, 22–23, 261–62; "Jay Gould and Party," *The Daily Cairo (Ill.) Bulletin*, January 15, 1882.

3. Robert Edgar Riegel, *The Story of the Western Railroads* (New York: Macmillan, 1926) 161–72; Klein, *Jay Gould*, 258–59; Grodinsky, *Jay Gould*, 261–62.

4. Klein, *Jay Gould*, 168–75, 258 (quote); White, *Railroaded*, 124–25, 205–6.

5. "Texas-Pacific Extension," *New York Times*, January 6, 1880; "Pulaski," *Nashville Daily American*, February 5, 1880.

6. "Pulaski," *Nashville Daily American*, February 5, 1880; "Governor John C. Brown's family," *Memphis Public Ledger*, February 7, 1880; "The Marshall (Tex.) Messenger," *The Ouachita Telegraph,* January 23, 1880; "The Nashville Centennial," *Memphis Public Ledger*, April 28, 1880; "Pulaski," *Nashville Daily American*, September 2, 1880; "Personal," *Memphis Public Ledger*, April 4, 1881.

7. "Over the State," *Galveston Daily News*, May 5, 1880; "The Dallas and Wichita Railroad," *Brenham Weekly Banner,* May 7, 1880; "Southern Gleanings," *The Milan Exchange*, May 13, 1880; "Gov. Brown Calls on the Next President," *Nashville Daily American*, July 4, 1880; "A Tennessean on Texas," *Galveston Daily News*, July 10, 1880.

8. "United States Railways," *Dallas Daily Herald*, August 14, 1880; "The Texas and Pacific Railroad," *New York Times*, August 11, 1880; "Other Rail News," *(Chicago) Daily Inter-Ocean*, November 12, 1880; "Col. Tom Scott and Party," *Galveston Daily News*, November 19, 1880; "The Texas Pacific Road," *Memphis Public Ledger*, November 16, 1880; "On the occasion," *Galveston Daily News*, November 27, 1880; "Governor John C. Brown" *Austin Weekly Democratic Statesman*, December 2, 1880; "Sketches of the Bench and Bar of Tennessee, *Nashville American*, September 20, 1897.

9. "Washington," *Boston Daily Advertiser*, December 28, 1880; Hart, *Redeemers, Bourbons and Populists*, 56–71; "John C. Brown's" *Memphis Daily Appeal*, October 7, 1880; "Ex-Gov. Brown on the Tennessee Situation," *Nashville Daily American*, February 21, 1882; Jones, *Tennessee at the Crossroads*, 128–42; Elliott, *Isham G. Harris*, 249–60.

10. "Railroad Matters" *Dallas Daily Herald*, January 22, 1881; "Thirty Miles of the T & P Received," *Dallas Daily Herald*, January 28, 1881; JCB to Dodge, 28 March 1881, G. M. Dodge Papers, Iowa Historical Society (hereafter cited as Dodge Papers); "Marshall," *Dallas Daily Herald*, April 21, 1881; "Railroad Magnates—The Texas & Pacific," *Dallas Daily Herald*, April 27, 1881; "Complimentary Reception," *Dallas Daily Herald*, May 18, 1881; "Pulaski," *Nashville Daily American*, May 5, 1881.

11. "Sketches of the Bench and Bar of Tennessee," *Nashville American*, September 20, 1897; White, *Railroaded*, 205–6; "The Texas Pacific and the Southern Pacific Lock Horns," *Galveston Daily News*, July 8, 1881; "The Texas & Pacific v. the Southern Pacific," *Dallas Daily Herald*, July 27, 1881.

12. "Sketches of the Bench and Bar of Tennessee," *Nashville American*, September 20, 1897; "Vanderbilt and Gould," *Galveston Daily News*, August 18, 1881; "Sad News," *Fort Worth Daily Gazette*, August 18, 1889; "Gould's Railroads," *Daily Arkansas Gazette*, October 1, 1881; "We learn from the St. Louis *Republican*," *Memphis Daily Appeal*, October 1, 1881; "Pulaski," *Nashville Daily American*, October 16, 1881 "Pulaski," *Nashville Daily American*, October 20, 1881; "We clip the following from the St. Louis Republican," *Dallas Daily Herald*, October 12, 1881; Klein, *Jay Gould*, 260; White, *Railroaded*, 196–97.

13. *The executive documents, printed by order of the Senate of the United States for the first session of the forty-eighth Congress, 1883–'84* (1884), Ex. Doc. No. 27, pp. 4–7; "The Land Grant Lobby," *Washington Post*, January 2, 1884; Evans, *Collis Porter Huntington*, 1:262–63; "Across the Continent," *Galveston Daily News*, March 1, 1882; "Gov. Brown at St. Louis," *Nashville Daily American*, April 3, 1882; "Gov. Brown Off for Mexico," *Nashville Daily American*, November 26, 1882; "Solicitor Brown on the Gould System," *St. Louis Globe-Democrat*, October 2, 1882; "Legal Appointments," *St. Louis Globe-Democrat*, January 4, 1882; "The Courts," *Washington Post*, April 4, 1884; "Home News,"

Austin Weekly Statesman, November 27, 1884; "Local News," *Dallas Daily Herald*, November 30, 1884; "The Gould Quo Warranto Suits," *Worthington (Minn.) Advance*, March 5, 1885.

14. "Austin," *Ft. Worth Daily Gazette*, March 23, 1883; "Railway Interests," *New York Tribune*, March 26, 1882; "Gov. John C. Brown," *Brenham Weekly Banner,* April 20, 1882; "The Railroads," *St. Louis Globe-Democrat*, October 19, 1883; "National Notes," *St. Louis Globe-Democrat*, January 27, 1884; "Interstate Commerce," *Ft. Worth Daily Gazette*, January 27, 1884; "The Texas Law Factory," *Ft. Worth Daily Democrat*, April 18, 1883; Dodge to JCB, 31 January 1884, Dodge Papers; "Railroad Grants," *(St. Paul) Daily Globe*, May 8, 1884; Dodge to JCB, 7 and 13 March 1884, Dodge Papers; "The Backbone Land Grant," *Colfax (La.) Chronicle*, April 4, 1885.

15. "The Florida Ship Canal," *Atlanta Constitution*, June 9, 1883; "Tennessee Capitalists in the Florida Ship Canal," *Memphis Public Ledger*, June 12, 1883; "The Florida Ship Canal," *Washington Post*, August 18, 1883; "A Cut Across Florida," *Washington Post*, August 21, 1883; Nelson M. Blake, *Land Into Water—Water into Land: A History of Water Management in Florida* (Tallahassee: Univ. Presses of Florida, 1980), 84; "An Internal Improvement," *Evening Critic*, January 4, 1884; "Notes of Various Interests," *New York Times*, November 10, 1883; "From Dallas," *Galveston Daily News*, April 9, 1884.

16. "St. Louis Letter," *Dallas Weekly Herald*, June 28, 1883; "Over the State," *Galveston Daily News*, February 23, 1884.

17. "To all Tennessee Ex-Confederate Captains," *Memphis Public Ledger*, September 22, 1882; "Confederate Reunion at McKinney, Texas," *Memphis Public Ledger*, July 11, 1883; "Pulaski," *Nashville Daily American*, November 12, 1883; "The nomination of a Southern man," *Memphis Public Ledger*, September 25, 1883; "The Memphis Appeal," *Milan Exchange*, September 29, 1883; "A Correspondent is right," *Memphis Daily Appeal*, September 6, 1884.

18. United States House of Representatives, *Investigation of Labor Troubles in Missouri, Arkansas, Kansas, Texas, and Illinois*, 2 parts (1887), 49th Congress, 2nd Session, Report No. 4174, 1:184, 192; "Affairs at Dallas," *Galveston Daily News*, June 10, 1884; "The New York Financial Chronicle," *Galveston Daily News*, December 5, 1884; "Texas and Pacific Reorganization Plan," *Dallas Daily Herald*, December 11, 1884; "Texas and Pacific Finances," *New York Times*, March 4, 1885; Klein, *Jay Gould*, 350; "The Many Friends," *Dallas Daily Herald*, April 29, 1885; "Railroad Accident," *Perrysburg (Ohio) Journal*, May 1, 1885; "A Bad Smash," *Jasper (Ind.) Weekly Courier*, May 8, 1885.

19. Theresa A. Case, *The Great Southwest Railroad Strike and Free Labor* (College Station: Texas A&M Univ. Press, 2010), 100–1, 108–17; Melvyn Dubofsky and Foster Rhea Dulles, *Labor in America: A History* (Wheeling, IL: Harlan Davidson, 2004), 128; *Investigation of Labor Troubles*, 1:i–iv.

20. Dubofsky and Dulles, *Labor in America*, 118–27.
21. *Investigation of Labor Troubles*, 1:3–4, 352–53.
22. "Death of Miss Daisy Brown," *Pulaski Citizen*, August 13, 1885; "Taken to Pulaski," *Nashville Daily American*, August 21, 1889; Elliott, ed., *Doctor Quintard*, 118.
23. Klein, *Jay Gould*, 350; *Investigation of Labor Troubles*, 1:184.
24. *Investigation of Labor Troubles*, 1:189–97.
25. "In the Hands of Receivers," *New York Times*, December 17, 1885; "Lionel A. Sheldon," *Donaldsonville (La.) Chief*, February 3, 1917; *Investigation of Labor Troubles*, 1:175, 209; *Biographical Dictionary of the United States Congress*, q. v. Sheldon, Lionel Allen; "Gould's Grab Game, " *(Abbeville, La.) Meridional*, January 30, 1886; "Judge John S. Wilkes," *Confederate Veteran* 16 (March 1908): 136.
26. *Investigation of Labor Troubles*, 1:175–76, 205, 213.
27. McBride and Robison, *Biographical Directory*, II:583–4; "Under the Marriage Bell," *New York Times*, January 6, 1886; "Brilliant Nuptials in Tennessee," *Atlanta Daily Constitution*, January 6, 1886; "It is Principally Personal," *Dallas Morning News*, January 11, 1886.
28. "It is Principally Personal," *Dallas Morning News*, January 11, 1886; "Texas Pacific Receivership," *New York Herald*, January 10, 1886; "Fighting for a Railroad," *New York Times*, January 11, 1886; "Railings," *Fort Worth Daily Gazette*, January 25, 1886; JCB to Grenville Dodge, 21 January 1886, Dodge Papers.
29. "Neill S. Brown," *(Jonesborough) Herald and Tribune*, February 4, 1886; "Local Paragraphs," *Memphis Daily Appeal*, June 2, 1878; "Harry A. Brown," *Memphis Public Ledger*, June 20, 1882; "Nashville," *Memphis Daily Appeal*, February 19, 1881; "50–4?," *Memphis Public Ledger*, September 28, 1882; "Nashville," *Memphis Public Ledger*, June 22, 1882; "Governor Bate's Luncheon," *Memphis Public Ledger*, May 29, 1883.
30. Maury Klein, *Jay Gould*, 358; Case, *The Great Southwest Railroad Strike and Free Labor*, 155–59.
31. *Investigation of Labor Troubles*, 1:173,176, 180, 317; White, *Railroaded*, 337.
32. Case, *The Great Southwest Railroad Strike and Free Labor*, 159, 164–65; "This End of the Wedge," *San Marcos (Tex.) Free Press*, April 1, 1886; *Investigation of Labor Troubles*, 1:176, 202, 204, 209.
33. *Investigation of Labor Troubles*, 1:xii, 176–77.
34. Ibid., 1:177–78.
35. Ibid., 1:181–82.
36. Ibid., 1:xiii, xvii, 179–80; "The Gould System Strike," *New York Times*, March 6, 1886.
37. Klein, *Jay Gould*, 358–60; *Investigation of Labor Troubles*, 1:179–82.

38. Klein, *Jay Gould*, 360–63; Case, *The Great Southwest Railroad Strike and Free Labor*, 222–23; "The Doom of the Boycott," *Fort Worth Daily Gazette*, March 21, 1886; "Working Men's War," *Sedalia Weekly Bazoo*, March 17, 1886; "The Railroad Strike," *Salt Lake Daily Tribune*, March 14, 1886; *Investigation of Labor Troubles*, 1:xx, 302

39. *Investigation of Labor Troubles*, 1:186–89; "Investigating Committee, *Austin Weekly Statesman*, May 3, 1886; "Crain's Sub-committee," *Fort Worth Daily Gazette*, May 11, 1886.

40. Dodge to JCB, 8 and 13 March 1886, and 23 April 1886, all in Dodge Papers; "Texas and Pacific," *New York Times*, July 14, 1886; MacArthur, "Charles McClung McGhee, Southern Financier," 151–53; JCB to C. M. McGhee, 3 August 1886, C. M. McGhee Papers, Lawson-McGhee Library, Knoxville, TN (hereafter cited as McGhee Papers); "English Steel Rail Despite Tariffs," *Baltimore Sun*, August 6, 1886.

41. Isaac Jones Wistar, *Autobiography: 1827–1905* (New York: Harper and Brothers, 1914), 2:150–53; MacArthur, "Charles McClung McGhee, Southern Financier," 148, 153–55; JCB to C. M. McGhee, 20 October 1887, McGhee Papers.

42. "In Old Giles," *Nashville Daily American*, November 2, 1886; "Pulaski," *Nashville Daily American*, November 18, 1886; "The Tennessee Senatorship," *New York Times*, January 3, 1887.

43. "Railroad Matters," *Galveston Daily News*, January 2, 1887; "The Railway World," *Galveston Daily News*, February 25, 1887; "Debating Rate Problems," *New York Times*, February 25, 1887.

44. JCB to C. M. McGhee, 6 August 1887, John A. Grant to C. M. McGhee, 8 December 1887, and JCB to C. M. McGhee, 17 December 1887, all in McGhee Papers; "Texas and Pacific Railroad Affairs," *St. Louis Globe-Democrat*, October 23, 1887; "Texas," *New Orleans Daily Picayune*, November 6, 1887; "News About the Railroads," *Dallas Morning News*, November 8, 1887; "Texas and Pacific Sold," *Galveston Daily News*, November 9, 1887; "The Texas Pacific Railroad," *Colfax (La.) Chronicle*, November 19, 1887; "The Railroads," *Fort Worth Daily Gazette*, December 2, 1887; Klein, *Jay Gould*, 411.

45. "Local Brevities," *Giles County Democrat*, December 7, 1887; "Death of an Estimable Lady," *Giles County Democrat*, December 14, 1887; "Rest, Eternal Rest," *Galveston Daily News*, August 18, 1889; "Pulaski's New Church," *Nashville Daily American*, December 18, 1887.

46. JCB to C. M. McGhee, 13 January 1888, and R. Fleming to C. M. McGhee, 7 August 1888, both in McGhee Papers; MacArthur, "Charles McClung McGhee, Southern Financier," 157–60.

47. "Why Set Aside," *Galveston Daily News*, February 1, 1888; "The Texas and Pacific," *Galveston Daily News*, March 14, 1888; Klein, *Jay Gould*, 411; "State News," *San Antonio Daily Light*, May 2, 1888; JCB to C. M. McGhee,

13 January 1888, I. J. Wistar to C. M. McGhee, 27 April 1888, and JCB to McGhee, 28 July 1888, all in McGhee Papers; MacArthur, "Charles McClung McGhee, Southern Financier," 156–57; "The Governor John C. Brown," *New Orleans Daily Picayune*, July 22, 1888.

48. "Tennessee Democrats Declare for Cleveland," *Washington Post*, May 11, 1888; "Political Odds and Ends," *New York Times*, December 18, 1888; see also "Political Situation," *Galveston Daily News*, January 29, 1889.

49. "Texas and Pacific Railway," *New Orleans Daily Picayune*, October 31, 1888; "In Gould's Grasp Again," *New York Times*, March 7, 1889; "Railroad Interests," *New York Tribune*, March 7, 1889; "Railroad Rumblings," *San Antonio Daily Express*, March 8, 1889; "The Texas Legislature," *Galveston Daily News*, January 29, 1889; "The Railroad Bill," *McKinney (Tex.) Democrat*, February 28, 1889.

50. MacArthur, "Charles McClung McGhee, Southern Financier," 156–61.

51. "A Sketch of the Deceased," *Nashville Daily American*, August 18, 1889; "Why Governor Brown Resigned," *New Orleans Daily Picayune*, April 15, 1889; "The Change in Management," *Atlanta Daily Constitution*, April 2, 1889; Ethel Armes, *The Story of Coal and Iron in Alabama* (Birmingham, AL: Chamber of Commerce, 1910), 360–93; "Ex-Gov. John C. Brown," *Nashville Daily Evening Herald*, August 17, 1889.

52. "The Railroad Budget," *Galveston Daily News*, April 7, 1889; "Railroad Notes," *Pulaski Citizen*, April 18, 1889; "Ex-Gov. John C. Brown," *Nashville Daily Evening Herald*, August 17, 1889.

53. White, *Railroaded*, xxviii (quote); Klein, *Jay Gould*, 411.

54. "Good-Bye to Governor Brown," *Pulaski Citizen*, May 2, 1889; "Gov. John C. Brown," *McKinney (Tex.) Democrat*, April 11, 1889; "Complimentary Resolutions," *Dallas Morning News*, May 15, 1889; "A Handsome Testimonial," *Galveston Daily News*, July 5, 1889; "Dallas," *Fort Worth Daily Gazette*, July 11, 1889.

55. "Cool Breezes at Cape May," *Philadelphia Inquirer*, August 2, 1889; "John C. Brown," *Cincinnati Commercial Tribune*, August 18, 1889; "Ex-Gov. Brown Dead," *Knoxville Journal*, August 18, 1889; "Ex-Gov. John C. Brown," *Nashville Evening Herald*, August 17, 1889; "The State Mourns," *Giles County Democrat*, August 21, 1889.

56. "Ex-Gov. Brown Dead," *Knoxville Journal*, August 18, 1889; "Ex-Gov. John C. Brown," *Nashville Evening Herald*, August 17, 1889; "An Honored Man," *Nashville Sunday Herald*, August 18, 1889; Butler, "The Life of John C. Brown," 117–18.

57. "Death of Ex-Governor Brown," *Knoxville Journal*, August 19, 1889; "John C. Brown," *Memphis Daily Avalanche*, August 18, 1889; "The Late John C. Brown," *Nashville Daily American*, August 26, 1889; "The State Mourns,"

Giles County Democrat, August 21, 1889; "Asleep in Death," *Pulaski Citizen*, August 22, 1889; "Governor Brown Dead," *Fort Worth Weekly Gazette*, August 22, 1889.

58. Ancestry.com, Tennessee Death Records, 1908–1958, http://search.ancestry .com/cgi-bin/sse.dll?indiv=try&db=TNDeathRecords&h=226914 (accessed July 5, 2015) (hereafter "Tennessee Death Records, 1908-1958"); "National Daughters of the Confederacy," *Confederate Veteran* 2 (October, 1894): 306; "United Confederate Daughters," *Confederate Veteran* 4 (January, 1896): 22; Caroline E. Janney, *Remembering the Civil War: Reunion and the Limits of Reconciliation* (Chapel Hill, NC: Univ. of North Carolina Press, 2013), 243; Gaines M. Foster, *Ghosts of the Confederacy: Defeat, the Lost Cause, and the Emergence of the New South, 1865 to 1913* (New York: Oxford Univ. Press, 1987), 116; Gilchrist, *Some Representative Women of Tennessee*, 12–16; Tennessee Biographical Questionnaires, TSLA; "A Society Event of the Civil War."

59. United States Census, 1900, Davidson County, Tennessee; "Mrs. Elizabeth Brown Burch," *Confederate Veteran* 12 (October 1904): 498–99; Tennessee Death Records, 1908–1958; Newman, *Brown Family Timeline*, 32; *Burch v. McMillin*, 15 S. W. 2d 86 (Tex. App. 1929).

60. John C. Brown Burch grave monument, Elmwood Cemetery, Memphis; "Memphis Alumnus Takes Presidency," *Sewanee Alumni News* 23 (November 1957): 3.

61. "Gov. Brown's Monument," *Pulaski Citizen*, February 19, 1891; John C. Brown grave monument, Maplewood Cemetery, Pulaski.

62. Caldwell, *Studies in the Constitutional History of Tennessee*, 296

63. White, *Messages*, 6:394.

64. "The Late John C. Brown," *(McMinnville) Southern Standard*, August 24, 1889.

Bibliography

PRIMARY SOURCES

Manuscript

Alexander P. Stewart Letter, in author's possession.
Chattanooga Public Library, Chattanooga, Tennessee
    David M. Key Papers
Chickamauga and Chattanooga National Military Park
    Third Tennessee File
        John Calhoun Higdon-Experiences and Life During the Civil War
    Twentieth Tennessee File
        Milton P. Jarnigan Reminiscences
Duke University, Durham, North Carolina
    Perkins Library
        James Longstreet Papers
        Pope-Carter Family Papers
    David M. Rubenstein Rare Book and Manuscript Library
        Confederate States of America Collection, 1850–1876
            Roll of Third Tennessee Regiment
Eastern Kentucky University, Richmond, Kentucky
    Thomas Osborne Papers
Florida State Library, Tallahassee, Florida
    Washington M. Ives Papers
Georgia Historical Society, Savannah, Georgia
    Confederate States Army Papers
Huntington Library, San Marino, California
    Simon Bolivar Buckner Collection
Lawson-McGhee Library, Knoxville, Tennessee
    C. M. McGhee Papers
Museum of the Confederacy, Richmond, Virginia
    Eleanor S. Brockenbrough Library
        Carter Stevenson Papers
        Ft. Donelson/Lloyd Tighlman Files

Morristown, and Morris Township Library North New Jersey History and Genealogy Center

    George Wise Diary

State Historical Society of Iowa, Des Moines, Iowa

    Grenville Mellon Dodge Papers

Tennessee State Library and Archives, Nashville, Tennessee

    David S. Bodenhamer Sketch

    John C. Brown Governor's Papers

    Gov. John C. Brown Autograph Album

    Neill S. Brown Governor's Papers

    G. W. Dillon Diary

    Lucy Virginia French Diary

    Thomas Hopkins Deavenport Diary

    Giles County Miscellaneous Records

        Louis Adams Diary

    Joseph Branch O'Bryan Papers

    Gen. Joseph B. Palmer Autograph Album

    James D. Porter Governor's Papers

    Tennessee Biographical Questionnaires

    Tennessee Election Returns

        Referendum of Secession Convention of the State of Tennessee and the Election of Delegates

University of Alabama, W. S. Hoole Special Collections

    Henry D. Clayton Papers

University of Florida, Smathers Libraries, Special and Area Studies Collections, P.K. Yonge Library of Florida History

    James Patton Anderson Papers

University of Georgia, Hargrett Rare Book and Manuscript Library

    Stone Family Papers

        Correspondence of Robert G. Stone

University of North Carolina, Chapel Hill

    Southern Historical Collection, Wilson Library

        William W. Mackall Papers

University of the South, Sewanee, University Archives and Special Collections

    Charles Todd Quintard Collection

        Charles Todd Quintard Diary

Western Kentucky University, Department of Library Special Collections

    Michael Walsh Cluskey Papers

Western Reserve Historical Society, Cleveland, Ohio

    William P. Palmer Collection of Braxton Bragg Papers

Newspapers

Anderson (SC) Intelligencer
Athens (GA) Southern Banner
Athens (TN) Post
Atlanta Constitution
Atlanta Journal
Atlanta Southern Confederacy
Augusta (GA) Chronicle
Austin Weekly Democratic Statesman
Baltimore Sun
Bangor Daily Whig and Courier
Boston Daily Advertiser
Boston Herald
Brenham Weekly Banner
Chattanooga Daily Rebel
Cincinnati Commercial Tribune
Clarksville Weekly Chronicle
Colfax (LA) Weekly Chronicle
Columbia Herald
Daily Arkansas Gazette
Daily Columbus Enquirer
Daily Nashville Patriot
Daily Nashville True Whig
Daily Evening Bulletin (Cairo, IL)
Daily Globe (St. Paul, MN)
Daily Inter-Ocean (Chicago, IL)
Dallas Daily Herald
Dallas Weekly Herald
Donaldsonville (LA) Chief
Evening Critic (Washington, DC)
Fayetteville Observer
Fort Worth Daily Gazette
Flake's Bulletin (Galveston, TX)
Galveston Daily News
Georgia Weekly Telegraph (Macon, GA)
Giles County Democrat
Herald and Tribune (Jonesborough, TN)
Jackson Whig and Tribune
Jasper (IN) Weekly Courier
Janesville (WI) Gazette
Knoxville Daily Chronicle

Knoxville Journal
Knoxville Register
Knoxville Weekly Whig and Chronicle
Knoxville Whig
Louisville Daily Journal
Macon Daily Telegraph
McKinney (TX) Democrat
Southern Standard (McMinnville, TN)
Memphis Commercial Appeal
Memphis Daily Avalanche
Memphis Daily Appeal
Memphis Public Ledger
Memphis Sunday Appeal
Milan Exchange
Nashville American
Nashville Banner
Nashville Daily American
Nashville Evening Herald
Nashville Republican Banner
Nashville Sunday Herald
Nashville Tennessean
Nashville Union and American
Nashville Union and Dispatch
National Tribune
New Hampshire Patriot
New Orleans Daily Picayune
New York Evening World
New York Herald
New York Herald-Tribune
New York Sun
New York Times
North American and United States Gazette (Philadelphia, PA)
The Ouachita Telegraph (Monroe, LA)
Perrysburg (OH) Journal
Philadelphia Evening Telegraph
Philadelphia Inquirer
Pulaski Citizen
Pulaski Gazette
Pulaski Western Star
Richmond Daily Dispatch
Richmond Examiner

Richland Beacon (Rayville, LA)
Salt Lake Daily Tribune
San Antonio Daily Express
San Antonio Daily Light
San Francisco Daily Evening Bulletin
San Marcos (TX) Free Press
Sedalia (MO) Weekly Bazoo
St. Louis Globe-Democrat
Sweetwater Enterprise (TN)
The Columbian (Bloomsburg, PA)
Washington Evening Star
Washington National Republican
Washington Post
Weekly Georgia Telegraph (Macon, GA)
Wilmington Journal (NC) `
Winchester Daily Bulletin (TN)
Worthington (MN) Advance

Government Publications and Records

State of Tennessee
    Civil War Centennial Commission. *Tennesseans in the Civil War.* 2 vols. 1964. Reprint, Knoxville: University of Tennessee Press, 2000.
    Public Acts of State of Tennessee
    Tennessee Reports
State of Texas
    Burch v. McMillin, 15 S. W. 2D 86 (Tex. App. 1929).
United States Government
    "Commission Sent by the President to Louisiana in April, 1877." Exec. Doc. No. 97. *Index to the Executive Documents of the House of Representatives for the Second Session of the Forty-Fifth Congress, 1877–78.* Vol. 17. Washington, DC: Government Printing Office, 1878.
    Congressional Record. 1877–1898. Washington, DC.
    The Executive Documents Printed by Order of the Senate of the United States for the First Session of the Forty-Eighth Congress, 1883–84. Ex. Doc. No. 27. 1884.
    National Archives and Records Administration
        Record Group 59
            Passport Applications 1795–1905. M-1372.
        Record Group 94
            Letters Received by the Office of the Adjutant General, Main Series, 1861–1870. M-619.

Records of the Adjutant General's Office, 1780s–1917.

Case Files of Applications for Former Confederates for Presidential Pardons. M-1003.

Record Group 105

Records of the Bureau of Refugees, Freedmen, and Abandoned Lands.

Records of the Assistant Commissioner for the State of Tennessee, Bureau of Refugees, Freedmen, and Abandoned Lands, 1865–1869.

Reports of Outrages, Riots, and Murders Affidavits Relating to Outrages, Mar. 1866–Aug. 1868. M-999.

Record Group 109

Compiled Service Records of Confederate General and Staff Officers and Non-Regimental Enlisted Men. M-331.

Compiled Service Records of Confederate Soldiers Who Served in Organizations from the State of Mississippi. M-269.

Compiled Service Records of Confederate Soldiers Who Served in Organizations from the State of Tennessee. M-268.

Letters Received by Confederate States Secretary of War. M-437.

United States Code

United States Department of the Interior.

Censuses for 1840, 1850, 1860, 1900.

United States House Journal

United States House of Representatives. *House Executive Documents, Report of the Secretary of War* (1867).

United States House of Representatives. *Investigation of Labor Troubles in Missouri, Arkansas, Kansas, Texas, and Illinois.* 2 Parts, 49th Congress, 2nd Session, Report No. 4174 (1887).

United States Public Laws

United States Reports

United States Senate. *The Executive Documents Printed by Order of the Senate of the United States for the Second Session of the Forty-Third Congress, 1874–75 and the Special Session of the Senate in March, 1875.* Ex. Doc. No. 12. Washington, DC: Government Printing Office, 1875.

United States Senate, U. S. Serial Set

Document No. 234, 58th Congress, 2nd Session

Journal of the Confederate Congress

United States Statutes at Large

United States Surgeon General's Office. *Cholera Epidemic of 1873 in the United States.* Washington, DC: Government Printing Office, 1875.

United States War Department. *War of the Rebellion: A Compilation of the Official Records of the Union and Confederate Armies.* 128 vols. Washington, DC: Government Printing Office, 1880–1901.

COLLECTED WORKS WRITTEN BY CONTEMPORARIES AND PARTICIPANTS, PUBLISHED PRIMARY SOURCES, MEMOIRS, AND UNIT HISTORIES

Abernathy, Martha. *The Civil War Diary of Martha Abernathy, Wife of Dr. Charles C. Abernathy of Pulaski, Tennessee.* Edited by Elizabeth Paisley Dargan. Beltsville, MD: Professional Printing, 1994.

Anderson, James Patton. "Autobiography of Gen. Patton Anderson, C. S. A." *Southern Historical Society Papers* 24 (1896): 57.

Barber, Flavel C. *Holding the Line: The Third Tennessee Infantry, 1861–1864.* Edited by Robert H. Ferrell. Kent, OH: Kent State University Press, 1994.

Brown, Campbell. *Campbell Brown's Civil War: With Ewell and the Army of Northern Virginia.* Edited by Terry L. Jones. Baton Rouge: Louisiana State University Press, 2001.

Brown, John C. *Argument of John C. Brown, Vice President Texas and Pacific Railway Company Before House Committee on Pacific Railroads, January 25, 1878, in Behalf of the Texas and Pacific Railway Company.* Washington: Thomas McGill and Co., 1878.

Buck, Irving. *Cleburne and His Command.* Wilmington, NC: Broadfoot Publishing Company, 1987.

Cate, Wirt A., ed. *Two Soldiers: The Campaign Diaries of Thomas J. Key C.S.A. and Robert J. Campbell U.S.A.* Chapel Hill: University of North Carolina Press, 1938.

Cheairs, N. F. *I'll Sting if I Can: The Life and Prison Letters of Major N. F. Cheairs, C. S. A.* Edited by Nathaniel Cheairs Hughes Jr. Signal Mountain, TN: Mountain Press, 1998.

Cheatham, Benjamin F. "The Lost Opportunity at Spring Hill, Tenn.—General Cheatham's Reply to General Hood." *Southern Historical Society Papers* 9 (October, November, and December, 1881): 524.

Chestnut, Mary Boykin. *A Diary From Dixie.* Edited by Ben Ames Williamson. Boston: Harvard University Press, 1949.

"Concerning Re-Enlistment at Dalton." *Confederate Veteran* 9 (January 1901): 12.

"Confederate Monument at Franklin." *Confederate Veteran* 8 (January 1900): 5.

Constitution of the Comrades of the Southern Cross. Macon, GA: Burke, Boykin and Company, 1863.

Corn, T. J. "Brown's Brigade at Chickamauga." *Confederate Veteran* 21 (March 1913): 124.

Cox, Jacob D. *The Battle of Franklin, Tennessee, November 30, 1864: A Monograph.* New York: Charles Scribner's Sons, 1897.

Cumming, Kate. *Kate: The Journal of a Confederate Nurse.* Edited by Richard Barksdale Harwell. Baton Rouge: Louisiana State University Press, 1959.

Dickert, D. Augustus. *History of Kershaw's Brigade with Complete Roll of Companies, Biographical Sketches, Incidents, Anecdotes, Etc.* Newberry, SC: E. H. Aull Company, 1899.

"Disastrous Campaign in Tennessee." *Confederate Veteran* 12 (July 1904): 340.

Dyer, Gustavus W., and John Trotwood Moore, comps. *Tennessee Civil War Veterans Questionnaires.* Easley, SC: Southern Historical Press, 1985.

Erskine, John H. "A Report on Yellow Fever As it Appeared in Memphis, Tennessee in 1873." *Public Health Papers and Reports.* Memphis, TN: American Public Health Association, 1873.

Field, H. M. *Bright Skies and Dark Shadows.* New York: Charles Scribner's Sons, 1890.

"Flag of the 20th Tennessee." *Confederate Veteran* 2 (April 1894): 118.

Foster, Samuel T. *One of Cleburne's Command: The Civil War Reminiscences of Capt. Samuel T. Foster, Granbury's Texas Brigade, CSA.* Edited by Norman T. Brown. Austin: University of Texas Press, 1980.

French, Samuel G. *Two Wars: An Autobiography of Gen. Samuel G. French.* Nashville: Confederate Veteran, 1901.

Garrett, Jill K., ed. *Confederate Diary of Robert D. Smith.* Columbia, TN: Captain James Madison Sparkman Chapter, UDC, 1997.

Gower, Herschel, and Jack Allen, eds. *Pen and Sword: The Life and Journals of Randal W. McGavock.* Nashville: Tennessee Historical Commission, 1959.

Graf, Leroy P., Ralph W. Haskins, Patricia P. Clark, and Paul H. Bergeron, eds., *The Papers of Andrew Johnson.* 16 vols. Knoxville: University of Tennessee Press, 1967–2000.

Grant, Ulysses S. *Personal Memoirs of U. S. Grant.* 2 vols. New York: Charles L. Webster and Company, 1886.

———. *The Papers of U. S. Grant.* Edited by John Y. Simon and John F. Marszalek. 31 vols. Carbondale: Southern Illinois University Press, 1967–present.

Green, John. *Johnny Green of the Orphan Brigade: The Journal of a Confederate Soldier.* Edited by A. D. Kirwan. Lexington: University of Kentucky Press, 1956.

Halstead, Murat. *Caucuses of 1860. A History of the National Political Conventions of the Current Presidential Campaign: Being a Complete Record of the Business of all the Conventions: with Sketches of Distinguished Men in Attendance Upon Them, and Descriptions of the Most Characteristic Scenes and Memorable Events.* Columbus: Follett, Foster and Company, 1860.

Hampton, N. J. *An Eyewitness to the Dark Days of 1861–65 or, A Private Soldier's Adventures and Hardships During the War.* Nashville: N. J. Hampton, 1898.

Hayes, Rutherford B. *Diary and Letters of Rutherford Birchard Hayes, Nineteenth President of the United States.* Edited by Charles Richard Williams. 5 vols. Columbus: The Ohio State Archeological Society, 1922–1926.

Hearn, W. C. "Forty-First Mississippi Regiment—A Lost Sword." *Confederate Veteran* 6 (April 1898): 152.

Hewett, Janet B., Noah A. Trudeau, Bryce A. Suderow, eds. *Supplement to the Official Records of the Union and Confederate Armies.* 100 vols. Wilmington, NC: Broadfoot Publishing Company, 1994–2001.

Hood, John Bell. *Advance and Retreat.* New Orleans: Beauregard, 1879.

Hood, Stephen M., ed. *The Lost Papers of Confederate General John Bell Hood.* El Dorado Hills, CA: Savas Beatie, 2015.

Jamison, Henry Downs and Marguerite Jamison McTigue, comp. *Letters and Recollections of a Confederate Soldier, 1860–1865.* 1964.

Johnston, Joseph E. *Narrative of Military Operations Directed During the Late War Between the States.* New York: D. Appleton and Company, 1874.

Johnston, William Preston. *The Life of Gen. Albert Sidney Johnston: His Service in the Armies of the United States, the Republic of Texas, and the Confederate States.* New York: D. Appleton and Company, 1879.

Journal of the Proceedings of the Convention of Delegates Elected by the People of Tennessee to Amend, Revise, or to Reform or Make a New Constitution for the State. Nashville: Jones, Purvis and Company, 1870.

"Judge John S. Wilkes." *Confederate Veteran* 16 (March 1908): 106.

Liddell, St. John Richardson. *Liddell's Record.* Edited by Nathaniel Cheairs Hughes Jr. 1985. Reprint, Baton Rouge: Louisiana State University Press, 1997.

Lindsley, John Berrian, ed. *The Military Annals of Tennessee: Confederate.* 2 vols. Nashville: J. M. Lindsley, 1886.

McCallie, David, ed. *THM: A Memoir.* Bloomington, IN: WestBow Press, 2011.

McKinnon, John L. *History of Walton County.* Atlanta: Byrd Printing Co., 1911.

McPherson, James M. *Battle Cry of Freedom: The Civil War Era.* New York: Oxford University Press, 1988.

"Memphis Alumnus Takes Presidency." *Sewanee Alumni News* 23 (November 1957): 3.

Monroe, Haskell M., Jr., James T. McIntosh, and Lynda Lasswell Crist, eds. *The Papers of Jefferson Davis.* 11 vols. Baton Rouge: Louisiana State University Press, 1971–2004.

Moore, John Trotwood, ed. *Tennessee Civil War Veterans Questionnaires.* Easely, SC: Southern Historical Press, 1985.

"Mrs. Elizabeth Brown Burch." *Confederate Veteran* 12 (October 1904): 498.

"National Daughters of the Confederacy." *Confederate Veteran* 2 (October 1894): 306.

Oeffinger, John C., ed. *A Soldier's General: The Civil War Letters of Major General Lafayette McLaws.* Chapel Hill: University of North Carolina Press, 2002.

Polk, William M. *Leonidas Polk, Bishop and General.* 2 vols. New York: Longmans, Green and Company, 1915.

Poore, Ben Perley. *Perley's Reminiscences of Sixty Years in the National Metropolis.* 2 vols. Philadelphia: Hubbard Brothers, 1886.

Porter, James D. *Confederate Military History—Tennessee.* 1899. Reprint, Wilmington, NC: Broadfoot Publishing Company, 1987.

Quintard, Charles Todd. *Doctor Quintard, Chaplain C. S. A. and Second Bishop of Tennessee.* Edited by Sam Davis Elliott. Baton Rouge: Louisiana State University Press, 2003.

Ramsey, J. G. M. *Dr. J. G. M. Ramsey: Autobiography and Letters.* Edited by William B. Hesseltine. 1954. Reprint, Knoxville: University of Tennessee Press, 2002.

Ratchford, James W. *Memoirs of a Confederate Staff Officer: From Bethel to Bentonville.* Edited by Evelyn Ratchford Sieburg and James E. Hanson II. Shippensburg, PA: White Mane Books 1998.

"Relics at the Centennial Exposition." *Confederate Veteran* 5 (November 1897): 562.

"Reminiscences—Mother of the Confederacy." *Confederate Veteran* 2 (April 1894): 108.

Ridley, Bromfield L. *Battles and Sketches of the Army of Tennessee.* 1906. Reprint, Dayton: Morningside Bookshop, 1995.

Riegel, Robert Edgar. *The Story of the Western Railroads.* New York: Macmillan, 1926.

Sherman, William T. *Home Letters of General Sherman.* Edited by M. A. DeWolf Howe. New York: Charles Scribner's Sons, 1909.

———. *Memoirs of General William T. Sherman.* New York: D. Appleton and Company, 1876.

Snell, William R., ed. *Myra Inman: A Diary of the Civil War in East Tennessee.* Macon, GA: Mercer University Press, 2000.

Stephenson, Philip D. *The Civil War Memoir of Philip Daingerfield Stephenson, D. D.* Edited by Nathaniel Cheairs Hughes Jr. Conway: University of Central Arkansas Press, 1995.

Stewart, Alexander P. "The Army of Tennessee: A Sketch." In *Military Annals of Tennessee: Confederate*, edited by John Berrien Lindsley, 2 vols. 1886. Reprint, Wilmington, NC: Broadfoot, 1995.

Stout, Samuel H. "Some Facts of the History of the Organization of Medical Service of the Confederate Armies and Hospitals." In *The Southern Practitioner.* Nashville: Jno. Rundle and Sons, 1901.

Sykes, E. T. "Walthall's Brigade, A Cursory Sketch With Personal Experiences of Walthall's Brigade, Army of Tennessee, 1862–1865." In *Publications of the Mississippi Historical Society*, edited by Dunbar Rowland. 14 vols. Jackson: Mississippi Historical Society, 1916.

Temple, Oliver P. *East Tennessee and the Civil War.* 1899. Reprint, Freeport, NY: Books for Libraries Press, 1971.

———. *Notable Men of Tennessee from 1833 to 1875: Their Times and Contemporaries.* New York: Cosmopolitan Press, 1912.

Thompson, Ed Porter. *History of the Orphan Brigade.* Louisville: Lewis N. Thompson, 1898.

Tower, R. Lockwood, ed. *A Carolinian Goes to War: The Civil War Narrative of Arthur Middleton Manigault.* Columbia: University of South Carolina Press, 1983.

"United Confederate Daughters." *Confederate Veteran* 4 (January 1896): 22.

Urquhart, David. "Bragg's Advance and Retreat." In *Battles and Leaders of the Civil War*, edited by Robert Underwood Johnson and Clarence Clough Buel, 3. 4 vols. 1887–1888. Reprint, New York: Youseloff, 1956.

Watkins, Sam R. *Co. Aytch: A Side show of the Big Show.* New York: Collier Books, 1962.

Wheeler, Joseph. "Bragg's Invasion of Kentucky." In *Battles and Leaders of the Civil War*, edited by Robert Underwood Johnson and Clarence Clough Buel, 3. 4 vols. 1887–1888. Reprint, New York: Youseloff, 1956.

White, William Lee, and Charles Denny Runion, eds. *Great Things are Expected of Us: The Letters of Colonel C. Irvine Walker, 10th South Carolina Infantry, C. S. A.* Knoxville: University of Tennessee Press, 2009.

Wistar, Isaac Jones. *Autobiography: 1827–1905.* 2 vols. New York: Harper and Brothers, 1914.

Young, J. P. "Hood's Failure at Spring Hill." *Confederate Veteran* 16 (January 1908): 25.

SECONDARY SOURCES

Abshire, David M. *The South Rejects a Prophet: The Life of Senator D. M. Key, 1824–1900.* New York: Frederick A. Praeger, 1967.

Alexander, Thomas B. *Political Reconstruction in Tennessee.* Nashville: Vanderbilt University Press, 1950.

———. "Kukluxism in Tennessee, 1865–1869." *Tennessee Historical Quarterly* 8 (September 1949): 195-219.

———. "Persistent Whiggery in the Confederate South, 1860–1877." *Journal of Southern History* 27 (August 1961): 305-329

———. "Whiggery and Reconstruction in Tennessee." *Journal of Southern History* 16 (1950): 291-305.

Allardice, Bruce S. "It Was Perfect Murder: Stephen D. Lee at Ezra Church." In *Confederate Generals in the Western Theater*, edited by Lawrence Lee Hewitt and Arthur W. Bergeron, 3:221-246. 4 vols. Knoxville: University of Tennessee Press, 2011.

Andrews, William J. "In the Days of the Past." In *Maury County, Tennessee Historical Sketches*, edited by Jill K. Garrett, 40-58. Columbia, TN: Privately published, 1967.

Armes, Ethel. *The Story of Coal and Iron in Alabama.* Birmingham: Chamber of Commerce, 1910.

Ash, Stephen V. *Middle Tennessee Society Transformed, 1860–1870: War and Peace in the Upper South.* Baton Rouge: Louisiana State University Press, 1988.

Atkins, Jonathan M. *Parties, Politics, and Sectional Conflict in Tennessee, 1832–1862.* Knoxville: University of Tennessee Press, 1997.

Austin, Linda T. "Escape from the Asylum: The End of Local Care of the Mentally Ill in Memphis and Shelby County." *Tennessee Historical Quarterly* 72 (Spring 2013): 50-67.

Ayers, Edward L. *The Promise of the New South: Life after Reconstruction.* New York: Oxford University Press, 1993.

Bailey, Anne J. *The Chessboard of War: Sherman and Hood in the Autumn Campaign of 1864.* Lincoln: University of Nebraska Press, 2000.

Baylen, Joseph O. "A Tennessee Politician in Imperial Russia, 1850–53." *Tennessee Historical Quarterly* 14 (1955): 227-252.

Bearss, E. C. "The Construction of Fort Henry and Fort Donelson." *West Tennessee Historical Society Papers* 21 (1967): 24-47.

Benedict, Michael Les. "Southern Democrats in the Crisis of 1876–1877: A Reconsideration of Reunion and Reaction." *The Journal of Southern History* 46 (November 1980): 489-524.

Bergeron, Paul H. *Andrew Johnson's Civil War and Reconstruction.* Knoxville: University of Tennessee Press, 2011.

Bergeron, Paul H., Stephen V. Ash, and Jeanette Keith. *Tennesseans and Their History.* Knoxville: University of Tennessee Press, 1999.

Bittle, George C. "Fighting Men View the Western War, 1862–1864." *Florida Historical Quarterly* 47 (July 1968): 25-33.

Blake, Nelson M. *Land into Water—Water into Land: A History of Water Management in Florida.* Tallahassee: University Presses of Florida, 1980.

Bohannon, Keith S. "'Witness the Redemption of the Army': Reenlistments in the Confederate Army of Tennessee, January–March, 1864." In *Inside the Confederate Nation: Essays in Honor of Emory M. Thomas*, edited by Lesley J. Gordon and John C. Inscoe, 111-127. Baton Rouge: Louisiana State University Press, 2005.

Bradley, Mark L. *Last Stand in the Carolinas: The Battle of Bentonville.* Campbell, CA: Savas Woodbury, 1996.

———. *This Astounding Close: The Road to Bennett Place.* Chapel Hill: University of North Carolina Press, 2000.

Bradley, Michael R. *Tullahoma: The 1863 Campaign for Control of Middle Tennessee.* Shippensburg, PA: Burd Street Press, 2000.

Bridges, Hal. *Lee's Maverick General: Daniel Harvey Hill.* New York: McGraw-Hill, 1961.

Brown, Russell K. *To the Manner Born: The Life of General William H. T. Walker.* Athens: University of Georgia Press, 1994.

Buell, Augustus C. *History of Andrew Jackson: Pioneer, Patriot, Soldier, Politician and President.* New York: Charles Scribner's Sons, 1904.

Burton, E. Milby. *The Siege of Charleston.* Columbia: University of South Carolina Press, 1970.

Caldwell, Joshua W. *Studies in the Constitutional History of Tennessee.* 2nd ed. Cincinnati: Robert W. Clarke and Company, 1907.

———. *Sketches of the Bench and Bar of Tennessee.* Knoxville: Ogden Brothers, 1898.

Cameron, Robert S. *Staff Ride Handbook for the Battle of Perryville.* Fort Leavenworth: Combat Studies Institute Press, 2005.

Campbell, Mary E. R. *The Attitude of Tennesseans Toward the Union.* New York: Vantage, 1961.

Capers, Walter B. *The Soldier Bishop, Ellison Capers.* New York: Neale Publishing, 1912.

Cardin, W. Thomas. "History of Pisgah." In *Flournoy Rivers' Manuscripts and History of Pisgah*, compiled by Clara M. Parker and Edward Jackson White. Pulaski, TN: n.d.

Case, Theresa A. *The Great Southwest Railroad Strike and Free Labor.* College Station: Texas A&M University Press, 2010.

Castel, Albert. *Decision in the West: The Atlanta Campaign of 1864.* Lawrence: University Press of Kansas, 1992.

Churella, Albert J. *The Pennsylvania Railroad.* Vol. 1, *Building an Empire, 1846–1917.* (Philadelphia: University of Pennsylvania Press, 2012).

Cohen, Nelle Roller. *Pulaski History, 1809–1850: The Beginning, The Building, The Development, The Institutions, And the People of the Town of Pulaski, Tennessee.* Pulaski, Tenn. Eighth Installment, 1951.

Coles, David J. "Ancient City Defenders: The St. Augustine Blues." In *Civil War Times in St. Augustine,* edited by Jacqueline K. Fretwell, 65-90. St. Augustine: St. Augustine Historical Society, 1988.

Combs, William H. "An Unamended State Constitution: The Tennessee Constitution of 1870." *The American Political Science Review* 32 (June 1938): 514-524.

Connelly, Donald B. *John M. Schofield and the Politics of Generalship.* Chapel Hill: University of North Carolina Press, 2006.

Connelly, Thomas L. *Army of the Heartland.* Baton Rouge: Louisiana State University Press, 1967.

———. *Autumn of Glory.* Baton Rouge: Louisiana State University Press, 1971.

Cooling, Benjamin Franklin. *Forts Henry and Donelson: The Key to the Confederate Heartland.* Knoxville: University of Tennessee Press, 1987.

Cooper, William James. *The South and the Politics of Slavery, 1828–1856.* Baton Rouge: Louisiana State University Press, 1978.

Corlew, Robert E. *Tennessee: A Short History.* 2nd ed. Knoxville: University of Tennessee Press, 1990.

Coulter, E. Merton. *William G. Brownlow: Fighting Parson of the Southern Highlands.* 1937. Reprint, Knoxville: University of Tennessee Press, 1999.

Cozzens, Peter. *The Shipwreck of Their Hopes: The Battles for Chattanooga.* Urbana: University of Illinois Press, 1994.

———. *This Terrible Sound: The Battle of Chickamauga.* Urbana: University of Illinois Press, 1992.

———. *No Better Place to Die: The Battle of Stones River.* Urbana: University of Illinois Press, 1990.

Crofts, Daniel W. *Reluctant Confederates: Upper South Unionists in the Secession Crisis.* Chapel Hill: University of North Carolina Press, 1989.

Cunningham, H. H. *Doctors in Gray: The Confederate Medical Service.* Baton Rouge: Louisiana State University Press, 1958.

Daniel, Larry J. *Battle of Stones River: The Forgotten Conflict Between the Confederate Army of Tennessee and the Union Army of the Cumberland.* Baton Rouge: Louisiana State University Press, 2012.

———. *Days of Glory: The Army of the Cumberland, 1861–1865.* Baton Rouge: Louisiana State University Press, 2004.

————. *Soldiering in the Army of Tennessee: A Portrait of Life in a Confederate Army.* Chapel Hill: University of North Carolina Press, 1991.

Davis, Stephen. *Atlanta Will Fall: Sherman, Joe Johnston, and the Yankee Heavy Battalions.* Wilmington, DE: SR Books, 2001.

————. "Hood and the Battles for Atlanta." In *The Campaign for Atlanta & Sherman's March to the Sea.* 1:40-82. 2 vols. Campbell, CA: Savas Woodbury, 1992.

Davis, Susan Lawrence. *Authentic History of the Ku Klux Klan, 1865–1877.* New York: Susan Lawrence Davis, 1924.

Dubofsky, Melvyn, and Foster Rhea Dulles. *Labor in America: A History.* Wheeling, IL: Harlan Davidson, 2004.

Dunn, John. "'An American Fracas in Egypt': The Butler Affair of 1872." *Journal of the American Research Center in Egypt* 42 (2005/2006): 153-161.

Durham, Walter T. *Nashville, The Occupied City: The First Seventeen Months—February 16, 1862, to June 30, 1863.* Nashville: Tennessee Historical Society, 1985.

Ecelbarger, Gary. *Slaughter at the Chapel: The Battle of Ezra Church, 1864.* Norman: University of Oklahoma Press, 2016.

————. *The Day Dixie Died: The Battle of Atlanta.* New York: St. Martin's Press, 2010.

Elliott, Sam D. *Isham G. Harris of Tennessee: Confederate Governor and United States Senator.* Baton Rouge: Louisiana State University Press, 2010.

————. "'I Regard Maj. Gen. Stewart as the Best Qualified of the Maj. Gens. of this Army': Alexander P. Stewart and His Division in the First Phase of the Atlanta Campaign." In *Confederate Generals in the Western Theater: Essays on America's Civil War*, edited by Lawrence L. Hewitt and Arthur W. Bergeron, 2:133-158. 4 vols. Knoxville: University of Tennessee Press, 2010.

————. "Tennessee's Declaration of Independence: Armed Revolt and the Constitutional Right of Revolution." *Tennessee Bar Journal* 44 (December 2008): 25-29.

————. "When the United States Attorney Sued to Remove Half the Tennessee Supreme Court: The Quo Warrants Cases of 1870." *Tennessee Bar Journal* 49 (August 2013): 20-27.

————. *Soldier of Tennessee: General Alexander P. Stewart and the Civil War in the West.* Baton Rouge: Louisiana State University Press, 1999.

Evans, Cerinda W. *Collis Potter Huntington.* 2 vols. Newport News, VA: The Mariner's Museum, 1954.

Feistman, Eugene G. "Radical Disfranchisement and the Restoration of Tennessee, 1865–1866." *Tennessee Historical Quarterly* 12 (June 1953): 135-151.

Fitzgerald, Oscar Penn. *John B. McFerrin: A Biography.* Nashville: Publishing House of the M. E. Church, 1888.

Foner, Eric. *Reconstruction: America's Unfinished Revolution, 1863–1877.* 1988. Updated edition, New York: Harper and Row, 2014.

Foster, Buck T. *Sherman's Mississippi Campaign.* Tuscaloosa: University of Alabama Press, 2006.

Foster, Gaines M. *Ghosts of the Confederacy: Defeat, the Lost Cause, and the Emergence of the New South, 1865 to 1913.* New York: Oxford University Press, 1987.

Freehling, William W. *The Road to Disunion: Secessionists Triumphant, 1854–1861*. New York: Oxford University Press, 2008.

Frisby, Derek W. "A Victory Spoiled: West Tennessee Unionists during Reconstruction." In *The Great Task Remaining Before Us: Reconstruction as America's Continuing Civil War*, edited by Paul A. Cimbala and Randall M. Miller, 9-29. New York: Fordham University Press, 2010.

Galloway, John Debo. *The First Transcontinental Railroad: Central Pacific, Union Pacific*. New York: Simmons-Boardman, 1950.

Garrett, Jill K., and Marise P. Lightfoot. *The Civil War in Maury County, Tennessee*. Columbia, TN: n. p., 1966.

"General John C. Brown." *Confederate Veteran* 3 (August 1895): 242.

Gilchrist, Annie Somers. *Some Representative Women of Tennessee*. Nashville: McQuiddy Printing Company, 1902.

Gillum, Jaime. *Twenty-five Hours to Tragedy: The Battle of Spring Hill and Operations on November 29, 1864, Precursor to the Battle of Franklin*. Spring Hill: n. p., 2014.

Gordon, Larry. *The Last Confederate General: John C. Vaughn and his East Tennessee Cavalry*. Minneapolis: Zenith Press, 2009.

Gott, Kendall D. *Where the South Lost the War: An Analysis of the Fort Henry-Fort Donelson Campaign, February 1862*. Mechanicsburg, PA: Stackpole Books, 2003.

Groce, W. Todd. *Mountain Rebels: East Tennessee Confederates and the Civil War, 1860–1870*. Knoxville: University of Tennessee Press, 1999.

Grodinsky, Julius. *Jay Gould: His Business Career 1867–1892*. Philadelphia: University of Pennsylvania Press, 1957.

Hafendorfer, Kenneth A. *Perryville: Battle for Kentucky*. Louisville: KH Press, 1991.

Hallock, Judith Lee. *Braxton Bragg and Confederate Defeat*. Vol. 2. Tuscaloosa: University of Alabama Press, 1991.

Hamilton, Milton W. "Augustus C. Buell: Fraudulent Historian." *Pennsylvania Magazine of History and Biography* 80 (October 1956): 478-492.

Harcourt, Edward John. "Who Were the Palefaces? New Perspectives on the Tennessee Ku Klux," *Civil War History* 51 (March 2005): 23-66.

Hart, Roger L. *Redeemers, Bourbons and Populists: Tennessee, 1870–1896*. Baton Rouge: Louisiana State University Press, 1975.

Hartman, David W., comp. *Biographical Rosters of Florida's Confederate and Union Soldiers, 1861–1865*. Wilmington, NC: Broadfoot, 1995.

Hattaway, Herman, and Archer Jones. *How the North Won: A Military History of the Civil War*. 1983. Reprint, Urbana: University of Illinois Press, 1991.

Hay, Thomas Robeson. "The South and the Arming of the Slaves." *The Mississippi Valley Historical Review* 6 (June 1919): 34.

Hess, Earl J. *Braxton Bragg: The Most Hated Man of the Confederacy*. Chapel Hill: University of North Carolina Press, 2016.

———. *The Battle of Ezra Church and the Struggle for Atlanta*. Chapel Hill: University of North Carolina Press, 2015.

———. *Kennesaw Mountain: Sherman, Johnston and the Atlanta Campaign.* Chapel Hill: University of North Carolina Press, 2013.

———. *The Civil War in the West: Victory and Defeat from the Appalachians to the Mississippi.* University of North Carolina Press, 2012.

———. *Banners to the Breeze: The Kentucky Campaign, Corinth and Stones River.* Lincoln: University of Nebraska Press, 2000.

Hesseltine, William B. *Confederate Leaders in the New South.* Baton Rouge: Louisiana State University Press, 1950.

Horn, Stanley F. *The Decisive Battle of Nashville.* 1956. Reprint, Baton Rouge: Louisiana State University Press, 1991.

———. *The Army of Tennessee.* 1941. Reprint, Wilmington, NC: Broadfoot Publishers, 1987.

———. *Invisible Empire: The Story of the Ku Klux Klan, 1866–1871.* Cambridge: Riverside Press, 1939.

Hoogenboom, Ari. *Rutherford B. Hayes: Warrior and President.* Lawrence: University Press of Kansas, 1995.

Hopkins, Anne H., and William Lyons. *Tennessee Votes, 1799–1976.* Knoxville: University of Tennessee Bureau of Public Administration, 1978.

Hughes, Nathaniel C., Jr. *Bentonville: The Final Battle Between Sherman and Johnston.* Chapel Hill: University of North Carolina Press, 1996.

———. *General William J. Hardee: Old Reliable.* Baton Rouge: Louisiana State University Press, 1965.

———. *The Battle of Belmont: Grant Strikes South.* Chapel Hill: University of North Carolina Press, 1991.

Hughes, Nathaniel C., Jr. and Gordon D. Whitney. *Jefferson Davis in Blue: The Life of Sherman's Relentless Warrior.* Baton Rouge: Louisiana State University Press, 2002.

Hughes, Nathaniel C., Jr. and Roy P. Stonsifer. *The Life and Wars of Gideon J. Pillow.* Chapel Hill: University of North Carolina Press, 1993.

Jacobson, Eric A., and Richard A. Rupp. *For Cause and Comrades: A Study of the Affair at Spring Hill and the Battle of Franklin.* Franklin, TN: O'More Publishing, 2006.

Janney, Caroline E. *Remembering the Civil War: Reunion and the Limits of Reconciliation.* Chapel Hill: University of North Carolina Press, 2013.

Jenkins, Robert D., Sr. *The Battle of Peach Tree Creek: Hood's First Sortie, 20 July 1864.* Macon, GA: Mercer University Press, 2014.

———. *To the Gates of Atlanta: From Kennesaw Mountain to Peach Tree Creek, 1–19 July 1864.* Macon, GA: Mercer University Press, 2015.

Jobe, James. "Forts Henry and Donelson: Disastrous and Almost Without Remedy." *Blue & Gray Magazine* 28, no. 4 (2011): 6-26, 43-50.

Jones, Evan C. "A 'Malignant Vindictiveness': The Rivalry Between Grant and Rosecrans." In *Gateway to the Confederacy: New Perspectives on the Chicka-*

mauga and Chattanooga Campaigns, 1862–1863, edited by Evan C. Jones and Wiley Sword, 172-226. Baton Rouge: Louisiana State University Press, 2014.

Jones, Robert B. *Tennessee at the Crossroads: The State Debt Controversy 1870–1883*. Knoxville: University of Tennessee Press, 1977.

———. "The Press in the Election." *Tennessee Historical Quarterly* 65 (Winter 2006/7): 320-341.

Jones, Robert B., and Mark E. Byrnes. "'Rebels Never Forgive': Former President Johnson and the Senate Election of 1869." *Tennessee Historical Quarterly 66* (Fall 2007): 250-269.

Kaestle, Karl F. *Pillars of the Republic: Common Schools and American Society, 1780–1860*. New York: Hill and Wang, 1983.

Klein, Maury. *Jay Gould*. Baltimore: Johns Hopkins Press, 1986.

Lester, Connie. *Up From the Mudsills of Hell: The Farmer's Alliance, Populism, and Progressive Agriculture in Tennessee, 1870–1915*. Athens: University of Georgia Press, 2006.

Lester, John C., and David L. Wilson. *Ku Klux Klan: Its Origin, Growth, and Disbandment*. Introduction and notes by Walter J. Fleming. 1884. Reprint, New York: Neale Publishing Company, 1905.

Levine, Bruce. *Confederate Emancipation: Southern Plans to Free and Arm Slaves During the Civil War*. New York: Oxford University Press, 2006.

Lindsley, Philip. *A History of Greater Dallas and Vicinity*. Chicago: Lewis Publishing Company, 1909.

Logsdon, David R., ed. *Eyewitnesses at the Battle of Perryville*. Nashville: Kettle Mill Press, 2007.

Losson, Christopher. *Tennessee's Forgotten Warriors: Frank Cheatham and His Confederate Division*. Knoxville: University of Tennessee Press, 1989.

Lundberg, John R. "Baptizing the Hills and Valleys: Cleburne's Defense of Tunnel Hill." In *The Chattanooga Campaign*, edited by Steven E. Woodworth and Charles D. Grear, 70-83. Carbondale, Ill: Southern Illinois University Press, 2012.

Maness, Lonnie. "Henry Emerson Etheridge and the Gubernatorial Election of 1867: A Study in Futility." *West Tennessee Historical Society Papers* 47 (1993): 37-49.

Martin, George Winston. *"I Will Give Them One More Shot": Ramsey's 1st Regiment Georgia Volunteers*. Macon, GA: Mercer University Press, 2010.

McBride, Mary Gorton. *Randall Lee Gibson of Louisiana: Confederate General and New South Reformer*. Baton Rouge: Louisiana State University Press, 2007.

McBride, Robert M., and Dan M. Robison. *Biographical Directory of the Tennessee General Assembly*. 6 vols. Nashville: Tennessee State Library and Archives and Tennessee Historical Commission, 1979–1991.

McCallum, James. *A Brief Sketch of the Settlement and Early History of Giles County, Tennessee*. Pulaski: Pulaski Citizen, 1928.

McClure, Wallace. "The Development of the Tennessee Constitution." *Tennessee Historical Magazine* 1 (December 1915): 292-314.

McDonough, James Lee. *Nashville: The Western Confederacy's Last Gamble.* Knoxville: University of Tennessee Press, 2004.

———. *War in Kentucky: From Shiloh to Perryville.* Knoxville: University of Tennessee Press, 1994.

———. *Stones River: Bloody Winter in Tennessee.* Knoxville: University of Tennessee Press, 1980.

McGinty, Garnie. *Louisiana Redeemed: The Overthrow of Carpet-Bag Rule 1876–1880.* 1941. Reprint, Gretna, LA: Firebird Press, 1999.

McKenzie, Robert Tracy. *Lincolnites and Rebels: A Divided Town in the American Civil War.* New York: Oxford University Press, 2006.

———. *One South or Many? Plantation Belt and Upcountry in Civil War Tennessee.* New York: Cambridge University Press, 1994.

McLain, Minor H. "The Military Prison at Fort Warren." In *Civil War Prisons*, edited by William B. Hesseltine, 32-46. Kent: Kent State University Press, 1972.

McMurry, Richard M. *Atlanta 1864: Last Chance for the Confederacy.* Lincoln: University of Nebraska Press, 2000.

———. *Two Great Rebel Armies: An Essay in Confederate Military History.* Chapel Hill: University of North Carolina Press, 1989.

McWhiney, Grady. *Braxton Bragg and Confederate Defeat.* Vol. 1. 1969. Reprint, Tuscaloosa: University of Alabama Press, 1991.

Mendoza, Alexander. *Confederate Struggle for Command: General James Longstreet and the First Corps in the West.* College Station: Texas A&M University Press, 2008.

Moore, John Trotwood, and Austin Foster. *Tennessee, The Volunteer State: 1769–1923.* Chicago: S. J. Clarke, 1923.

Neall, Dianne, and Thomas W. Kremm. *Lion of the South: General Thomas B. Hindman.* Macon, GA: Mercer University Press, 1993.

Nelson, Scott R. *Iron Confederacies: Southern Railways, Klan Violence, and Reconstruction.* Chapel Hill: University of North Carolina Press, 1999.

Newman, George W. *Brown Family Timeline: 1745–1919.* N. p., 2001.

Newton, Steven H. *Lost for the Cause: The Confederate Army in 1864.* Boston: DaCapo Press, 2000.

Noe, Kenneth W. *Perryville: This Grand Havoc of Battle.* Lexington: University Press of Kentucky, 2001.

Overdyke, W. Darrell. *The Know-Nothing Party in the South.* Baton Rouge: Louisiana State University Press, 1950.

Parker, Clara M. *Giles County, Tennessee Will Abstracts, 1815–1900.* n.p. Pulaski, TN; 1988.

Parsons, Elaine Frantz. *Ku-Klux: The Birth of the Klan During Reconstruction.* Chapel Hill: University of North Carolina Press, 2015.

Patton, James Welch. *Unionism and Reconstruction in Tennessee, 1860–69.* 1934. Reprint, Gloucester, MA: Peter Smith, 1966.

Perman, Michael. *The Road to Redemption: Southern Politics, 1869–1879*. Chapel Hill: University of North Carolina Press, 1984.

Peskin, Allan. "Was There a Compromise of 1877." *The Journal of American History* 60 (June 1973): 63–75.

Powell, David A. *The Chickamauga Campaign: Barren Victory: The Retreat into Chattanooga, the Confederate Pursuit, and the Aftermath of the Battle, September 21 to October 20, 1863*. El Dorado Hills, CA: Savas Beatie, 2016.

——. *The Chickamauga Campaign: Glory or the Grave: The Breakthrough, the Union Collapse and the Defense of Horseshoe Ridge, September 20, 1863*. El Dorado Hills, CA: Savas Beatie, 2015.

——. *The Chickamauga Campaign: A Mad Irregular Battle: From the Crossing of the Tennessee River Through the Second Day, August 22–September 19, 1863*. El Dorado Hills, CA: Savas Beatie, 2014.

Powell, David A., and David A. Friedrichs. *The Maps of Chickamauga*. New York: Savas Beatie, 2009.

Prim, G. Clinton, Jr. "Born Again in the Trenches: Revivals in the Army of Tennessee." *Tennessee Historical Quarterly* 43 (Fall 1984): 250–72.

Prokopowicz, Gerald J. "Last Chance for a Short War: Don Carlos Buell and the Chattanooga Campaign of 1862." In *Gateway to the Confederacy: New Perspectives on the Chickamauga and Chattanooga Campaigns, 1862–1863*, edited by Evan C. Jones and Wiley Sword, 36-59. Baton Rouge: Louisiana State University Press, 2014.

Rayburn, Larry. "'Wherever the Fight is Thickest': General James Patton Anderson of Florida." *The Florida Historical Quarterly* 60 (January 1982): 313-336.

Riegal, Robert Edgar. *The Story of Western Railroads*. New York: Macmillan, 1926.

Roberts, Derrell C. *The Gray Winter of 1864 in Dalton*. Dalton, GA: Whitfield-Murray County Historical Society, 1991.

Robertson, William Glenn. "A Tale of Two Orders: Chickamauga, September 20, 1863." In *Gateway to the Confederacy: New Perspectives on the Chickamauga and Chattanooga Campaigns, 1862–1863*, edited by Evan C. Jones and Wiley Sword, 129-158. Baton Rouge: Louisiana State University Press, 2014.

——. "The Chickamauga Campaign: The Fall of Chattanooga." *Blue & Gray Magazine* 23 (Fall 2006): 6-28, 43-50.

——. "The Chickamauga Campaign: McLemore's Cove: Rosecrans' Gamble, Bragg's Lost Opportunity." *Blue & Gray Magazine* 23 (Spring 2007): 6-26, 42-50.

——. "The Chickamauga Campaign: The Armies Collide: Bragg Forces His Way Across Chickamauga Creek." *Blue & Gray Magazine* 24 (Fall 2007): 6-28, 40-50.

——. "The Chickamauga Campaign: The Battle of Chickamauga Day 1, September 19, 1863." *Blue & Gray Magazine* 24 (Spring 2008): 6-29, 40-52.

——. "The Chickamauga Campaign: Day 2, September 20, 1863." *Blue & Gray Magazine* 25 (Summer 2008): 6-31, 40-50.

Roland, Charles P. "Albert Sidney Johnston and the Loss of Forts Henry and Donelson." *Journal of Southern History* 23 (February 1957): 45-69.

Scharf, John Thomas. *History of Saint Louis City and County From the Earliest Periods to the Present Day, Including Biographical Sketches of Representative Men.* Philadelphia: Louis H. Evarts and Company, 1883.

Schott, Thomas E. "Lieutenant General William J. Hardee, the Historians, and the Atlanta Campaign." In *Confederate Generals in the Western Theater*, edited by Lawrence Lee Hewitt and Arthur W. Bergeron, Jr., 2:159-186. 4 vols. Knoxville: University of Tennessee Press, 2010.

Schroeder-Lein, Glenna R. *Confederate Hospitals on the Move: Samuel H. Stout and the Army of Tennessee.* Columbia: University of South Carolina Press, 1994.

Scrabec, Quentin R., Jr. *The 100 Most Significant Events in American Business: An Encyclopedia.* Santa Barbara, CA: ABC-CLIO, 2012.

Secrist, Philip L. *The Battle of Resaca.* Macon: Mercer University Press, 1998.

Severance, Ben H. *Tennessee's Radical Army: The State Guard and Its Role in Reconstruction.* Knoxville: University of Tennessee Press, 2005.

Shaler, Nathaniel S. *Kentucky: A Pioneer Commonwealth.* Boston: Houghton, Mifflin and Company, 1885.

Shapiro, Karin A. *A New South Rebellion: The Battle Against Convict Labor in the Tennessee Coalfields, 1871–1896.* Chapel Hill: University of North Carolina Press, 1998.

Sheppard, Johnathan C. *By the Noble Daring of Her Sons: The Florida Brigade of the Army of Tennessee.* Tuscaloosa: University of Alabama Press, 2012.

Sikes, Lewright B. "Gustavus Adolphus Henry: Champion of Lost Causes." *Tennessee Historical Quarterly* 50 (Fall 1991): 173.

Simpson, Brooks D. *The Reconstruction Presidents.* Lawrence: University Press of Kansas, 1998.

Slap, Andrew L. *The Doom of Reconstruction: The Liberal Republicans in the Civil War Era.* New York: Fordham University Press, 2006.

Smith, Jean Edward. *Grant.* New York: Simon and Schuster, 2001.

Smith, Mark A., and Wade Sokolosky. *"No Such Army Since the Days of Julius Caesar": Sherman's Carolinas Campaign from Fayetteville to Averasboro.* Fort Mitchell, KY: Ironclad Publishing, 2005.

Smith, Timothy B. *Grant Invades Tennessee: The 1862 Battles for Forts Henry and Donelson.* Lawrence: University Press of Kansas, 2016.

Sparks, Edwin Erle. *National Development, 1877–1885.* New York: Harper and Brothers, 1907.

Speer, William S. *Sketches of Prominent Tennesseans.* Nashville: Albert B. Tavel, 1888.

Stryker, Lloyd Paul. *Andrew Johnson: A Study in Courage.* New York: Macmillan, 1929.

Summers, Mark W. *Railroads, Reconstruction, and the Gospel of Prosperity: Aid under the Radical Republicans, 1865–1867.* Princeton: Princeton University Press, 1984.

———. *A Dangerous Stir: Fear, Paranoia, and the Making of Reconstruction.* Chapel Hill: University of North Carolina Press, 2009.

———. *The Ordeal of the Reunion: A New History of Reconstruction.* Chapel Hill: University of North Carolina Press, 2014.

Sword, Wiley. "'Our Fireside in Ruins': Consequences of the 1863 Chattanooga Campaign." In *Gateway to the Confederacy: New Perspectives on the Chickamauga and Chattanooga Campaigns, 1862–1863,* edited by Evan C. Jones and Wiley Sword, 227-253. Baton Rouge: Louisiana State University Press, 2014.

———. *Mountains Touched With Fire: Chattanooga Besieged, 1863.* New York: St. Martin's Press, 1995.

———. *The Confederacy's Last Hurrah: Spring Hill, Franklin, and Nashville.* Lawrence: University Press of Kansas, 1992.

Symonds, Craig R. *Stonewall of the West: Patrick Cleburne and the Civil War.* Lawrence: University Press of Kansas, 1997.

———. "War and Politics: Jefferson Davis Visits the Army of Tennessee." In *Gateway to the Confederacy: New Perspectives on the Chickamauga and Chattanooga Campaigns, 1862–1863,* edited by Evan C. Jones and Wiley Sword, 159-171. Baton Rouge: Louisiana State University Press, 2014.

Tennessee Civil War Centennial Commission. *Tennesseans in the Civil War.* 2 vols. Nashville: N. p., 1964.

Texas and Pacific Railway. *From Ox-Teams to Eagles: A History of the Texas and Pacific Railway.* Dallas: Texas and Pacific Railway, 1946.

Tollison, Grady. "Andrew J. Kellar, Memphis Republican." *West Tennessee Historical Society Papers* 16 (1962): 29-55.

Trefousse, Hans L. *Andrew Johnson: A Biography.* New York: W. W. Norton and Company, 1989.

Trelease, Allen W. *White Terror: The Ku Klux Klan Conspiracy and Southern Reconstruction.* New York: Harper and Row, 1971.

Tucker, Glenn. *Chickamauga: Bloody Battle in the West.* 1961. Reprint, Dayton: Morningside, 1981.

Vandiver, Margaret. *Lethal Punishment: Lynchings and Legal Executions in the South.* New Brunswick, NJ: Rutgers University Press, 2006.

Warner, Ezra. *Generals in Gray.* Baton Rouge: Louisiana State University Press, 1959.

Watters, Zack C., ed. "Lines of Battle: Maj. Gen. William B. Bate's Partial Reports of the Atlanta Campaign." In *The Campaign for Atlanta & Sherman's March to the Sea,* 1:169-188. 2 vols. Campbell, CA: Savas Woodbury, 1992.

White, Elizabeth W., comp. *Giles County Chancery Court Extracts.* Pulaski, 1990.

White, Richard. *Railroaded: The Transcontinentals and the Making of Modern America.* New York: W. W. Norton and Company, 2011.

White, Robert Hiram. *Messages of the Governors of Tennessee.* 11 vols. Nashville: The Tennessee Historical Commission, 1952-1998.

White, William Lee. "A. P. Stewart at Chickamauga." In *The Chickamauga Campaign,* edited by Steven E. Woodworth, 84-101. Carbondale: Southern Illinois University Press, 2010.

Wiley, Bell I. "A Story of 3 Southern Officers." *Civil War Times Illustrated* 3 (April 1964): 28–34.

Williams, Frank B. "The Poll Tax as a Suffrage Requirement in the South." *Journal of Southern History* 18 (November 1952): 469-496.

Woodward, C. Vann. *The Origins of the New South*. Baton Rouge: Louisiana State University Press, 1951.

———. *Reunion and Reaction: The Compromise of 1877 and the End of Reconstruction*. 1951. Reprint, New York: Oxford University Press, 1991.

———. "Yes, There Was a Compromise of 1877." *The Journal of American History* 60 (June 1973): 215-223.

Woodworth, Steven E. "'In Their Dreams': Braxton Bragg, Thomas C. Hindman, and the Abortive Attack in McLemore's Cove." In *The Chickamauga Campaign*, edited by Steven E. Woodworth, 50-67. Carbondale: Southern Illinois University Press, 2010.

———. *Nothing But Victory: The Army of the Tennessee 1861–1865*. New York: Alfred A. Knopf, 2005.

———. *Six Armies in Tennessee: The Chickamauga and Chattanooga Campaigns*. Lincoln: University of Nebraska Press, 1998.

———. *Jefferson Davis and His Generals: The Failure of Confederate Command in the West*. Lawrence: University Press of Kansas, 1990.

Zebley, Kathleen R. "Unconditional Unionist: Samuel Mayes Arnell and Reconstruction in Tennessee." In *Tennessee History: The Land, the People and the Culture*, edited by Carroll Van West, 180-200. Knoxville: University of Tennessee Press, 1998.

MONUMENTS AND MARKERS

Chickamauga and Chattanooga National Military Park
    Brown's Brigade markers
Elmwood Cemetery, Memphis, Tennessee
    John C. Brown Burch grave marker
Maplewood Cemetery, Pulaski, Tennessee
    John C. Brown grave marker
    Ann P. Brown grave marker
    Marie Brown grave maker
    Elizabeth Brown Burch grave marker
Tennessee Historical Commission
    Colonial Hall marker

THESES AND DISSERTATIONS

Barnett III, Luke J. "Alexander P Stewart and the Tactical Employment of His Division at Chickamauga." Master's thesis, U. S. Army Command and General Staff College, 1989.

Butler, Margaret. "The Life of John C. Brown." Master's thesis, University of Tennessee, 1936.

Chesney, William M. "The Public Career of William B. Bate." Master's thesis, University of Tennessee, 1951.

Eresman, Raymond S. "Union and Confederate Infantry Doctrine in the Battle of Chickamauga." Master's thesis, U. S. Army Command and General Staff College, 1991.

Hardy, William Edward. ""Fare well to all Radicals": Redeeming Tennessee, 1869–1870." PhD diss., University of Tennessee, 2013.

MacArthur, William Joseph, Jr. "Charles McClung McGhee, Southern Financier." PhD diss., University of Tennessee, 1975.

Zebley, Kathleen R. "Rebel Salvation: The Story of Confederate Pardons." PhD diss., University of Tennessee, 1998.

ONLINE RESOURCES

Ancestry.com. U. S., Sons of the American Revolution Membership Applications, 1889–1979. [database on-line]. Provo, UT, USA: Ancestry.com Operations, Inc., 2011. Accessed September 13, 2013. Available through subscription.

———. *John Henry Pointer Family Tree.* http://person.ancestry.com/tree/21827151/person/19984700221/story. Accessed September 28, 2013.

———. Tennessee Death Records, 1908–1958. http://search.ancestry.com/cgi-bin/sse.dll?indiv=try&db=TNDeathRecords&h=226914. Accessed July 5, 2015. Available through subscription.

Benson, T. Loyd, and Trina Rossman. "Re-Assessing Tom Scott, the 'Railroad Prince.'" http://eweb.furman.edu/~benson/col-tom.html. Accessed July 21, 2013.

Bioguide.congress.gov. *Biographical Directory of the United States Congress, 1774–Present.* http:// bioguide.congress.gov. Accessed September 30, 2013.

Hamilton County, Tennessee, GIS data.

Logsden, David. "Middle Tennessee Eyewitnesses to the Civil War." http://www.midtneyewitnesses.com. Accessed June 22, 2014.

Index

Bristol, Tenn., 198

Bristol *News*, 198

Brown, Aaron V., 3, 4, 5, 7

Brown, Angus, 2, 284n3

Brown, Anne Pointer, 8–9, 11, 12, 17, 86, 286n18

Brown, B. Gratz, 192

Brown, Daisy, 180, 256, 260, 261, 271, 275

Brown, Duncan, 2–3, 5

Brown, Elizabeth Childress ("Bettie"), x, 70, 89–91, 142–43, 149–50, 152, 190, 224–25, 234, 243, 248, 252, 255, 256, 262, 275, 276, 277, **278**

Brown, Hugh, 5, 285n11

Brown, James Trimble, 100, 263, 295n59

Brown, John (of Harper's Ferry), 11–12

Brown, John C., **119**, **170**

—anti-Radical activities, 153, 158–9

—argues in United States Supreme Court, 249, 256

—at Atlanta, Battle of, 105–11

—and at-large congressional election of 1872, 193–97

—attitude toward Brownlow's government, 156

—before Congressional committees, 207, 231–32, 244, 246, 247, 265–67

—birth and boyhood, 3–4

—brigade(s) of, 21–22, 23–27, 28–33, 42–43, 45–47, 49–50, 53–56, 60, 62–68, 73, 76

—at Chattanooga, Battle of, 73–83

—at Chickamauga, Battle of, 60–69, 300n33

—children born, 150, 180, 209

—civic endeavors of, 4, 8, 256

—and Cleburne's slave proposal, 85–87

—commands post at Murfreesboro, 49

—and Compromise of 1877, 235–38

—as Confederate veteran, 243, 258

—and constitutional convention of 1870, 168–73

—courtship and marriage, 8–9, 11, 70, 89–91

—death and burial, 274–75

—as Democrat, 158, 175–76, 177, 179, 189, 193–94, 197, 209, 211, 215–16, 222, 232–33, 234, 237–38, 239–40, 243, 249, 253, 272

—descendants of, 262, 276–77

—destruction of "army papers" of, 180

—divisional commands: Bate's, 118–27; Cheatham's, 127–40, 312n11; Cleburne's (brigades of Govan and Smith), 145; Hindman's, 101–117; Loring's, 118; Stevenson's, 77–79, 100–101; Stewart's, 57, 101

—early Confederate service, 19–24

—education of, 3–4

—elections of: 1869 delegate to constitutional convention, 168; 1870 governor, 177–80; 1872 governor, 195–99; 1875 senator, 220–23

—at Ezra Church, Battle of, 113–17

—at final surrender of Army of Tennessee, 145–146, 315n35

—as former Whig, 158, 166, 169, 175–76, 189, 211, 215, 221, 223, 237, 280, 281

—at Fort Donelson, Battle of, 25–35, 290n15

—at Franklin, Battle of, 136–40

—as general solicitor of Gould System, 256–57, 257–58, 260

—as Governor of Tennessee: administration of, 189–92, 194, 202, 218; analysis of, 218–220, 281; asylum issue, 202, 208–209; civil rights, 209, 210–14; comptroller controversy, 204–206; educational initiatives, 187–88, 200–201; fears Federal interference, 191–92, 213; prison/prisoner issues, 188–89, 199, 209; state debt/finances, 184–187, 200–202, 203–204, 206–207, 210

—and Great Southwest Railroad Strike of 1886, 263–267

Munfordville, Ky, 43
Murfreesboro, Tenn., 23, 48, 49, 63, 70, 178, 260; Battle of, 49–50, 73, 102
Murfreesboro *Monitor*, 192

Nashville, Tenn., vii, 6, 8, 9, 11, 16, 20, 24, 28, 31, 38, 39, 40, 43, 49, 50, 70, 104, 130, 137, 140, 141, 149, 154, 158, 159, 163, 165, 168, 174, 178, 180, 183, 188, 191, 192, 194, 195, 196, 197, 202, 204, 206, 210, 211, 216, 221, 222, 224, 232, 234, 239, 249, 273, 274–75, 276, 277; Battle of, 141
Nashville *Banner*, 205, 220
Nashville *Bulletin*, 204
Nashville *Republican Banner*, 13, 17, 167, 169, 181, 196
Nashville *Union and American*, 14, 165, 175, 178, 183, 186, 190, 191, 192, 194, 197, 199, 203, 214, 217, 229
National Tribune, 34, 139
Nebraska (steamboat), 36
Negley, James, division of, 59
Nelson, T. A. R., 158
Nelson, William "Bull," 43–44
Netherland, John, 166, 168, 169, 175, 181
Newman, Tazewell W., 64
New Orleans, La., 40, 238, 239, 240–43, 247, 257, 258, 261, 262, 270, 272
New York, N.Y., vii, 192, 196, 204, 206, 207, 219, 243, 246, 249, 251, 253, 257, 262, 268, 272
Nicholls, Francis T., 239, 241–242
Nicholson, Alfred Osborne Pope, 168, 169, 170, 171, 172, 173, 174, 181, 215, 281
Noble, George, 255, 264

O'Bryan, Lawrence, 4
Ocean Queen (steamship), 40
Orr, J. L., 222

Packard, Stephen B., 238–239, 241, 242
Paducah, Ky., 36

Palmer, Joseph B., 23, 27, 29, 30, 31, 37, 39–40, 49, 50, 63, 64, 69, 101, 106, 141, 147, 160
Palmer, Joseph E., 42, 46
Pardee, Don A., 261, 262, 266, 267, 270, 272
Patterson, David, 164
Pegram, John, 60
Pemberton, John C., 54
Pettus, Edmund, 79; brigade of, 73, 77, 78, 92, 98
Peyton, Balie, 167
Philadelphia, Pa., vii, 183, 234, 254, 259
Pickettsville, Tenn., 213
Pillow, Gideon J., 25–29, 31–33, 50, 53, 160, 180, 292n42, 296n68
Pointer, John A., 8–9, 180
Pointer, Major, 39, 291n19
Pointer, Martha A., 8–9
Polk, Andrew J., 130
Polk, James K., 4, 25, 38, 70
Polk, Leonidas, 21, 22, 23, 24, 41, 44, 45, 48, 49, 56, 57, 61, 62, 66, 71, 88, 89, 93, 99, 100, 101, 102, 112, 117; corps of, 48, 93, 97, 98
Polk, Lucius E., 71, 85–86, 142
Polk, Lucius J., 130
Polk, Major William, 85–86
Polk, Sarah Childress, 38, 70, 149, 180, 224, 316n1
Porter, James C., 166, 168, 211, 216, 217, 222, 225, 240, 247, 249, 258
Porter, Nimrod, 130
Porter, Thomas K., 27; battery of, 32
Powderly, Terence V., 259, 263, 266
Preston, William, 59, 71
Pulaski, Pisgah, and Bradshaw Turnpike Company, 224
Pulaski, Tenn., x, 1, 3, 4, 6, 8, 11, 12, 13, 19, 20, 39, 86, 129, 130, 141, 147, 148, 150, 152, 155, 157, 159, 163, 164, 176, 178, 180, 183, 190, 193, 204, 207, 209, 211, 214, 217, 218, 223, 224, 225, 234, 239, 242–43, 252, 255, 256, 258, 261, 262, 268, 271, 273, 275, 276, 277, 279

Walthall, Edward C., 78, 101, 102, 130, 145, 218, 253, 301n38; brigade of, 78, 83, 106; division of, 116–117
Wartrace, Tenn., 54, 55, 84a
Washington, D. C., vii, 44, 55, 58, 72, 146, 149, 162, 165, 166, 171, 173, 179, 181, 191, 193, 194, 207, 217, 225, 231, 232, 234–35, 237, 239, 240, 242, 243, 248, 253, 262, 271, 280
Watts, Thomas H., 91
Waynesboro, Tenn., 129
Welles, Gideon, 167
Wheeler, Joseph, 44, 144
Whitaker, Walter, brigade of, 94
White, Hugh Lawson, 3
White, Richard, 274
Whitthorne, Washington C., 160, 191, 217–218, 234

Wilkes, John S., 190, 199, 204, 207, 211, 233, 244, 261
Williams, John, 189
Wilson, D. L., 275
Wilson, Henry, 224
Winchester, Tenn., 41, 55
Wise, George, 92, 96
Wisener, William A., 177–178
Withers, Jones, division of, 102
Wood, Sterling A. M., 67; brigade of, 47, 67, 68
Woodward, C. Vann, ix, 166, 219, 235, 283n3; criticism of, 341n24
Wright, Marcus J., 62, 63, 118; brigade of, 62, 128
Wurtemburg Academy, 4

Zollicoffer, Felix, 24

- Secession politics

- Ft. Donelson

- captivity?

- Perryville, VA

- N'boro? Bragg resigns?
  1863

- Chickamauga, VA
- signs and Bragg problems — MANNERS!
       attacks behind the RR   P90
- Chattanooga
       — Battle of Lookout Mtn (reunion, 1911)
              Tunnel Hill
                                      Cleburne idea?
  Atlanta Campaign   p85
       — girl in dress
       — dividend, p125
       — rebel retreat, p113
- Spring Hill
       — another night, p134?
- Franklin, VA
- NC campaign
_____

6/65 oath pardon (not valid til 1865)
Pulaski TN
       KKK — Pisani's vets. Brown member, p153
vs. Brownlow — Radical governor, State Guard
       won 1867 elections, CSA disenfranchised

1868 resistance — KKK
              nat'l — establish like Brown
                     unite w/ Dems
       Brown did lose control of KKK,
       Brownlow calls out State Guard, martial
       law — 1869 — then goes to US Senate
       "Redeemers" [not used ironically?] — ex-Whigs?
              illegal election of Senter

1870 Const'l Convention — Dem progressives
       — universal suffrage
       — poll tax

Governors race
       — conservatives became Dems
                    vs
              radicals
       Brown elected

1871
       debt reduction
       also ed, penal system,
              road stuff, tax

1872 re-elected
       — long running issues are
       debt, education

1874 — Fed intervention,
       racial violence
       — Senate campaign vs AJ

1876   Texas Pac RR
       Tom Scott
       fed subsidy

       La Commission

1880   T+ PRR,
       Scott
       Jay Gould
       move to Texas?
       RR lawyer p54
       K of L, strike